Understanding
Data
Communications

Understanding
Data
Communications
Third Edition

Second & Third
Editions
Revised by: Gilbert Held

First
Edition by: George E. Friend, M.S.; John L. Fike, Ph.D., P.E.;
H. Charles Baker, Ph.D., P.E.; and John C. Bellamy, Ph.D.
With Contributions by Gerald Luecke and Charles W.
Battle

SAMS

A Division of Prentice Hall Computer Publishing

11711 North College, Carmel, Indiana 46032 USA

Trademarks

Publisher: *Richard K. Swadley*
Publishing Manager: *Joe Wikert*
Acquisitions Manager: *Charlie Dresser*
Development Editor: *James Rounds*
Managing Editor: *Neweleen Trebnik*
Technical Reviewer: *David Hanson*
Production Editor: *Don Herrington*
Keyboarder: *ASEC International, Los Angeles, California*
Cover Photography: *David Kadlec*
Designer: *Scott Cook*
Indexer: *Sharon Hilgenberg*

Production Team: *Joelynn Gifford, Debbie Hanna, Matthew Morrill, Dennis Sheehan, Mary Beth Wakefield, Corinne Walls*

Contents

Preface .... **ix**

Chapter   **Page**

1 *An Overview of Data Communications* **1**
        Quiz **29**

2 *Data Terminals* **31**
        Quiz **64**

3 *Messages and Transmission Channels* **67**
        Quiz **88**

4 *Asynchronous Modems and Interfaces* **89**
        Quiz **125**

5 *Synchronous Modems and Digital Transmission* **127**
        Quiz **159**

6 *Multiplexing* **161**
        Quiz **180**

7 *Fiber Optic and Satellite Communications* **183**
        Quiz **208**

8 *Protocols and Error Control* **211**
        Quiz **239**

9 *Alternatives in Local Area Networks* **241**
        Quiz **276**

10 *Architectures and Packet Networks* **279**
        Quiz **301**

11 *Network Design and Management* **305**
        Quiz **329**

12 *ISDN* **331**
        Quiz **341**

Glossary **343**
Bibliography **349**
Index **351**
Answers to Quizzes **367**

Preface

The communication of information of all kinds by means of binary signals—the ones and zeros that are used by computers—has gained such an important place in American society that it is fair to say that successful operation of the U.S. economy would be impossible without it. Information sent using data communications controls a major portion of the long distance telephone network, enables the rapid authorization of credit purchases and cashing of checks, and provides for the inventory and ordering of goods in stores of all kinds from fast-food franchises to photo finishers. Data communications technology allows the simultaneous printing in widely separated cities of national magazines and newspapers, whose entire text and picture copy is transmitted from a central source to the city in which they are to be printed on a daily basis.

A basic knowledge of such a pervasive force in our lives is as necessary for all of us as some knowledge of the workings of another transportation system—the automobile. We have attempted to cover the basic principles of data communications and to explain those areas of application which have a daily impact: communications between terminals and computers, including local area networks and packet networks; communication of telephone conversations and control of the telephone network; and the use of light rays and satellites for carrying the ever-increasing volume of data helping to make our lives more comfortable and sometimes a great deal more confusing.

This book is arranged somewhat like a textbook. Each chapter starts by saying what it covers, ends by saying what has been covered, and provides a short multiple-choice quiz on the chapter contents. Like other books in the series, this book builds understanding step-by-step. Try to master each chapter before going on to the next one.

If your objective is to obtain general information about the subject, the more detailed portions of the text and the quiz can be bypassed. This will allow you to absorb the information more easily and, hopefully, enjoy the style of presentation. If you need more basic information about the telephone system and telephone electronics, a companion book in the series titled *Understanding Telephone Electronics* should be helpful. For more detailed and more advanced information about data communications, refer to the books listed in the bibliography.

G. H.

An Overview of Data Communications

ABOUT THIS BOOK

This book is intended to explain how data communications systems and their various hardware and software components work. It is not intended to tell you how to build the equipment, nor will it tell you how to write computer programs to transmit data between two computers. What can be learned is a basis for understanding data communications systems in general, and some tips for setting up your own system to communicate between your personal or professional computer and another personal computer, a data base service, an information utility, or an electronic bulletin board.

To understand data communications, it is necessary to have some understanding of the telephone channel because it is the medium used by most data communications systems to move information from one place to another. Therefore, part of this book is devoted to describing the public telephone network and the equipment used to interface between it and a computer.

ABOUT THIS CHAPTER

This chapter presents some history of data communications and a general description of a data communications system. Explanations of bits, bytes, two-state communications systems, and codes help lay the foundation for further discussions in the remainder of the book.

WHAT IS DATA COMMUNICATIONS?

Data communications is often referred to as computer communications due to the ever increasing use of computers and their support equipment.

Data communications is the process of communicating information in binary form between two points. Data communications is sometimes called computer communications because most of the information interchanged today is between computers, or between computers and their terminals, printers, or other peripheral devices. The data may be as elementary as the binary symbols 1 and 0, or as complex as the characters represented by the keys on a typewriter keyboard. In any case, the characters or symbols represent information.

WHY IS DATA COMMUNICATIONS IMPORTANT?

It is important for us to understand data communications because of its significance in today's world. Data communications is commonly used in the world of business and it is being used more and more in homes as well. Whether it is the transmission of bank account information from a central computer to a convenient electronic teller machine, or the downloading of a video game from a computer bulletin board to a home computer's memory, data communications is becoming an integral part of our daily activities. In fact, for many readers hardly a day goes by without the recipient of an activity performed or enhanced through the use of data communications. For example, many traffic lights are controlled via the transmission of signals from computer systems, while large retailers routinely transmit sales information which allows timely distribution of warehouse inventory to retail locations. Thus, the more modern a society, the more dependent that society is upon the use of data communications.

THE FIRST DATA COMMUNICATIONS SYSTEMS

Modern data communications involves the use of electrical or electronic apparatus to communicate information in the form of symbols and characters between two points. Since electricity, radio waves, and light waves are all forms of electromagnetic energy, it is stretching things only a bit to say that early forms of communication, such as the puffs of smoke from the Indian's signal fire (Figure 1.1), or reflections of sunlight from a hand-held mirror, also were forms of the same type of data communications. To carry this idea further, think of the puffs of smoke as discrete symbols, just as the symbols used in today's communications systems are discrete.

Early Uses of Electricity

Originally, data communications depended on codes transmitted by visual systems such as mirrors, flags, and smoke. Electrical data communication systems transmit codes by switching electrical current.

The discovery and harnessing of electricity introduced many new possibilities for communications codes beyond the smoke signals, mirrors, signal flags, and lanterns in use in eighteenth and nineteenth centuries.

One of the early proposals, submitted to a Scottish magazine in 1753, was simple but had profound implications for hardware. This idea was to run 26 parallel wires from town to town, one wire for each letter of the alphabet. A Swiss inventor built a prototype system based on this 26-wire principle, but the technology of wire making eliminated that idea from serious use.

In 1833, Carl Friedrich Gauss used a code based on a 5 by 5 matrix of 25 letters (I and J were combined) to send messages by deflecting a needle from one to five times, right or left. The first set of deflections indicated the row; the second the column.

The Telegraph

The first notable development in data communications occurred in the nineteenth century when an American, Samuel F. B. Morse, invented the electric telegraph. Although other inventors had worked on the idea of using electricity to communicate, Morse's invention was by far the most important because he coupled the human mind (intelligence) with the communications equipment.

**Figure 1.1.
Looks Like Trouble
Ahead**

The first data communications did not rely on electricity.

Samuel F. B. Morse perfected the telegraph, the first mass data communications system based on electric power.

A basic telegraph system is diagrammed in Figure 1.2. When the telegraph key at station A was depressed, current flowed through the system and the armature at station B was attracted to the coil, clicking as it struck the stop. When the key was released, it opened the electrical circuit and the armature of the sounder was forced to its open position by a spring, striking the other stop with a slightly different click. Thus, the telegraph sounder had two distinctive clicks. If the time between successive clicks of the sounder was short, it represented a dot; if longer, a dash. Morse developed a code, similar to the one shown in Figure 1.3, to represent characters by a series of these dots and dashes. The transmitting operator converted the characters in the words of a message to be sent into a series of dots and dashes. The receiving operator interpreted those dots and dashes as characters; thus, the information was transmitted from point A to point B.

**Figure 1.2.
Basic Telegraph
System**

**Figure 1.3.
International Morse
Code**

*Much of
Morse
terminology
is still in
use today.*

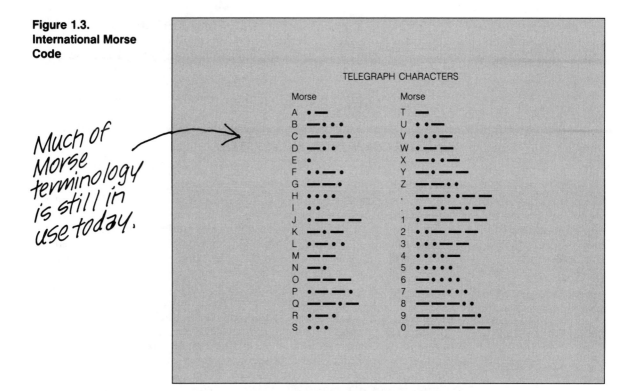

When Morse developed his code, legend has it that he examined the quantity of type in boxes a typesetter used for storing English characters and digits. Morse assigned short codes to frequently occurring characters and digits while longer codes were assigned to less frequently occurring characters and digits. This explains why a dot was assigned to the letter E which is the most frequently occurring character in the English language while a dash was assigned to the letter T, which is the second most frequently occurring character.

Morse first developed the telegraph in 1832, but it wasn't until much later that he successfully demonstrated its use. The best-known demonstration took place in 1844, when Morse transmitted over a wire from Washington to Baltimore the message, "What hath God wrought!"

The telegraph system was the first electrically based communications system to connect the east and west coasts of the United States, and both sides of the Atlantic.

Since mail delivery by the Pony Express was the typical means of communication before the telegraph, the telegraph quickly became a success because of its much greater speed. The equipment was simple and rugged; the key and the sounder each contained only one moving part. Both the system's strength and weakness (and its only real complexity) was the human mind—the transmitting and receiving operators. By the time of the Civil War, a telegraph line spanned the continent, crossing the prairies and deserts to connect California with the rest of the United States. It was from this historic technological breakthrough that the Western

Union Telegraph Company made its legacy and indeed was named; their line connected the *West* with the *Union*. By the time the telephone was invented some thirty years later, the telegraph industry was large and prosperous, with many companies providing service to almost every city and town in the United States. In 1866, the telegraph connected the nations of the world with the laying of the trans-Atlantic cable between the United States and France.

TWO-STATE COMMUNICATIONS SYSTEMS

Much of the telegraph's terminology and principles of operation is still used today. The most important of these is the two-state communications system.

The importance of the Morse telegraph is not just historical; it illustrates the simplicity of a complete data communications system. Much of the terminology that developed around the Morse system still is in use today. For example, consider the terms "mark" and "space." If a device were arranged so that paper continually moved under a pen attached to the telegraph sounder armature, then a mark would be made on the paper when the armature was attracted to the coil. Thus, we could refer to the state of current flow in the line as the marking state and the state of no current flow in the line as the spacing state. Worldwide standards for data communications today still use the terms mark and space, with the idle condition on the transmission channel called the marking condition.

The wire ("telegraph channel") between the operators, therefore, is in one of two states; either current is flowing, or it is not. This illustrates a simple idea which has been repeated over and over again in the development of data communications systems. A two-state communications system is the simplest, the easiest to build, and the most reliable. The two states can be On and Off (as in the telegraph), Plus and Minus (with current flowing in opposite directions), Light and Dark (like turning a flashlight on and off to send code), 1 and 0 (the concept used in the computer), or some other design with only two possible values. A two-state or two-valued system is referred to as a binary system.

BITS AND BYTES

The 0 and the 1 are the symbols of the binary system. A binary digit is commonly referred to as a bit. The individual line changes in digital data (like the mark and space) are called bits and each bit is assigned a value of 0 or 1.

Transmission codes in the binary system are made up of digits called bits. Each bit can have one of two possible states (high or low, on or off). Several bits combined in a uniform group are called a byte.

The binary system uses positional notation, just as the familiar decimal system does, except that each position has only two possible values, rather than ten. For example, the number 345.27 in decimal means three hundreds plus four tens plus five ones plus two tenths plus seven hundredths. The *weight* of each position is a power of ten, thus:

$$345.27 = (3 \times 100) + (4 \times 10) + (5 \times 1) + (2 \times 1/10) + (7 \times 1/100)$$
$$= 3 \times 10^2 + 4 \times 10^1 + 5 \times 10^0 + 2 \times 10^{-1} + 7 \times 10^{-2}$$

Note the use of positive and negative exponents, and remember the definition that *any* number raised to the zero power is equal to 1. In the decimal system, as shown by the preceding example, ten is the *base*, and the weight of each digit position is a power of ten.

Similarly, we can define powers of two in the binary positional system, where the weight of each position is two times the weight of the one to the immediate right. A table of powers of two can be quite useful when dealing with binary numbers because most of us don't want to memorize them. Table 1.1 is such a table for powers of two up to 2^8 which will be sufficient for this book. Using this table makes it easy to convert a binary number to its decimal equivalent. For example;

$$1101001 = 1 \times 2^6 + 1 \times 2^5 + 0 \times 2^4 + 1 \times 2^3 + 0 \times 2^2\ 0 \times 2^1 + 1 \times 2^0$$
$$= 64 + 32 + 0 + 8 + 0 + 0 + 1$$
$$= 105 \text{ decimal}$$

Table 1.1
Powers of Two

Power of Two	Positional Weight	9-Bit Binary Number
2^0	1	000000001
2^1	2	000000010
2^2	4	000000100
2^3	8	000001000
2^4	16	000010000
2^5	32	000100000
2^6	64	001000000
2^7	128	010000000
2^8	256	100000000

Computers are more efficient if their internal paths and registers are some power of two in length (two bits, four bits, eight bits, sixteen bits, etc.). A commonly used grouping is eight bits and this 8-bit group is called a byte or an octet. From Table 1.1, you can see that a byte can represent 2^8 or 256 unique sequences of 1s and 0s.

COMMUNICATIONS CODES

The use of simplified and standardized binary codes allowed information to be encoded and decoded by mechanical or electrical means, and made it possible to automate data communications.

A common characteristic of data communications systems is the use of an intelligent device to convert a character or symbol into coded form and vice versa. In the Morse system, the intelligent "devices" were the telegraph operators who converted the characters into dots and dashes.

Skilled telegraph operators were always in short supply and the work was difficult and exhausting, so an electrical or mechanical means of coding the characters was needed. However, it was essentially impossible to automate the transmitting and receiving operations because of the varying duration of the dots and dashes in the Morse code, and the fact that the codes for the characters were made up of different quantities of dots and dashes. Therefore, a code that had an equal number of equal duration signaling elements for each character was needed.

Some Definitions

A code is a previously agreed upon set of meanings that define a given set of symbols and characters.

Before we go any further, let's establish the following definitions in order to discuss communication codes:

Codes: Standard (agreed-upon-in-advance) meanings between signaling elements and characters. The key idea is *standard*. The codes used in data communications systems are already defined and the code set is built into the equipment. About the only time the user might need to deal with codes is when interfacing two machines (computers, printers, etc.) from different manufacturers.

Characters are the letters, signs and symbols on an input device's keyboard; some are used to control the system.

Characters: The letters, numerals, space, punctuation marks, and other signs and symbols on a keyboard. (Remember that the space character is just as important as any other even though we tend to think of it as "nothing" or "blank.") For example, A 7# is a sequence of four characters. Communication systems also use control characters which do not print, but they also must be coded. Some of these (such as Carriage Return or Tab) may be on a keyboard, but many are not.

Symbols are the representations of characters that are transmitted over transmission lines. It is easier to design and build machines to recognize symbols rather than characters.

Signaling Elements: Something that is sent over a transmission channel and used to represent a character. The dots and dashes (or marks and spaces) of the Morse code are signaling elements, as are the ones and zeros in this sequence:

0100000101 0000001011 0111011011 0110001011

This is the way A 7# might look when transmitted between a personal computer and another computer or printer. You will see later that the code is ASCII, with even parity and one start and one stop bit.

The definitions for characters and signaling elements illustrate why machines and people need different ways to represent information. People quickly and reliably recognize printed characters by their distinctive shapes, but that is difficult and expensive for a machine to do. On the other hand, machines can easily handle long strings of two-valued signaling elements such as marks and spaces or ones and zeros, but that is hard for a person to accomplish with any accuracy.

Baudot Code

Emile Baudot developed one of the more successful codes suited for machine encoding and decoding. However, it was limited because it used only five symbols.

As stated before, the Morse code was unsuitable for machine encoding and decoding because of the problems caused by the varying lengths of the codes for the characters. When, early in the twentieth century, interest developed in replacing human telegraph operators with machines, several suitable codes already existed. The most prominent of these had been invented in the 1870s by a Frenchman named Emile Baudot. Since Baudot's code, similar to the one shown in Figure 1.4, used the same number of signaling elements (marks and spaces) to represent each character, it was better suited to machine encoding and decoding.

Unfortunately, the number of signaling elements was limited to five by problems in timing the electromechanical devices. The 5-bit code could generate only 32 possible combinations, fewer than was needed to represent the 26 characters of the alphabet, the 10 decimal digits, the punctuation marks, and the space character. In addition, Baudot used two shift-control characters—the letters (LTRS) shift and the figures (FIGS) shift—to permit the code set to represent all the characters which seemed necessary at the time. The shift codes do not represent printable characters, but select one of two character sets, each composed of 26 to 28 characters. Receipt of the letters shift (11111) code causes all following codes to be interpreted as letters of the alphabet; receipt of the figures shift code (11011) causes all the following characters to be interpreted as numerals and punctuation marks. Notice that the LTRS and FIGS codes, as well as the other control codes and the space character, always have the same interpretation no matter which shift mode the machine is currently in. Although Baudot's invention did not immediately revolutionize telegraphy (because of the difficulty that human operators had in sending equal length codes), it did provide a basis for the later development of the teleprinter.

Modern Codes

There was a need for new codes that could represent all characters, be able to check for errors, and leave room for further expansion.

The Baudot code and variations of it were the backbone of communications for almost half a century, but they clearly left much to be desired. The newspaper industry found the lack of differentiation between upper- and lowercase letters to be a problem and devised a six-level code to designate the difference between upper- and lowercase letters. This was just one example of a general need; modern communications required a code that could represent all printable characters and still leave room for error checking. The code had to permit decoding without reliance on correct reception of previous transmissions, and also had to permit decoding by machine. Perhaps most important of all, the new code needed to be expandable.

During the 1960s, a number of data transmission codes were developed. Most of these have fallen by the wayside, leaving three predominant codes: a single 5-bit code (CCITT International Alphabet No. 2) still used for telex transmission; the Extended Binary-Coded-Decimal Interchange Code (EBCDIC, pronounced "eb-see-dik") developed by IBM and primarily used for synchronous communication in systems attached to large mainframe computers; and the American Standard Code for Information Interchange (ASCII, pronounced "as-key") code defined by the American National Standards Institute (ANSI) in the United States and by the International Standards Organization (ISO) worldwide.

**Figure 1.4.
Five-Level Teleprinter
Code**

Start	1	2	3	4	5	Stop	LTRS Shift	CCITT Standard International Telegraph Alphabet No. 2 Used for Telex	North American Teletype Commercial Keyboard
	●	●				●	A	—	—
	●			●	●	●	B	?	?
		●	●	●		●	C	:	:
	●			●		●	D	Who are you?	$
	●					●	E	3	3
	●		●	●		●	F	Note 1	!
		●		●	●	●	G	Note 1	&
			●		●	●	H	Note 1	#
		●	●			●	I	8	8
	●	●		●		●	J	Bell	Bell
	●	●	●	●		●	K	(	(
		●			●	●	L	)	)
			●	●	●	●	M	.	.
			●	●		●	N	,	,
				●	●	●	O	9	9
		●	●		●	●	P	0	0
	●	●	●		●	●	Q	1	1
		●		●		●	R	4	4
	●		●			●	S	'	'
					●	●	T	5	5
	●	●	●			●	U	7	7
		●	●	●	●	●	V	=	;
	●	●			●	●	W	2	2
	●		●	●	●	●	X	/	/
	●		●		●	●	Y	6	6
	●				●	●	Z	+	"
						●		Blank	
	●	●	●	●	●	●		Letters shift (LTRS)	
	●	●		●	●	●		Figures shift (FIGS)	
			●			●		Space	
				●		●		Carriage return	
		●				●		Line feed	

Code Signals — ● Denotes positive current

FIGS Shift

Notes:
1. Not allocated internationally; available to each county for internal use.

EBCDIC

EBCDIC is a modern
code using 8-bits to
represent 256 charac-
ters. It was developed
by IBM to provide a
standard code for its
own products.

When a clear need arises for standardization, standards can come into
existence in two ways. A single manufacturer (especially a dominant one)
can define a standard for its own products, and the rest of the industry may
follow. This is what IBM did. It created the EBCDIC 8-bit code, allowing
256 characters to be represented. The world would probably be better
off if EBCDIC had become the standard, because it has enough unique
characters to allow almost any representation. However, only IBM and
firms who build IBM-compatible equipment adopted EBCDIC. Since
EBCDIC is primarily used in large IBM-compatible computing systems, it
will not be used in most of the examples in this book.

ASCII

The ANSI developed
the 7-bit ASCII data
communications code
that is in general use
today. It can represent
128 characters.

The other, more common method of creating a standard is through a
committee, which serves as a forum for examination of needs, discussion
between interested parties, and compromise. This process produced the
ASCII 7-bit code, formally known as ANSI Standard X3.4-1977. ASCII can
represent 128 characters, but not all of them represent printed symbols.
Included in the character set are all the letters of the English alphabet
(both uppercase and lowercase), the numerals 0–9, punctuation marks,
and many symbols. This standard code set is used in virtually all small
computers and their peripherals, as well as in large computers in most of
the world.

A variation of ASCII, commonly referred to as "extended ASCII,"
gained wide acceptance with the introduction of the IBM Personal
Computer in 1981. The IBM PC supports an 8-bit code, with the first
7 positions supporting the ANSI standard. The additional bit position
extends the computer's ASCII, enabling an additional 128 characters to be
represented. This extension enables software developers to use extended
codes for such functions as end-of-paragraph markings and bold printing
indicators in a word processing system.

Figure 1.5 shows the ANSI standard ASCII characters and their
associated codes. Compare this chart to the Morse code in Figure 1.3 and
the 5-bit teleprinter code in Figure 1.4. The Morse code had a varying
number of elements (dots and dashes) for each character, and was quite
restricted—only letters, numerals, and a few punctuation marks. The 5-bit
code had a constant number of elements and a few more special characters,
but still couldn't distinguish between upper- and lowercase letters.

The ASCII format is
arranged so that lower-
case letters can be
changed to uppercase
by changing only one
bit. Bits 4 through 1 of
the numeric characters
also are the BCD value
of the number.

ASCII not only has upper- and lowercase, but also has a great deal of
regularity that may not be readily apparent. For example, to convert any
uppercase alphabetic character (A through Z) to lowercase, it is only
necessary to change bit 6 from zero to one! Another feature is that bits 4
thorough 1 of the numeric characters (0, 1, 2, 3, 4, 5, 6, 7, 8, and 9) are
the binary-coded-decimal (BCD) value of the character. Another advantage
of standard ASCII is that 128 different characters can be represented by
the seven bits used in the code, rather than only 32 characters from the
5-bit code.

Figure 1.5.
American Standard
Code for Information
Interchange (ASCII)

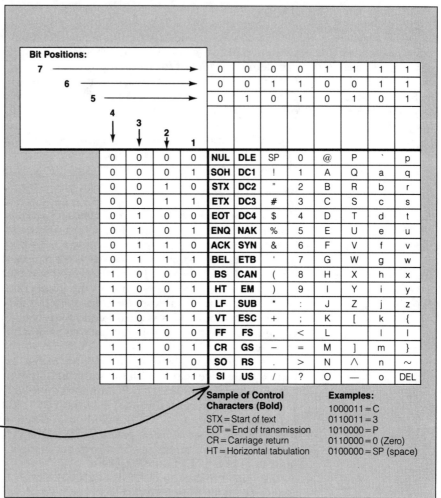

Bit Positions:

7 →	0	0	0	0	1	1	1	1
6 →	0	0	1	1	0	0	1	1
5 →	0	1	0	1	0	1	0	1

4	3	2	1								
0	0	0	0	**NUL**	**DLE**	SP	0	@	P	`	p
0	0	0	1	**SOH**	**DC1**	!	1	A	Q	a	q
0	0	1	0	**STX**	**DC2**	"	2	B	R	b	r
0	0	1	1	**ETX**	**DC3**	#	3	C	S	c	s
0	1	0	0	**EOT**	**DC4**	$	4	D	T	d	t
0	1	0	1	**ENQ**	**NAK**	%	5	E	U	e	u
0	1	1	0	**ACK**	**SYN**	&	6	F	V	f	v
0	1	1	1	**BEL**	**ETB**	'	7	G	W	g	w
1	0	0	0	**BS**	**CAN**	(	8	H	X	h	x
1	0	0	1	**HT**	**EM**	)	9	I	Y	i	y
1	0	1	0	**LF**	**SUB**	*	:	J	Z	j	z
1	0	1	1	**VT**	**ESC**	+	;	K	[	k	{
1	1	0	0	**FF**	**FS**	,	<	L	\	l		
1	1	0	1	**CR**	**GS**	–	=	M	]	m	}
1	1	1	0	**SO**	**RS**	.	>	N	∧	n	~
1	1	1	1	**SI**	**US**	/	?	O	–	o	DEL

Sample of Control
Characters (Bold)

STX = Start of text
EOT = End of transmission
CR = Carriage return
HT = Horizontal tabulation

Examples:
1000011 = C
0110011 = 3
1010000 = P
0110000 = 0 (Zero)
0100000 = SP (space)

Non-Printable Control Characters

ASCII also has several control codes which, in addition to their defined control functions, have been used by some manufacturers to represent specialized functions.

The two left-most character columns in the chart of Figure 1.5 represent the nonprinting control characters which may be used to control the operation of the receiving device. For example, the control codes for carriage return (CR) and linefeed (LF), which are commonly used on a typewriter, are shown. Other control codes include formfeed (FF), bell (BEL), horizontal tab (HT), and vertical tab (VT). These control codes were designed for printing or display devices, although some manufacturers have used the control codes for all manner of special functions. Also, some codes control how a receiving device will interpret subsequent codes in a multiple character function or command. Two shift characters called Shift In (SI) and Shift Out (SO) are used to shift between ASCII and character sets other than those used in English. ANSI standards

X3.41-1974 and X3.64-1979 expand the definition of the escape (ESC) control code for even greater flexibility. Other control codes delimit text, such as start of text (STX) and end of text (ETX). These codes are used primarily in block or synchronous data transmission, and you'll see more of them in later chapters.

Escape Character

Escape sequences are code sequences made up of noncontrol characters that are to be interpreted as control codes.

The escape (ESC) character designates that the codes that follow have special meaning. Characters received in an escape sequence are not interpreted as printing characters, but as control information to extend the range of the "standard" character set by allowing other definitions. The escape character has the effect of making all character codes available for control of a device. Graphics characters, foreign language character sets, and special applications sets have been developed which are accessible via escape character sequences; thus, they permit a much richer variety of displayed symbols than is possible with any single code.

The CRT terminal probably has benefited most by the escape sequence. The serial communications link to these terminals is the same as for a teleprinter, and ordinarily, any characters received via this channel are displayed on the terminal screen as expected. But the people who developed the ASCII standard did not foresee (thus did not make provision for) capabilities for character and line deletion, and display enhancements such as inverse video, underlining, and blinking that are available on the CRT terminal. Unfortunately, little standardization of these sequences existed until the ANSI X3.64 standard came out in 1979. Before then, and without standardization, designers felt free to exercise their creativity. For example, one major feature now found on most video display terminals is absolute cursor positioning. The computer can send a command to the terminal that will place the cursor anywhere on the screen. This capability is important for many types of form-filling operations. Unfortunately, there are almost as many escape sequences to do cursor positioning as there are terminal manufacturers. Even different models in a manufacturer's line may use different escape sequences to do the same thing.

The result of this "creativity" with the character set is that some manufacturers' equipment will not operate correctly with that of most of the rest of the world. An example is a printer that automatically inserts a linefeed after receiving a carriage return. Since most computers send both a carriage return and linefeed in response to only a carriage return input, the printout will not be spaced as desired because of the extra linefeed supplied by the printer.

To promote compatibility, many terminal and personal computer manufacturers provide implicit or explicit support of the ANSI standard. Explicit support of that standard includes those terminals and personal computers designed explicitly to support the ANSI X3.64 standard. Implicit support is provided by terminals and personal computers that have the ability to load a program and read the contents of a predefined memory area or memory cartridge to enable support of the ANSI X3.64

standard. Perhaps the most commonly available device capable of supporting that standard is the IBM PC and compatible personal computers. Those computers, which use the Microsoft MS-DOS or PC DOS operating system, can be configured to use device driver ANSI.SYS, which is a file on the operating system diskette that will be loaded into memory during subsequent startups once specified. The execution of that file results in the personal computer becoming an ANSI compatible terminal, including support for standardized escape code sequences.

Teleprinters

The technology and techniques used in teleprinting have provided the basis for asynchronous data communication.

The teleprinter was the next major step after the telegraph in data communications. Teleprinter equipment has been the backbone of nonvoice business communications for over half a century. As recently as the mid-1970s, a teletypewriter (TTY), which is a teleprinter with a keyboard for input, was the standard terminal for small- and medium-sized computers. Many companies have nationwide and even worldwide private teleprinter networks. Two nationwide public teleprinter networks are the TWX and TELEX services. Several common carriers will transmit telex messages to any teleprinter in the United States, and companies called "international record carriers" will deliver them to any teleprinter in the world. A company's telex number can be found in a directory similar to a telephone directory.

Like the telegraph, teleprinters are important not only in their own right because they were the principal data communication method for almost fifty years, but also because most of the standards and terminology for low-speed or asynchronous data communications came from the world of teleprinters. We'll discuss asynchronous transmission more thoroughly in Chapter 2; for now, it is sufficient to realize that the transmission of each of the coded characters begins with a "start" symbol and ends with a "stop" symbol. Although this technique permitted synchronization of teleprinter equipment thousands of miles apart, it also added to the already high overhead (in terms of extra time) required for transmission of each character.

Teleprinter equipment was inherently limited to slow transmission speeds because it was electromechanical: solenoids had to be energized to attract armatures; motors had to start, turn and stop; and clutches had to engage and disengage. All of these mechanical operations limited the maximum speed at which teleprinters could operate reliably to less than thirty characters per second. International telex operates even slower—less than ten characters per second! Either speed is much too slow for a computer to communicate efficiently with another computer, or even with a modern printer or CRT terminal.

DATA COMMUNICATIONS IN COMPUTING

The introduction of the electronic computer provided greater speed and capabilities to the data communications system.

Further improvements in data communications were necessitated by the widespread use of electronic computers which were introduced in the early 1950s. These computer systems were capable of storing large quantities of information and of processing it quickly. Input and output equipment were much improved over the teletypewriter and teleprinter so they could operate much faster. As more computers were used, it became necessary for computers to communicate with each other. Since this communication did not need any electromechanical equipment, data transfer theoretically could occur at extremely fast rates. Practically, however, data transfer rates are limited by the transmission medium— primarily the public telephone network.

The 1950s

The first computer systems had little need for data communication because they were located close together, I/O was usually direct, and information was processed in discrete batches.

The typical computer system of the 1950s, shown in Figure 1.6, used punched cards for input, printers for output, and reels of magnetic tape for "permanent" mass storage. There was little or no data communications in these systems because the input devices, output devices and computer were all located close together and were directly connected by short cables. Information was processed on a "one job at a time" or "batch" basis.

**Figure 1.6.
Typical Data
Processing System of
the 1950s** *(Courtesy
International Business
Machines Corporation)*

For example, a wholesale grocery company would receive orders by mail and telephone during the day. At the end of the day, these would be collected and punched into cards which were then assembled as a batch. The data on the cards were read into the computer for processing at night. During the processing, the computer would do such things as check the customer's credit. If satisfactory, the computer would generate a pick list for the warehouse so the order could be filled and shipped the next day. The quantity ordered for the different types of items would be deducted from the quantity on hand, and the invoices and various warehouse tickets would be printed. This system worked well except that the person taking the order from the customer during the day, whether on the phone or at the customer's premises, was never certain whether the ordered items were available in the warehouse. Although an updated inventory report was available each morning, a running inventory was not kept during the day as orders were received.

The 1960s

In the 1960s, the use of outlying, on-line terminals required communications links to connect them to the main computer.

Batch processing systems such as the one just described are the most efficient in the use of computer time and equipment; however, they are relatively inefficient in the use of the order clerks, sales people and other resources of the company. While the costs of people were increasing, the solid-state revolution caused the cost of computer logic and memory to decrease sharply. This meant that companies could invest in more computer equipment to reduce the costs of personnel, as well as to make themselves more competitive in business.

In the 1960s, batch processing was largely replaced by on-line processing (Figure 1.7). In the example of the wholesale grocery company, the clerks took the orders over the phone and used on-line terminals to enter the orders into the computer at the same time. Some of these terminals were directly connected to the computer by parallel communication channels, but many of the terminals were teleprinter devices which used serial data communications over dedicated private cables to the computer.

As the order was entered, the computer checked the inventory to see if the goods were on hand. If so, the customer was given a delivery date; if not, he was told that the goods were out of stock, and was given the option of placing a back order or selecting another item. While more expensive than batch processing in terms of computer time and equipment, this method of doing business made the wholesale grocery company more competitive because it gave the customer better service.

In the 1970s, the introduction of the minicomputer and the very portable microcomputer required that these units have increased communications with their mainframe computer.

The 1970s

The 1970s changed this process still further (Figure 1.8). Other computers, sometimes called minicomputers, could communicate with the larger computer in the wholesale grocer's central office. The on-line order terminals were not necessarily in the room next to the computer; they might have been on a different floor, in a different building, or even in a different city. Toward the end of the decade, even smaller computers, called microcomputers or personal computers, began to be seen not only in the homes of some of the employees, but also on their desks at the office. Sometimes the employees would communicate with the main computer through these smaller computers. The company salesmen began carrying portable computer terminals with them on their sales calls. They could enter their orders from the customers' office directly into the main computer over a standard telephone line.

Figure 1.7. Typical Data Processing System of the 1960s (Courtesy Control Data Corporation Archives)

True data communications was everywhere in the system. There was more equipment around than anyone would have thought possible in the 1950s—more computers, more terminals, more communications channels—and businesses were run more efficiently because of it.

The 1980s

Advances in technology increased the capabilities, reduced the size and power requirements of computers, and provided a new communications link—the satellite.

As the wholesale grocery company grew, they decided to produce some of the food products that they sold, so they set up producing operations in California, Texas, and Florida. Because their wholesale business is primarily in the northeast, they have major warehouse facilities in New Jersey, Pennsylvania, and Ohio, and sales offices in Chicago, Philadelphia, and New York City. The company headquarters is also in New York City.

**Figure 1.8.
Typical Data
Processing System of
the 1970s** *(Courtesy
Mohawk Data Sciences
Corporation)*

With the expansion to the south and west, the company's data communications system also needed expansion. They decided to use the relatively new satellite communications to tie the New York office with the Texas and California operations. (Satellite communications are discussed in later chapters.) The satellite could be used for other points as well, but the company (for various reasons) uses leased terrestrial circuits to the Florida, Chicago, and Philadelphia sites. The smaller sales offices in the states where the company operates are tied together with a network of low-speed teletypewriter-like terminals that allow order entry and some communication with the home office. The company's salesmen still carry portable terminals, but advances in technology have reduced the size of the terminal while increasing its capabilities. A typical one is shown in Figure 1.9.

As low-cost personal computers became more widely available during the mid-1980s, many managers acquired them for departmental use. Although the original intention was to use the local processing capability of personal computers for such tasks as budgeting with spreadsheet programs and word processing, corporate management quickly began to integrate personal computers into their company communications networks. Some personal computers replaced CRT terminals and served as both terminals and local processing devices. Other PCs were linked together into a local area network, which enabled users to share peripheral devices and provided the capability of sending electronic messages to other users on the network.

Figure 1.9.
TI 703KSR Teleprinter
*(Courtesy Texas
Instruments, Inc.)*

Introduced in mid-1981, more than ten million IBM PC and compatible computers had been manufactured by 1987, when the Personal System/2 Model 30 computer replaced the IBM PC. Figure 1.10 illustrates the major components of an IBM PC computer system. Today, the personal computer is as prevalent in many organizations as is the office typewriter.

The 1990s

The growth in the distribution of personal computers throughout organizations during the 1980s was linked to a requirement to provide communications capability between these devices. In addition, many personal computer users required access to corporate mini and mainframe computers, further increasing requirements for communications between different types of computers.

For the grocery company previously discussed, their personal computers were installed in their sales offices in Chicago, Philadelphia, and New York City. Initially used for a variety of functions ranging from "what-if" computations using spreadsheets to word processing and the maintenance of small databases of sales and marketing information, eventually it was recognized that productivity could be increased by

Figure 1.10.
IBM PC System
(Courtesy IBM
Corporation)

providing a capability for various PC users within each office to
communicate with one another. Through the installation of an appropriate
adapter card in each personal computer (Figure 1.10), cabling, and
software, local area networks (LANs) were installed in each sales office.
This specialized type of network allowed persons within a building or
campus to communicate with one another, share peripheral devices such
as laser printers and plotters, and to share access to common software
programs and database information residing on special types of personal
computers known as file servers.

As the grocery company continued to grow, it was recognized that
LANs were essentially islands of information isolated from one another.
Commencing in the late 1980s and gaining momentum in the 1990s,
vendors introduced a number of internetworking products consisting of
software and hardware which enabled diverse LANs to be connected to one
another and information to flow between devices connected to one another
and between devices connected to different LANs and other computer
systems. Taking advantage of this technology, the wholesale grocery
company installed devices known as gateways, bridges, and routers.

Gateways

Gateways enabled personal computers on selected LANs to access a
corporate mainframe computer. Here the corporate mainframe acted as a
central repository for large databases and intensive computing programs
that are not suitable for execution on personal computers. For example,
database information, including inventory, customer accounts, and
historical ordering and pricing information, could require billions of
characters of storage whereas most personal computers are limited to
hundreds of millions of characters of storage. Concerning intensive
computing applications, the grocery company now used the mainframe for

execution of linear programs that optimize delivery schedules based upon an analysis of thousands of variables. Although personal computer users can access the linear programming results produced on the mainframe via gateways, the execution of this type of program on a personal computer might require 10 or 20 hours while the results might be obtainable in 15 minutes when executed on a mainframe.

Bridges

Bridges enable data to be transmitted between two LANs supporting the same transmission protocol, allowing electronic messages, data files, and programs to be sent between users on different networks. A bridge examines the destination address of data flowing on a LAN to determine if its destination is on that LAN. If it is, the bridge simply functions as a transparent device and allows the data to continue to flow on the LAN to its destination. If the data destination is a different LAN, the bridge then transmits the data via a communications facility to a distant LAN where another bridge functions in a similar manner.

Routers

With a need to add automation to the company's warehouse facilities also served through the installation of LANs, sales personnel upon occasion found it necessary to access information from personal computers connected to warehouse LANs. In fact, the number of LANs installed within the grocery company would have required the establishment of a mesh network with a large number of long distance lines if only bridges were used. Fortunately, the development of routers which examine data destination addresses and route data over different circuits based upon those addresses enabled a lesser number of lines to be used for interconnecting many LANs.

Figure 1.11 illustrates in a block diagram format the relationship of bridges, routers, and gateways for internetworking. In this example, a pair of bridges interconnect two sales office LANs, while a router is used to provide a link from one LAN to many warehouse LANs. The gateway provides a mechanism which allows LAN users to access the mainframe computer. In fact, when sophisticated hardware and software are used, it may be possible for a PC user attached to the LAN at the top of Figure 1.11 to be "bridged" to the second LAN and provided, via the gateway, access to the mainframe—a key goal of internetworking. As we move forward toward the year 2000, it can be reasonably expected that this broad term which defines the connection of diverse equipment and network facilities will represent the method by which organizations integrate their data transmission requirements.

**Figure 1.11.
Internetworking Using
Bridges, Routers, and
Gateways**

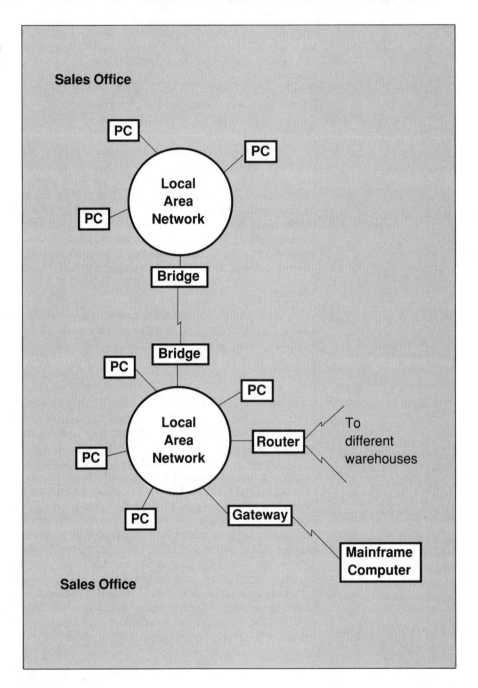

CHANGES IN THE INDUSTRIES

Besides the technological revolution, the breakup of the Bell System changed the way business used and paid for communications.

The hardware and software are not the only things changing. Both the computer industry and the communications industry have changed in ways that would have been unimaginable twenty years ago. The rise of the minicomputer, and later the microprocessor in personal computers, and programmable controllers for equipment, created a situation where computing power was rather inexpensive. The suppliers of large main frame computers, such as IBM, UNISYS, Control Data, and Honeywell, were joined by companies such as Texas Instruments, Apple, Radio Shack, and Commodore, that had not previously made computers. With many more computers used by many more people to create and use much more data, interest in data communications increased. In communications, the advent of satellites followed by optical fiber transmission offered the promise of far greater bandwidths (range of usable frequencies), thus, faster data transmission speeds.

The revolution in computing and data transmission was paralleled by an upheaval in the structure of the communications industry. The telephone companies' monopoly of almost a century disappeared forever, beginning in the late 1960s and accelerating until the Bell System was broken up in 1984. For the first time, other firms not only could compete with the telephone companies in offering long distance service; but they also could sell equipment, including data communications devices, to be connected to the telephone network.

These two forces, the advent of the microprocessor-based personal computer and the increase in competition in both the computing and communications industries, brought about dramatic changes and accelerated technological advances in the communications field. They also brought communications and computing closer together. In the example wholesale grocery company of the 1980s, it is hard to say where communications stops and computing begins. Is the sales person's portable terminal or the manager's personal computer a communications device or a computer? The answer, of course, is that they are both, because they do whatever combination of tasks is required for the job at hand.

In modern computer-communications systems, we can interconnect equipment of many different sizes and capabilities from a variety of suppliers. One of the purposes of this book is to explain how to interconnect, or interface, these different kinds of equipment so it all works together in a system.

GENERAL DESCRIPTION OF A DATA COMMUNICATIONS SYSTEM

The most accurate way to separate a data communications system's parts is in terms of the Universal Seven-Part Data Circuit.

A data communications system can be described simply in terms of three components: the transmitter (also called the "source"), the transmission path (usually called the channel, but sometimes the line), and the receiver (occasionally called the "sink"). In two-way communications, however, the source and the sink may interchange roles; that is, the same piece of equipment may transmit and receive data simultaneously. Therefore, it is easier to think of a data communications system between point A and point B (Figure 1.12) in terms of the Universal Seven-Part Data Circuit which consists of:

1. The data terminal equipment (DTE) at point A.
2. The interface between the DTE and the data circuit-terminating equipment (or data communications equipment) (DCE) at point A.
3. The DCE at point A.
4. The transmission channel between point A and point B.
5. The DCE at point B.
6. The DCE-DTE interface at point B.
7. The DTE at point B.

In our Seven-Part Data Circuit, the DTE can be a terminal device or computer part, while the DCE can be a modem if an analog channel is used or a Data Service Unit (DSU) if a digital channel is used.

    The function of the various parts of the data communications system, both hardware and software, now can be described more easily. The DTE is the source, the sink, or both in the system. It transmits and/or receives data by utilizing the DCE and data transmission channel. Don't be misled by the name "data terminal equipment"; these could indeed be CRT or Teletype terminals, but they also may be personal computers, printers, front-end processors for large mainframe computers, or any other device that can transmit or receive data. The whole purpose of the data communications system is to transmit useful information between point A and point B; the information may be used directly by the DTE, or the DTE may process and display the information for use by human operators.

Form and Content of Information

The data communications system is only concerned with the correct transmission of data, in its coded form, between two points.

    The DCE and the transmission channel perform the function of moving the data from point A to point B. In general, they neither know nor care about the content of the information transmitted; it could be stock market quotations, a display for a video game, or recipes for Aunt Martha's fudge.

    This brings us to an important point about data communications— the difference between the *form* and *content* of the information transmitted. The form of the information might be English language text represented by code for a telegram; the content might advise you that a rich uncle had just left you a million dollars. Clearly, the average user of data communications is much more interested in the content of the information, and really is not concerned about the mechanics of the communication process so long as the information is received correctly. It would be rather disappointing if, in fact, your uncle had left you only $100.00, but because of errors in transmission, the telegram you received stated that you had inherited $1,000,000.00.

**Figure 1.12.
The Universal Seven-
Part Data Circuit**

CRT's, teletypes, personal computers or printers

POINT A

POINT B

DTE

DCE

TRANSMISSION
CHANNEL

DCE

DTE

DTE/DCE INTERFACE

DCE/DTE INTERFACE

The DTE
can be the
source, the
sink, or
both.

a. Block Diagram

TELEPHONE LINES

MODEM

MODEM

MAINFRAME COMPUTER
AND FRONT-END
PROCESSOR

PERSONAL
COMPUTER

b. Pictorial

The data communications system itself is concerned only with the correct transmission between points A and B of the information given it; the system does not operate on the content of the information at all. This means that where we talk about the "correctness" of the transmitted information in this book, we mean only that the information received has the identical form as the information transmitted. If someone gave a message to the telegraph operator stating that your uncle had left you a million dollars, when he had left you only a hundred dollars, the inaccuracy of that information would not be the fault of the telegraph operator or the data communications equipment.

Protocol is the name given to the hardware and software rules and procedures for making sure that any transmission errors are detected. These may be as simple as transmitting an extra bit of information in each character to detect errors, as used with personal computers, or as complex as some systems use for satellite data communications. The satellite system not only sends extra information to allow the receiver to detect transmission errors, but also to correct the errors and to make the receiver appear to be in the room next to the DTE, rather than about 50,000 transmission miles away.

DTE-DCE Interface

The DTE-DCE interface consists of the input/output circuitry in the interface, as well as the cables and connectors that link DCE and DTE.

We've mentioned the DTE-DCE interface several times as though it is something special. It is. The interface consists of the input/output circuitry in the DCE and in the DTE, and the connectors and cables that connect them. In most systems, this interface conforms to the RS-232 standard as published by the Electronics Industry Association (EIA) in the United States. (The RS-232 and other standard DTE-DCE interfaces will be discussed later in this book.) The RS-232 interface, and other serial interfaces which use some of the RS-232 specification, but depart from it in some important way, are by far the most commonly-used interfaces in data communications. The RS-232 standard specifies the rules by which data is moved across the interface between the DTE and the DCE, and, therefore, ultimately from point A to point B. The word serial means that the bits cross the interface one at a time in series.

DTEs are a very important part of the process of moving data between points A and B. Not only are basic input and output capabilities important, but today's intelligent electronic terminals can perform many complex software-driven functions whose goal is to ensure better performance and accuracy of the data transfer. We'll look at these functions in several of the chapters to follow.

Similarly, while we devote a great deal of discussion to the interface between the DTE and the DCE, we spend less time on the interface between the DCE and the communications channel. This is because the latter interface is quite simple (either two wires or four wires, rather than two to twenty-four as in the RS-232 interface), and because there is not a problem with the sequencing of the electrical signals across this interface.

We won't spend a great deal of time discussing the transmission channel either, even though it is obviously crucial to the data communications system. The various electrical characteristics of the channel itself (such as its bandwidth, relative delay at various frequencies, and other parameters) usually conform to published specifications, and these specifications are often contained in the tariffs published by the telephone companies or other carriers. We have very little control over the transmission channel itself (except to hang up and redial), and the equipment used for data communications is tolerant of a wide range of channel characteristics. We will discuss some of these characteristics and some of the problems, but unless the data transmission rate is at a very high speed, the communications channel usually does not cause any trouble.

So we really don't care much about how the channel works, so long as a standard voice-grade channel between points A and B is available. A standard voice-grade channel is a telephone line which normally would be used for voice communication, that is, a telephone conversation. Thus, a fundamental problem in data communications is that the transmission of digital data must be accomplished over facilities that were designed for voice (analog) communications. The modem, a type of DCE which is used to convert digital data to an analog form (like speech or tones) for transmission over the telephone channel, is described later in this book.

WHAT HAVE WE LEARNED?

Now that we have revealed the fundamental secrets of data communications, let's briefly review the problem, the terms and the parts of the system:

1. Problem: To encode information using some kind of standard code, convert it to a form that can be transmitted over the existing telephone network, transmit it between point A and point B without introducing errors, and reverse the process at the receiving end to recover the original information.
2. Channel: A transmission facility connecting points A and B. It's usually a voice-grade telephone channel provided by the telephone company. The channel can be established for the duration of a call (dial up) or from a permanent connection (leased line).
3. Data Terminal Equipment (DTE): At one end, the source of the data to be transmitted; at the other end, the sink which receives the transmitted data.
4. Data Circuit-Terminating (or Communications) Equipment (DCE): The conversion equipment between the DTE and the transmission channel. One type of DCE, the modem, converts the data into tones for transmission over the voice channel.
5. RS-232 Interface: The interface wiring and electronics between the DTE and the DCE equipment at either end of the system. Although there are other important interface standards, this is the most common.
6. Information: The data to be transmitted between A and B. It could be as simple as a command to turn on an indicator light, or as complex as the commands for drawing a multicolor illustration on a CRT display. In either case, the communications system itself is concerned only about moving the data between A and B without any error. The data communications system does not respond to, nor act on, the content of the data transmitted.
7. Internetworking: Hardware and software which enables information to flow between devices connected to different LANs and other computer systems.
8. Protocol: The rules for transmission of information between two points. They include rules for handling such questions as what to do if a transmission error occurs, or how to determine if the receiver is ready to receive the transmission.
9. LAN and WAN: A local area network (LAN) interconnects devices within a building or campus, while a wide area network (WAN) interconnects devices within a city or locations in different cities.

Quiz for Chapter 1

1. Which is *not* an example of data communications?
   a. A Teletype printing news bulletins.
   b. A computer transmitting files to another computer.
   c. An automatic teller machine checking account balances with the bank's computer.
   d. A salesman telephoning orders to the office.

2. Two-state (binary) communications systems are better because:
   a. They can interface directly with the analog telephone network.
   b. The components are simpler, less costly, and more reliable.
   c. People think better in binary.
   d. Interstate calls are less costly.

3. Which is not a positional notation system?
   a. Roman (MCMXXXVII)
   b. Binary (01111110)
   c. Decimal (1492)
   d. Hexadecimal (3A2B)

4. Codes are always:
   a. Eight bits per character.
   b. Either seven or eight bits per character.
   c. Agreed upon in advance between sender and receiver.
   d. The same in all modern computers.

5. The Baudot code:
   a. Was invented by the Baudot brothers, Mark and Space.
   b. Requires the escape character to print numbers.
   c. Requires shift characters to provide sufficient combinations.
   d. Was invented by Emile's sister, Bridgette.

6. The standard ASCII:
   a. Is version II of the ASC standard.
   b. Has 128 characters, including 32 control characters.
   c. Is a subset of the 8-bit EBCDIC code.
   d. Is used only in the U.S. and Canada.

7. Extended ASCII:
   a. Adds extra digits to standard ASCII.
   b. Provides 128 additional character definitions beyond standard ASCII.
   c. Doubles the bit length of each ASCII character.
   d. Provides extra characters that you define.

8. Escape sequences:
   a. Use the ESC character to indicate the start of a special control sequence.
   b. Are used to switch (escape) between ASCII and EBCDIC codes.
   c. Are a popular daydream for inmates.

9. The principal difference between batch processing and on-line processing is:
   a. Computer resources are used more efficiently for on-line processing.
   b. Teleprinters are used for batch processing; CRTs are used for on-line processing.
   c. Transactions are grouped for batch processing; transactions are processed as needed for on-line processing.

10. DCE and DTE:
   a. Mean "digital communications equipment" and "digital termination equipment."
   b. Are connected by either two or four wires.
   c. Refer to the modem and the computer or terminal, respectively.

11. The correctness and accuracy of the transmitted message content is:
   a. Verified by the modem.
   b. Determined by the sender and receiver, not by the communications system.
   c. Ensured by use of digital techniques.

Data Terminals

ABOUT THIS CHAPTER

Having defined data communications in an overall sense, we now begin describing the various equipment and software which make up the system. We'll start with the part of the system that is most visible to the user—the terminal. Terminals are one of the most dynamic areas of the computer industry; they are associated with convenience, speed, and glamour. The great majority of data terminals used through the early to mid-1980s fell into two categories: teleprinter terminals and CRT terminals. Growing additions to the later category are small business computers and personal computers used as terminals. In fact, by the early 1990s more personal computers were used as terminals than teleprinters and CRT terminals combined. We'll discuss both the older teleprinter terminals and the newer CRTs as well as their rivals.

TELEPRINTERS

The teleprinter, the next step in data communications after the Morse telegrapher, is a low-speed printer that has a serial communications interface.

The device that was invented to replace the Morse telegrapher was called the *teleprinter*. It was actually a form of specialized telegraph which used the 5-bit character code. An early teleprinter is shown in Figure 2.1. The largest manufacturer of teleprinters in the United States was the Teletype Corporation, and because of this, the word "Teletype" has been commonly used to refer to any teletypewriter or teleprinter. This usage is improper, however, because "Teletype" is a trademark of Teletype Corporation.

A teleprinter may be defined as any device that combines a low-speed printer with a serial communications interface. Although a keyboard is an important component of most teleprinters, it is not required to fit this definition (which is used in the commercial marketplace). Thus, the common line printer qualifies if it has a serial interface.

Teleprinter Communications

Teleprinters transmit characters using a simple but slow asynchronous transmission method that either reverses current flow or turns it on and off.

Teleprinters use start-stop asynchronous transmission which is the most widely used method of data communications for a serial interface. It is the simplest technique, but it's also the least efficient (the price paid for simplicity).

Teleprinters transmit at a speed much lower than the capacity of a telephone voice grade line. Common teleprinter speeds in North America are 75 and 110 bits per second (bps). Common speeds elsewhere in the world are 100 and 200 bps. The international teleprinter (telex) network and many European lines operate at 50 bps. Teleprinter signals are formed simply by switching an electrical current on and off or by reversing its direction of flow. The current is either 20 or 60 milliamperes, and the equipment is called current-loop equipment. (Most teleprinters today use RS-232 as the external interface, but current-loop circuitry still may be used internally). The on and off pulses form a code which is interpreted by the receiving device. Single-current teleprinter signaling, also known as neutral or unipolar signaling, is common in the United States; but double-current signaling, also called polar or bipolar signaling, is more common in Europe. We'll discuss current-loop signaling more in a later chapter.

Teleprinter Terminals

The speed of the tele-printer's printing mechanism is very important in applications where most of its time will be spent in receiving and printing incoming data.

Two types of teleprinters are available: those with typewriter-style keyboards (called keyboard send-receive or KSR), and those without keyboards (called receive-only or RO). The typical teleprinter is capable of printing from 10 to 30 characters per second (cps) or from 100 to 300 words per minute (wpm) which is much faster than most typists. However, because much of the terminal's time may be devoted to printing output from a computer rather than entering data, it is usually desirable to have the fastest possible printing mechanism. Thus, teleprinters are available with printing speeds of up to 120 cps.

In the usual operation of a teleprinter, a user enters inputs to the computer via the keyboard. The inputs are transmitted back (called echo) from the computer character-by-character to the printer and printed to verify receipt. Output originating in the computer or another source is printed as it is received, thus, a "hard copy" of both the inputs and the outputs is available. While many teleprinters are utilized in this way, some are strictly on-line printing devices; thus, they don't require a keyboard.

The classic and perhaps best application for teleprinter terminals is in interactive sessions with a computer, such as timesharing or bulletin boards. Here the comparative slowness of the teleprinter is not restrictive, and the printed copy is often quite useful. The slow speed of operation is not as noticeable as in other applications because much of the operator's time is spent in thinking, rather than in waiting for output.

Teleprinters that use microprocessors can be programmed for a variety of different applications. This has reduced their cost and extended the machine's life.

Modern teleprinters, such as the one illustrated in Figure 2.2, utilize a variety of printing techniques and operate at a wide range of print speeds. They provide features such as programmable format control, adjustable forms control, upper- and lowercase printing, interchangeable character styles (fonts), bidirectional printing and paper feeding, selectable character and line spacing, status indicators, portability, and additional keys such as a numeric keypad.

Manufacturers have incorporated the microprocessor into teleprinters to reduce design, development, and production costs, while providing a variety of applications that can be implemented by either the vendor or user. The microprocessor delays the time when a particular teleprinter design will become obsolete because future applications can be accommodated by reprogramming the microprocessor to do other jobs. From the user's point of view, microprocessor technology also offers the major advantage of lower cost because the manufacturer's cost savings resulting from using microprocessors are passed on to the customer.

Compared to total terminal sales, few new teleprinter units are sold outside of the traditional record services markets (telex, twx, and private teleprinter network). Even most of these are specialized. An example is the portable printing terminal often used by a traveling businessperson whose needs are satisfied by a small, lightweight (13 to 18 pounds), hand-carried terminal. Such terminals are available from Texas Instruments and other vendors.

The rapid decrease in the price of portable computers means that they can be used now for applications that previously were reserved for portable terminals. Not only can portable personal computers communicate with large corporate computers, but these portables permit the traveling businessperson to compose memorandums and letters and to analyze business decisions with spreadsheet programs. Although portable terminals communicating with corporate computers could perform such functions, the personal computer can complete these tasks in a local mode of operation, which eliminates many long distance communication sessions.

Although many vendors call their personal computers portable, the word transportable may be more appropriate in certain cases. Personal computers that weigh between 20 and 30 pounds are best categorized as transportable, whereas truly lightweight (weighing under 12 pounds)

Figure 2.2.
TI 820 KSR Teleprinter
(Courtesy Texas
Instruments, Inc.)

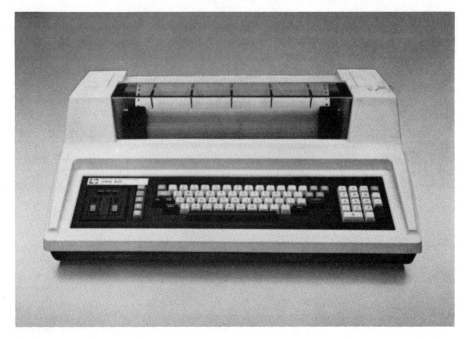

personal computers can be considered portable, especially when you carry them through an airport.

Fortunately for the executive who travels, two new types of personal computers became available in the late 1980s—laptops and palmtops. Laptops, so named because they could literally be placed on a person's lap, normally weigh under 12 pounds, and many can fit into an attache case. Palmtops, so named because they can be lifted by closing one's hand around the device, usually weigh under two pounds. Both laptop and palmtop computers can perform most, if not all, computing functions associated with conventional personal computers while providing a high level of portability.

Although they have a high level of portability, both laptops and palmtops do have some drawbacks. The chief drawbacks of these portable computers include a compressed keyboard in which multiple key depressions may be required to generate some of the key functions for normal keyboards, and poor screen readability. The latter is now a problem mainly associated with palmtops.

TELEPRINTER VERSUS CRT TERMINALS

A teleprinter's disadvantages are: slower speed, little or no variability in format, and limited reliability due to mechanical wear.

The drawbacks to teleprinters are speed, formatting, and reliability. They are far slower in operation than CRT terminals; even their highest print speed doesn't compare to the 300 or 1200 characters per second on the CRT. Because teleprinters are designed primarily for message communications, they do not provide sophisticated capabilities for data editing or formatting. It is quite difficult to create a form on a teleprinter, and of course such attributes as blinking, highlighting, and similar enhancements that are available on a CRT terminal are impossible on a teleprinter. While teleprinters are quite reliable, they are, nevertheless, electromechanical devices that are subject to wear and misalignment. CRT terminals on the other hand, generally have higher reliability because of far fewer parts, most of which do not move.

Serial Printers

Teleprinter terminal serial printers, either impact or nonimpact, print one character at a time sequentially.

Teleprinter terminals utilize serial (or character) printers, so named because they print one character at a time. Such printers may be classified into two categories: impact printers that mechanically strike the paper to produce a printed image, and nonimpact printers that produce an image by some other means. Impact printers are further divided into two subcategories: those that produce a ''fully-formed'' character (where the character is created by impact from a single piece of type), and ''dot matrix'' printers, where the character image on the paper is formed by a matrix of dots. Nonimpact teleprinters form characters by the dot matrix method only, using either an electrothermal or ink-jet printing method.

Impact Printers

Impact printers are those that use mechanical action to strike a ribbon against the paper to print the desired character, either completely formed, or in a dot matrix.

Impact printing mechanisms include replaceable type-ball elements (as used on the IBM Selectric typewriters), daisy wheels (a flat disk with petal-like projections for the character elements), elements shaped like a cup with finger-like projections, moving type belts with the characters engraved on the belt, a rotating cylinder containing the characters, and a type block with characters embedded in the block. All of these share the same advantages of fully-formed characters in almost any style and shape, and the ability to make carbon copies. They also share the same disadvantages of low speed and mechanical complexity. No matter how the character is mounted or engraved on the type element, it must be positioned in front of the platen and then struck against an inked ribbon and paper to produce an image. This limits the speed of the printer to a maximum of 120 cps (but it's usually much lower), as well as creating a large amount of noise in the process.

This speed limitation was an incentive for printer manufacturers to seek a different approach that would extend the upper limit of printing speed for serial impact printers. Their search led to the development of the dot matrix printer. Dot matrix printers are a compromise (and often a successful one) between decreased character quality and substantially higher print speeds of 180 cps or more. The printed image is formed from a rectangular matrix of dots, which was initially 9 dots high by 7 dots wide. Printing is performed by moving a print head containing a column of 9 pins across the paper and selectively actuating the pins at 7 successive intervals to form each character. Developments in dot matrix printer technology increased the number of pins that could be placed on the print head, resulting in the availability of 18- and 24-pin print-head printers. Dot matrix printers with these high density print heads result in the printing of characters whose pin dots overlap to produce a near solid character format. This type of printing which provides the appearance of an impact printer output is referred to as near letter quality. Though they contain comparatively few moving parts, dot matrix printers are subject to a large amount of wear and heat within the print head as a result of the succession of pin movements required to create each character.

Dot matrix teleprinters are typically less expensive than similarly featured fully-formed character teleprinters. With the improved print quality now available with higher-resolution dot matrix printing, most teleprinter users are satisfied with dot matrix printers.

Another development that has improved speed in newer teleprinters is the bidirectional print head with logic-seeking control. The print head can print while moving in either direction (left to right or right to left). The logic-seeking control circuitry determines the shortest horizontal distance to move the print head to print the next line. Thus, on full pages of text, one line is printed left to right and the next is printed right to left, etc. This feature, which is available on both fully-formed character printers and dot matrix printers, eliminates the time required for a full carriage return to the left side for every line.

NonImpact Printers

Nonimpact printers use electrothermal or ink-jet printing techniques. They are more reliable, quieter, and faster than impact printers.

The nonimpact types of teleprinters employ various electronic and chemical techniques to produce printed images. All nonimpact teleprinters currently on the market utilize dot matrix character formation. Some of the printing techniques have been developed from xerography and facsimile communications techniques. Others were specifically developed for use in high speed printing applications where print speeds of more than 2000 lines (that's lines, not characters) per minute are not uncommon. Still others were designed to meet a specific goal, such as quiet operation.

The electrothermal printing technique is one nonimpact technique. The print head applies heat through the matrix pins to chemically coated paper. The heat causes a chemical reaction which produces a matrix of colored dots that forms the character. It is quiet and efficient, but some people object to having to supply special paper.

The ink-jet technique uses a stream of electrically charged ink droplets sprayed onto ordinary paper to produce the characters as shown in Figure 2.3. Dot placement is accomplished by electrostatic deflection plates that control the direction of the charged ink droplets in much the same manner as electron beam position is controlled within a cathode ray tube. By electronic control of switching between reservoirs of different colored ink, instant color changes can be made as the printer operates. Ink-jet printers were very expensive, but prices have been reduced substantially in the last few years.

**Figure 2.3.
Basic Ink-Jet Printing
Technique**

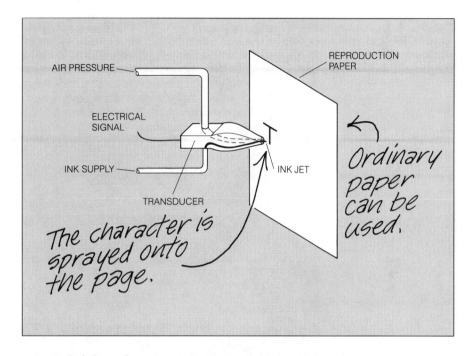

Reliability of nonimpact printers is high compared to impact printers because they have few mechanical parts. Their inability to produce more than one copy at a time (no carbon copies) might sometimes be a disadvantage, but their quiet and reliable operation is certainly an advantage.

CRT TERMINALS

In many applications, the CRT terminal has replaced the teleprinter terminal as the interface between computers and people.

The cathode ray tube (CRT) terminal, also called a video display terminal (VDT), is a common interface between people and computers. Originally developed as an alternative to teleprinter terminals, its introduction in 1965 revolutionized the data communications environment where the teleprinter had been the only interface device. Although many companies entered the marketplace, prices remained high due to low-volume production and the cost (price and assembly labor) of discrete components. The advent of the integrated circuit, followed by large-scale integration, brought prices down, although they were still out of reach of the average individual. Then came the microprocessor, which replaced much of the integrated circuit logic and drove prices still lower. The result is high-quality, high-performance and relatively low-cost CRT terminals that even the hobbyist can afford. A CRT terminal designed for businesses is shown in Figure 2.4.

Figure 2.4.
TI 931 CRT Terminal
*(Courtesy Texas
Instruments, Inc.)*

ASCII Terminals

A CRT terminal that can operate without a separate controller, and can transmit and receive asynchronous data using the ASCII Code is called an ASCII terminal.

In the computer industry, the term "ASCII display terminal" usually refers to a CRT terminal that operates without a separate controller, uses the ASCII code, and transmits and receives asynchronous data. This term originated with CRT terminals (the glass Teletype) designed to replace Teletype ASR 33/35 teleprinter terminals; and ASCII terminals are still described as being "Teletype-compatible". ASCII terminals are available in a wide range, from low-end dumb units that do little more than emulate a teleprinter (or which emulate another CRT terminal, such as the ADM-3, which emulates a teleprinter), up to 132-column split-screen editing terminals with several pages of electronic memory storage.

CRT terminals have three capabilities in common:

1. A keyboard that can generate a full alphanumeric character code set.

CRT terminals can be classed in one of three general categories: dumb terminals, smart terminals, and user-programmable terminals.

2. A CRT monitor that can display the characters of that code set.

3. The capability to send and receive data via communications lines to a remote host computer.

CRT terminals fall into one of three general categories: dumb, smart, and user-programmable. Of course, there is some overlap between categories, but we'll define them as follows:

1. Dumb terminals are Teletype-compatible and offer a limited number of functions; perhaps none beyond keyboarding and display. They are the lowest cost, but often the difference in price between them and the smart terminals is small compared to the difference in performance and features.

2. Smart terminals offer extended functions, such as editing and formatted data entry. The user may be able to tailor the terminal to fit his or her application through limited programming, such as format creation, parameter definition, or input checking.

3. User-programmable (or intelligent) terminals feature software support. The manufacturer provides an operating system (an assembler, compiler, or interpretive programming language), subroutines (I/O utilities; one or more protocol emulators), and one or two application programs, such as data entry and text editing. They provide some form of program storage and more memory for text.

Dumb Versus Smart Terminals

The description of the capabilities of teleprinters also describes the capability of the dumb CRT terminals except for print speed. These essentially consist of a CRT, video (display) memory, and interface electronics. Few truly dumb terminals are still manufactured; virtually all CRT terminals currently manufactured are microprocessor controlled, making them smart terminals according to our definition. The microprocessor chips cost only a few dollars, which is less than the cost of the logic they replace.

Microprocessor control has given CRT smart terminals the flexibility and capabilities to perform many operations beyond simple display and keyboarding.

The microprocessor programs (firmware) reside in read-only memory (ROM) or programmable ROM (PROM). ROM-resident programs control those features which are "permanent" while PROM-resident programs are typically produced in smaller quantities and implement customized or modifiable features. Either type can be replaced by a different type with a different program by simply removing the old chip and putting in a new one, although this feature is more talked about than actually used. In addition to controlling basic terminal functions, the microprocessor can provide protocol emulation, define the character code sets to be generated by the keyboard, implement special features, set control parameters, etc. Moreover, the microprocessor delays obsolescence, since future needs can be implemented via reprogramming.

In addition to the ability to simply display alphabetic and numeric characters, microprocessor control provides the capability to highlight characters by means of underscoring, reverse video, blinking, differing levels of brightness, and combinations of these attributes. One of the most impressive capabilities of these terminals is the ability to display a predefined form and let the operator "fill in the blanks" while checking the entries as they are made.

Many CRT terminals can display double size characters, and most have a graphics character set for creating forms and formats. Some also support business graphics; for example, bar, column, and pie charts to graphically show sales, income and expense, inventory levels, etc. Interactive or engineering graphics, on the other hand, is a highly specialized area usually requiring a completely different, high-resolution graphics terminal.

User-Programmable Terminals Versus Personal Computers

Because of the need for increased requirements, the emphasis has shifted to using microcomputers for terminal functions.

Taken separately, the words programmable and terminal are precisely definable. But when combined to describe one class of equipment, their meaning becomes vague and difficult to define with precision. In 1979, a popular periodical defined a user-programmable terminal as a terminal which permits local file updating and accommodates user-written applications programs. At that time, this definition stirred up quite a bit of controversy because such a terminal would have to provide for the following in addition to the basic terminal functions:

1. The availability of, and the support and documentation of, at least one general-purpose programming language for development of programs by customer personnel.

2. Entry of programs via the terminal keyboard.

3. The ability to access and retrieve programs stored in the host computer memory, and the ability to execute (use) those programs at the terminal.

Much of the value of user-programmable terminals is their off-line processing capability provided by the above listed items. All user-programmable terminals have built-in main memory that the user can use to store and execute programs, but the capacity varies from as little as 1 kilobyte (usually written as 1K or 1K byte), which will accommodate only a very small program to as much as 512K bytes (which will accommodate a large program and much data). Most (though not all) user-programmable terminals also provide for local mass storage using floppy, hard, or cartridge disks; or cassette or cartridge magnetic tape.

With disks, tapes, memory, an operating system, and a programming language, the user-programmable terminal sounds a lot like a personal or professional computer, doesn't it? This is the revolution in the terminal market. Dumb terminals and low-end smart terminals are rapidly being squeezed aside by personal and professional computers running terminal programs, which relegates terminals to specialized tasks. Many office workers now have a personal or professional computer on their desks, which can be used either standalone as a computer or placed on-line to the large host computer. Files can be up- and down-loaded and processed wherever it makes the most sense to do so. All because of data communications and the microprocessor!

Emulation

When the personal computer operates a communications program that enables the computer to duplicate the attributes of a terminal, the software is known as a *terminal emulator program*. Such programs permit the personal computer to communicate with main frame application programs developed to work with predefined types of terminals.

Depending on the terminal emulation software marketed for the personal computer, you may be able to replace several types of terminals with one computer. For an example, consider the organization that has both Hewlett Packard (HP) and Digital Equipment Corporation (DEC) main frame computers. With HP 2645 and DEC VT100 terminal emulation software, one can use a personal computer to emulate common Hewlett Packard and Digital Equipment Corporation terminal devices and thereby obtain full screen access to two different computer systems that are designed to operate with two specific types of terminals.

Non-ASCII Terminals

This section describes CRT terminals that do not fit the ASCII label, together with some specialized terminals that use other displays. Of these, the most important are the batch or cluster type.

Batch Terminals

Two different methods of terminal-computer communications, interactive and batch, effectively mesh user needs with the communications techniques.

Communications between a terminal and its computer tends to fall into two basic categories, interactive and batch, which are distinguished by the types of functions to be performed. Terminals and software designed for interactive communications between the terminal and the host support conversational inquiry/response, interactive data entry, and other such applications. Batch communications, on the other hand, supports either remote job entry or remote batch data communications. Remote job entry (RJE), in which the terminal acts as a remote console for the central computer, allows local users to load and execute applications programs. For remote batch data communications, the terminal acts as a remote input/output device for an application program being performed in the host.

The reasons for these distinctions are efficiency and accuracy. An interactive terminal designed to communicate in asynchronous character-by-character mode is not a very efficient method for transmitting large blocks of data as required in the batch mode, nor is the error checking (if any) adequate to ensure correct transmission. On the other hand, it would be wasteful to tie up a complete remote batch terminal just to allow one user to use the keyboard to ask questions about particular data stored in the host computer with the answers sent back by the computer.

Although batch terminals were commonly used to access a remote computer during the 1960s and 1970s, the computer also affected the use of this type of terminal device. The widespread use of personal computers during the 1980s resulted in the development of hardware and software that enables many types of personal computers to function as remote job entry type terminals.

Clustered Terminals

Clustered terminals are generally used in remote, high-volume key-entry locations to facilitate the transfer of large quantities of data to a main computer.

When a remote location generates a large amount of data via key entry, the use of a clustered system may be indicated. This is typical in large-scale data processing installations where it is common practice to control many peripheral units, such as CRT terminals and key-to-disk data input devices, at one location with a single control unit. Data entered through the keyboard devices are stored in a buffer for transmission or transfer to magnetic tape or disk. Then the output of many operators is transmitted in one block to the main computer at much higher speed than that used by teleprinters and ASCII CRT terminals. In addition to the key entry devices, storage, and controller, the cluster may include printers and mass storage. This type of architecture is fundamental to modern data processing, and a widely-used example is the IBM 3270 series.

IBM 3270 Series

The IBM 3270 is not a terminal per se, but is a designation for a family of devices designed for use in clusters. The 3270 series has had a strong impact on the synchronous terminal market since its introduction in 1971. The first generation, which was discontinued in 1982, included the 3271/3272 control units, 3275 display station, 3277 display, and 3284/3286/3288 printers. In 1977, the product line was expanded and updated with the 3274 control unit, 3276 control/display, 3278 display, and 3287/3289 printers. In 1979, color displays and printers were added. In 1983, IBM made some long-awaited changes and enhancements to the 3270 product line. Added were the 3178 display station, a new 3274 control unit, the 3290 information panel (a gas plasma display) and the 3299 terminal multiplexer.

A few years after the introduction of the new 3274, IBM announced its 3174 control unit in 1986. The device in some respects is similar to a personal computer as it can be customized through the addition of special adapter cards. Two of the key functions that can be added to a 3174 control unit are asynchronous ASCII terminal support in which the control unit performs protocol conversion and Token-Ring interface. The latter permits devices on a LAN to access a mainframe via the 3174 which then functions as a gateway.

The 3299 multiplexer is normally used to reduce the amount of cable required to connect terminals to a control unit when the distance between the location of the terminals and the control unit exceeds a few hundred feet. Up to eight terminals can be connected to a 3299, with only one cable required to connect the 3299 to a control unit.

Newer terminals in the 3270 series include the 3179 color display station, the 3279G color graphics display station, the 3180 and 3191 monochrome display stations, and the 3192 and 3194 color display stations. The latter two are most notable for their design, which minimizes the desk space that they require compared with earlier terminals in the 3270 series.

In the area of personal computer connectivity to the 3270 series, IBM has introduced many products. Two of the more significant products are adapter cards that are installed into a system expansion slot of a computer in the IBM PC and PS/2 series and a new control unit. The adapter card permits direct connection of the personal computer to a control unit, which enables the PC to function as a 3270 terminal. With this configuration, personal computer users also can transfer files and do local processing, both of which are beyond the capability of conventional 3270 terminals. As previously mentioned, in 1986, IBM introduced the 3174 control unit, which features an optional token-ring gateway. This feature permits one member of the IBM PC series to be cabled to the 3174 as a gateway device on a token-ring local area network. Other personal computers are then connected to the gateway personal computer, enabling many personal computers on the network to obtain access via one personal computer.

The IBM 3270 family of clustered synchronous terminals is receiving strong competition from microcomputers.

In providing the PC interface, IBM finds itself in an interesting quandary. The 3270 line has been quite profitable over the years; now it faces competition from personal computers, especially those manufactured by IBM! As personal computing becomes the rule instead of the exception in most major corporations, the terminal industry is on the verge of the biggest change since the introduction of the CRT.

The many other firms which offer 3270-compatible products must likewise compete with personal computers. In order to remain competitive, these companies have traditionally offered some combination of lower prices, improved price-performance, and shorter delivery times in order to penetrate the IBM "plug-compatible" market. In addition to the 3270-compatible vendors, some ASCII terminal manufacturers have invaded the 3270 market through protocol conversion. On a 3270 network, synchronous terminals can be replaced with asynchronous terminals coupled with "black boxes" that convert the asynchronous data to synchronous form with the proper headers, check bits, etc. These devices allow an ASCII terminal to support the functional characteristics of the 3270 terminal. The advantage of this strategy is that ASCII terminals are considerably less expensive than their 3270 counterparts.

Other Types of Terminals

The majority of terminals manufactured today employ a keyboard and a CRT. The popularity of this device stems from its flexibility, high character capacity, and relatively low cost. However, specialized needs have led to the development of a broad range of other terminals which include optical bar code readers, voice response units, portable terminals, and the ordinary tone dialing telephone. In addition, such things as supermarket cash registers, portable communicating terminals for inventory management, and a host of other types of equipment now employ data communications. By the DTE/DCE definition, all of these are terminals.

PARTS OF A TERMINAL

Having discussed the various types of terminals, let's now discuss the components of a typical CRT terminal. The average user is concerned only with the components with which he or she interacts—the keyboard and the display. But first, let's talk about one of the current buzz words in the terminal business—ergonomics.

Ergonomics

ANSI standards define ergonomics as: "A multidisciplinary activity dealing with the interactions between man and his total working environment, plus such traditional environmental aspects as atmosphere, heat, light, and sound, as well as the tools and equipment of the workplace."

Terminal manufacturers have become increasingly aware of the need to consider ergonomics in the design of their equipment. The trend toward making CRT terminals more "operator-friendly" began in Europe, and most people agree that European manufacturers still lead in this area. Recent developments in terminals, such as sloped keyboards and green or amber displays, have come about because of ergonomic considerations.

Keyboards

Although terminal keyboards have been improved for user comfort and utility (ergonomics), little has been done to improve and standardize the keyboard layout.

The majority of display terminals now have keyboards that are detached or detachable. Most of these are connected to the console via a coiled cable, usually three to six feet long, which allows the operator to place the keyboard in a comfortable position while using the terminal. A more recent development is the "light-link" or cordless keyboard, where an infrared transmitter/receiver replaces the cable to allow even more freedom of movement.

Another design factor is the slope and thickness of the keyboard. Most keyboards today are either sloped or stepped, with the angle being 5 to 15 degrees. Most recent terminals have sculptured key caps instead of flat key caps, which speeds data entry and improves operator comfort. Audible keyboard feedback may be provided by a beep or key click from a speaker, and tactile feedback may be provided by a unique "feel" when the stroke is registered. Like most other ergonomic considerations, the above features are not, in themselves, the most important criteria for choosing one terminal over another; what they do indicate is the manufacturer's commitment to providing equipment that is up-to-date and easy to use.

Keyboard Layout

The layout of the keyboard is a primary concern of ergonomics. The de facto standard typewriter key layout is that of the IBM Selectric typewriter illustrated in Figure 2.5. A keyboard that has this arrangement of the alphabetic keys is called a QWERTY (pronounced quir-t) keyboard because these are the first six letters of the top row of alphabetic keys. The QWERTY is far from the best layout. In fact, the QWERTY keyboard layout was designed for early mechanical typewriters to arrange the key hammers to reduce key hangups. This arrangement also slowed the typist, so that he or she could not key faster than the early typewriters could operate! In the 1890s, there were over a hundred different typewriter keyboards because almost every company that made a typewriter used a different keyboard. Some of these keyboard types were: the Crandall (ZPRCHMI), the American (CJPFUBL), the Hall (KBFGNIA), and the Morris (XVGWSLZ).

**Figure 2.5.
IBM Selectric
Typewriter Keyboard
Layout**

Various attempts have been made to improve keyboard layout. Some had the letters of frequently used words close together. One proposed by Dr. August Dvorak put the five vowels under one hand and the five most common consonants under the other hand. There were circular keyboards, semicircular keyboards, keyboards with six rows, and keyboards with one long row. The idea of a shift key didn't come along until 1875; prior to that, upper and lower case letters were on different keys.

Programmable Keyboards

The ability to program the keyboard provides the opportunity to rearrange the layout and/or key functions to suit personal taste.

You may be thinking that the operator has no choice but to adapt since the keyboard is built-in and the key arrangement is fixed. Ten years ago that was true, but no it may not always be. Alternate keyboard arrangements (including the Dvorak) are available from some manufacturers, either as standard equipment, or as add-on devices for several terminals and computers. More importantly, many keyboards are programmable. The processor in the terminal considers each key depression simply as a contact closure in a matrix of contacts. The matrix location represented by that row and column is used by the processor to look up the character in the corresponding location in a table in memory. Thus, the keyboard layout may be changed by simply reprogramming the table; that is, the "C" key could be defined in the table so that a "?" is printed instead of "C". This suggests that the terminal of the future might have several keyboards which can be changed by plugging in the new one and telling the program which table to use.

Numeric Keypads

Most terminals have some form of numeric keypad with the numerals 0 through 9 grouped like those on a ten-key adding machine to provide faster entry of numeric data. Other keys such as +, −, and . also may be included. The numeric keypad may be entirely separate from the main keyboard or it may be implemented through an alternate definition of alphabetic keys (usually the "IOP", "KL;", and "M,." groups). Using the main keyboard's number keys to enter numbers requires the use of both hands, thus, number entry is faster with a numeric keypad because all of the numerals are under the fingers of the right hand.

Other Keys

Special keys provide access to functions unique to computer input. While there are a large number of these keys, no uniformity exists as to their positioning on the keyboard.

In addition to the alphabetic and numeric keys, terminal keyboards offer a variety of special keys that are unique to computer input. Unfortunately, there is no standard arrangement of these keys. These may include the CTL (control) key (which allows input of some or all of the ASCII control characters), TAB (usually programmable), ESC, arrow keys (which control cursor movement), and programmable F (function) keys.

For example, on the Wyse WY-50 terminal, the LINE DELETE key sends ESC R. Some keys send different codes in the shifted and unshifted positions. Thus, the unshifted PAGE key means scroll one page forward, and the shifted PAGE key means scroll one page backward. The eight function keys are capable of producing 16 code sequences by using the SHIFT key. When the terminal is powered up, these are set to Ctrl A@ through Ctrl-AO, but they may be changed by the computer program, which sends the terminal a series of escape sequences. For example, the sequence ESC z A DIR B: CR DEL will reprogram the F2 key to send DIR B: followed by a carriage return. Each function key may be programmed with up to eight characters. Like most modern terminals, the WY-50 has the ability to display function key labels on the bottom line of the CRT screen.

Those users who feel that the more keys the merrier should be very merry indeed because many terminals now have over one hundred keys. However, the keys sometimes are not laid out in the most useful way. For example, the cursor arrow keys may be in a row, rather than in a diamond pattern where their direction can be felt. These additional keys may be packed close around the regular keyboard, or arranged in logical groups and slightly separated from the main keyboard. When keys have unusual or unexpected placement, the operator is likely to hit them by mistake. The result can be devastating.

Other Input Devices

Alternatives to keyboard input, which can make entry of specialized data easier, include light pens, touch-sensitive screens, graphic tablets, a "mouse" (a cursor positioning device), and even speech input. Proponents of all of these devices, and more, suggest that they will eventually replace the keyboard for most input. Don't bet on it. Buy the most comfortable, best designed, easiest-to-use keyboard that you can find; it and the display are your window into the computer. The other devices can be quite useful (especially the mouse), but most input probably will be through the keyboard for a long time to come.

Display

The display provides the visualization of the terminal inputs and outputs. Most use dot matrix character formation with 24 text lines having 80 characters per line.

There has been more discussion recently about CRT displays than any other part of the terminal. Some researchers have noted eyestrain, headaches, dizziness, back pains, nausea, and nervous symptoms in workers whose jobs require that they operate CRT terminals for long periods of time. Eyestrain and fatigue are considerations which must be dealt with when designing a CRT display screen. Most CRT tubes are etched or contain a bonded faceplate to reduce glare; tilt and swivel adjustments are also popular for the same reason. The latter also allow the operator to place the screen at the most comfortable viewing angle. The phosphor color and character size is important, too. White, green, or amber phosphors are generally used in the United States, with green probably the most popular.

Most display terminals use the dot matrix technique to form characters. The more dots that are contained in the character cell, the better defined the character will appear on the screen. For years, 5 by 7 dot characters were standard, but today 7 by 7 and 7 by 9 as well as 9 by 11 dot characters are more common. Some manufacturers use high screen refresh rates and noninterlaced scanning to reduce image flicker and improve legibility. The size of the characters generated depends on the size of the screen and the display format used. Characters will be larger on 15-inch screens than on 12-inch screens; likewise, characters will be larger in an 80 character-per-line format than in a 132 character-per-line format. Display enhancements such as double-height and double-width characters can make characters larger, but these are intended for highlighting important data, not for routine use.

Most CRT terminals display 24 text lines of 80 characters each. Many also provide a twenty-fifth line which is used for labels, status, or other terminal or program related information. The status line sometimes is displayed in reverse video.

Memory-Mapped Displays

The majority of ASCII terminals use a technique called memory-mapped video. An advantage of the memory-mapped technique is that the microcomputer can write to and read from the video memory in the same way as ordinary memory because a portion of the ordinary memory is used for the video memory. The difference is that whatever characters are stored in video memory are displayed on the CRT when addressed by the microprocessor.

When memory-mapped displays are used, the microcomputer can write into and read from the video memory just as from ordinary memory.

An 8-bit microprocessor uses two bytes (16 bits) for a memory address; thus, it can directly address 2^{16} or 65,536 memory locations. If each memory location can hold one character (which is the usual arrangement), and if the display size is 80 characters by 24 lines, then 1920 character locations are needed in video memory. If the program memory is restricted to addresses below 63,615, then memory locations from 63,615 through 65,535 could be used for video memory to store an array of characters for the display.

Assume that the upper left-hand corner of the CRT display receives the character from the first location (63,615) in video memory, the next horizontal position on the CRT receives the character from the second location (63,616), etc. Thus, if the first video memory location contains "J", the second "O", the third "H", and the fourth "N"; the upper left-hand corner of the CRT will display "JOHN".

Memory-mapped displays are fast and inexpensive. Because the character set is translated into dots within the dot matrix using a table lookup technique, it is also possible to redefine the character set by simply changing the table entries (if the table is user-accessible). Line insertion and deletion, scrolling, and other effects are easily accomplished by moving data around in video memory, or even simpler, by changing starting addresses. The principal disadvantage of memory-mapped video of the type described is that it takes up space in the memory used to store programs and data. This usually is not a problem for terminals, but for computers, video memory is now usually separate. Also, computer video memory now is often "bit-mapped" rather than "character-mapped" as discussed in the preceding paragraphs. With bit-mapping, each dot on the screen has a separate memory location. This feature allows high-resolution graphic displays, but it requires much more video memory.

Other Types of Displays

Although the CRT is the dominant display device today, there are other devices for displaying information. These include solid-state devices such as light-emitting diodes and liquid crystal displays, and plasma (gas discharge) matrices such as those used in the IBM 3290. These alternate types of displays provide extremely sharp images, but the dominance of the CRT remains unchallenged for now.

Features of a Typical Low-Cost Terminal

The Wyse WY-50 is an asynchronous terminal that also is capable of block-mode transmission. Special functions are available to display the dot matrix characters.

The Wyse WY-50 (Figure 2.6) is fairly typical of current terminal technology; thus, an examination of its operating features will illustrate some of the previous points. When power is turned on, the WY-50 performs self-tests on the microprocessor, memory, communications and printer ports, keyboard, and display. The terminal halts all further operation if a fault is detected, and an error message pointing to the fault is displayed. The main display is 24 lines of 80 characters, plus a top line for local and host messages, and a bottom line for function-key labels. The main 24 by 80 display can be split horizontally into two screens. An escape sequence initiates this feature. For example, ESC x 1 + will split the screen horizontally, with the lower screen starting at line 12.

Figure 2.6.
Wyse WY-50 CRT
Terminal *(Courtesy*
Wyse Technology)

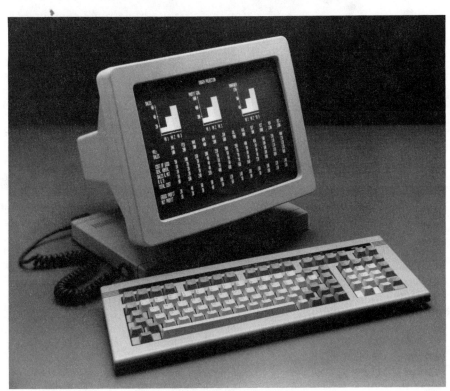

Characters are formed by an 8 by 10 dot matrix in a 10 by 11 cell which provides very good character definition. The terminal can display the 128 ASCII characters and a number of graphics characters. Normal and reverse video, underscore, dim, blink, and blank attributes may be assigned in any combination on a line-by-line basis; for example, ESC A1T creates a reverse video, half-intensity function-key labeling line. Actual labels are entered with another escape sequence; for example, ESC z 3

DEL CHAR will enter DEL CHAR into the label field for the fourth function key (keys are numbered 0 through 7). Attributes and text are entered into the local and host message fields in a similar manner.

In addition to asynchronous character-by-character transmission, the WY-50 is capable of block-mode transmission. When in the block mode, the terminal performs editing and validation for data entered through the keyboard. This function requires a second page or screen of video memory. One 24 by 80 page is used as the data "form" and the second page is used to define the data-validation parameters. Local editing features include line insert and delete, character insert and delete, and automatic word wrapping.

PC Terminals

The growth in the use of personal computers resulted in its adoption as a standard terminal device by many organizations. Some organizations, including several airlines, purchased tens of thousands of IBM PC and compatible personal computers for use with their on-line reservation systems during the 1980s. Other organizations use personal computers for both terminal emulation and local processing functions and have PCs coexisting with conventional terminals. Regardless of the application or utilization, the processing capability of the personal computer can be used with appropriate hardware and software to provide terminal capabilities not available through the use of conventional terminals.

Figure 2.7 shows an IBM PS/2 Model 30 computer with keyboards and graphics monitor. This computer is similar to other members of the PS/2 family in that it contains a built-in serial port. The connector for this port, which is located at the rear of the computer, can be cabled to a modem. When appropriate communications software is loaded into the computer, it can then function as an asynchronous terminal.

For synchronous transmission, IBM and third party vendors manufacture a variety of adapter cards that can be installed in system expansion slots in the system unit of that computer. Some adapter cards enable the PS/2 to be directly attached to IBM 3174 or 3274 control units. When terminal emulation software is loaded, the computer then functions as a 3278- or 3279-type terminal, providing the user with full screen access to mainframe computer applications. Other hardware adapter cards can be used to provide the PS/2 with batch terminal emulation capability to enable it to emulate a variety of IBM and non-IBM remote job entry devices.

The use of a personal computer as a terminal enables hardware and software manufacturers to take advantage of the processing capability of the computer to provide additional capabilities. For example, by using a portion of the memory of the computer for temporary printer data storage, the personal computer can be programmed to accept a mixed data stream of video and printer destination data. This allows the personal computer operator to maintain his or her interactive transmission with a mainframe computer while a print job is routed to their computer, stored in memory,

**Figure 2.7.
The IBM Personal
System/2 Model 30
Computer** *(Courtesy
IBM Corporation)*

and dumped from memory to their printer. A second advantage obtained
from the use of personal computers as terminals includes the
expandability and upgradability of PCs. For example, additional memory
can be easily added to most personal computers. Concerning
upgradability, many personal computers obtain their display capability
from the use of display adapters in a system expansion slot in the
computer's system unit or through the use of a special chip set installed
on the computer's system board. When a new video standard gains
acceptance, most personal computers can have their existing video display
adapters removed and a new adapter that supports the new standard
installed. If video support was obtained from the use of a chip set installed
on the system board, the installation of a video display adapter will
normally override the chip set, enabling the personal computer to support
the new video standard.

DATA TRANSMISSION

Serial and Parallel Transmission

Data are commonly transferred between computers and terminals by
changes in the current or voltage on a wire or channel. Such transfers are
called parallel if a group of bits move over several lines at the same time,

or serial if the bits move one-by-one over a single line. Figure 2.8 illustrates parallel and serial data transmission.

In parallel data transmission, each bit of a character is sent over its own wire. In serial transmission, all bits travel over the same wire one after another.

In parallel transmission, each bit of a character travels on its own wire. A signal, called the strobe or clock, on an additional wire indicates to the receiver when all of the bits are present on their respective wires so that the values can be sampled. Computers and other digital systems that are located near one another (within a few feet) usually use parallel transmission because it is much faster. As the distance between equipment increases, the multiple wires not only become more costly, but also the complexity of the line drivers and receivers increases because of the difficulty of transmitting and receiving pulse signals on long wires.

Serial transmission is used for transmission over long distances. The conversion from parallel to serial and vice versa is accomplished with shift registers. Transmission of serial data is called synchronous if the exact sending or receiving time of each bit is determined before it is transmitted or received, or asynchronous if the timing of the bits in a character are not determined by the timing of a previous character.

Timing

Bit timing is critical to the accurate transmission and reception of data.

Figure 2.9 illustrates a series of bits transmitted serially over a line. Note that while both the sender and receiver use the same nominal clock rate, the receiver must somehow determine a more exact clock for decoding the data. This is one of the fundamental problems of data communications. In this case, the receiver retimes its clock on the negative-going edge of the transition (change) from one to zero of the start bit, then uses its new timing to find the middle of the start bit as shown in Figure 2.9a. Notice in Figure 2.9b that although the receiver clock is slightly fast, it doesn't cause an error because the sample strobe still occurs within each bit time.

Figure 2.9c shows a different situation. Here, the receive clock is so much slower than the transmit clock that the sample strobe does not sample bit 4 at all, thus, an error occurs in the output. This illustrates the fact that the communications system must somehow ensure that the receive clock is timed so that errors do not occur. Although bit timing is very important, it alone isn't enough to complete the communications process.

Framing

The framing method used in asynchronous transmission defines a character by using start and stop bits to separate it from other characters.

Framing is the next step in timing after bit timing. In the example of Figure 2.9, it could be called character timing, since the start and stop bits frame one character for the receiver. This is the framing used in asynchronous data transmission which will be discussed in association with teleprinter operation in the next section. Synchronous data communications systems utilize different methods of framing, and these will be discussed in later chapters.

**Figure 2.8.
Parallel and Serial
Data Transfer**

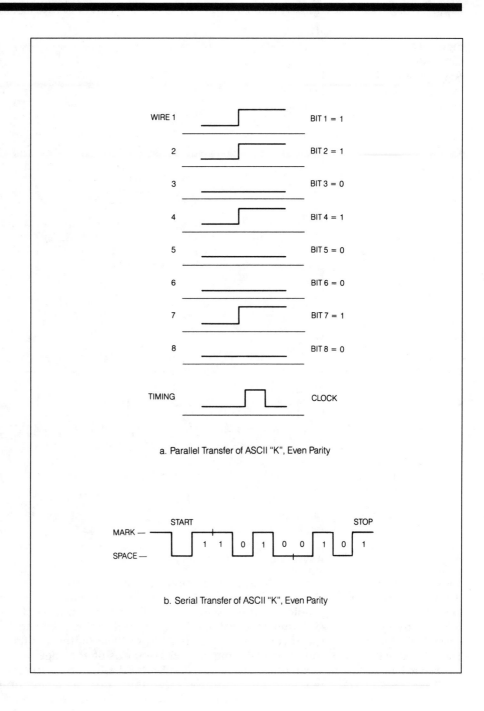

a. Parallel Transfer of ASCII "K", Even Parity

b. Serial Transfer of ASCII "K", Even Parity

**Figure 2.9.
Clocking of
Asynchronous Data**

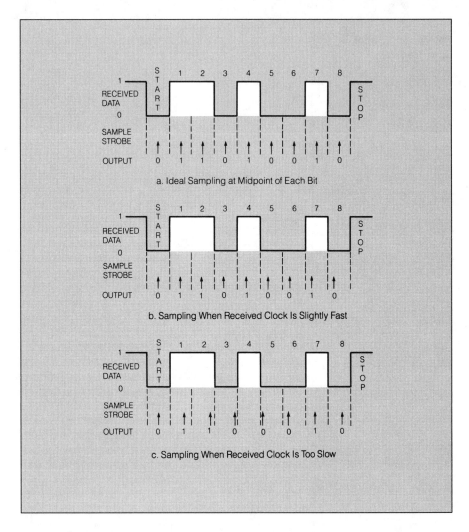

a. Ideal Sampling at Midpoint of Each Bit

b. Sampling When Received Clock Is Slightly Fast

c. Sampling When Received Clock Is Too Slow

Asynchronous Transmission

The first asynchronous
communication systems
used electric motors
driving rotating
contacts at each end.
The rotation of the mo-
tors had to be synchro-
nized.

Asynchronous communications systems evolved before electronic
systems, therefore, electromechanical systems had to be used. The
problem in those systems was the synchronization of the operation of two
electromechanical devices (motors), one at each end of the line, whose
speed could not be easily adjusted. The timing and framing problem was
solved by resuming each character using the edge of the start bit, which
was required to be the first bit on the line. Nevertheless, if the difference
in motor speeds was too great, the bit timing would drift with each
successive bit until the sampling of the last received data bit in the
character could be incorrect. Thus, five bits became the standard for the

low speed teleprinter code because the chance of error increased significantly if more bits were used.

Imagine an operator keying a teleprinter keyboard to produce characters for transmission. The framed character generated by each key depression begins with a start bit and ends with one or two stop bits. The stop condition is a mark or positive voltage on the line (negative voltage with double-current signaling). The positive voltage remains on the line until the next character starts because the line idle condition is internationally defined as current flow or mark, rather than no current or space. As soon as a space (start bit) is detected, the receiving device starts and will be in synchronization with the transmitting device.

Electromechanical Method

Current pulses, placed on the line by the sender's rotating armature, select the character to be printed through the synchronized receiver contacts.

The diagram in Figure 2.10 illustrates the operation of an electromechanical start-stop teleprinter machine. The sending device and the receiving device each have an armature, A, which rotates at a constant speed when a clutch connects it to an electric motor in the machine. Contacts on the armature connect an outer ring of contacts, B, to the transmission line. In the diagram, the armature is in its stop position. Current from the battery in the sender flows through the contact labeled stop, through the armature, and through the line to the receiver. This current causes the receive relay to remain energized, keeping the clutch disengaged, the armature stationary, and the teleprinter in the idle condition.

Now suppose that an operator at the sending device presses the H key on the keyboard. In accordance with the 5-bit code in Figure 1.4, data contacts 3 and 5 close to encode the H, and the start contact at the sending machine closes. This energizes the start magnet to engage the clutch to turn the armature of the sending device counterclockwise. The armature connects the contacts on the outer ring to the line in sequence: start, 1, 2, 3, 4, 5, stop. Notice that the start contact and data contacts 1, 2, and 4 do not conduct current.

As soon as the armature of the sender travels to its start contact, the current through the line and the receive relay ceases. The receive relay is de-energized, and current flows through the other set of relay contacts and through the start magnet of the receiver. This engages the clutch, and the receiver armature begins turning counterclockwise at approximately the same speed as that of the sender armature. When the sender armature is over data contact 3, current flows through the line and the receive relay. The receive relay is energized, and as the armature of the receiver passes over data contact 3 on the outer ring, current flows through select magnet 3. Select magnet 5 is operated similarly. The operation of these two magnets cause the letter H to be selected on the type mechanism of the receiver. When the sender armature reaches its stop contact, the receiver armature passes over contact C, current flows to the print magnet, and the letter H is printed. Both armatures then come to rest in the position shown in the illustration, unless the sender is ready to transmit another character immediately.

**Figure 2.10.
Electromechanical
Start-Stop Coding and
Decoding**

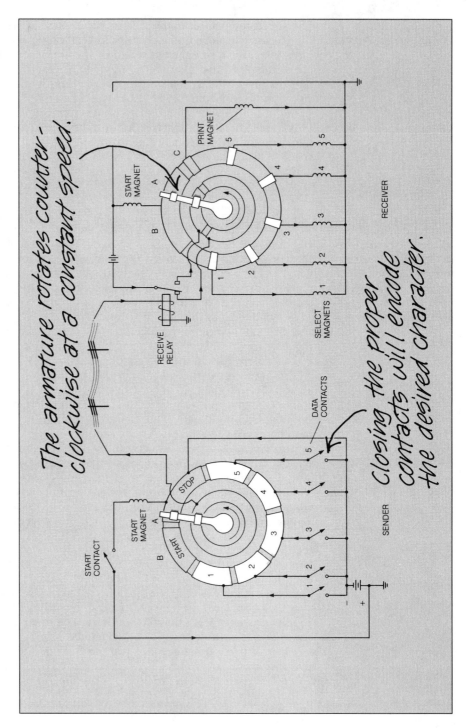

Bit timing within a character must be precise to prevent errors. However, the timing between characters is of not importance for accuracy.

Note that the start and stop elements have those exact functions; that is, they start and stop the armature rotation. As you can visualize, if there were much variation in the rotational speed of the sending and receiving armatures, the armatures would not be in synchronization and the character would be decoded incorrectly. As discussed previously, this is one reason that the Baudot code was limited to five symbols.

With start-stop transmission, a new character can begin at any time after the stop bits of the preceding character have been received. The time between one character and the next is indeterminate, but within a character, the timing is precisely defined. For that reason, it might be better to call this technique "self-synchronized" or "internally synchronized", rather than asynchronous, meaning "not synchronized." (The lack of a continuous synchronous agreement between the transmitter and the receiver—specifically, the lack of a clocking signal within or accompanying the data channel—is the reason for the name "asynchronous.")

Electronic Receiving Circuit

The electromechanical arrangements of the early teleprinters have been replaced with electronic circuits. Since these can be synchronized within closer tolerances, an 8-bit code can be used. An electronic circuit for receiving asynchronous serial data in an 8-bit code is shown in Figure 2.11. It utilizes a clock which runs at 16 times the symbol rate of the incoming data. This rapid rate is used in order to detect the 1 to 0 transition (when the start bit begins) as soon as possible after it occurs. The circuit which detects the 1 to 0 transition enables a spike detection circuit. Eight "ticks" of the 16X clock (one-half a bit time) are counted, then the line is checked to see if it is still in the 0 state. If it is not, it is assumed that the initial 1 to 0 transition was due to noise on the line, the spike detection circuit is reset, and no further action is taken.

If the line is still at 0, a valid start signal has arrived, and a counter is enabled which divides the 16X clock by 16 to produce a sampling clock which ticks once per bit time for the shift register. This tick occurs roughly at the center of the bit being sampled. The off-center error can be made smaller by sampling at 32 times the bit rate, and even further reduced by sampling at 64 times the bit rate. However, when higher sampling rates are used, the counter in the spike detection circuit and the counter in the bit sampler circuit must count proportionately higher.

The bit sampler circuit strobes the shift register eight times to sample the state of the line to get the eight bits into the serial-to-parallel shift register. Then a signal, called a flag, is sent to the computer or controller with which it is associated to announce that a character has been received. The computer then signals the shift register to transfer the eight bits in parallel into the processing circuits.

Figure 2.11.
Asynchronous
Receiver *(Source:*
McNamara, John E.,
Technical Aspects of
Data Communications,
2nd Ed., Digital Press,
© 1982)

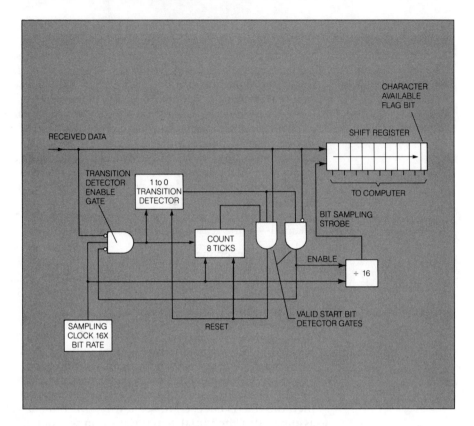

A single-buffered
interface requires the
receiving computer to
read each character as
soon as it is received
with no break before
the next one begins.

A problem with using only one shift register (called a single-buffered
interface) is that, when characters are arriving continuously, the computer
has only the duration of the stop bit to read the received character before
the next character begins entering the register. A simple improvement is
to provide a holding register into which the received character can be
parallel transferred as soon as the eighth bit has been sampled. A character
available flag is sent to the computer when the parallel transfer occurs,
and the receiving register becomes available for the next character. This
arrangement, called a double-buffered interface, is shown in Figure 2.12.
In either case, the arrival of a character which cannot be handled because
the previous character has not been read is called a data overflow. If
overflow occurs, most receiver circuits overwrite the old character with
the new one (the old one is lost), and place an error signal on a separate
lead to the computer.

Figure 2.12.
**Double-Buffered
Interface** *(Source:
McNamara, John E.,
Technical Aspects of
Data Communications,
2nd Ed., Digital Press
© 1982)*

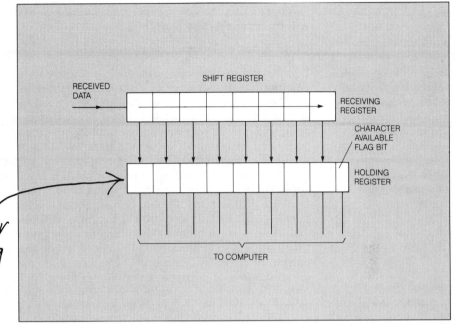

*Allows time
to read the
character
while another
one is being
received.*

Stop Bits and Timing Errors

With a double-buffered interface, the stop bit arrival time is no longer the only time available to the computer for reading the character, so there is time for circuitry to check the stop bit (sometimes called the ninth bit) to confirm that it is a 1. If it is not a 1, one of the following conditions exists: the communications channel is broken, receiver timing is confused, or the transmitting station is sending a special signal. The existence of one of these conditions typically provides an error signal on a lead in the asynchronous receiver.

A double-buffered interface provides a holding register to hold the character for reading, while the next character received fills the receiving register.

Such an error occurs when the receiver has lost track of which zeros in the transmission are the start bits and which are just zeros in the data. If, for some reason, the receiver treats a data bit as a start bit, it will assemble the next eight bits as a character. Since these eight bits are really parts of two characters (the end of one and the beginning of another) the ninth bit to arrive will not be the stop bit, but rather a data bit from the second character. If it is a zero, the error checking circuit will detect an error. Since framing is the process of deciding which groups of eight bits constitute characters, and this error is due to a failure in that process, it is called a framing error.

Failure in the framing process generally can be avoided. The idle line condition is a mark condition, and any amount of idle time more than a character time in length will correct this condition. Even if characters are sent continuously, the receiver will eventually become realigned to the correct start elements, no matter which zero bit is chosen as the start bit.

Of course, the characters received while the framing is not in alignment will be decoded incorrectly.

Other Types of Transmission

Large data communications systems normally do not use asynchronous transmission because the start-stop codes takes too much time, and error detection and correction methods are impractical.

Asynchronous transmission is the most common in data communications simply because there are more low-speed terminals and small computer applications in which it is used. Large systems and computer networks usually utilize other methods in addition to asynchronous. This is because of the large overhead penalty of 20% associated with start-stop codes; that is, two (the start and stop bits) out of the ten bits transmitted are for control rather than information. This is not a problem in conversational timesharing or many other types of interactive applications, where more time is spent in looking at the screen and thinking than in transmission, but it would be a heavy price to pay when transferring a file of 500,000 characters (4 million bits) at 9600 bps.

A second problem in such large transfers is error checking. The timesharing user originally had to check his or her own input and output for errors by looking at the screen, and rekeying or asking for retransmission of portions that contain errors. Such a procedure is clearly impractical for long file transfers that occur at fast rates and often without an operator present. Although transmission protocols have been developed to provide error free asynchronous transmission, the use of this type of communications is oriented for relatively short transmission sessions, normally under a few hours. Prolonged transmission requirements, such as applications requiring large-volume, high-speed data transfers require a different method of data transfer. This method is called synchronous transmission.

In synchronous transmission, start and stop bits are not used. Characters are sent in groups, called blocks, with special synchronization characters placed at the beginning of the block and within it, to ensure that enough 0 to 1 or 1 to 0 transitions occur for the receiver clock to remain accurate. Error checking is done automatically on the entire block. If any errors occur, then the entire block is retransmitted. This technique also carries an overhead penalty (nothing is free), but the overhead is far less than 20% for blocks of more than a few dozen characters. Figure 2.13 compares asynchronous and synchronous transmission of a sequence of characters.

In addition to asynchronous and synchronous transmission methods to achieve receiver timing, there is now a third method called *isochronous transmission*. This technique is used in a few computer networks. It involves timing that is controlled by the network rather than the DCE or DTE, as is true for synchronous and asynchronous transmission. Synchronous and isochronous data transmission will be discussed later in this book.

Figure 2.13.
Comparison of
Asynchronous and
Synchronous Data
Transmission

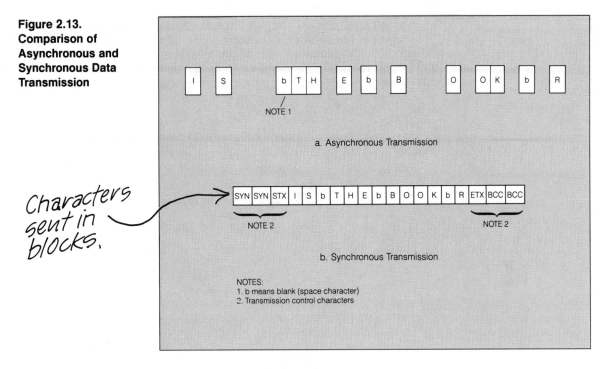

Characters sent in blocks.

a. Asynchronous Transmission

b. Synchronous Transmission

NOTES:
1. b means blank (space character)
2. Transmission control characters

WHAT HAVE WE LEARNED?

1. Compared to CRT terminals, teleprinters are much slower in printing, have limited formatting capability, don't have enhancements such as blinking and highlighting, and are less reliable in operation.

2. A serial or character printer prints one character at a time. The printer may be either an impact or a nonimpact printer. An impact printer may produce fully-formed characters or characters formed by a dot matrix. A nonimpact printer usually uses a thermal or ink-jet method.

3. CRT terminals may be classified as dumb, smart, and user-programmable. A dumb terminal is essentially the same as a teleprinter except for printing speed. A smart terminal has capabilities such as editing, formatting, highlighting, and blinking. A user-programmable terminal has a built-in programming language and the capability to store and execute programs.

4. As applied to terminals, ergonomics has to do with the color, character size, and nonglare surface of the display, and with the shape, position, and layout of the keys. It also is concerned with the physical position of both the display and the keyboard with respect to the operator.

5. In serial transmission, the bits are transmitted one at a time over a single wire. In parallel transmission, each bit of a group moves over its own wire, and all bits of the group move at the same time.

6. Both bit timing and framing are necessary to maintain synchronization for proper decoding in data communications. Bit timing usually is accomplished by clocking the bits. Framing usually is accomplished by inserting special bits or characters in the data stream just for that purpose.

7. In asynchronous transmission, each character is sent by itself and is framed by a start bit and a stop bit. This is the transmission method used by teleprinters and ASCII terminals.

8. In synchronous transmission, many characters are sent together in groups called blocks. Each block is framed by special synchronization characters.

Quiz for Chapter 2

1. Teleprinters:
   a. Are only for printing at remote locations, not for input.
   b. Offer both high speed operation and a variety of formatting controls.
   c. Have a printer for output and may have a keyboard for input.

2. Impact printers:
   a. Strike a ribbon against the paper to produce character images.
   b. Include ink-jet and thermal devices.
   c. Are rapidly becoming obsolete.

3. Glass Teletypes:
   a. Are among the most recent developments in CRT terminals.
   b. Were so-named because they had the same interface as a teleprinter.
   c. Are teleprinters designed to interface with fiber-optic transmission systems.

4. Electromechanical teleprinters:
   a. Use a complex mechanical buffer to match speed between transmitting and receiving machines.
   b. Use start/stop codes to synchronize sending and receiving equipment.
   c. Are rarely used today.

5. ASCII terminals are generally defined as:
   a. Terminals using synchronous transmission in EBCDIC.
   b. Terminals using synchronous transmission in ASCII.
   c. Terminals using asynchronous transmission in ASCII.
   d. Any terminal having an American (dollar-sign) keyboard.

6. ''3270'' terminals refer to:
   a. Asynchronous terminals made by IBM.
   b. Any terminal which is painted blue.
   c. Synchronous terminals that interface with an IBM-type cluster controller.

7. The difference between timing and framing is:
   a. Timing is concerned with the individual bits; framing is concerned with the boundaries between characters.
   b. Timing refers to serial transmission; framing refers to parallel.
   c. Timing is concerned primarily with asynchronous systems; framing is concerned with synchronous systems.

8. Escape codes are so called because:
   a. In effect, they provide a means to temporarily "escape" from the standard meanings of the character set.
   b. They initiate operation of the escapement mechanism in teleprinters.
   c. They cause the cursor to escape from the boundaries of the CRT screen and roam around in memory.

9. The QWERTY keyboard:
   a. Is still considered to be the layout allowing the greatest typing speed.
   b. Is the most popular keyboard, but not necessarily the best.
   c. Is a key layout that is rarely used.

10. Memory-mapped displays:
    a. Are associated with electromechanical teleprinters.
    b. Have the advantage that they do not take up memory space.
    c. Allow direct addressing of display locations by the processor.

11. Serial printers:
    a. Are used to transmit grain prices.
    b. Are faster than CRT terminals, and offer more flexibility.
    c. Print one character at a time.
    d. Usually use serial interfaces.

12. Nonimpact printers:
    a. Are normally quieter than impact printers.
    b. Generate carbon copies easily.
    c. Produce fully-formed characters.

13. CRT terminals:
    a. Are the most widely-used hardcopy terminals.
    b. Offer high-speed display and formatting flexibility.
    c. Do not normally utilize microprocessors.

14. User-programmable terminals:
    a. Are replacing personal and professional computers.
    b. Offer more flexibility at lower cost.
    c. Are being replaced by personal and professional computers.

15. Ergonomics:
    a. Involves the interface between people and machines, such as terminals.
    b. Is the application of ergo-economics to communications.
    c. Utilizes three-level ergo-coding for transmission over certain channels.

16. Serial and parallel transmission:
    a. Differ in how many bits are transferred per character.
    b. Are used in synchronous and asynchronous systems, respectively.
    c. Differ in whether the bits are on separate wires or all on one.

17. Memory-mapped displays:
   a. Are utilized for high-resolution graphics, such as maps.
   b. Use ordinary memory to store the display data in character form.
   c. Store the display data as individual bits.

18. Asynchronous transmission:
   a. Is less efficient than synchronous, but simpler.
   b. Is much faster than synchronous transmission.
   c. Is another name for isochronous transmission.

19. Single-buffering:
   a. Is more efficient than double-buffering.
   b. Is less efficient than no buffering.
   c. Provides very little time to unload the incoming character from the register.

20. Most terminal keyboards:
   a. Provide numerous additional specialized keys.
   b. Are strictly typewriter-style, with few extra keys.
   c. Use the Dvorak layout.

Messages and Transmission Channels

ABOUT THIS CHAPTER

Useful communication requires four elements as shown in Figure 3.1: a message (information) to be communicated, a sender of the message, a medium or channel over which the message can be sent, and a receiver. Messages usually are information that is useful to people, but the sender and receiver may or may not be human. The medium must be one suitable to convey the type of message. In this chapter, we will examine in more detail the types of messages and the media which carry them.

WHAT IS INFORMATION?

Information as a Quantity

The unit of information used in data communications is the bit which has only two possible values, 1 and 0. Seven bits are needed to select any one of 128 different symbols in ASCII.

"Information," according to one definition, "is the communication or reception of knowledge or intelligence." Information is also "a numerical quantity that measures the uncertainty in the outcome of an experiment to be performed." This second definition has an application in the sending of messages. For example, suppose we have a machine that can send only two symbols, A1 and A2. We can then say that the "experiment" is the accurate recognition of the two symbols (A1 and A2) being sent from one machine to another. As far as the receiving machine is concerned, it is just as likely to receive one symbol as the other. So we can say that the "numerical quantity" in this experiment is a unit of information that will allow a selection between two equally likely choices. This quantity, or unit of information is usually called a bit (a contraction of *bi*nary dig*it*), and has two possible values, 0 and 1. If these two values are used to represent A1 and A2, then A1 could be represented by the bit value 0, and A2 by the bit value 1. The number of bits per symbol is 1, but we still need a way of selecting which symbol (bit) we want to use. A machine which needs only two symbols only needs a 1-bit select code (0 and 1).

A machine that uses only two symbols is not of much use for communication, but suppose the machine used 128 symbols (like the standard ASCII character set). Then the number of equally likely choices to be handled is 128, and the number of bits (information) required to represent each of those 128 symbols is seven (refer to Table 1.1). You can see, then, that if the knowledge (or intelligence) to be communicated can be represented by a set of equally likely symbols, then the amount of

Figure 3.1.
The Elements of
Communication

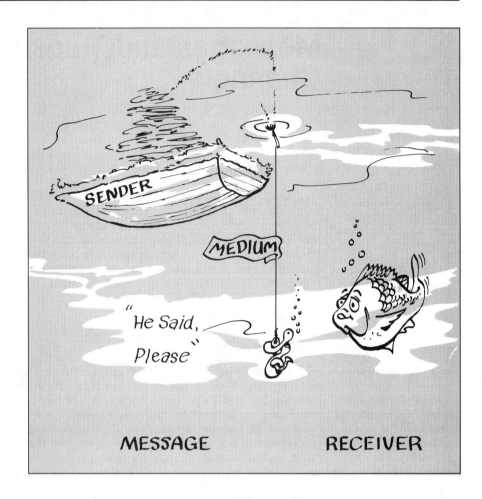

information required per symbol to communicate it is necessarily
dependent upon the total number of bits of information. The standard
ASCII character set is particularly useful for selecting the information to
be communicated since it can select one of 128 ASCII symbols with only
one 8-bit byte, a common bit grouping in computers (the eighth bit is not
used in this case).

Information Content of Symbols

In many information systems, not every symbol is equally likely to be
used in a given communication. The English language is a good example.
In a message written in English, the letter e is 12 times more likely to
occur than the letter s. This uneven distribution is also characteristic of
particular groups of letters and of words. What this means, then, is that
each of the 128 symbols in ASCII is not likely to occur an equal number
of times in any given communication. For example, notice that the use of

the letters e and g, and the letter combinations th and er, is unequal in this paragraph.

Redundancy is the measurement of the probability of occurrence of any particular character in a character set.

In 1949, Claude Shannon published a book titled *The Mathematical Theory of Communication*. In this book, he discusses the uncertainty or amount of disorder of a system, which he called entropy. The entropy of a set of equally likely symbols (like the digits 0–9 in a table of random numbers) is the logarithim to the base 2 of the number of symbols in the set. The entropy of the English *alphabet*, which contains 26 letters and a space, is then $\log_2(27) = 4.76$ bits per symbol. Because of the uneven use of letters in the English *language*, however, its entropy was estimated by Sharnon as 1.3 bits per symbol. This means that the language is about 70% redundant, and that it should be possible to reconstruct English text accurately if every other letter is lost or changed due to noise or distortion. Obviously, redundancy is desirable in order to raise the chances of receiving a good message when the medium is noisy. (The words noise and noisy in this book refer to electrical noise; that is, an electrical signal that is not supposed to be present.)

Using Redundancy in Communications

Redundancy can be used to reconstruct a message even if part of the message is lost during transmission. It is very important in verifying data accuracy.

So, you wonder, what does all this have to do with the real world of data communications? Quite a bit, since almost every scheme in current use for sending data uses redundancy in an attempt to verify that the data have been received exactly as sent; that is, no errors have been introduced by the sending mechanism, the transmission medium, or the receiver. The redundant information may consist simply of a retransmission of the entire original message. Although simple to implement, retransmission is not efficient; therefore, special techniques are used to generate redundant information that is related to the message in a way that is known to both the sender and receiver. The sender generates the redundant information during transmission and sends it along with the message. The receiver regenerates and checks the redundant information when the message is received. This scheme is represented by Figure 3.2. Verification usually occurs at the end of each link in the chain making up the transmission path. The details of this process and various methods in current use are described in a later chapter.

WHAT CARRIES THE MESSAGES?

Bounded data channels confine the signals within wires, coaxial cable, or optical fiber cable. Unbounded channels permit the signal to radiate in all directions.

The physical channels (the media) that carry data are of two types— bounded and unbounded. In a bounded medium, the signals are confined to the medium and do not leave it (except for small leakage amounts). A pair of wires, coaxial cable, waveguide, and optical fiber cable are examples of a bounded media. The atmosphere, the ocean, and outer space are examples of unbounded media, where electromagnetic signals originated by the source radiate freely into the medium and spread throughout the medium. The unbounded media are utilized by various radio frequency transmitting schemes to carry messages. The main feature of unbounded media is that once the signal is radiated from the

**Figure 3.2.
Error Checking Points**

Redundant code generated here.

Redundant code regenerated and vertified here.

transmitter, it radiates equally in all directions (unless restricted) and continues forever onward. As it moves farther from the source, the energy is spread over a larger area so the level continually gets weaker at greater distances. As the wave moves through the medium, it is affected by natural disturbances which can interfere with the signal.

Wire Pairs

Wire pairs are the simplest type of bounded carrier. The two wires which provide a go and return signal path, when balanced to ground, provide the most protection from induced noise.

The simplest type of bounded medium is a pair of wires providing a go and return path for electrical signals. Early telegraph systems used the earth itself instead of a wire for one of the paths as shown in Figure 3.3a. Repeaters were inserted along the line to reduce the effects of noise and attenuation (loss of signal strength). However, this scheme did not work well because the earth is not always a good conductor and the path was susceptible to large noise currents induced by lightning. Losses were reduced by using two wires as shown in Figure 3.3b, but the line was still unbalanced to ground so it was subject to picking up noise from almost every noise-producing device. Finally, the balanced two-wire line shown in Figure 3.3c was used to greatly reduce noise pickup.

The most common type of bounded medium consists of wire pairs twisted together and made up into cables of from 4 to 3000 pairs. The size of the wire used varies from 16 AWG (American Wire Gauge) with a wire diameter of 0.05082 inch to 26 AWG with a diameter of 0.01594 inch. In modern cables, each wire is insulated with a polyethylene or a polyvinyl chloride jacket; however, there is still a large quantity of older cable in use in which the insulation for each wire is paper.

**Figure 3.3.
Types of Transmission
Circuits**

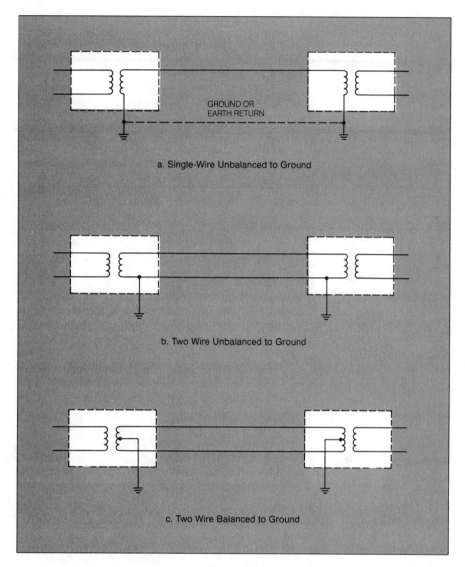

a. Single-Wire Unbalanced to Ground

b. Two Wire Unbalanced to Ground

c. Two Wire Balanced to Ground

The size of the wires used and the distance between them affect the attenuation. Twisted wire pairs are limited to a maximum frequency of about 1 MHz.

Open-wire lines have low attenuation of voice frequencies due to the large size of the wire and the relatively large distance between the two wires when mounted on a crossarm of a utility pole. A typical value of attenuation for 104 mil (0.104 inch) diameter open wire lines is 0.07 decibel (dB) per mile; while 19 gauge (0.03589 inch diameter) twisted wire pairs in a multipair cable have a voice frequency attenuation of about 1 dB per mile.

The attenuation of twisted wire pairs rises rapidly with increasing frequency, and the amount of crosstalk between adjacent pairs also increases with frequency. The maximum usable frequency for wire pairs in cables is around 1 MHz without special treatment.

The Effect of Inductance

A concept that may not be obvious about paired wire circuits is that the addition of inductance in the line can help reduce attenuation at voice frequencies. The line impedance (ac resistance) is increased, so that a given amount of power can be transmitted with less current, but at a higher voltage. The result is a reduction in the series losses and an increase in the shunt losses. Since the series losses are usually the most severe, there is a net reduction in attenuation until the inductance rises to the point where series and shunt losses are equal.

Adding inductance to wire pairs is called loading, and a circuit to which inductance has been added is called a loaded line or loaded circuit. The effect of loading is illustrated in Figure 3.4. The typical frequency versus attenuation performance is shown for a nonloaded 19 gauge cable pair and a 19 gauge cable pair loaded with 88 millihenrys of inductance every 6000 feet. (The standard notation for this is 19H-88 loaded pair.) Figure 3.4 shows that the attenuation of the loaded circuit is less than that of the unloaded one, and that it changes very little with increasing

> By loading a circuit with added inductance, attenuation can be reduced at higher frequencies so the circuit response is relatively constant over the voice band.

Figure 3.4.
Effect of Inductance
Loading

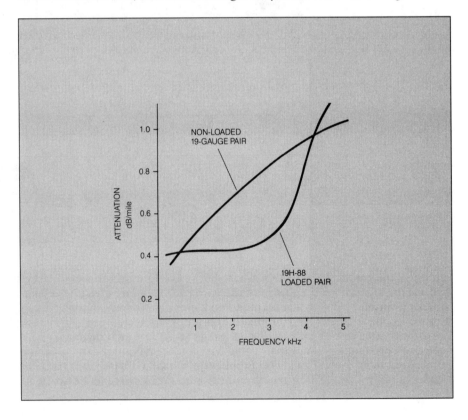

frequency up to a certain point above 3 kHz. This point is called the cutoff point or cutoff frequency.

Loading was introduced around 1900 on long distance open wire lines to reduce losses due to attenuation, since there were no amplifiers for the signals.

Electronic Amplifiers

In 1883, Thomas Edison discovered the rectifying properties of the thermionic vacuum tube. A thermionic vacuum tube is one in which a stream of electrons is emitted by an incandescent substance. Edison's tube was a two-element tube (called a diode) consisting of a cathode (the incandescent substance) and an anode.

Electronic amplifiers eliminate the requirement to load long distance circuits because amplification can compensate for the line losses.

However, the principle of thermionic vacuum tubes lay unused until 1904 when Sir John Ambrose Fleming, an English physicist and engineer, adapted the diode for use as a demodulator (detector) of radiotelegraph signals for the Marconi Wireless Telegraph Co. In 1906, Lee DeForest introduced a third element, called a control grid, to the diode and created the triode. By 1912, the triode and its associated circuits were developed for use as an amplifier.

When the use of the DeForest triode as an amplifier began in 1914, it was no longer necessary to load long distance circuits because the losses in the line could be compensated for by amplification. However, loading is still used on longer local loops (from the telephone office to the customer), since it is cheaper than adding active components for amplification. The presence of loading on local circuits has a considerable effect on their ability to carry high-frequency data signals which causes problems for some new types of telephone service.

Coaxial Cable

To put more data transmissions onto one channel at the same time, the transmissions must be at frequencies higher than those practical for wire pairs. Coaxial cables can be used for signals with frequencies of 10,000 MHz.

In order to make telephone service economical, a way had to be found to put more than one conversation onto a channel. Indeed, the invention of the telephone arose out of Alexander Bell's experiments on a "harmonic telegraph," an attempt to put more than one telegraph signal on a channel. Putting more conversations or more data on a single channel requires a larger bandwidth (ability to carry more frequencies), which, as a practical matter, means higher frequencies. Since the practical limit for wire pairs is around 1 MHz, some other method had to be developed.

Some significant and interesting effects occur in the vicinity of a wire carrying an alternating current signal. One of these effects is that both an electric field and a magnetic field are created around the conductor. The magnetic field can induce the signal it is carrying into adjacent conductors. (In communications, the induced and unwanted signal is called crosstalk.) However, if one conductor of the pair is the ground side of the circuit, and is made to surround the other conductor, both the radiated electric field and the magnetic field can be confined within the tube formed by the outer conductor as illustrated in Figure 3.5.

Figure 3.5.
Structure of Coaxial
Cable

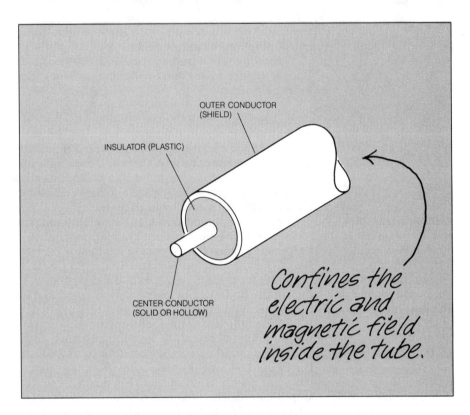

This medium is called a coaxial cable, because the two conductors have a common axis. The self-shielding works well at frequencies above about 100 kHz, but at low frequencies the "skin depth" of the current is comparable to the thickness of the outer conductor and the shielding becomes ineffective. The resistive loss of coaxial cable increases as the square root of the frequency, making coaxial cable generally usable at frequencies of up to 2000 MHz, although some types may be used up to 10,000 MHz.

Waveguide

Waveguides can be used to frequencies of 2,000 MHz.

If the frequency of transmission is high enough, the electric and magnetic components of a signal can travel through free space, requiring no solid conductor at all. However, to avoid interference and losses due to signal spreading, and to be able to route the signal as desired, it is sometimes useful to confine these waves to another bounded medium called a waveguide.

Fiber optic systems can handle high capacity, high frequency transmissions economically because they have low loss, are free of electromagnetic interference, are nonconductive, noninductive, and do not radiate energy.

Waveguides are commonly used at frequencies from 2000 MHz up to 110,000 MHz to connect microwave transmitters and receivers to their antennas. Waveguides are pressurized with dry air or nitrogen to drive out moisture from inside the waveguide because moisture attenuates the microwaves. Older waveguides were constructed with a rectangular cross section, but common practice today is to make the guides circular as shown in Figure 3.6. Waveguides remain in use as a conductor of high-power, high-frequency signals, but optical fiber cables are being used in newer systems.

Figure 3.6.
Circular Waveguides
(Source: Members of the Technical Staff, Bell Telephone Laboratories, Engineering and Operations of the Bell System, © 1977, AT&T Bell Telephone Laboratories, Inc.)

No conductor is required; the signal is simply confined and directed.

HIGH-LOSS DIELECTRIC

COPPER WIRE

STEEL PIPE

COPPER PLATING

STEEL PIPE

LOW-LOSS DIELECTRIC

a. Helix

b. Dielectric Lined

Fiber Optic Systems

The capacity of a transmission system is a direct function of the highest frequency it can carry; therefore, progress in transmission technology has been measured by the bandwidth of the media available to carry signals. Recent developments in the use of glass fibers to carry binary signals have shown these systems to be extremely well-suited to high data rate applications. Fiber optic systems are attractive for several reasons:

1. The low transmission loss, as compared with wire pairs of coaxial cable, allows much greater separation between repeaters. A fiber optic system with no repeaters has been demonstrated which transmits 420 megabits per second (Mbps) over a span of 75 miles with an error rate several times lower than high-quality coaxial cable systems.

2. Since the optical fibers carry light rays, the frequency of operation is that of light. The transmission wavelength used for current single-mode fibers is 1.2 micrometers, equivalent to a frequency of around 800 terahertz (800,000,000,000,000 Hz). Such frequencies allow data transmission rates of 20,000 Mbps over short distances.

3. Optical fiber cables do not radiate energy, do not conduct electricity, and are noninductive. They are essentially free from crosstalk and the effects of lightning-induced interference, and present no security problem from an inductively coupled "wire tap."

4. Optical fiber cables are smaller, lighter, and cheaper than metallic cables of the same capacity. It is economically feasible to provide several unused fibers in a cable for spares and for future growth. A cross section of a typical fiber optical cable is shown in Figure 3.7.

One standard fiber optic system currently in service is the AT&T FT3 lightwave system which can carry 80,000 two-way voice conversations at the same time. The cable for this system is one-half inch in diameter and contains 144 fibers. Each fiber pair operates at 90 Mbps for a total data rate of about 6000 Mbps. The system provides one spare fiber for every operating one, and switchover to a spare is automatic upon loss of signal in a fiber. A more detailed discussion of fiber optic systems is given in a later chapter.

High-Frequency Radiotelephone

By convention, radio transmission in the frequency band between 3 MHz and 30 MHz is called high-frequency (HF) radio. Frequency bands within the HF spectrum are allocated by international treaty for specific services, such as mobile (aeronautical, maritime, and land), broadcasting, radio nagivation, amateur radio, space communications, and radio astronomy. HF radio has properties of propagation that make it less reliable than some other frequencies; however, HF radio does allow communications over great distances with small amounts of radiated power.

HF radio waves transmitted from antennas on the earth follow two paths as indicated in Figure 3.8 when they leave the antenna. The groundwave follows the earth's surface and the skywave bounces back and forth between the earth's surface and various layers of the earth's ionosphere. The groundwave is useful for communications up to about 400 miles, and works particularly well over water. The skywave propagates signals for up to 4000 miles with a path reliability of about 90%. Data signals are carried on HF radio systems as continuous wave

High frequency (HF) signals radiate from an antenna over two paths: a ground wave following the earth's surface and a skywave that bounces between the earth and ionosphere.

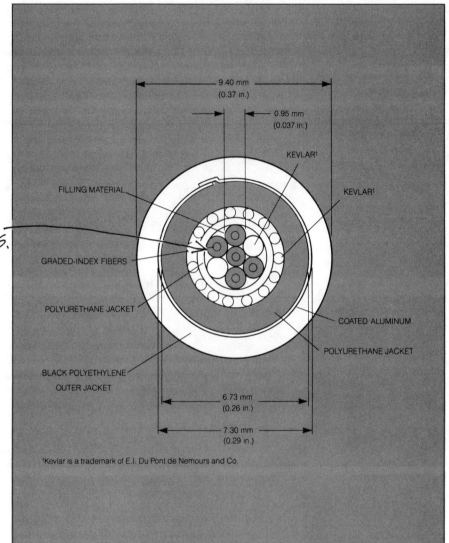

**Figure 3.7.
Typical Five-Fiber
Optical Fiber Cable for
Direct Burial** *(Source:
R.L. Freeman,
Telecommunication
Transmission
Handbook, 2nd Ed.,
John Wiley & Sons,
1981, Copyright ©
1981 by John Wiley and
Sons, Inc.)*

*Carry the
light waves.*

9.40 mm
(0.37 in.)

0.95 mm
(0.037 in.)

KEVLAR[1]

FILLING MATERIAL

KEVLAR[1]

GRADED-INDEX FIBERS

POLYURETHANE JACKET

COATED ALUMINUM

POLYURETHANE JACKET

BLACK POLYETHYLENE
OUTER JACKET

6.73 mm
(0.26 in.)

7.30 mm
(0.29 in.)

[1]Kevlar is a trademark of E.I. Du Pont de Nemours and Co.

(CW) radio telegraphy at about 15 bits per second (bps), and frequency shift keyed (FSK) single sideband signals are carried on HF at 75 bps. Higher data bit rates (up to 4800 bps) are converted to standard 3-kHz voice channel analog signals by modems and these analog signals are transmitted on voice frequency (VF) carrier systems using HF radio.

**Figure 3.8.
Paths of HF Radio
Waves**

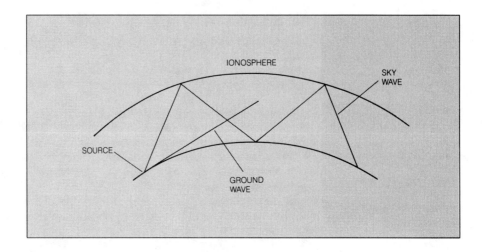

Microwave Radio

Microwave radio is used by line-of-sight carrier systems to carry large quantities of voice and data signals. It is affected adversely by atmospheric conditions and solid objects.

The tall towers with large horns and/or dish antennas that you see while driving through the country are the repeater stations for line-of-sight (LOS) microwave radio systems (sometimes called radiolink systems). Such systems can carry large quantities of voice and data traffic for several reasons:

1. They require no right-of-way acquisition between towers.

2. They can carry very large quantities of information per radio system, due to their high operating frequency.

3. They require the purchase or lease of only a small area of ground for installation of each tower.

4. Because the wavelength of the transmitted signal is short, an antenna of reasonable size can focus the transmitted signal into a beam. This provides a much greater signal strength at the receiver without increasing transmitter power.

Radiolink systems are subject to transmission impairments which limit the distance between repeater points and cause other problems. The microwave signals are:

1. Attenuated by solid objects (including the earth) and, in addition, the higher frequencies are attenuated by rain, snow and fog.

2. Reflected from flat conductive surfaces (water, metal structures, etc.).

3. Diffracted (split) around solid objects.

4. Refracted (bent) by the atmosphere so that the beam may travel beyond the line-of-sight distance and be picked up by an antenna that is not supposed to receive it.

In spite of all these possible problems, radiolink systems are highly successful and until the late 1980s carried a substantial part of all telephone, data, and television traffic in the U.S. Beginning in the early 1980s, most long distance communications carriers installed tens of thousands of miles of optical fiber. Since the late 1980s, a majority of long distance transmission has been moved off microwave systems to fiber optic transmission systems. The microwave range of radio frequencies is allocated for various purposes by international treaty . Some of the frequency assignments for the United States are shown in Table 3.1.

Table 3.1. Frequency Assignments for Microwave Radiolink Systems

Service	Frequency, GHz	Service	Frequency, GHz
Military	1.710–1.850	Common Carrier and Satellite (uplink)	5.925–6.425
Operational Fixed	1.850–1.990	Operational Fixed	6.575–6.875
Studio Transmitter Link	1.990–2.110	Studio Transmitter Link	6.875–7.125
Common Carrier	2.110–2.130	Common Carrier and Satellite (downlink)	7.250–7.750
Operational Fixed	2.130–2.150	Common Carrier and Satellite (uplink)	7.900–8.400
Common Carrier	2.160–2.180	Common Carrier	10.7–11.7
Operational Fixed	2.180–2.200	Operational Fixed	12.2–12.7
Operational Fixed (TV)	2.500–2.690	CATV Studio Links	12.7–12.95
Common Carrier and Satellite (downlink)	3.700–4.200	Studio Transmitter Link	12.95–13.2
Military	4.400–4.990	Military	14.4–15.25
Military	5.250–5.350	Common Carrier	17.7–19.3

Although there are microwave systems that send data in digital form, most send data as analog signals.

Most common carrier radiolink systems carry analog signals, principally frequency modulation (FM). There are a few systems, however, which carry digital signals. Two examples in extensive service in the U.S. are the AT&T 3A-RDS radio system which operates in the 11 GHz band, and the AT&T DR-18 radio system which operates in the 18 GHz band. The 3A-RDS system carries DS-3 digital signals at 44.736 Mbps, and the DR-18 system carries DS-4 digital signals at 274.176 Mbps. The DS-3 and DS-4 signals, which are made up of several lower bit-rate signals, will be discussed in more detail later in this chapter.

Terrestrial radiolink systems are point-to-point; that is, the signal is transmitted in a beam from a source microwave antenna across the earth's surface to the antenna at which it is aimed. The width of the beam transmitted by a microwave antenna varies between 1 degree and 5 degrees as a function of the frequency of transmission and antenna size. As a result, the transmission is highly directional, which is desirable if the information is intended for only one destination (for example, a telephone conversation). For many applications, however, the information has multiple destinations (for example, television broadcasts), which makes the satellite radiolink system more practical and desirable.

Satellite Radiolink Systems

Figure 3.9 is a simple model of a satellite radiolink system. The satellite contains several receiver/amplifier/transmitter sections, called transponders, each operating at a slightly different frequency. Each of the 12 transponders on each satellite has a bandwidth of 36 MHz. Individual transmitter sites, called uplink earth stations, send narrow beams of microwave signals to the satellite. The satellite acts as a relay station. A transponder receives the signal from a single transmitter, then amplifies it and retransmits it toward earth on a different frequency. Note that the transmitting earth station sends to only one transponder on a single satellite. The satellite, however, sends to any and all downlink receiving earth stations in its area of coverage, called its footprint.

A satellite radio link consists of an uplink transmitter signal to the satellite and a down link retransmitted signal to receiving stations on earth.

Figure 3.9.
Satellite Radio Link
System

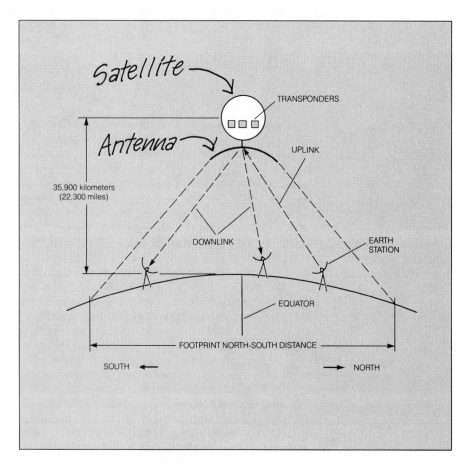

Commercial communications satellites are launched into geostationary orbit at an altitude of 35,900 kilometers (22,300 miles) above the equator. This means that the geostationary satellite is orbiting the earth at a constant speed and in the same direction as the earth's rotation about its axis. The orbiting speed is such that it causes the satellite to have a fixed location with respect to the earth. The earth station antennas, therefore, can be fixed in position and do not have to track a moving target in the sky. The angle of view for a geostationary satellite is almost 120 degrees wide. In principle, three such satellites equally spaced around the equator could cover the earth from 60 degrees north latitude to 60 degrees south latitude. In practice, the coverage angle is restricted to less than 110 degrees because the earth station's antenna must be elevated above the local horizon by more than five degrees.

Several types of signals are carried by satellite systems. For example, 6-MHz bandwidth standard televisions programs, multiplexed 64 kilobits per second (kbps) telephone channels, and high-speed data all can be carried simultaneously. One privately operated system, the Satellite Business System, which was merged with Hughes Network Systems is all digital with each of the 10 transponders per satellite capable of carrying 43 Mbps of digital data.

Cellular Radio Systems

The introduction of cellular radio systems effectively increased the number of radio channels available to mobile telephone systems.

Americans have demonstrated an insatiable desire to communicate with each other, anywhere, at any time. It seems that no location is too private, too noisy (audible noise), or too busy to exclude the installation of a telephone or a data terminal. Since Americans spend a lot of time in their cars, mobile telephones and data terminals are in great demand. Each telephone conversation requires a separate radio channel, and since only a limited number of such channels were available in the past, the demand for mobile telephone channels far outstripped the radio frequencies available to provide them. However, in 1982, a system allowing the reuse of channels within a metropolitan area, called the cellular radio system, began trial operation in Chicago. This system provides many more mobile telephone channels and rapidly gained acceptance throughout the United States in the late 1980s.

A diagram of a simple cellular system is shown in Figure 3.10. A metropolitan area is divided into several cells, each of which is served by a low-powered transmitter and associated receiver. The radio channels are suitable for data transmission up to 9.6 kbps as well as voice. The number of radio channels assigned to each cell is sufficient for the predicted number of users in that cell at any one time. When a caller makes a call, his mobile unit automatically seizes a free channel in his current cell. When the caller moves out of the cell, the cell controller automatically switches control of the call from the cell being left to the one being entered. Even a different radio channel may be used, but the caller doesn't have to do anything and is never aware of anything happening. The call is linked from the cell controller to a central switching system. The central switching system can link the caller via radio to another mobile or can access the public telephone network for connection to any fixed telephone.

**Figure 3.10.
Cellular Radio System**

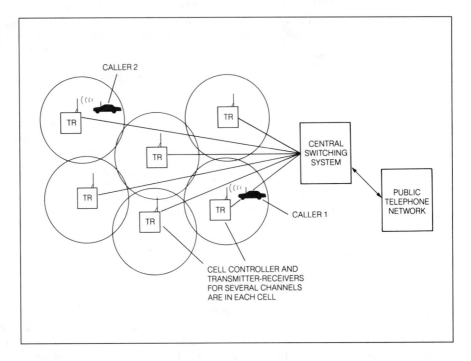

EFFECTS OF BANDWIDTH ON A TRANSMISSION CHANNEL

All transmission channels of any practical interest are of limited frequency bandwidth. The limitations arise from the physical properties of the channel or from deliberate limitations on the bandwidth to prevent interference from other sources. For primarily economic reasons, most data communications systems seek to maximize the amount of data that can be sent on a channel.

Theoretical Information Handling Capacity of a Channel

Claude Shannon proved that the maximum capacity of an ideal channel whose only impairments are finite bandwidth and noise randomly distributed over that finite bandwidth is:

$$C = W \times Log_2[1 + (P/N)] \text{ bits per second}$$

where:
      P is the power in watts of the signal through the channel,
      N is the power in watts of the noise out of the channel,
      W is the bandwidth of the channel in hertz.

Theoretically, a channel's data rate can be increased as desired as long as the signal-to-noise ratio increases. The practical maximum data rate limit was defined by Nyquist's theory to be two times the bandwidth.

Neglecting all other impairments, some typical values for a voice-grade analog circuit used for data are: W = 3000 hertz, P = 0.0001 watts (−10 dBm), N = 0.0000004 watts (−34 dBm). According to Shannon's Law, the value of C is:

$$3000 \times \text{Log}_2(1 + 250) = \text{about } 24{,}000 \text{ bits per second}$$

Shannon's value of C is never achievable because there are numerous impairments in every real channel besides those taken into account in Shannon's Law. Also, there are no ideal modems. However, Shannon's Law provides an upper theoretical limit to a binary channel. It is important to note that, due to the nature of the function Log_2, the value of C in the formula can be increased more readily by increasing W than by increasing (P/N).

Intersymbol Interference Reduces Capacity

One of the factors which tends to reduce the achievable capacity of a channel below the value of C in the formula is a problem called intersymbol (or interbit) interference. If a rectangular pulse like that shown in Figure 3.11 is input to a bandlimited channel, the bandwidth limitation of the channel rounds the "corners" of the pulse as shown in the output waveform and causes an undesired signal to appear. The "tail" or overshoot part of this new signal interferes with previous and subsequent pulses, adding uncertainty to the signal; that is, the signal may be incorrectly interpreted at the destination.

**Figure 3.11.
Pulse Response
Through a Band-
Limited Channel**

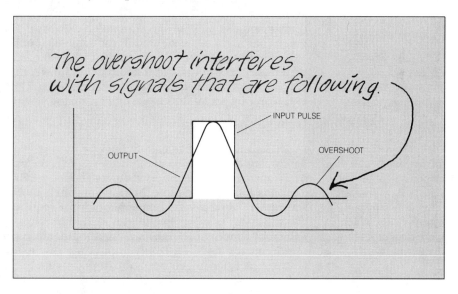

Harry Nyquist analyzed the problem of intersymbol interference and developed an ideal rounded pulse shape for which that impairment is minimized. Nyquist also did much theoretical research dealing with sampling of analog signals for representation in binary form. Nyquist's Sampling Theorem says that if an analog signal is sampled 2f times per second, then the samples may be used to perfectly reconstruct the original signal over a spectrum f hertz. For example, if a signal is sampled at the rate of 8000 times per second, then those samples can be used to reconstruct the original signal with perfect accuracy over the range of 0–4000 hertz.

BANDWIDTH REQUIREMENTS FOR VARIOUS SIGNALS

Analog Signals

As improved analog signal processing techniques continue to evolve, a given bandwidth can be used more efficiently.

Transmission rates for data communications seem to follow a corollary of Parkinsons's Law; that is, data rates increase to fill the bandwidth available. A good example is the introduction of low-cost modems operating at 1200 and 2400 bps for personal computers, which are four and eight times faster than the rate of 300 bps that was used for a long time. Large scale integrated circuits made possible the remarkable increases in performance and decreases in price of these analog modems. In 1974, a 300-bps full-duplex modem cost $600 to $800. Now, a 1200-bps modem can be bought for under $100, whereas 2400-bps modems in the $175 to $250 range are readily available from many vendors. In 1988 9600-bps modems designed for use on dial-up lines cost over $3000. By 1991 several vendors were selling such modems for under $600.

The 300-bps full-duplex signals use two bands of frequencies, each occupying about 300 Hz. Thus, the total 600 Hz used out of the 3000 Hz available bandwidth is inefficient. The 1200-bps modems also are full-duplex and use most of the available bandwidth. Therefore, four times as much information can be sent in the same channel in a given time period. Modern 9600 modems use a sophisticated echo cancelling technique which enables both transmit and receive signals to flow on a common wire pair. Through sophisticated signal processing techniques, modems can even carry up to 19,200 bps using an analog signal over a voice channel.

Digital Signals

Digital signals require a greater bandwidth than an equivalent analog signal. The advantages offered by transmitting signals in digital form more than offset this disadvantage.

Transmission of signals in binary form can require considerably more bandwidth than an equivalent analog signal. For example, the transmission of 24 analog voice channels requires about 96 kHz (24 × 4 kHz). Transmission of these same 24 voice channels in digital form using the standard T1 time division multiplex format requires about 776 kHz, or about 8 times as much bandwidth (776/96). However, the advantages gained by sending the signals as binary data more than offset the requirement for greater bandwidth. (For a discussion of the tradeoffs and advantages, refer to another book in this series: Stephen Bigelow, *Understanding Telephone Electronics*).

CARRIER SYSTEMS

In general, carrier systems are systems that provide a means to send signals from more than one source over a single physical channel. The bandwidth available to carry signals in a particular medium can be allocated in two ways; by frequency or by time intervals.

Analog Carrier Systems

In FDM, the total available channel bandwidth is divided into smaller bandwidth portions (subchannels), each with its own signal source.

The frequency spectrum represented by the available bandwidth of a channel can be divided into smaller bandwidth portions, with each of several signal sources assigned to each portion. This is the principle of frequency division multiplexing (FDM). FDM is still used in some simple data communications systems, and the long-haul part of the public telephone network. One common example of a frequency division multiplexing system is a standard low-speed (300-bps) modem, which divides the spectrum available in a voice channel into two portions—one for transmit and one for receive (this is discussed more and illustrated in a later chapter).

The electronic systems that implement FDM are called analog carrier systems. The carrier in an analog carrier system is a signal generated by the system and the carrier is modulated by the signal containing the information to be transmitted. Table 3.2 shows the standard analog carrier systems in use in the public telephone network.

Table 3.2. Analog Carrier Systems

Multiplex Level	No. of Voice Circuits	Frequency Band, kHz
Voice Channel	1	0–4
Group	12	60–108
Supergroup	60	312–552
Mastergroup	600	564–3,084
Jumbogroup	3600	564–17,548

Digital Carrier Systems

TDM is used in digital carrier systems because many bits can be packed into the very narrow time blocks allotted to each of several signal sources.

The second method of dividing the capacity of a transmission channel among several separate signal sources is to allocate a very short period of time on the channel in a repeating pattern to each signal. This technique is called time division multiplexing (TDM). It is well-suited to binary signals consisting of pulses representing a one or a zero. These pulses can be made of very short duration and still convey the desired information; therefore, many of them can be squeezed into the time available on a digital carrier channel.

The original signal may be an analog wave which is converted to binary form for transmitting as in the case of speech signals in the telephone network, or the original signal may already be in binary form as in the case of a business machine. The electronic systems that perform this TDM process are called digital carrier systems. As with the analog carrier systems, there is a standard heirarchy of digital carrier systems in the public telephone network as shown in Table 3.3. The reader is referred to Chapter 6 for specific information concerning time division multiplexing and the operation and utilization of a T1 multiplexer that can be used with DS-1 digital carrier system.

**Table 3.3.
Digital Carrier
Systems**

Digital Signal No.	No. Voice Circuits	Bit Rate, Mbps
DS-1	24	1.544
DS-2	96	6.312
DS-3	672	44.736
DS-4	4032	274.176

WHAT HAVE WE LEARNED?

1. Information is a numerical quantity that measures the randomness of a system.
2. Symbols such as letters have an information content. Not every symbol is equally likely to occur.
3. The redundancy of a system measures how likely symbols are to be repeated.
4. Data communications systems use redundancy to detect and correct errors in transmission.
5. Signals can travel through guided and unguided transmission media.
6. Adding inductance to pairs of wires is called loading. Loading is used to reduce high-frequency attenuation over the wire pair.
7. Fiber optic transmission systems send data signals as light rays. These systems have much higher bandwidth and have immunity from external interference.
8. Transmission rates over channels are limited by the bandwidth of the channel, the signal-to-noise ratio, and the amount of intersymbol interference in the transmitted waveform.

Quiz for Chapter 3

1. The amount of uncertainty in a system of symbols is also called:
   a. Bandwidth.
   b. Loss.
   c. Entropy.
   d. Quantum.

2. Redundancy measures:
   a. Transmission rate of a system.
   b. How likely symbols are to be repeated.
   c. Time between failure.
   d. System cost.

3. An example of a bounded medium is:
   a. Coaxial cable.
   b. Waveguide.
   c. Fiber optic cable.
   d. All of the above.

4. Loading refers to the addition of:
   a. Resistors.
   b. Capacitors.
   c. Bullets.
   d. Inductance.

5. Coaxial cable has conductors with:
   a. The same diameter.
   b. A common axis.
   c. Equal resistance.
   d. None of the above.

6. Fiber optic cables operate at frequencies near:
   a. 20 MHz.
   b. 200 MHz.
   c. 2 GHz.
   d. 800 THz.

7. HF radio waves follow how many basic paths on leaving the transmitter?
   a. Two.
   b. Four.
   c. One.
   d. Many.

8. The area of coverage of a satellite radio beam is called its:
   a. Beamwidth.
   b. Circular polarization.
   c. Footprint.
   d. Identity.

9. Transmission of binary signals requires:
   a. Less bandwidth than analog.
   b. More bandwidth than analog.
   c. The same bandwidth as analog.
   d. A license from the FAA.

10. The standard first-level digital multiplex system in the U.S. operates at:
    a. 2.048 Mbps.
    b. 44.736 Mbps.
    c. 1.544 Mbps.
    d. 9600 bps.

Asynchronous Modems and Interfaces

ABOUT THIS CHAPTER

Having laid the groundwork by describing the form of the data (codes), the source of the data to be transmitted (terminals), and the transmission media; we now can discuss *how* the data are transmitted. This chapter explains how modems work in terms of frequency, bandwidth, and modulation; and describes the data terminal equipment/data communication equipment (DTE/DCE) interface.

WHY DATA CAN'T BE TRANSMITTED DIRECTLY

Digital information cannot be transmitted directly over the switched telephone network because the portion of the network beyond the central office cannot carry direct current.

Although it may not have been obvious at the time, the reasons that modems are necessary were discussed in Chapter 3. Remember that the switched telephone network utilizes a variety of transmission methods from wire pairs to microwave, but only in the local area (primarily within the area served by a Central Office) does an actual metallic path (wire) exist from one telephone to another. This means that we cannot transmit data in its original form as a series of pulses much farther than from our telephone to the Central Office (CO). Actually, if loading coils are used in the local loop, we can't even transmit it that far. As discussed in Chapter 3, the bandwidth (the passband) of the telephone channel beyond the CO after it has been filtered and amplified is approximately 300 to 3400 Hz as shown in Figure 4.1. Since direct current (zero Hz) is below 300 Hz, it is not within the passband; thus, data in its original pulsed DC or "baseband" form cannot be transmitted over this channel.

SOLVING THE PROBLEM WITH MODEMS

A transmitting modem changes the digital signals produced by computers to an analog signal with a frequency bandwidth that can be transmitted over the telephone network.

Because we are interested in transmitting data beyond the CO using the existing telephone network, we need to change the data pulses to another form that can be transmitted over the telephone channel. Since the telephone network is designed and optimized for transmission of analog signals in the voice band, why not make the data look like these analog signals for transmission? This is exactly the function of a modem. The ones and zeros of the data stream from the DTE are converted to tones (or analog waveforms resembling tones) having frequencies within the 300 to 3400-Hz range. Thus, the modem is nothing more than a rather complex interface device.

**Figure 4.1.
Telephone Channel
Bandwidth** *(Source: S.
Bigelow, Understanding
Telephone Electronics,
© 1991, Sams, Division
of Macmillan Computer
Publishing)*

A receiving modem converts the analog signal back to its original digital form so that the receiving computer can use the data.

At the transmitting end, incoming pulses from the DTE are converted to tones and transmitted over the telephone channel; at the receiving end, the tones are converted back to pulses which are passed to the DTE. In other words, the transmitting modem modulates an analog signal, called a carrier, with the data (more about modulation in the next section) and uses the analog signal to carry to the other end of the telephone circuit. The receiving modem demodulates the analog signal to recover the data in their original pulse form and passes it to the receiving DTE. In fact, the name "modem" is a contraction of the words *mo*dulator-*dem*odulator. One important fact to remember is this: A modem does not operate on the content of the data; it merely changes the form for transmission.

Telephone Channel Restrictions on Modems

In addition to the bandwidth limits, another restriction of the telephone channel which affects modem design is inherent in any analog transmission facility; that is, the transmission is best at frequencies near the center of the passband and poorer for frequencies toward the upper and lower limits of the passband. High-speed modems use almost all of the voice band for one channel; therefore, most high-speed modems in North America utilize a carrier frequency of 1700 to 1800 Hz because these frequencies are very near the middle of the voice band. Low-speed modems, because of their narrower bandwidth requirements, can use more than one carrier frequency within the voice band and still operate in the "good" portion of the band.

Modems cannot use the frequencies in the transmission channels that are used for telephone network signaling.

Still another restriction of the telephone channel is that certain frequencies cannot be used. The telephone network uses the transmission channel for passing information and control signals between the switching offices. This process, called in-band or in-channel interoffice signaling, utilizes tones at frequencies within the voice band. A modem cannot use these same frequencies because the network might interpret them as control tones with disastrous results to the call.

Modem Interfaces

A modem has an interface to the telephone network and an interface to the DTE. The one to the telephone network is the simpler because that interface consists of only two wires called the "tip and ring." As long as the modem adheres to the voltage, current, power, and frequency rules of the telephone company, the telephone channel is really just a pipe to move analog tones from one place to another.

A protocol establishes the procedures which are used by the transmitting and receiving equipment in establishing and maintaining communications. "Handshaking" assures the equipment is ready to go.

The interface wiring between the modem and the DTE is more complex and is governed by standards which will be discussed later in this chapter. This interface also requires that certain procedures (called a protocol) be observed in establishing communications between the two ends. First, the DTE and the modem at the transmitting end must establish communication with one another. The DTE indicates to the modem that it wishes to transmit, and this modem signals to the modem at the other end of the circuit to see if it is ready to receive. Since, in general, modems do not store data, the receiving modem must contact its DTE to see if it is ready to receive. (This communication between the equipment often is referred to as "handshaking.") After the transmitting modem knows that the receiving modem and DTE are listening on the line, it notifies the transmitting DTE which then begins passing data to the transmitting modem for modulation and transmission. On the receiving end, the receiving modem demodulates the incoming signal and passes the received data to the receiving DTE.

In half-duplex transmission (only one direction at a time), when the transmitter is finished and wants a reply from the other end, the channel must be "turned around." To do this, much of the handshaking must be done again to establish transmission in the opposite direction and this turn-around handshaking must occur each time the direction is changed. In full-duplex transmission (both directions simultaneously), the transmission uses two different carrier frequencies, thus, the handshaking is necessary only for the initial set up.

A sine wave signal often is used as the carrier in an analog modulation process. A sine wave can be easily generated by electromechanical generators and electronic oscillators.

ANALOG MODULATION

Modulation is the process of using some medium as a carrier to carry information between two points. For example, we could send Morse code by turning a flashlight on and off to modulate the light beam. Reflecting on this process, we see that we are changing some property of the carrier to represent the data; in this instance it is the intensity of the beam. (This might be more easily understood if we imagine that we use a bright light for a mark and a dim light for a space. In this case, we are modulating the brightness or "amplitude" of the light beam to send data.)

A sine wave that might be used as a carrier in a modem is illustrated in Figure 4.2. Sine waves are not only mathematical functions; they also are fundamental phenomena of the physical universe. Sine waves are generated by devices such as electromechanical generators and electronic oscillators.

A man named Fourier discovered that any series of pulses, sounds, voltages, or similar waves may be broken down into a series of sine waves of varying frequencies and amplitudes. This means that human speech, in the air or on a telephone wire, can be analyzed in terms of the sine waves it contains. That is not to say that the human larynx creates speech by combining sound waves at different frequencies; it simply means that Fourier analysis is a fundamental and useful tool for analyzing the characteristics of any transmission channel or device, whether it be a modem or the speakers of a high fidelity sound system.

Frequency, amplitude, and phase are the characteristics of a sine wave that can be varied to achieve modulation.

As illustrated in Figure 4.2a, a sine wave can be defined by its frequency and amplitude. Frequency is measured in cycles per second with the unit of measurement termed the Hertz (Hz). That is, one cycle per second equals one hertz. Amplitude can be measured in units of volts peak-to-peak, volts peak, and volts root mean square (rms) as indicated in the illustration.

Another parameter of a sine wave is the phase of the wave, but it only has meaning in reference to another wave of the same frequency. Two different sine waves having the same frequency can be compared by the amount by which one leads or lags the other. Since one complete cycle of a sine wave occurs in 360 degrees, we can consider the difference between the two waves in terms of degrees as indicated in Figure 4.2b. The amplitude of the two waves so compared does not have to be the same, but the frequency has to be exactly the same.

Since the frequency, amplitude, and phase completely characterize a sine wave, these are the only parameters of the carrier sine wave that can be changed to modulate the carrier for transmitting information from one modem to another. All modems, therefore, utilize either amplitude, frequency, or phase modulation, or some combination of these.

The modem converts the 1s and 0s of the data stream into an analog signal that is within the telephone voice band so the data can be transmitted over the telephone network.

Figure 4.3 illustrates amplitude, frequency, and phase modulation. Notice that the same sequence of 1s and 0s of the data stream affect the carrier in different ways. After modulation, the pulses are represented by an ac signal having frequencies within the voice band, thus, the information can be transmitted over telephone channels. Actually, simple amplitude modulation is not used for data communication because it is very susceptible to electrical noise interference which can cause errors in the received data. Low-speed modems use frequency modulation; higher speed modems use phase modulation; and the very highest speed modems for voice-band transmission use a combination of phase and amplitude modulation.

**Figure 4.2.
Sine Wave
Fundamentals** *(Source:
D.L. Cannon,
Understanding Digital
Troubleshooting,* ©
*1991, Sams, Division of
Macmillan Computer
Publishing)*

*Sine wave is
defined by
frequency
and
amplitude.*

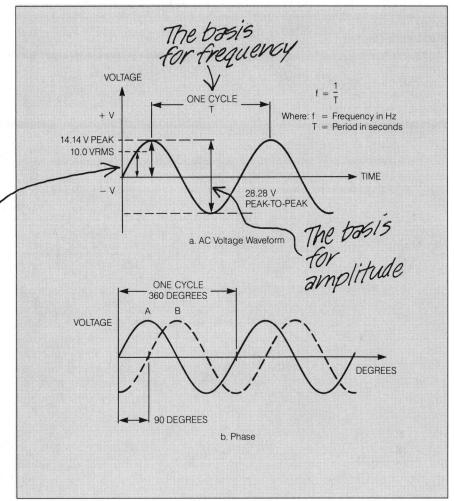

*The basis
for frequency*

a. AC Voltage Waveform

*The basis
for
amplitude*

$$f = \frac{1}{T}$$

Where: f = Frequency in Hz
T = Period in seconds

b. Phase

LOW-SPEED MODEM OPERATION

By separating the total channel bandwidth into two bands, modems can transmit and receive data simultaneously over the same channel. The calling modem is set to the originate mode and the answering modem to the answer mode.

With this background, we can describe how a standard 0–300-baud low-speed modem works. Figure 4.4 shows the voice band divided into two sub-bands for transmission in both directions simultaneously. Recall that such two-way transmission is called full-duplex, meaning that the same bandwidth is available in both directions at the same time.

For some people, the process of transmitting data over one channel in two directions at the same time may be hard to visualize. One could think of it as being similar to two people talking on the same local call simultaneously. Both people can talk and hear at the same time, although they may have trouble understanding each other because the entire bandwidth of the channel is available to both parties in both directions.

Figure 4.3.
Types of Analog
Modulation *(Source:*
D. Doll, Data
Communications;
Facilities, Networks and
System Design, John
Wiley & Sons, © *1978,*
John Wiley & Sons, Inc.)

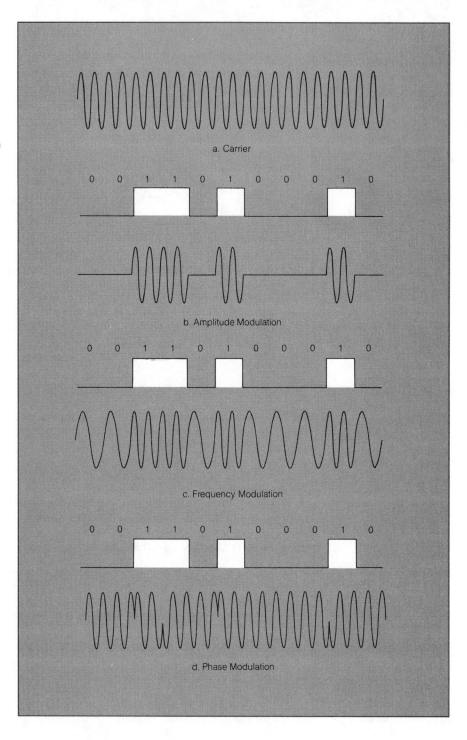

**Figure 4.4.
Frequencies Used for
300-Baud Full-Duplex
Transmission**

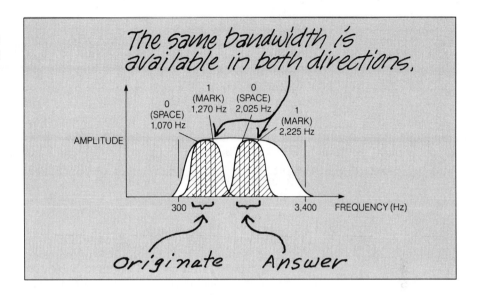

However, the modems completely separate the data into the two bands shown, one for each direction, so that each can understand the other.

The separation is accomplished when one modem is set to the "originate" mode, and the other to the "answer" mode, by a switch on each modem or through the issuance of commands to each modem from attached DTEs. The terms originate and answer come from the use of low-speed modems in dial-up computer applications where a user calls a computer. The calling modem is usually in the originate mode, and the called modem in the answer mode (makes sense, doesn't it?). By doing things this way, the marking tone of the answer modem (the high-pitched "whistle" heard when it answers) also disables any echo suppressors and companders (which interfere with data transmission) that may be in the circuit.

FSK is a simple, economical modulation technique used in low-speed modems. The mark and space each are assigned a particular frequency, then transmitted simply by switching the appropriate frequency on and off.

In Figure 4.4, notice that the originate modem transmits 0s (spaces) at 1070 Hz and 1s (marks) at 1270 Hz. The answer modem also transmits spaces and marks, but at 2025 and 2225 Hz, respectively. This type of modulation is called frequency-shift keying (FSK). (The term "keying" means turning a transmitter on and off.) The appropriate mark or space frequency is simply turned on and off by the transmitting modem as it wishes to send a one or zero. If you listen on a telephone line which is carrying low-speed FSK modem transmissions, you may hear a warbling sound as the frequencies shift back and forth.

If the originating modem transmits 0s at 1070 Hz and 1s at 1270 Hz, at what frequency does it receive 0s and 1s? For compatibility with the answer modem that transmits 0s and 1s at 2025 and 2225 Hz, respectively, the originating modem receives 0s and 1s at those frequencies. Similarly, the answer modem receives 0s and 1s at 1070 Hz and 1270 Hz, respectively, to maintain transmission compatibility with the originating modem.

The FSK modem just described is more commonly known as a Bell System 113 type device. Originally, the Bell System supplied all modems that could be attached to the switched telephone network. By the time other vendors were permitted to sell modems for use on the switched network, the Bell System's monopoly had created a large base of telephone company devices, which encouraged vendors to manufacture modems compatible with Bell System products.

High-speed modems use phase modulation because it requires less bandwidth for the same data rate.

FSK is a straightforward and economical modulation method that works well over telephone channels, so the logical question is: "Why not use it for higher speed modems?" The answer is "between the lines" (no pun intended) of Figure 4.4. Higher data rates require more bandwidth; thus, if we wanted to transmit at higher speeds, then the mark and space frequencies for each sub-band would have to be farther apart, and the two sub-bands would have to be separated further to provide enough bandwidth. Soon we would be outside of the telephone channel; in other words, we would require more bandwidth than is available. Therefore, higher speed modems use some form of phase modulation because phase modulation requires the least bandwidth of the three analog modulation methods.

BELL SYSTEM 212A AND V.22 MODEMS

Until the mid-1980s, the Bell System 212A modem was the most popular upgrade for Bell System 113 type modem users. The 212A modem can be considered two modems in one because it employs FSK modulation using the Bell System 113 frequency assignments at 300 bps. At its higher 1200-bps rate, it uses dibit phase shift keyed (DPSK) modulation. Under DPSK modulation, two bits at a time are encoded into one phase shift or signal change. Thus, the signal rate of modem (commonly known as its baud rate) is 600 or one-half of its 1200-bps data rate. The phase shift encoding of 212A type modem is illustrated in Table 4.1.

**Table 4.1.
212A Type Modem
Phase Shift**

Dibit	Phase Shift (Degrees)
00	90
01	0
10	180
11	270

When a 212A modem operates at 1200 bps, it can transmit data either asynchronously or synchronously. One key advantage to using 212A type modems is that when connected to a computer they can receive transmission from terminal devices operating at either 300 or 1200 bps.

The V.22 standard is similar to the 212A at 1200 bps. However, at the 212A's lower data rate, the two modems are incompatible. The V.22

modem's second data rate is 600 bps compared with the 212A's lower data rate of 300 bps. A second major difference between the lower speed of the two modems is in the method of modulation used. The 212A uses FSK modulation at 300 bps, whereas the V.22 uses 2-phase PSK at 600 bps. Fortunately, the V.22 modem is used primarily in Europe, whereas the 212A type modem is used primarily in North America.

V.22 bis

The CCITT V.22 bis (bis meaning second in Latin) has received widespread acceptance throughout the United States and Europe during the last few years and represents one of the few modems that can be used for worldwide communications. The V.22 bis recommendation governs modems designed for asynchronous data transmission at 2400 bps over the switched telephone network, with a V.22 fallback method of operation. When the V.22 bis modem operates in its fallback mode, incompatibility problems can arise because of the different methods used to manufacture this modem.

In the United States, most if not all V.22 bis modems follow the Bell System 212A specifications for fallback operations—DPSK at 1200 bps and FSK at 300 bps. In Europe, most V.22 bis modems follow the V.22 specifications for fallback operations, which includes 2-phase PSK at 600 bps. Thus, at their lowest fallback rate, V.22 bis modems manufactured for use in North America are incompatible with those manufactured for use in Europe.

NONSTANDARD MODEMS

The requirements of personal computer users for higher transmission rates for file transfer and interactive full screen display operations resulted in several vendors designing proprietary operating modems to achieve data rates that would have been beyond belief several years ago. To achieve data rates up to 19.2 kbps over the switched telephone network, some modems incorporate data compression and decompression algorithms, whereas other modems attempt to transmit data on up to 512 distinct frequencies over the communications link bandwidth.

Modems incorporating compression really operate at variable data rates because their throughput depends on the susceptibility of the data to the compression algorithms in the modem. As an example of how a modem can compress data, consider the sequence ACCOUNT ƀƀƀƀƀƀƀ AMOUNT where ƀ indicates a blank or space character. This sequence could represent the column headings of a report and is similar to most accounting reports that contain columns of data with each column separated by spaces from the next column. If the modem uses a special character denoted as S_c to show space compression, the sequence is transmitted as ACCOUNT S_c7 AMOUNT between modems. At the receiving modem, the character S_c indicates the occurrence of space compression, and the numeric 7 indicates the number of space characters compressed.

This information provides the receiving modem with the ability to decompress the data into its original form.

To prevent the natural occurrence in the data stream of a character indicating space compression and thus falsely affecting the modem at the opposite end of the data link, the originating modem is programmed to stuff an extra space compression indicating character into the transmission sequence. Thus, if the data stream into the modem is $XYZS_cABC$, the modem transmits the sequence $XYZS_cS_cABC$. At the receiving modem, the occurrence of the first S_c character causes the modem to examine the next character. If the receiving modem finds a second S_c character following the first, it will disregard the second S_c character, restoring the data stream to its original form while preventing a false decompression of the data.

Until 1990, most compression modems used a mixture of compression algorithms. Although the actual throughput is variable, the net effect of compression is roughly double the data transfer rate of the device. In 1990 the CCITT promulgated its V.42 bis recommendation. V.42 bis defines a modified Lempel-Ziv compression algorithm for use in modems. This data compression technique was adopted by over 20 modem vendors by the beginning of 1991 and is expected by the mid-1990s to be incorporated by most modems. Until then, a competitive data compression method known as MNP Class 5 is expected to provide the primary mechanism by which modems compress data. The MNP modem protocol is discussed later in this chapter. For further information covering data compression techniques and applications, the reader is referred to the book *Data Compression 3rd Edition* by Gilbert Held. Published by John Wiley & Sons in 1991, this book explains eleven compression algorithms and contains BASIC language programs that can be used to compress and decompress data.

PACKETIZED ENSEMBLE PROTOCOL MODEM

A second type of nonstandard modem gaining widespread acceptance is known formally as a Packetized Ensemble Protocol Modem. This modem incorporates a high-speed microprocessor and roughly 70,000 lines of instructions built into read-only memory (ROM) chips to obtain a revolutionary advance in modem technology.

Under the Packetized Ensemble Protocol mode of operation, the originating modem simultaneously transmits 512 tones onto the line. The receiving modem determines which tones are usable and reports back to the originating device the usable frequencies over which data can be transmitted. The originating modem then selects a transmission format most suitable to each tone, forms a group of bits into a packet for transmission on each tone and adds an error checking group of bits that covers the data to be transmitted before actually transmitting the data over the full bandwidth. The receiving modem performs a check based on the same algorithm used by the first modem to develop the error checking group of bits. If the transmitted and locally generated check group of bits do not match, the receiving modem requests the transmitting modem to retransmit the data, which results in error corrections by retransmission that is transparent to the modem user.

One of the prime advantages of a Packetized Ensemble Protocol Modem is its capability of adjusting automatically to the usable frequencies on a line. This capability enables the modem to lower its fallback data rate in small increments to correspond to the loss of a few tones at one time.

Figure 4.5 illustrates the transmission rate of a Packetized Ensemble Protocol Modem compared with a conventional modem as the noise level on a circuit increases. The Packetized Ensemble Protocol Modem loses its capability of transmitting on one or a few tones as the noise level increases, resulting in a gradual decrease in the data rate of that modem. In comparison, most conventional modems, such as a 9600-bps device, are designed to fall back to a predefined fraction of their main data rate, such as 7200 or 4800 bps.

Figure 4.5.
Transmission Rate
Versus Noise Level

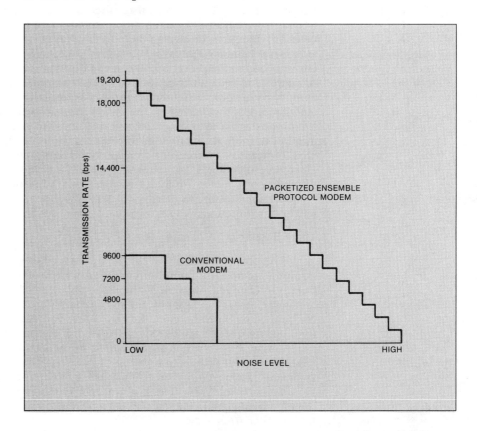

The original Packetized Ensemble Protocol Modem was developed by Telebit Corporation and is marketed as the Trailblazer. Other vendors, including GTE, Digital Communications Corporation, and Racal-Vadic, have entered into various marketing agreements with Telebit that enable them to market this modem.

INTERFACE AND SIGNALING STANDARDS

There are many ''standards'' and ''recommended practices'' used to define data communications interfaces and signaling; in fact, the entire problem of data communications may be looked at as the task of passing information through a series of interfaces and transmission channels without loss of meaning.

Correct interfacing between equipment is of utmost importance to achieve error-free data communications. The most common interface standard is RS-232.

The interface that is of the greatest interest is the one between the equipment which originates and/or receives the data, the Data Terminal Equipment (DTE), and the equipment which handles the problem of transmitting them from place to place, the Data Communications Equipment (DCE). Computers are called Data Terminal Equipment (whether or not they look or act like a CRT or other terminal). Modems are called Data Communications Equipment (also called data circuit-terminating equipment or data sets), because their function is to communicate the data rather than consider, compute, or change them in any way.

Terms like RS-232, V.24, RS-422, RS-423, RS-449, X.21, X.25, current loop, and several others are the designations of the various standards and recommendations designed to make the task of connecting computers, terminals, modems, and networks easier. As we'll see, manufacturers have in many cases used the standardized interfaces for functions that were never intended; this helps by not increasing the number of interfaces, but adds to the confusion of the user.

In terms of the present computer and communications world, the Electronic Industry Association (EIA) RS-232 is *the* standard; therefore, we'll describe it and use it as a way to explain interfaces in general. We'll consider some of the limitations of RS-232, and we'll discuss some of the newer developments which eventually may replace RS-232.

The RS-232 and V.24 Interface

The proper name of RS-232 is ''Interface Between Data Terminal Equipment and Data Communication Equipment Employing Serial Binary Data Interchange.'' Currently, the most popular version of RS-232 is revision C, which is formally referred to as RS-232C. In the late 1980s, revision D was introduced and its use will eventually supersede RS-232C. Both versions of the RS-232 standard have a large core of common functions and operating features which we will collectively refer to as RS-232. We will designate revision C or D to describe specific functions associated with each revision. What we say here also applies to CCITT Recommendation V.24, which is almost identical with RS-232; however, the electrical signal characteristics are specified separately in CCITT Recommendation V.28.

The RS-232 standard covers the mechanical and signal interface between data terminal equipment and data communication equipment employing serial binary data interchange.

In addition to explanatory notes and a short glossary, the RS-232 standard covers four areas:

1. The mechanical characteristics of the interface (which has some surprises).
2. The electrical signals across the interface.
3. The function of each signal.
4. Subsets of signals for certain applications.

Mechanical Interface

Connector shape and pin arrangement are not covered in the standard, but the assignment of signals to connector pins, the connector gender, and cable length and capacity are.

Like any standard, the purpose of RS-232 is primarily as a reference for designers of equipment; therefore, it is not tutorial, and not particularly easy reading. (Perhaps that explains why it seems that many people who write about RS-232 have never read it.) Almost anyone in the computer or communications field, including authors, will tell you that the DB-25 connector is defined in the standard. That is simply not true when referencing RS-232C. It wasn't until reference D was introduced that the 25-pin interface connector was formally specified. Until RS-232D was introduced, all that the mechanical section covered was the assignment of signals to the connector pins (discussed in the next section), which piece of equipment has the female connector (the DCE), the recommended maximum cable length (50 feet), and the maximum cable capacitance (2500 picofarads). Because the DB-25 connector *became* almost universally associated with RS-232C, its pin arrangement is shown in Figure 4.6. However, it was not defined in the standard until revision D, and some manufacturers (notably IBM) use a different connector on some of their equipment. RS-232D additions and changes to RS-232C are indicated in parenthesis in Figure 4.6

Electrical and Functional Interfaces

The standard covers the specifications for current and voltage, special electrical considerations, and the sequencing of signals across the interface.

Although it doesn't make much sense to say that one part of a standard is more important than another, the heart of RS-232 is certainly the electrical and functional sections. The electrical portion covers the all important voltage and current specifications for each pin, along with such features as the requirement that the equipment not be damaged if any two pins are shorted together. (We didn't say the equipment would still work, but it's not supposed to burn up.) The functional portion, perhaps the most important of all, defines the sequencing of the signals and the action taken by the DTE and DCE in response.

Although the RS-232 standard defines the procedure for automatic answering by the modem and for reversing the transmission direction in half-duplex communications, it does not define automatic dialing. This is covered in EIA Standard RS-366. As we will see later, many newer modems incorporate automatic dialing in ways that the authors of RS-232 and RS-366 did not imagine.

Figure 4.6.
Typical RS-232 Female
Connector

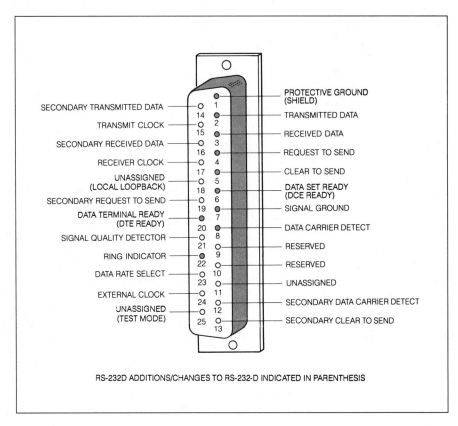

RS-232D ADDITIONS/CHANGES TO RS-232-D INDICATED IN PARENTHESIS

A Pin by Pin Tour of RS-232C

In Figure 4.7, the signals are numbered and named according to three standard systems, plus a fourth that isn't a standard but which many people use. The first is by pin number, which is the way that people who deal regularly with the interface think of the signals: pin 2, pin 3, pin 5, etc. The second is the EIA designation: BA, BB, CB, etc. The third is the CCITT designation: 103, 104, 106, etc. The fourth is an abbreviation of the signal description: TD for Transmitted Data, RD for Received Data, CTS for Clear To Send, etc. A given signal often has more than one of these abbreviations because they aren't standard. Let's now take a pin-by-pin tour and look at the signals by category and function.

Pins 1 and 7, Protective Ground (GND) and Signal Ground (SG)

Two grounds are provided. Chassis (frame) ground (Pin 1) for the system, and a reference signal ground (Pin 7) for the signals on all the other pins.

If provided, Pin 1 is connected to the chassis of the equipment and is intended to connect one end of the shield if shielded cable is used. Shielded cable can be used to minimize interference in high-noise environments. Never connect the shield at both ends of the cable. Pin 7 is the common reference for all signals, including data, timing, and control signals. Pin 7

**Figure 4.7.
RS-232 Pin
Designations**

PIN NO.	EIA CKT.	CCITT CKT.	Signal Description	Common Abbrev.	From DCE	To DCE
1	AA	101	Protective Chassis Ground (Shield)	GND		
2	BA	103	Transmitted Data	TD		X
3	BB	104	Received Data	RD	X	
4	CA	105	Request to Send	RTS		X
5	CB	106	Clear to Send	CTS	X	
6	CC	107	Data Set Ready (DCE Ready)	DSR	X	
7	AB	102	Signal Ground/Common Return	SG	X	X
8	CF	109	Received Line Signal Detector	DCD	X	
9			Reserved			
10			Reserved			
11			Unassigned			
12	SCF	122	Secondary Received Line Signal Detector		X	
13	SCB	121	Secondary Clear to Send		X	
14	SBA	118	Secondary Transmitted Data			X
15	DB	114	Transmitter Signal Element Timing (DCE)		X	
16	SBB	119	Secondary Received Data		X	
17	DD	115	Receiver Signal Element Timing		X	
18			Unassigned (Local Loopback)			X
19	SCA	120	Secondary Request to Send			X
20	CD	108/2	Data Terminal Ready (DTE Ready)	DTR		X
21	CG	110	Signal Quality Detector	SQ	X	
22	CE	125	Ring Indicator	RI	X	
23	CH	111	Data Signal Rate Selector (DTE)			X
23	CI	112	Data Signal Rate Selector (DCE)		X	
24	DA	113	Transmitter Signal Element Timing (DTE)			X
25			Unassigned (Test Mode)		X	

RS-232D Additions/changes to RS-232C indicated in parentheses

must be connected at both ends in order for the DTE and DCE to work properly across the serial interface. Under RS-232D, pin 1's use is modified to provide shielding and this conductor is referred to as the shield.

Pin 7 is the reference signal ground for all of the other pins, thus, it is very important. The interface will not work without it because none of the signal circuits would be completed. One difficulty of RS-232C is the use of two separate grounding wires; grounding of distributed analog systems is often difficult, and having two ground paths doesn't help any. For example, suppose there is an RS-232C cable between two pieces of equipment where the Protective Ground is open (or not connected), but where the Signal Ground is connected to the power outlet ground at both ends. However, due to problems in the building ground circuit, the two ends are at different ground potentials. This causes a current to flow through the Signal Ground wire, and the resistance in the wire causes a difference in potential to develop between pin 7 at one end and pin 7 at the other end. If this potential is large enough, it could cause the data to be received incorrectly.

Pins 2 and 3, Transmitted Data (TD) and Received Data (RD)

The voltage polarities transmitted and received on the data lines (Pin 2 and 3) range from 5 to 25 volts for logic 0 and 1, and are reversed on the control lines.

At last we're getting down to the nitty-gritty. These are the pins that count; if it weren't for the data that passes through them, all the rest would be unnecessary. One important point to remember is that all signal names in the RS-232 standard are as viewed from the DTE. Thus, the DTE transmits on pin 2 and receives on pin 3, but the DCE transmits on pin 3 and receives on pin 2. If you imagine yourself as a computer (easier than imagining yourself as a modem), then the names are easier to understand.

For people accustomed to more modern electronic interfaces, RS-232 signal levels may be a bit surprising because they are not TTL levels. In RS-232C, a positive voltage between 5 and 15 volts on pin 2 or 3 with respect to pin 7 represents a logic 0 level, and a negative voltage between −5 and −15 volts on either pin represents a logic 1. These are the levels for data; the voltage polarities are reversed for logic 0 and 1 on the control lines. Under RS-232D the ON and OFF voltage ranges were extended to +25 V and −25 V, respectively.

Pins 4 and 5, Request to Send (RTS) and Clear to Send (CTS)

The signals on pins 4, 5, 6, and 20 are the handshaking signals which establish the communications link.

Terminals may not transmit until Clear to Send (CTS) is received from the DCE. For private-line transmission, CTS is usually linked to Request to Send (RTS); in such cases, the DTE may use RTS to turn on the modem transmission carrier if the modem is so optioned. In this type of application, the relationship between RTS and CTS is usually a simple count-down timer which is optioned when the DCE is installed. The time delay will be set to such a value as to allow time for the carrier to turn on and become stable before CTS is returned to the DTE. If the DCE is optioned for constant carrier (without regard to RTS), then the RTS/CTS delay is usually set to zero.

Pin 6 and 20, Data Set Ready (DSR) and Data Terminal Ready (DTR)

Data Set Ready (DSR), that is, Modem Ready, is used to indicate that the modem is powered on and is not in test mode. In dial-data applications, Data Terminal Ready (DTR) is used to create the equivalent of an off-hook condition. When the modem is in auto-answer mode, DTR may be asserted in response to the ring indicator to tell the modem to answer the incoming call. Under RS-232D the signal on pin 6 was renamed DCE Ready while the signal on pin 20 was renamed DTE Ready.

Pin 8, Received Line Signal Detector (DCD or CD)

The Received Line Signal Detector is asserted when the modem receives a carrier of sufficient strength for reliable communications.

The Received Line Signal Detector signal is usually called Data Carrier Detect (DCD) or Carrier Detect (CD); however, CD should be avoided as it can be confused with the EIA designation of CD for pin 20. The modem asserts DCD whenever it receives a signal on the telephone line that meets its internal criteria for amount of energy at the carrier frequency. Many DTEs require this signal before they will transmit or accept data; for this reason, in applications where no modem is present, pin 8 usually is tied to pin 20, which in most cases is asserted whenever the DTE is turned on.

Pin 22, Ring Indicator (RI)

When the DCE detects a ringing signal on pin 22, it tells the DTE that the phone is ringing. The DTE tells the modem to answer the phone by asserting pin 20.

The Ring Indicator (RI) signal is the means by which the DCE tells the DTE that the phone is ringing. Virtually all modems that are designed to be directly connected (via an FCC-approved modular plug) to the telephone network are equipped for auto answer. This means that the modem is able to recognize the standard ringing voltage, indicate the ringing to the DTE, and answer (take the line off-hook) when told to do so by the DTE. Pin 22 is asserted by the DCE in time with the cadence of the ringing signal on the line; that is, when the ringing voltage is present, RI is true (on); between rings, RI is not true (off). The DTE tells the modem to answer the phone by asserting pin 20, DTR.

The ten pins and signals described in the foregoing are by far the most often used of those defined in RS-232 and V.24. It is very unlikely that equipment or cables for the small computer market will be equipped with any other proper RS-232 signals, although sometimes (unfortunately) other pins are used in nonstandard ways which can cause problems when equipment is interconnected. We will now quickly cover the functions of the remaining pins in the specification.

Pins 15, 17, 21, and 24

Pins 15, 17, and 24 are used by synchronous modems to control bit timing. Pin 21 indicates that the quality of the received carrier is satisfactory.

Synchronous modems use the signals on pins 15, 17, 21, and 24. Because the transmitting modem must send something (a 1 or 0) at each bit time, the modem controls the timing of the bits from the DTE. Similarly, the receiving modem must output a bit and associated timing whenever received. Pin 15 (Transmitter Signal Element Timing—DCE source), and pin 17 (Receiver Signal Element Timing—DCE source) are used for these purposes. In instances where the transmitter timing comes from a source other than the transmitting modem (such as another modem in a multiplexing situation), pin 24 (Transmitter Signal Element Timing—DTE source) is used. Pin 21 (Signal Quality Detector) indicates that the received carrier meets some predetermined criterion for quality.

Pin 23, Data Signal Rate Selector

Pin 23 looks like two pins in the chart of Figure 4.7, but actually it is either Data Signaling Rate Selector (DTE source) or Data Signaling Rate Selector (DCE source). Some modems, called dual-rate or "gearshift" modems, allow switching between two transmission speeds. Sometimes the speed is selected automatically by the modem during the training (initializing) sequence, or it may be selected by the transmitting DTE. The signal on pin 23 controls whether the modem uses the high or low speed. Usually the modem at the calling end sets the speed for the connection and informs its DTE. The calling modem signals the speed to the answering modem, which informs the called DTE by asserting Data Signaling Rate Selector (DCE source).

Secondary Channels: Pins 12, 13, 14, 16, and 19

In modems equipped with primary and secondary channels, the secondary channels carry signals in the reverse direction and at a much lower data rate.

Some modems are equipped with both primary and secondary channels. The five secondary signals—Secondary Transmitted Data, Secondary Received Data, Secondary Request To Send, Secondary Clear To Send, and Secondary Received Line Signal Detector—allow control of the secondary channel in the same way as described for the primary channel. In these modems, the primary transmission channel usually has the higher data rate, and the secondary channel transmits in the reverse direction with a much lower data rate (for example, 75 bps).

SOME EXAMPLES OF RS-232 CONNECTIONS

Not all of the RS-232 pins are used in every application, but the minimum DTE-DCE interface connections are: transmitted data, received data, signal ground, and frame ground.

Now that you understand the functions of the various signals, let's look at some examples of RS-232 interfaces. Let's begin with a simple example where the interface is used in the proper way; later we'll discuss how the interface is used in ways for which it was not intended.

Computer to Modem Interface

When you call from your home computer to another computer over telephone lines, you are using the Universal Seven-Part Data Circuit that we defined in Chapter 1 and illustrated in Figure 1.9. Your computer is connected to a modem through an RS-232 interface, and the modem is connected to the telephone network. At the far end, whether it is a local or long-distance call, the other computer is similarly connected to a modem through an RS-232 interface. Figure 4.8a shows an absolutely minimum RS-232 interface for the "normal" DTE-DCE connection.

Computer to Video Display Terminal Interface

The video display terminal (VDT) uses the simplest possible interface, as Figure 4.8 shows. If both the computer and the VDT are set up as DTE, pins 2 and 3 must be interchanged at the VDT end of the cable, as Figure 4.8b shows. Otherwise, each would expect to transmit data on the same wire.

This interchange usually is done at one of the cable connectors; however, an adapter with the wiring interchange done between its back-to-back connectors may be inserted between one end of a standard cable and the equipment. This adapter, often called a modem eliminator or null modem, permits the standard cable wiring to be left as is. These adapters are available in any combination of connector gender; that is, male-to-male, male-to-female, and female-to-female.

Computer to Serial Printer Interface

When a RS-232 cable is used to connect peripheral equipment to a computer, it may have to be modified.

The label on the box for your new printer says, "Serial interface connects directly to the RS-232 port of your computer." When you open the box, you see a connector on the back of the printer that looks just like the RS-232 connector on your modem. (The manufacturer also charges you quite a bit extra for the absolutely essential printer cable, but that's

**Figure 4.8.
Minimum RS-232
Interface**

*Pins 2 and 3
must be
interchanged
if both
computer
and VDT
are set up
as DTE.*

another story.) So, it appears that the RS-232 interface on your computer does double duty; it can connect to a modem or to a printer. But the RS-232 was never intended for connecting peripheral devices such as printers to DTEs such as computers. It's not that it won't work; the problem comes in the confusion of identities. The computer is almost always (when talking about RS-232, it *always* pays to say "almost always") internally wired as a DTE, and modems are always wired as DCEs (yes, always, because the role of the modem is defined precisely in the standard), but what about the poor printer? Is it DTE or DCE; fish or fowl? Does it use the same signals (and pins) that the modem uses, or are some different? Can you get by without buying that expensive special printer cable, or can you use your modem cable which, after all, looks just like the printer cable, even to having the same connectors.

Nonstandard Use of a Standard

You probably have already guessed that the answer is bad news, or we wouldn't be talking about it. The RS-232 and other standards are intended to define the interface between DTEs and DCEs for communications over networks, usually telephone facilities. They don't address the idea of using the interface as a general serial input/output port. The wiring and control of

Modified RS-232 cables often have pins that are not connected, or they are interchanged or jumpered to adapt the cable for the desired interface connections.

a peripheral device in the same room, such as a printer (or another computer), is simply not considered in the standard. This means that the manufacturers are presented with a useful solution to the interfacing problem, but few guidelines (and no hard-and-fast rules) on how to apply it. The result is a certain amount of confusion in the marketplace, and the purpose of this section is to help the reader understand what happens across the interface so she or he can solve the problem if necessary.

One source of the confusion is that printers and similar peripherals simply don't do the same things that modems do; therefore, they don't need the same control signals. The printer doesn't need to send and receive some of the signals that the modem needs, and needs some that the modem doesn't. One question is whether pin 2 or pin 3 of the RS-232 connector will be used for data transfer. In the sense of the standard, both the computer and printer are DTE, and when a DTE is connected directly to another DTE most of the signals defined in RS-232 are unnecessary. Although the manufacturer's special printer cable looks like an RS-232 cable, some of the pins aren't connected at all and some of the pin connections are interchanged or jumpered together to adapt the interface on both ends. So, the printer manufacturer's claim that its product is ''RS-232 compatible'' really means that the equipment accepts and generates only a small fraction of the RS-232 signals, and (hopefully) doesn't violate any other parts of the standard.

Flow Control

Let's imagine that we decide to write our own software (called a printer driver) to pass data through the RS-232 port to the printer. We bought the manufacturer's cable, and we've checked things like bit rate, parity, number of stop bits, and character code. Suppose the printer is set up for ASCII 7-bit characters, odd parity, and 1 stop bit. The printer manual says it can operate at 9600 bits per second, and since that's the fastest our computer can output serial data, we'll use that speed. Now we send a page of text to the printer, using our driver program. What happened? After the first line or two, there were more missing characters than were printed. Looks like they never made it to the printer! There doesn't seem to be any rhyme or reason, but every time we try to print using our program, data are lost. Why?

The RS-232 assumes that the flow control needed by modems would be furnished by the software at either end of the communications network.

Let's compare data rates. Asynchronous ASCII uses 7 bits for the character code, 1 for the parity bit, 1 for the stop bit, and 1 for the start bit, for a total of 10 bits per character. Since the computer is transmitting 9600 bits per second to the printer, the character rate must be 960 characters per second.

Digging out the printer manual one more time, we see that the printer's maximum rate is 80 characters per second. That means we are sending 12 times as much data as it can accept. No wonder the data were getting lost. The printer buffer would fill up, then data would be lost until buffer space became available again. What we need is a simple handshake mechanism to stop the computer from sending data when the buffer fills up, and turn it on again when the buffer empties. This is called flow control, and RS-232 is bound to have it, right? Wrong! RS-232 was designed for communicating between computers over telephone channels; the assumption is that any flow control mechanism needed is built into the software at either end. As we'll see next, various schemes have been used for flow control with varying degrees of success.

Methods Used For Flow Control

The RTS and CTS lines should not be used for flow control because it is very likely that data will be lost.

From the previous discussion about RTS and CTS (pins 4 and 5), it would seem that these signals could be used for flow control; although they often are, they shouldn't be, for many reasons. The problem is that the DCE is not allowed to drop Clear to Send until the DTE drops Request to Send. RTS and CTS are indeed handshake lines; the problem is that they indicate something besides that the DCE is ready to accept data. The RTS and CTS signals are intended to allow the terminal to request control of the communications link from the modem. The terminal assumes that it will keep the link as long as it needs it, and the DCE cannot arbitrarily drop Clear to Send whenever it desires to do so. That means that CTS cannot properly be used by the DCE as a flow control indicator; the DCE (or equipment such as a printer posing as DCE) can't raise and lower Clear to Send to tell the DTE to pause or restart transmission. Put another way, the DTE and the communications link are handshaking, not the DTE and the DCE; the handshake is for the purpose of establishing message transmission, not character-by-character or line-by-line acknowledgement for a printer.

Suppose that we decide to use RTS and CTS for flow control anyway (as some manufacturers who should know better have done). If the printer drops Clear to Send in the middle of a character transmission, what does that mean? If the transmitter stops immediately in the middle of the character, that character is sure to be garbled because timing is important in serial communications. If the transmitter waits until the character is transmitted and then stops, there may be no room in the printer's buffer for the last character. Because this possibility is not considered in the standard, the success of RTS-CTS as a flow control mechanism cannot be predicted without studying the manuals for both of the devices involved. Even doing that is no guarantee of success, but the odds are better.

A way to achieve flow control is for the peripheral equipment to send special characters to the computer, which uses software to recognize the characters.

Some manufacturers avoid the conflict by using the Data Terminal Ready or Data Set Ready (DTR or DSR) pins, depending on whether their printer thinks it is DTE or DCE. For example, if pin 6 (DSR) is used to provide flow control; the printer turns off pin 6 when it can accept no more data, and turns it on again when its buffer is nearly empty. Still, there is no assurance that the device on the other end of the cable will recognize the signal or interpret it correctly because none of these lines was intended to be used for flow control.

Another method for flow control is for the printer to send special characters for pause and return over the data line (pin 3, RD) to the computer. The software driver recognizes the special characters and controls the terminal output according to the character received. ASCII codes DC1 and DC3 (device control 1 and 3) are often used, but usually are called XON and XOFF. On the standard keyboard, these characters correspond to Control-Q (resume) and Control-S (pause). The printer logic transmits Control-S when its buffer is approximately 80% full and Control-Q when the buffer is below 20% full.

Some printer manufacturers use both the DSR line and the RD line (XON/XOFF). However, problems may occur with either method. In instances where the printer is connected to a modem (perhaps a short-haul modem on another floor of the building), there is no connection between the DSR circuits at the opposite ends (nor between RTS/CTS), so use of other pins is impossible. XON/XOFF should work fine in this instance, provided the software recognizes it, and provided that the printer logic anticipates buffer overflow in time. Problems also can occur if several terminals are multiplexed together because the reverse characters are stored for a short time in the multiplexer.

In summary, RS-232 is not very reliable for flow control because it was not designed for this application.

Of course, these problems occur because RS-232 was never intended for flow control or for DTE-to-DTE connections. We should not be surprised when individually arranged flow-control methods don't always work; they simply are not part of the standard.

LIMITATIONS OF RS-232

It would seem that the lack of a flow control mechanism is the major drawback of RS-232, but actually that isn't the case. Flow control is much better handled through software than through hardware, and that is the direction that new systems are moving. Small computer peripherals just haven't gotten there yet. However, RS-232 does have some limitations that restrict its use. After we discuss these, we'll look at some standards that don't have these limitations and offer other advantages as well.

Distance Limitations

The RS-232 standard of 2500 picofarads for stray capacitance may be restrictive in direct computer-to-terminal connections.

The principal problem with RS-232 is its distance limitation of 50 feet. With all but the highest data rates, much longer cable runs can be successful, but they never seem quite long enough and there's always a risk of losing data. The distance restriction is not a serious disadvantage when the modem is close to the computer or terminal, and the long-haul transmission to a remote computer takes place over telephone lines. In local applications, however, RS-232 cables often are used to connect terminals directly to computers because it is convenient to use the same terminal and computer interface whether or not a modem connection is used. (Also, the RS-232 connector is probably the only one provided.) For these connections, the 50-foot limit becomes restrictive.

An RS-232 transmitter generates a voltage between +5 and +25 volts for one of the two possible signal states (space), and a voltage between −5 and −25 volts for the opposite state (mark). Unfortunately, these voltage levels are not the same as those inside the computer and terminal, which use standard TTL and MOS logic. This means an additional power supply (usually ±12 volts) is required for the RS-232 levels. As Figure 4.9 shows, an RS-232 receiver circuit recognizes voltage of above +3 V as spaces and voltages of below −3 V as marks. When a signal changes from one condition to the other, the specification limits the amount of time in the undefined region to 4% of a bit period. This requirement determines the maximum amount of stray capacitance allowable in the cable because capacitance limits the rise time (or transition time) of the signal. RS-232 specifies that the capacitance must not exceed 2500 picofarads (pF). Because the cables generally used for RS-232 have a capacitance of 40 to 50 picofarads per foot, RS-232 limits cables to 50 feet (2500/50 = 50).

**Figure 4.9.
RS-232 Data Signal
Levels at the Receiver**

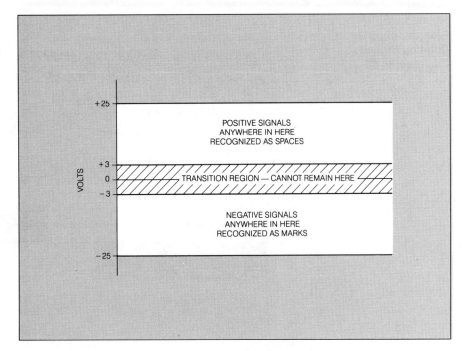

Speed Limitations

Improper grounding of control and data signal grounds can cause signals to be misinterpreted.

A second limitation is the maximum transmission speed of 20,000 bps, although this is not usually a disadvantage in applications between computers and terminals. The data rate between a computer and a terminal is usually less than or equal to 19,200 bps at best, and it is difficult (and expensive, in terms of modem costs) to transmit data even at this rate over the switched telephone network.

Ground Limitations

The third disadvantage of RS-232 is, as we have discussed previously, its grounding method. The problem is not so much with the protective (chassis) ground, but with the control and data signals that all are referenced against the same signal ground wire (pin 7). This method, called unbalanced transmission, works satisfactorily most of the time.

However, if there is a difference in ground potential between the two ends of the cable (quite likely for long runs), the transition region between a space and a mark is narrowed. When this occurs, the possibility exists that a signal will be misinterpreted, as Figure 4.10 shows. Just as the various parts of the standard work together (speeds within the standard will usually work fine over cables that are also within the standard), so the various restrictions interact. If you try to drive cables that are too long at speeds that are too high, all these problems tend to bite you at once.

Figure 4.10.
Problems Because of
Differing Ground
Potentials in RS-232

OTHER INTERFACES

An Old Standby: The Current Loop

When the serial data transmission format is defined by the presence or absence of current, the signal interface is called a current loop.

RS-232, for all its faults, at least defines connector pins and signal levels. No such standards exist for teleprinters. The serial transmission format is defined, with start and stop bits, data bits, and parity bits, but the electrical interface varies with the manufacturer, and control signals are unknown. In teleprinters, the signal interface is called the current loop. Instead of positive and negative voltages representing logic 1s and 0s, the current loop uses presence or absence of current. Presence may be either 20 or 60 milliamperes, depending on the teleprinter model and manufacturer. No standard connector or standard pinouts exist for current-loop operation.

The idea of the current loop is to switch a current on and off. The active side of the transmission line generates the current, while the passive side switches or detects it. Since either the receiver or transmitter can be active, there are four possibilities: active receiver, active transmitter, passive receiver, and passive transmitter. Because of the convenience of locating the power supply at just one end of the link (usually at the computer), all four of these signals are found in a single computer-to-terminal connection.

Despite the lack of standards, designers of serial devices for computers like to include current-loop interface capability. It's a useful interface because teleprinters are still a cost-effective solution as a combination printer and terminal, and many devices other than teleprinters use it. Where RS-232 is limited to a 50-foot cable, a current loop can be up to 1500 feet long and handle data rates of up to 9600 bps without a special power supply. Unfortunately, the current-loop interface is completely incompatible with RS-232 and requires either hardware that has both interfaces built-in or interface boxes. The interface boxes can be built to adapt to any of the four possible interfaces. For example, if two microcomputers that are to be connected both contain the active interface, an active-to-active converter is required to directly connect them. Similarly, to connect a passive terminal directly to another passive terminal, a passive-to-passive converter is required. Fortunately, the converters can be easily constructed using an optoisolator. The active-to-active converter does not even need a power supply, although the passive-to-passive must have one to generate the current.

Data rates up to 9600 bps can be handled using current loops, even when cable lengths are longer than those allowed for RS-232 interfaces.

RS-422A, RS-423A, and RS-449

Useful though the current loop may be in some cases, most of the world is not moving away from RS-232 back to teleprinters. Instead, the movement is toward three types of interfaces. Two are similar to RS-232, but with some of the warts removed; the other quite different, with hardware functions replaced by software. We'll examine the ones more like RS-232 first.

In the early 1970s, the EIA introduced the RS-422A, RS-423A, and RS-449 standards to overcome the defects of RS-232 while at the same time incorporating and improving upon the advantages of the current-loop interface. A major change was to unbundle the electrical, mechanical, and functional specifications of RS-232 into separate documents. RS-422A and RS-423A cover only electrical specifications, while RS-449 covers control functions.

RS-422A

To allow transmission at high data rates, RS-422A uses two separate wires for each signal. This technique, called balanced transmission, doubles the number of wires in the cable, but permits very high data rates and minimizes the problem of varying ground potential. Since ground is not used as a voltage reference, RS-422A grounding requirements are much less critical than those of the RS-232, and the use of the Signal Ground wire is optional with RS-422A.

By using balanced transmission based upon the RS-422A standard, greater speed in data transmission is obtained and ground potential problems are eliminated.

Another major difference between RS-422A and RS-232 is the transition region between mark and space states. With the elimination of the ground potential problem, the transition region can be much narrower. In RS-422A, the difference between the voltages on the two wires determines whether a mark or a space is sent. This difference is only 0.4 V in RS-422A, whereas it is 6 V (+3 V and −3 V) in RS-232. If the difference signal between the two wires is positive and more than 0.2 V, the receiver reads a mark; if it is negative and more than −0.2 V, the receiver reads a space. These voltage values allows suitable transmitters and receivers to be implemented with the ±5 V power supply commonly available in computers.

RS-423A

The RS-423A standard defines an adapter for use between RS-232C and RS-422A which enables RS-232C equipment to interface with RS-422A equipment.

RS-423A transmits at lower speeds and uses one wire as a common return path for all signals in a given direction (unbalanced transmission like RS-232, but with two return wires). The RS-423A standard operates in both RS-232 and RS-422A environments. It provides users of existing RS-232 interfaced equipment with a way to move to the new RS-422A regime, including a defined RS-232 to RS-422A adapter connector.

Because of the much smaller transition region, RS-422A transmitters will not drive RS-232 receivers correctly. RS-423A equipment, on the other hand, will interface with RS-232 signals. Each direction of transmission uses a common return path that is connected to ground only at the transmitter end. The receiver determines whether a mark or space is present by examining whether the signal wire is negative or positive with respect to the common return. Because this return path does not connect to ground in the receiver, the problem of ground currents does not arise.

In an RS-423A transmitter, the voltage difference between the signal line and the common return must be at least 4 V, positive for a space and negative for a mark. This gives an 8 V transition region, which is compatible with RS-232 receiver circuitry, but which presents the same power supply problem that occurs with RS-232. Because the RS-423A receiver must properly respond to the same 0.4 V transition region as a RS-422A receiver, RS-422A transmitters can be used with RS-423A receivers.

RS-449

The RS-449 standard, which uses two connectors instead of one, is intended to replace the functional portion of RS-232. Even so, it has no provision for automatic dialing.

RS-449 is the intended successor to the functional portion of RS-232, including the mechanical specification of the plugs and sockets. Apart from its improved speed and distance specifications, RS-449 offers some minor functional enhancements over RS-232 in automatic modem testing and provision for a standby channel, but it still does not incorporate outward dialing. The acceptance of RS-449 in the marketplace seems questionable at this time.

Figure 4.11 shows the RS-449 signals with the corresponding RS-232 and V.24 signals. Notice the similarity between the new and old standards. The major differences are in the grounding arrangements (Send Common and Receive Common) and testing facilities. Apart from these, only a few miscellaneous signals have been added. All signals use the RS-423A transmission standard except those that may optionally use the RS-422A for higher-speed links. (Two wires are specified for each of these.) The signals are divided between a 37-pin and a 9-pin connector, and the ground and common signals are handled separately for each cable. Many applications will not need the smaller cable because it contains only signals relevant to the secondary channel.

**Figure 4.11.
Comparing RS-449
With RS-232 Signals**
*(Source: EIA Standard
RS-449. Electronic
Industries Association)*

RS-449		RS-232*		CCITT Recommendation V.24	
SG	Signal Ground	AB	Signal Ground (Shield)	102	Signal Ground
SC	Send Common			102a	DTE Common
RC	Receive Common			102b	DCE Common
IS	Terminal in Service				
IC	Incoming Call	CE	Ring Indicator	125	Calling Indicator
TR	Terminal Ready	DC	Data Terminal Ready (DTE Ready)	108/2	Data Terminal Ready
DM	Data Mode	CC	Data Set Ready (DCE Ready)	07	Data Set Ready
SD	Send Data	BA	Transmitted Data	103	Transmitted Data
RD	Receive Data	BB	Received Data	104	Received Data
TT	Terminal Timing	DA	Transmitter Signal Element Timing (DTE Source)	113	Transmitter Signal Element Timing (DTE Source)
ST	Send Timing	DB	Transmitter Signal Element Timing (DCE Source)	114	Transmitter Signal Element Timing (DCE Source)
RT	Receive Timing	DD	Receive Signal Element Timing	115	Receiver Signal Element Timing (DCE Source)
RS	Request to Send	CA	Request to Send	105	Request to Send
CS	Clear to Send	CB	Clear to Send	106	Ready for Sending
RR	Receiver Ready	CF	Received Line Signal Detector	109	Data Channel Received Line Signal Detector
SQ	Signal Quality	CG	Signal Quality Detector	110	Data Signal Quality Detector
NS	New Signal				
SF	Select Frequency			126	Select Transmit Frequency
SR	Signaling Rate Selector	CH	Data Signaling Rate Selector (DTE Source)	111	Data Signaling Rate Selector (DTE Source)
SI	Signaling Rate Indicator	CI	Data Signaling Rate Selector (DCE Source)	112	Data Signaling Rate Selector (DCE Source)
SSD	Secondary Send Data	SBA	Secondary Transmitted Data	118	Transmitted Backward Channel Data
SRD	Secondary Receive Data	SBB	Secondary Received Data	119	Received Backward Channel Data
SRS	Secondary Request to Send	SCA	Secondary Request to Send	120	Transmit Backward Channel Line Signal
SCS	Secondary Clear to Send	SCB	Secondary Clear to Send	121	Backward Channel Ready
SRR	Secondary Receiver Ready	SCF	Secondary Received Line Signal Detector	122	Backward Channel Received Line Signal Detector
LL	Local Loopback	(LL)	(Local Loopback)	141	Local Loopback
RL	Remote Loopback			140	Remote Loopback
TM	Test Mode	(TM)	(Test Mode)	142	Test Indicator
SS	Select Standby			116	Select Standby
SB	Standby Indicator			117	Standby Indicator

*RS-232D Additions/changes to RS-232C indicated in parentheses

One of the major problems that prevented more than a token acceptance of the RS-449 standard is its use of two connectors, with each connector differing in size and conductor connection from the RS-232 connector used with tens of millions of DTEs and DCEs. Recognizing that RS-449 would probably not fulfill its intended role, the EIA announced the RS-530 standard in the late 1980s as the successor to RS-449. Both RS-442 and RS-423 standards will continue to exist and are referenced by the RS-530 standard.

RS-530

RS-530 is similar to RS-449 in that it provides equipment with the ability to transmit data above the RS-232 limit of 20 kbps. Like RS-232, RS-530 uses the near universal 25-pin D-shaped interface connector.

The RS-530 standard obtains its ability to transmit data above 20 kbps by the utilization of balanced signals in place of several RS-232 secondary signals and the Ring Indicator signal. This balanced signalling technique is accomplished by the use of two wires with opposite polarities for each signal to minimize distortion.

Figure 4.12 summarizes the RS-530 interchange circuits based upon their pin assignments. Although no equipment conforming to this new standard was marketed at the time this book revision was prepared, its elimination of the Ring Indicator signal suggests that its use will be reserved for non-PSTN applications.

RS-366

The RS-366 standard is different because it deals with automatic dialing under computer control.

None of the RS-standards we've discussed provide for automatic dialing of calls by a computer. RS-232 and RS-449 provide specifications for answering calls, but not for dialing. A different standard, RS-366, covers automatic calling units. The reason is that, until recently, equipment for placing calls under computer control was expensive because the actions required in making a telephone call can be quite complicated. The dialing equipment must be able to determine whether the line is free, take the phone off hook (in effect), wait for and recognize dial tone, dial the number, and understand and respond to the various call progress tones (such as the busy signal) that the telephone system provides to indicate the status of a call.

The principal use of RS-366 automatic dialing equipment in data communications is for dial backup of private-line data circuits, and for automatic dialing of remote terminals to allow them to transmit data. For example, a company's central computer could be programmed to dial automatically the computer in each branch office each evening, and to cause (via software) the day's transactions to be transmitted to the main office.

**Figure 4.12.
RS-530 Interchange
Circuits**

Pin number	Circuit	Description
1	-	Shield
2	BA	Transmitted Data
3	BB	Received Data
4	CA	Request to Send
5	CB	Clear to Send
6	CC	DCE Ready
7	AB	Signal Ground
8	CF	Received Line Signal Detector
9	DD	Receiver Signal Element Timing (DCE Source)
10	CF	Received Line Signal Detector
11	DA	Transmit Signal Element Timing (DTE Source)
12	DB	Transmit Signal Element Timing (DCE Source)
13	CB	Clear to Send
14	BA	Transmitted Data
15	DB	Transmitter Signal Element Timing (DCE Source)
16	BB	Received Data
17	DD	Receiver Signal Element Timing (DCE Source)
18	LL	Local Loopback
19	CA	Request to Send
20	CD	DTE Ready
21	RL	Remote Loopback
22	CC	DCE Ready
23	CD	DTE Ready
24	DA	Transmit Signal Element Timing (DTE Source)
25	TM	Test Mode

CCITTX X.21

The CCITT standards are aimed toward direct digital data communications. CCITT X.21 covers both automatic dialing and answering, and uses full-duplex synchronous transmission.

The CCITT has charted a course different from the RS-standards, a course that was predicated on the eventual availability of direct digital connection to a digital telephone network. Then all data transmission will be synchronous, and the communication equipment will provide bit and byte timing signals. The CCITT X.21 recommendation, introduced in 1976, includes the protocol for placing and receiving calls and for sending and receiving data using full-duplex synchronous transmission. Byte-timing signals are an option, but one which the vast majority of digital telephone exchanges will almost certainly provide. In sharp contrast to RS-232, RS-449, and RS-530, X.21 uses only six signals. The electrical specifications are contained in recommendations X.26 (corresponding to EIA RS-422A) and X.27 (corresponding to EIA RS-423A).

The eventual minimum line speed under X.21 is likely to be 64,000 bps, the data rate now used to encode voice in digital form in the telephone network. In Europe, British Telecom offers X.21 customer data rate access to its Kilostream digital service at 2.4, 4.8, 9.6, 48, and 64 kbps. Customer data rates up to 9.6 kbps are converted to a line rate of 12.8 kbps, whereas data rates of 48 and 64 kbps both use a line rate of 64 kbps for transmitting through the Kilostream network.

The circuits used in X.21 are given in Figure 4.13. The first two circuits listed provide the voltage reference and ground connections. The computer sends data to the modem on the Transmit line, and the modem returns data on the Receive line. The Control and Indication circuits provide control channels in two directions. The Signal Element Timing line carries the bit timing, and the Byte Timing line carries the byte timing. Although the Control and Indication lines are control lines, most of the controlling information uses the Transmit and Receive lines. The computer changes the state of Control when it wants to place a call, just as you lift the handset when you want to dial. To end the call, the computer changes Control back to the idle state. Similarly, the modem changes the state of Indication when the remote telephone is answered and changes it back if it shuts down. All the dialing information travels on the Transmit line in coded form, and all the information about tones comes back on the Receive line.

Figure 4.13.
CCITT X.21 Signals
(Source: CCITT Recommendation X.21, CCITT, Geneva, C.H.)

Interchange Circuit	Name	To DCE	From DCE
G	Signal Ground or Common Return	(Note)	
Ga	DTE Common Return	X	
T	Transmit	X	
R	Receive		X
C	Control	X	
I	Indication		X
S	Signal Element Timing		X
B	Byte Timing		X

NOTE: See Recommendation X.24.

The major advantage of X.21 over RS-232, RS-449, and RS-530 is that the X.21 signals are encoded in serial digital form. For example, when a dial tone is received, a continuous sequence of ASCII "+" characters is sent to the computer on the Receive wire. In effect, this is a digital dial tone. The computer dials the number by transmitting it as a series of ASCII characters on the Transmit line, one bit at a time. After dialing the call, the computer receives call progress signals from the modem on the Receive wire. These signals indicate such things as number busy, access disallowed, and network congestion.

> X.21, with its signal encoded in serial digital form, permits a few signal lines to accomplish all functions.

By using serial digital coding instead of dedicated wires for special functions, X.21 establishes a basis for providing special services in computer communication. A short-code-dialing or repeat-last-call facility would be extremely useful, for example, to reconnect a call every time you complete a line of typing at the terminal. (Some European nations are trying this approach to networking right now.) If the line could be disconnected while you are typing, long-distance calls would be much cheaper. Of course, this would also depend on the tariff policies of the telecommunication carriers. Using X.21 could allow many of the advantages of telecommunications by the packet-switching technique without the associated complexity.

Although X.21 is defined as the lowest (or "physical") level of the international X.25 packet-switching protocol, it is far ahead of its time because direct digital connection to public telephone networks is hardly possible now. For this reason, CCITT offers the X.21 bis recommendation as an interim measure to connect existing computer equipment to packet communication services. X.21 bis is virtually identical to CCITT V.24 and RS-232. (Packet switching and CCITT protocols are discussed more in a later chapter.)

TYPES OF MODEMS

Asynchronous (300 or 300/1200 Baud) Auto-Answer Modem

> The asynchronous 300 or 300/1200-baud auto-answer modem is usually used with unattended personal computers that are connected to dial-up circuits.

Asynchronous 300- or 300/1200-baud modems are usually used with personal computers. The signals needed are: Protective Ground, Signal Ground, Transmitted Data, Received Data, Request To Send, Clear To Send, Data Terminal Ready, Ring Indicator, Received Line Signal Detector, and possibly Data Set Ready. Pin 20 (DTR) indicates that the computer is ready to receive calls, while Pin 22 (RI) indicates that the modem is receiving the telephone ringing signal, going high and low as the ringing current goes off and on. (This is the way a modem can count how many rings to wait before answering.) If the computer leaves pin 20 (DTR) on all the time, the modem answers incoming calls without delay. If DTR is off, the computer will turn it on in response to RI to tell the modem to answer the call. At the completion of the call, the computer will turn off pin 20 (DTR) to cause the modem to disconnect the line (go on hook).

The following sequence of events is one possible set that can happen when a computer receives a call from another computer via a 300-baud asynchronous modem: When the modem detects ringing, it turns on pin 22 (RI), the DTE responds by asserting pin 20 (DTR), and the modem goes off hook to answer the phone. The answering DTE asserts pin 4 (RTS), which commands the modem to turn on its transmitter. After the RTS-CTS delay, the modem responds by asserting CTS. At the other end of the line, the computer operator hears the carrier signal and either pushes the data button or puts the telephone handset into the acoustic coupler. Now the calling modem's transmitter turns on, producing its own carrier tone. When the modem at the receiving computer hears this carrier, it turns on pin 8 (DCD). Upon receiving this signal, the receiving computer begins transmitting data to tell the sending computer to log in, etc. Some operating systems wait for the caller to transmit a special character to begin the log-on process.

At the end of the session, the caller logs off, causing the receiving computer to terminate the call. It turns off pin 4 (RTS), which causes the receiving modem to turn off its carrier signal. The receiving computer then drops pin 20 (DTR), causing the modem to go on hook to "hang up" the telephone line. At the calling end, pin 8 (DCD) goes off, the operator replaces the handset, and the action is complete.

Full-Duplex Asynchronous Private Line Modem

A private line modem does not have the capability for automatic answering because it's not needed, the modem is always on-line.

The full-duplex asynchronous modem could be used on switched lines as well; it is called a private line modem because it is not equipped for automatic answer. Signals used are: Protective Ground, Signal Ground, Transmitted Data, Received Data, Received Line Signal Detector (Pin 8), and Data Set Ready (Pin 6). Pin 8 (DCD) says in effect, "I hear something like a modem talking to me," in other words, that another modem is trying to make contact on the line. Pin 6 (DSR) usually is not used in asynchronous modems, but could indicate that the modem is ready and not in voice or test mode.

Half-Duplex Asynchronous Private Line Modem

The signals used in the half-duplex asynchronous modem are: Protective Ground, Signal Ground, Transmitted Data, Received Data, Request To Send, Clear To Send, Received Line Signal Detector, and possibly Data Set Ready. Pins 4 and 5, (RTS and CTS) control the transmission direction in the half-duplex operation. The computer asserts pin 4 (RTS) when it wants to transmit. The modem responds by turning on pin 5 (CTS) to indicate that it is ready to receive characters to be transmitted. There is a built-in delay (typically 200 milliseconds) between the Request To Send and the Clear To Send response because the modem must generate the carrier waveform and allow it to stabilize. When transmission is completed in that direction, the computer drops pin 4 (RTS), causing the modem to turn off the transmitter and to drop CTS. The process of determining who transmits when, and how to tell when the other end is finished, is the responsibility of the software protocol which is outside the modem and the RS-232 interface.

Smart Modems

By combining a micro-processor with a modem, both data com-munications and auto-matic dialing can be realized in one unit—a "smart modem."

The so-called "smart" or "intelligent" modem combines a standard modem (300, 300/1200, or 2400 baud) and a microprocessor to provide both data communications and automatic dialing in one unit. (One of the best known is the Smartmodem 1200 made by Hayes Microcomputer Products, Inc.) A smart modem accepts commands in ASCII form over the same RS-232 interface used for data transmission and can respond over the same interface with either status codes or sentences. For example, the computer operator would turn the modem on and load the terminal software, then type a code such as "AT TD1-800-772-5942". This tells the modem to take the phone line off hook, wait for a dial tone, then tone dial (using DTMF tones) the number 1-800-772-5942. The modem will attempt to do this. If the number is busy, the modem's response, "number busy," would appear on the computer's screen. Modems of this type usually can redial the last number entered, and many of these modems automatically keep trying a number at preset intervals if they encounters a busy signal. Some modems can store a list of frequently called numbers (such as the one above) that the user can select by entering only a two- or three-digit code.

The smart modem contradicts our previous statement that modems don't look at the data that passes through them, since it does examine some of the information coming over the RS-232 interface for its commands. Smart modems are being used increasingly by business and individual computer users, and a number of software products exist to support these modems. Virtually all of the software utilizes the Hayes interface protocol, and most (but not all) smart modems accept commands in the Hayes format, which has become a de facto standard. Thus, if you are considering the purchase of a smart modem, it would be wise to consider one that is compatible with the Hayes commands.

The Hayes command set consists of a basic set of commands and command extensions. The basic commands, such as placing the modem off hook and dialing a number, are applicable only to modems designed to transmit and receive data at that speed.

Commands in the Hayes command set are initiated by transmitting an attention code to the modem, followed by an appropriate command or set of commands. The attention code is the character sequence AT, which must be input by the user or sent to the modem by a software program in all uppercase or all lowercase letters. The requirement to prefix all command lines with the code AT has led many modem manufacturers to denote their modems as Hayes AT compatible or simply AT compatible.

A Hayes Smartmodem can hold up to 40 characters in its command buffer, permitting a sequence of commands to be transmitted to the modem on one command line. This 40-character limit does not include the attention code, nor does it include spaces placed in a command line to make it more readable. Table 4.2 lists the major commands included in the basic Hayes Command Set. Other modems, such as the Telebit Trailblazer, employ a command set that is a superset of the Hayes command set.

Although communications software that uses the Hayes command set operates with this modem, such software cannot use the modem's full potential because the Hayes command set in 1991 supported a data rate selection only up to 9600 bps, whereas the Trailblazer modem could be set to data rates of up to 19,200 bps by proprietary software commands.

**Table 4.2.
Major Commands of
the Hayes Command
Set**

Command	Description
A	Answer call
A/	Repeat last command
C	Turn modem's carrier on or off
D	Dial a telephone number
E	Enable or inhibit echo of characters to the screen
H	Hang up telephone (on hook) or pick up telephone (off hook)
I	Request identification code or request check sum
M	Turn speaker off or on
O	Place modem on-line
P	Pulse dial
Q	Request modem to send or inhibit sending of result code
R	Change modem mode to "originate-only"
S	Set modem register values
T	Touch-Tone dial
V	Send result codes as digits or words
X	Use basic or extended result code set
Z	Reset the modem

The basic format required to transmit commands to a Hayes compatible modem is shown below.

AT Command[Parameter(s)]Command[Parameter(s)] ..Return

Each command line includes the prefix AT, followed by the appropriate command and the command's parameters. The command parameters are usually the digits 0 or 1, which serve to define a specific command state. As an example, C1 is the command that tells the modem to turn on its carrier signal, whereas C0 is the command that causes the modem to turn off its carrier signal. Up to 40 characters can be entered into a command line, and each command line must be terminated by a carriage return character.

To illustrate the use of the Hayes command set, suppose that you want to dial automatically information for New York City. The number is 212/555-1212. First, you tell the modem to go off hook, which is similar to picking up a telephone handset. Then, you tell the modem the type of telephone system that we are using—pulse or touch-tone—and the telephone number to dial. If you have a terminal or personal computer connected to a Hayes compatible modem, the following commands would be sent to the modem:

AT H1

AT DT9,1,212-555-1212

In the first command, the 1 parameter used with the H command places the modem off hook. In the second command, DT tells the modem to dial a telephone number using touch-tone (T) dialing. The digits 9 and 1 are included in the telephone number because we assumed that you had to dial 9 to gain access to an outside line through your company's switchboard and 1 for long distance. The commas between the outside line (9), long distance access number (1), and the area code (212) causes the modem to pause for two seconds before dialing the area code. Usually, two seconds is long enough for you to hear the outside line and long distance dial tones before the modem dials the next number.

Because a smart modem automatically goes off hook when dialing a number, the first command line is not required and is normally used for receiving calls. In the second command line, the type of dialing does not have to be specified if a previous call was made because the modem automatically uses the last type specified. Although users with only pulse dialing availability must specify P in the dialing command when using a Hayes Smartmodem, other vendors offer modems that can determine automatically the type of dialing facility that the modem is connected to, then use the appropriate dialing method without requiring the user to specify the type of calling.

WHAT HAVE WE LEARNED?

1. A modem (modulator-demodulator) changes data pulses to analog tones that the telephone channel will pass.
2. Frequency-shift keying is the type of modulation used by most low-speed modems. Phase modulation or a combination of phase and amplitude modulation is used in high-speed modems.
3. Data terminal equipment (DTE) is the equipment that originates or receives the data in digital form.
4. Data communications equipment (DCE) is the equipment that converts the data from the DTE to the form required for the transmission channel. A modem is DCE.
5. The signal levels, signal identification, and wiring between the DTE and the DCE are governed by standards.
6. The RS-232 and CCITT V.24 standards for the DTE-DCE interface are the ones used most in the present computer and communications world.
7. RS-422A, RS-423A, and RS-449 are relatively new standards that overcome the defects of RS-232; however, the widespread adoption of RS-449 will probably be superseded by the RS-530 standard.

Quiz for Chapter 4

1. Flow control is:
   a. What people do who open and close floodgates on dams.
   b. The process whereby the modem matches the rate of the receiver.
   c. The process of starting and stopping the terminal output to avoid loss of characters by the receiving device.

2. Buffering is:
   a. The process of temporarily storing data to allow for small variations in device speeds.
   b. A method of reducing the severity of communications headaches.
   c. Storage of data within the transmitting modem until the receiver is ready to receive.

3. Direct machine-to-machine transmission over long distances without modems is not practical because:
   a. Copper wire does not transmit DC efficiently.
   b. A DC path that will handle data in pulse form does not exist.
   c. Data comes from the computer in the form of tones, not pulses.

4. Modulation is the:
   a. Varying of some parameter of a carrier, such as its amplitude, to transmit information.
   b. Utilization of a single transmission channel to carry multiple signals.
   c. Transmission of pulses in DC form over a copper wire.

5. RS-232, RS-449, RS-530, V.24, and X.21 are examples of:
   a. Standards for various types of transmission channels.
   b. Standards for interfaces between terminals and modems.
   c. Standards for interfaces between modems and transmission facilities.
   d. Standards for end-to-end performance of data communications systems.

6. A smart modem can:
   a. Detect transmission errors and correct them automatically.
   b. Correctly answer multiple-choice quizzes.
   c. Accept commands from the terminal via the RS-232 interface.

7. RTS/CTS:
  a. Is the way the modem indicates ringing, and the way the terminal indicates it is ready for the call to be answered.
  b. Is the way the DTE indicates that it is ready to transmit data, and the way the DCE indicates that it is ready to accept data.
  c. Are the pins that represent received transmissions and carrier transmissions.

8. Pin 7, the Signal Ground:
  a. Completes the circuit for control and data signals.
  b. Indicates a failure in the ground side of the transmission line.
  c. Completes the circuit for control signals but not data signals.

9. Pin 22, the Ring Indicator:
  a. Must be present on all modems connected to the switched network.
  b. Is used on acoustic-coupled modems but not on direct-connect types.
  c. Is asserted when ringing voltage is present on the line.

10. The reason that many cables have "RS-232" connectors with some wires crossed or connected to each other is:
  a. There are various RS-232 standards.
  b. Many computers and peripherals use RS-232 serial interfaces but not as DTE-to-DCE.
  c. Asynchronous modems reverse the direction of transmitted and received data from the standard.

Synchronous Modems and Digital Transmission

ABOUT THIS CHAPTER

In this chapter, you will be introduced to the signaling methods used by synchronous modems, the American and International standards which apply to synchronous data modems, and the concepts used in higher speed (above 19,200 bits per second) wideband devices. In addition, the techniques of direct transmission of binary signals without modems, called digital transmission, will be discussed.

SYNCHRONOUS SIGNALING AND STANDARDS

A Search for Higher Data Rates

Like the Olympic athlete, whose motto is "alitus, cititus, fortitus," the aims of the data communications systems designer in the development of high-technology products are to pack more data per channel, deliver it at a faster speed, and deliver it at a lower cost. The transmission of a larger quantity of data through a channel of a given bandwidth with smaller and cheaper devices is a natural target. Since in many cases the channel available is a standard voice-grade line, and the cost of the channel dominates the cost of the system, a large amount of design effort has gone into the production of devices that will send the largest number of bits per unit time through standard (voice-grade) channels. One result has been synchronous signaling.

Sending the Clock With the Data

Binary signals have two basic parameters: amplitude and duration. As the number of information bits sent per unit of time increases, the bit duration decreases.

Binary signals sent over a channel represent the quantization of data in two dimensions: amplitude (voltage of the electrical wave), and time (the duration of each signaling element). As the number of signaling elements per unit time (the "baud rate") increases, the duration of each element must decrease as illustrated in Figure 5.1. If, as is the case with the asynchronous modems described in a previous chapter, the time base for the transmitter and receiver are independent, small differences between the two clocks become increasingly likely to cause errors due to the sampling of the data at the wrong time. This problem is overcome in synchronous modems by deriving the timing information for the received data.

**Figure 5.1.
Baud Rate Versus
Element Duration**

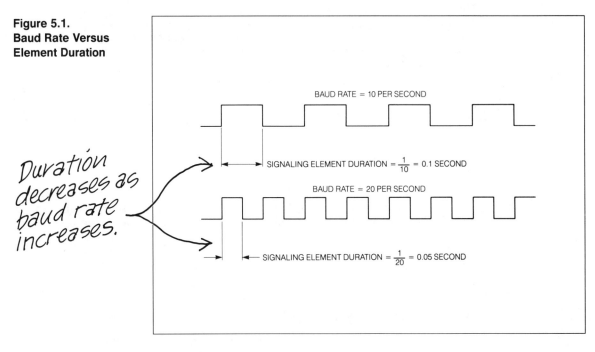

*Duration
decreases as
baud rate
increases.*

More Bits per Baud

The data rate is limited by the bandwidth of the voice-band channel to about 2400 baud. One way to increase the data rate is to pack two or more bits in a baud.

Recall that in a previous chapter it was stated that for a channel of given bandwidth, the maximum signaling rate is fixed by the channel bandwidth and the signal-to-noise ratio (Shannon's formula). Since voice-grade channels have a fixed bandwidth (about 3000 Hz), they have a fixed maximum baud rate (about 2400 baud). The solution to this dilemma is to pack more than one bit into one signaling element; that is, two or more bits per baud.

TYPICAL SYNCHRONOUS COMPONENTS

The greater complexity and cost of synchronous modems over asynchronous units is due to the circuitry necessary to derive the timing from the incoming data and to pack more than one bit into one baud. Synchronous modems typically consist of four sections as shown in Figure 5.2: transmitter, receiver, terminal control, and power supply. We will look at the first three of these in some detail.

**Figure 5.2.
Synchronous Modem
Block Diagram**

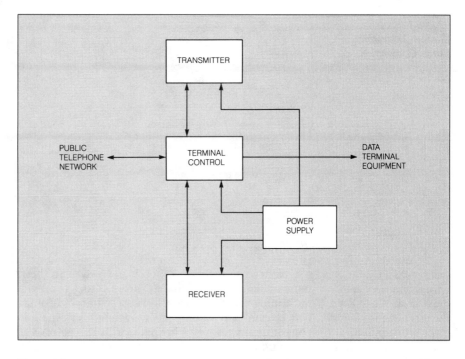

Transmitter

As shown in Figure 5.3, the transmitter section of a synchronous modem typically consists of timing (clock), scrambler, modulator, digital-to-analog converter, and equalizer circuits.

Timing Circuit

The internal clock of the transmitting modem is phase locked with the external clock source when the DTE or another modem provides the timing.

The timing circuit provides the basic clocking information for both the modem and the data terminal equipment (DTE) that is providing the data to be transmitted. Certain data circuit arrangements require that the clocking for the transmitted data be supplied by the DTE (which may be another modem). In these cases, an option is usually provided in the modem to phase lock the internal clock to an external clock source input through the DTE interface. The internal timing is usually controlled by a crystal oscillator to within about 0.05% of the nominal value.

**Figure 5.3.
Modem Transmitter
Block Diagram**

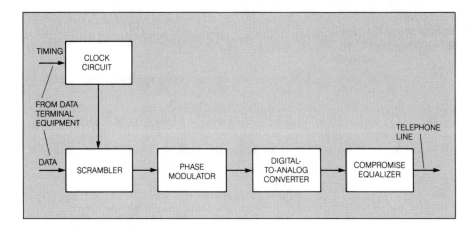

Scrambler

Enough 0 to 1 to 0 changes must exist in the data stream to keep the receiving modem's clock synchronized. The scrambler ensures that the changes occur by modifying the data stream in a controlled way.

Since the receiver clock is derived from the received data, those data must contain enough changes from 0 to 1 (and vice versa) to assure that the timing recovery circuit will stay in synchronization. In principle, the data stream provided by the associated terminal or business machine can consist of any arbitrary bit pattern. If the pattern contains long strings of the same value, the data will not provide the receiver with enough transitions for synchronization. The transmitter must prevent this condition by changing the input bit stream in a controlled way. The part of the transmitter circuitry that does this is called the scrambler.

Scramblers are usually implemented as feedback shift registers, which may be cascaded (connected in series) as shown in Figure 5.4. Input bit No. 1 is modified by adding the state of selected bits of the 7-bit register to the incoming bit. Input bits 2, 3, etc. are modified by the preceding bits as indicated in the illustration. The scramblers are designed to ensure that each possible value of phase angle is equally likely to occur to provide the receiver demodulator with enough phase shifts to recover the clocking signal. Although scrambling is necessary for the reasons cited previously, it increases the error rate, since an error in one bit is likely (and in some cases is certain) to cause an error in subsequent bits. To counteract this problem, some modems encode the input to the scrambler into the Gray code so that the most likely error in demodulation (picking an adjacent phase state) will cause only a 1-bit error when decoded at the receiver. As shown in Table 5.1, the Gray code has the property that, between any two successive binary numbers (tribit numbers in this case), only one bit changes state.

Figure 5.4.
Tribit Scrambler

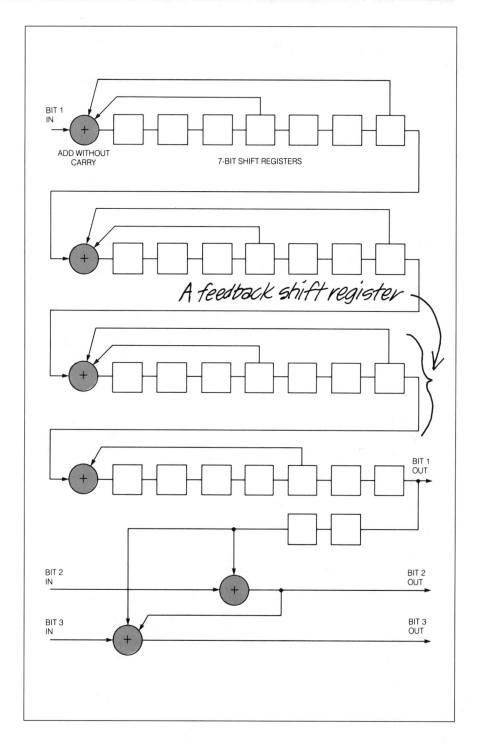

**Table 5.1.
Binary and Gray Code
Equivalence for 3-bit
Code**

Decimal	Binary	Gray Code
0	000	000
1	001	001
2	010	011
3	011	010
4	100	110
5	101	111
6	110	101
7	111	100

Modulator

Specific modulator characteristics such as the baud rate, number of bits per baud and modulation techniques vary for modems of different rates and from different manufacturers.

The modulator section of the transmitter converts the bit patterns produced by the scrambling process into an analog signal representing the desired phase and amplitude of the carrier signal. The carrier frequency, baud rate, and number of bits represented by each baud is different for modems of different data rates. The modulator collects the correct number of bits and translates them into a number giving the amplitude of the electrical signal that is correct for the carrier frequency and phase of the carrier at that instant in time. Modulation techniques differ for modems of different speed and from different manufacturers. Some of the more common ones are discussed in the section on standard modems later in this chapter.

Digital-to-Analog Converter

The digital-to-analog converter changes the binary encoded signal from the modulator into the required analog voltage.

The binary encoded signal from the modulator is fed to a digital-to-analog converter which produces the actual analog voltage required. This in turn goes through a low-pass filter to remove frequencies outside of the voice band, then through a circuit called an equalizer which compensates for transmission impairments on the line.

Equalizer

The transmitter equalizer corrects amplitude distortion and group delay based upon the average characteristics of the transmission medium.

The transmitter equalizer is called a compromise or statistical equalizer because it is set to compensate for the nominal or average characteristics of the transmission medium. The equalizer compensates for amplitude distortion in the medium and for the problem called group delay. Group delay measures the amount by which a signal of one frequency travels faster in the transmission medium than a signal of a different frequency. Group delay usually is expressed in microseconds (μs) at a given frequency. Nominal values of delay variation versus frequency for some commonly available voice grade channels are given in Table 5.2.

Receiver

As shown in Figure 5.5, the receiver section of a synchronous modem typically consists of an equalizer, timing (clock) recovery, demodulator, descrambler, and DTE interface.

Table 5.2.
Group Delay Variation
Versus Frequency for
Conditioned
Transmission Lines

Conditioning Applied to Voice Grade Channel	Frequency Range (Hz)	Delay Variation (μs)
Basic (none)	800–2600	1750
C1	800–2600	1750
C2	600–2600	1500
C3	600–2600	260–300
C4	800–2800	500
C5	600–2600	300

Figure 5.5.
Modem Receiver
Block Diagram

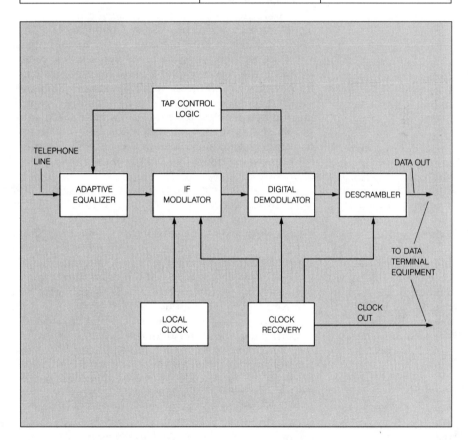

Equalizer

The receiving equalizer must deal with actual errors in the received signal. The errors are measured and corrected by adjusting specific circuit parameters.

The equalizer section of the transmitter is relatively simple since it can compensate only for the average of expected errors on the output channel. The receiver equalizer, however, must compensate for the actual errors introduced in the transmission path. This is done by using an adaptive equalizer which measures errors observed in the received signal and adjusts some parameter of the circuit (usually the receiver clock frequency) to track slowly varying changes in the condition of the transmission line.

Delay distortion has the greatest effect on transmission of an analog signal. As mentioned previously, analog signals of different frequencies travel at different rates through a transmission medium. Since each signaling element contains many frequencies, each signaling element arrives at the receiver over a period of time instead of all at once. The frequencies which travel faster (leading frequencies) arrive earlier and those traveling slower (lagging frequencies) arrive later. The leading and lagging frequencies not only fail to make their proper contribution to the proper signaling element, but also cause interference with signaling elements behind and ahead of the proper element. The equalizer must get the parts of each element back together and cancel their effects on other elements.

The adaptive equalizer compensates for delay distortion by temporarily storing the analog signal in a tapped delay line. The signals from each tap, amplified by a different amount as determined by the amount of error detected, are summed to form the corrected signal.

The adaptive equalizer does this by use of a tapped delay line which stores the analog signal for a period of time. This time period includes the main signaling element to be corrected at the center, and several element times before and after the center as shown in Figure 5.6. The taps in the delay line allow the analog voltage representing the signal to be picked off at specified time intervals before and after the element of interest. The time interval between each tap is the reciprocal of the baud rate. The voltage from each tap is amplified by a variable gain amplifier whose gain is controlled by an amount determined by the correction calculator circuit.

In response to a phase error signal developed by the demodulator circuit, the correction calculator determines the amplitude and polarity of the signal needed from each tap amplifier. What makes the equalizer adaptive is that the error signal is continuously derived from the difference between the phase of the received signal and a nominal phase value determined by the demodulator.

Start-up bits (training sequences) are sent at the beginning of a transmission to allow the adaptive equalizer to prepare itself for the incoming message.

The circuit adapts itself fairly slowly to changing line conditions because of all of the delays. This can be a disadvantage for half-duplex operation, or at start-up on a one-way link, so a start-up or training sequence of bits usually is sent first to allow the receiver to adapt more rapidly than it would on random data. This is called training. The amount of time required by the modem to retrain after changing direction of transmission must be less than the turnaround time or request-to-send, clear-to-send (RTS-CTS) delay. This delay effectively reduces the data transmission rate on the circuit. Contemporary 4800-bps modems have RTS-CTS delays in the 10 to 20 millisecond (ms) range (about 50 to 100 bit times).

**Figure 5.6.
Adaptive Equalizer**

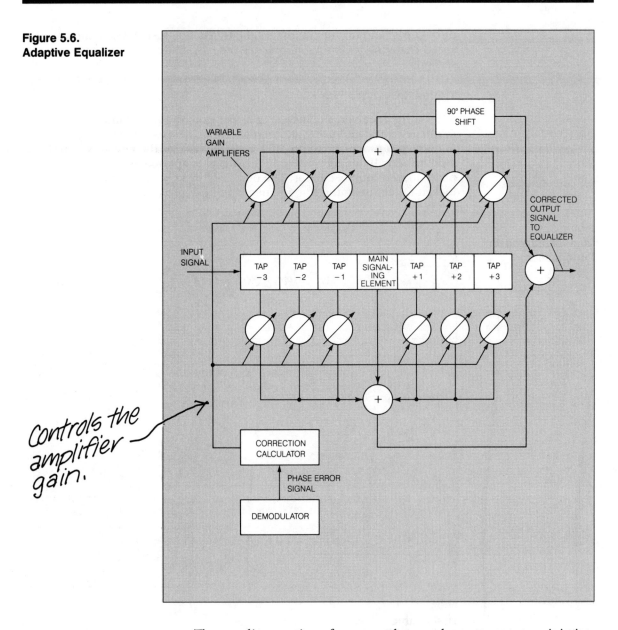

Controls the amplifier gain.

The equalizer section of some modern modems attempts to minimize the amount of line time lost in turnaround by a dual speed or "gearshift" technique. This technique causes the modem pair to start at a lower data rate (say 2400 bps) at which training is very fast, and to transmit data at that rate while the adaptive equalizer goes through its training cycle. The modems then "shift gears" to run at the full data rate as shown in Figure 5.7. Since for short messages the RTS-CTS delay is the controlling factor in throughput, and for long messages the transmission speed is dominant, the speed changing technique minimizes the first while still providing the second.

Timing Recovery

At the receiver, the incoming signal from the line is modulated or frequency translated using an internal clock. The resulting intermediate frequency is processed to produce a clock signal at the rate at which the data are actually being received. This signal is applied as the reference to a phase locked loop oscillator. The output of this oscillator is a stable signal locked to the incoming line frequency in both phase and frequency.

**Figure 5.7.
Dual-Speed Modem
Performance**

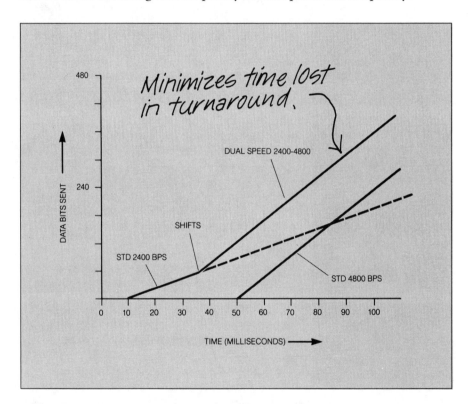

Descrambler

The descrambler section of the receiver performs an operation that is the inverse of the scrambler described in the section on the transmitter. If the data have been Gray coded by the transmitter prior to scrambling, they are converted back to straight binary, then applied to the DCE interface circuit.

Terminal Control Section

Each of the terminal control interface points requires different control and response signals.

The control section of synchronous modems must deal with two external interfaces: the telephone line at one end and the business machine at the other. If it is to be used on the public dial telephone network, the modem must:

1. Sense the ringing signal.

2. Provide line supervision (connecting and disconnecting the modem with the telephone line).

3. In some cases it must be able to provide a busy indication to the incoming line without tying up telephone central office equipment.

At the other end, the control section must connect to the associated business machine or data terminal equipment (DTE). The DTE interface for most modems conforms to one of two standards—the Electronic Industries Association (EIA) RS-232, or the International Telephone and Telegraph Consultative Committee (CCITT) Recommendation V.24. These standards were covered in a Chapter 4.

Interface Circuits

Most synchronous modems support the set of interface circuits shown in Table 5.3. The backward channel circuits (CCITT circuit numbers 118 through 122) are required only in modems that provide a reverse or backward channel for control information in the opposite direction to normal data flow. The Data Terminal Ready circuit (CCITT circuit No. 108.2) is required only for modems used on the dial-up connections.

The Clear-to-Send signal is returned to the DTE in response to assertion of the Request-to-Send signal, but is delayed by the modem by the amount of time necessary for the modem to "turn the line around"; that is, to send the required training pattern to the distant end.

External Timing

Systems which have terminals remote from the terminating modem on the main channel require that the remote modem be synchronized to the originating modem.

Standard 9600-bps modems usually contain internal time division multiplexers which allow more than one terminal to operate simultaneously over a single channel. In many cases, one or more channels are carried to terminals remote from the first modem terminating the circuit as shown in Figure 5.8. In such cases, which apply only to full-duplex operation, the clock signal for all of the modems in the path must be synchronized to only one of the modems. The external clock input (EIA circuit DA) for the extension modem circuit is fed from the receive clock from the primary modem (EIA circuit DD), causing the clocks in all of the modems to be slaved to the single modem at the originating end. Refer to Chapter 6 for information concerning the operation and utilization of time division multiplex.

**Table 5.3.
Synchronous Modem
DTE Interface Circuits**

Circuit Number		Designation
EIA	CCITT	
AA	101	Equipment Ground
AB	102	Signal Ground
BA	103	Transmitted Data
BB	104	Received Data
CA	105	Request to Send
CB	106	Clear to Send
CC	107	Modem Ready
CD	108.2	Data Terminal Ready
CE	125	Ring Indicator
CF	109	Received Line Signal Detector (Carrier)
CG	110	Signal Quality Detector
CH	111	Data Signal Rate Detector (DTE Source)
CI	112	Data Signal Rate Detector (DCE Source)
DA	113	Transmitted Signal Element Timing (DTE Source)
DB	114	Transmitted Signal Element Timing (DCE Source)
DD	115	Received Signal Element Timing (DCE Source)
SBA	118	Secondary (Backward Channel) Transmitted Data
SBB	119	Secondary Received Data
SCA	120	Secondary Request to Send
SCB	121	Secondary Clear to Send
SCF	122	Secondary Received Line Signal Detected (Carrier)

STANDARD MODEMS

Let's now examine the implementations of some currently available modems, and the CCITT recommendations to which synchronous modems used in Europe are designed. Four types of modems are considered:

1. 2400-bps half-duplex and full-duplex
2. 4800-bps half-duplex and full-duplex
3. 9600-bps half-duplex and full-duplex
4. 9600-bps full-duplex modems that operate over 2-wire dial-up circuits.

**Figure 5.8.
Multiple Modem
Circuit Requiring
External Clocking**

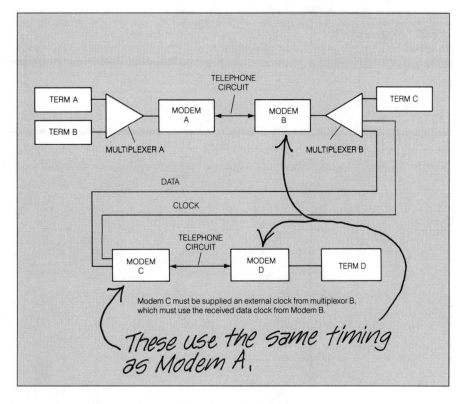

Modem C must be supplied an external clock from multiplexor B, which must use the received data clock from Modem B.

These use the same timing as Modem A.

2400-bps Half-Duplex 2-Wire or Full-Duplex 4-Wire (DPSK)

Western Electric 201

The Western Electric 201 is representative of standard 2400-bps synchronous modems. This modem encodes two bits per baud using differential phase shift keying (DPSK).

A good example of the basic synchronous modem is the Western Electric (WE) 201 diagrammed in Figure 5.9. It operates at 1200 bauds with a carrier frequency of 1800 Hz. It uses a kind of phase shift modulation called the differential phase shift keying (DPSK) technique, and encodes two bits (called a dibit) into one signaling element (2 bits per baud). Phase shift keying encodes the binary values as changes of the phase of the carrier signal as discussed in a previous chapter. Differential phase shift means that the reference point from which the phase angle is measured at any signaling interval is the phase angle of the immediately previous interval. The WE 201 shifts the phase by multiples of 45 degrees according to Table 5.4.

**Figure 5.9.
WE 201 Modem Block
Diagram**

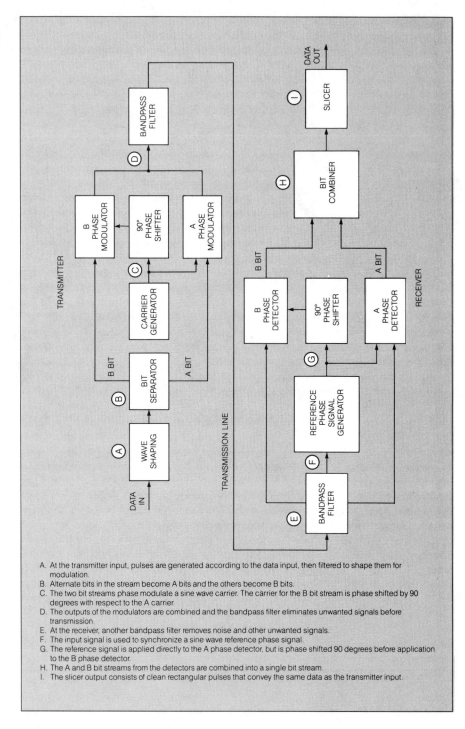

A. At the transmitter input, pulses are generated according to the data input, then filtered to shape them for modulation.
B. Alternate bits in the stream become A bits and the others become B bits.
C. The two bit streams phase modulate a sine wave carrier. The carrier for the B bit stream is phase shifted by 90 degrees with respect to the A carrier.
D. The outputs of the modulators are combined and the bandpass filter eliminates unwanted signals before transmission.
E. At the receiver, another bandpass filter removes noise and other unwanted signals.
F. The input signal is used to synchronize a sine wave reference phase signal.
G. The reference signal is applied directly to the A phase detector, but is phase shifted 90 degrees before application to the B phase detector.
H. The A and B bit streams from the detectors are combined into a single bit stream.
I. The slicer output consists of clean rectangular pulses that convey the same data as the transmitter input.

Table 5.4.
WE 201 Phase Coding

Dibit	Phase Change in Degrees
00	45
10	135
11	225
01	315

DPSK requires no absolute phase information to be transmitted. It has its own clock which is phase locked to the phase of the received signal.

With this technique, the signal is self-referenced; that is, no separate absolute phase information needs to be transmitted, and the most likely error (picking an adjacent phase value) will cause only a 1-bit error. The WE 201 contains a local clock which is phase locked to the detected phase of the incoming signal. Differences between the nominal phase values given in Table 5.4 and the detected phase of the incoming signal referenced to the phase of the local clock are used to measure the quality of the incoming line signal. Since the phase of the received signal changes for each signaling interval, there is always sufficient energy at the 1200-baud rate to recover the baud clock.

CCITT V.26

The CCITT V.26 2400-bps modem is similar to the WE 201, but one significant difference is the alternate set of phase codes.

The CCITT has published a recommendation for a standard 2400-bps modem with the designation, "Recommendation V.26—2400 bits per second modem standardized for use on leased telephone-type circuits." It specifies a full-duplex, 1200-baud DPSK modem with a modulation rate of up to 75 baud in each direction on an optional "backward channel." In Europe, V.26 modems are commonly built into television receivers to provide a transmission capability for accessing Videotext systems. When used in this manner, pressing buttons on a TV remote control results in the transmission of "page" selection numbers to a Videotext system. The Videotext system, in turn, transmits the requested "page," which is displayed on the TV set. Since a small quantity of data flows from the TV set to the Videotext system in the form of page number requests, the use of the V.26 modem is reversed. That is, the 75-baud "backward channel" is used to transmit page number requests while Videotext information flows on the primary channel to the TV set. The V.26 recommendations are generally similar to the specifications for the WE 201 (in large part because the WE 201 had by 1968 become a de facto standard). One interesting difference is that the assignment of dibits to phase change values is allowed alternative sets of values. Alternative A is given in Table 5.5 and alternative B is the same as that given in Table 5.4 for the WE 201. Use of alternative A leads to the problem of no phase change at all for long strings of 00 dibits; thus, the energy content in the transmitted stream at the 1200-baud rate is greatly reduced, making baud clock recovery uncertain.

**Table 5.5.
V.26 Alternative A
Phase Coding**

Dibit	Phase Change in Degrees
00	0
01	90
11	180
10	270

Recommendation V.26 specifies the form of the synchronizing signal between two modems to be continuous transmission of dibit 11 (giving continuous 180 degree phase shifts) during the RTS-CTS sequence. It also specifies incoming signal levels of −26 dBm or higher for the modem to assert the Carrier Detect (Circuit 109) and −31 dBm or lower for it to negate Carrier Detect. It is recommended that the modem be designed so that the operator cannot control the send level or receive sensitivity.

4800-bps Half-Duplex 2-Wire or Full-Duplex 4-Wire Modems (DPSK)

CCITT V.27

The CCITT Recommendation V.27 specifies a 4800-bps modem for use on leased telephone-type circuits. The modem:

1. Can operate in either half or full-duplex.
2. Uses differential phase shift keying with eight phases.
3. Provides an optional 75-bps backward channel in both directions for supervisory signaling.
4. Has a manually adjustable equalizer.

Although the manual equalizers mentioned in CCITT V.27 are no longer used, most of the standard is still used as the basis for many modems today, particularly in Europe.

This recommendation was promulgated in 1972, and the state of the modem art has progressed far beyond the manually adjustable equalizer. However, the remainder of the recommendation is the basis for many current modems, particularly for the European market. The carrier frequency is 1800 Hz, the modulation rate is 1600 baud, and the basic phase shift interval is 45 degrees. To signal at 4800 bps with 1600 baud requires that each baud represent three bits (tribits). The tribit to phase-change amount for V.27 is given in Table 5.6.

**Table 5.6.
V.27 Phase Coding**

Tribit Value	Phase Change in Degrees
001	0
000	45
010	90
011	135
111	180
110	225
100	270
101	315

The synchronization pattern for the V.27 modem is comprised of continuous ones in tribits for at least 9 ms to train the demodulator, plus continuous ones at the input to the transmit scrambler until the CTS lead (circuit 106) is asserted by the transmitting modem to synchronize the scramblers. The general operation of a scrambler has been described earlier in the chapter, but the details of the V.27 scrambler follow.

The scrambler implements dividing the message polynomial by a generating polynomial by means of a feedback shift register.

The transmitter scrambler divides the message polynomial, of which the input data bits are the coefficients in descending order, by a generating polynomial, which for V.27 is equal to $1 + X^{-6} + X^{-7}$. This division is continuously performed as each bit enters the scrambler and the result taken as the transmitted data pattern. The transmitted pattern is then searched continuously over 45 bits for repeating patterns of 1, 2, 3, 4, 6, 9, and 12 bits, which are eliminated. The result is sent as the scrambled data pattern. Figure 5.10 shows a feedback shift register which implements the polynomial division process.

**Figure 5.10.
CCITT V.27 Scrambler**

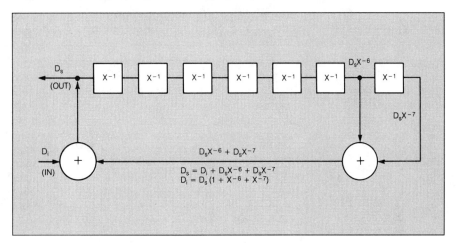

Western Electric 208

The WE 208 modem is another 4800-bps modem which is widely used in the U.S. It has been supplied by AT&T and the Bell Operating Companies when they were part of the Bell System. It is a DPSK unit, using eight phase angles to represent eight different groups of three bits. The coding pattern (after Gray coding the binary input) for the WE 208 is given in Table 5.7.

**Table 5.7.
WE 208 Phase Coding**

Tribit	Relative Phrase in Degrees
001	22.5
000	67.5
010	112.5
011	157.5
111	202.5
110	247.5
100	292.5
101	337.5

The carrier frequency for the WE 208 is 1800 Hz and the baud rate is 1600 baud. The WE 208 is not equipped with an internal multiplexer because the 1600-baud rate of the modem is not a standard data rate for any other modem or business machine. The design of the WE 208 is as covered in the previous section on typical synchronous modem components, including the scrambler implementation as four 7-bit feedback shift registers to randomize the first bit of each tribit.

The WE 208 uses DPSK to encode tribits to transmit 4800 bps at 1600 bauds. Its design and operation are similar to the typical standard synchronous modem.

The demodulator in the WE 208 multiplies the carrier frequency by eight, then measures the interval between the 1600-baud clock transition and the first positive value of the current carrier cycle. This measurement is done digitally, and successive values of the count are compared to determine the phase shift which occurred during the previous signaling interval. The measured phase shift, with any errors that may be present due to line noise, demodulator errors, baud clock errors, etc. is rounded to the nearest permitted value (22.5 degrees, 67.5 degrees, etc.) and the transmitted tribit sequence is extracted and decoded from Gray code to binary. An error feedback signal is developed as the difference between the actual phase of the signal, as demodulated, and the nominal value. This error signal is monitored and used to cause the modem to retrain if it becomes too large.

The WE 208 modem normally operates with a basic retraining time of 50 ms, but it can be changed with internal strapping (jumper wires) to 150 ms for operation on long circuits (over 2000 miles). Even this delay probably is still too short for operation on satellite links, due to the very long (about 650 ms) round trip propagation delay.

9600-bps Half-Duplex 2-Wire or Half/Full-Duplex 4-Wire

Modulation Types

The data rate of the standard 9600-bps modem is increased by increasing its baud rate to 2400 bauds and increasing the number of bits per baud to four.

In order to increase the data rate of a synchronous modem over 4800 bps, it is necessary to either increase the baud rate, or increase the number of bits per baud. Standard 9600-bps modems do both. The baud rate is increased to 2400 bauds, and the input data are taken four bits at a time (quadbits) for controlling the output of the modulator. Two modulation schemes are commonly used to reach these extreme data rates: vestigial sideband modulation (VSB), and quaternary amplitude modulation (QAM).

The choice between modems using one or the other of the two modulation schemes is less a matter of performance than of economics. Some VSB modems require little or no line conditioning, whereas a few QAM unit manufacturers generally recommend at least C2 conditioned circuits. The VSB units are less complex internally, which usually allows a price advantage over QAM units.

Vestigial Sideband Modulation

The VSB transmitter modulator takes two bits at a time and constructs a four-level signal which modulates the carrier to transmit 9600 bps.

Since it is possible to transmit a double-sideband frequency-modulated (FM) signal (with a WE 202 type modem) at 1800 bps, one would think that it should be possible to send at 3600 bps using only one sideband since the entire bandwidth would be available for the one sideband. However, this is not possible with an FM signal (the signal can't be recovered), but it is possible to use an amplitude-modulated (AM) single-sideband signal to transmit at 4800 bauds. Four different carrier amplitudes are used to represent the four different values of bits taken two at a time, thus, each baud represents two bits which gives an effective rate of 9600 bps.

A VSB transmitter has a scrambler and Gray coder similar to those of 4800-bps modems. The modulator, however, takes the bits two at a time to form a four-level signal which modulates a 2853-Hz carrier. The carrier and upper sideband are suppressed, and a 2853-Hz pilot signal is added back to what remains, but 90 degrees out of phase. A signal that is 90 degrees out of phase is called a quadrature signal because "in quadrature" means at right angles to the original carrier. The quadrature signal does not interfere with the modulated single-sideband signal, but it is necessary for the receiver to recover the exact frequency and phase of the original carrier so it can recover the data.

The receiver's local 2853-Hz oscillator is locked to the phase and frequency of the pilot signal recovered from the received signal. This adjusted clock is used to demodulate the received single-sideband signal into the four-level 4800-baud baseband signal. The signal is processed by a 60-tap adaptive equalizer to remove intersymbol interference, then put through a decision circuit to recover the dibits, which are then unscrambled.

Training a 60-tap equalizer is a lengthy process which reduces the cost effectiveness of using 9600-bps modems on half-duplex circuits. A four-segment training sequence must be sent to:

1. Set the automatic gain control circuits.
2. Acquire the phase of the carrier tone.
3. Set the equalizer tap coefficients.
4. Synchronize the scrambler.

In the CCITT Recommendation V.29 for a 9600-bps modem, the total four-segment sequence takes about 250 ms.

Quadrature Amplitude Modulation

Modems using quadrature amplitude modulation achieve a data rate of 9600 bps by encoding four bits per baud, and by using a baud rate of 2400.

QAM modems use some combination of differential phase shifts and amplitudes totaling sixteen states of encode four bits per baud. This combined with a baud rate of 2400 gives the desired 9600 bps. The CCITT Recommendation V.29 specifies eight phases with two possible signal amplitudes at each phase change. The WE 209 modem uses twelve phases and three amplitudes, but some combinations of phase and amplitude are not allowed. Constellation patterns are shown in Figure 5.11. The choice of the number of phases and level spacing represents the modem manufacturer's best guess at the type and severity of various transmission line errors the modem is likely to experience.

CCITT Recommendation V.29 9600-bps Modem

The CCITT V.29 modem's maximum data rate is 9600 bps, but has automatic fallback to 7200 and 4800 bps if the error rate is too high.

The carrier frequency for the CCITT V.29 modem is 1700 Hz and it operates at 2400 bauds. This modem is specified to operate at 9600 bps with fallback rates of 7200 and 4800 bps. It has an automatic adaptive equalizer, and may optionally contain a multiplexor for carrying up to four separate data streams whose aggregate (combined) rate does not exceed 9600 bps. The combined data stream to be transmitted is scrambled, then divided into sets of four bits (quadbits). The first bit (in time) of each quadbit determines the amplitude of the transmitted signal as illustrated in Figure 5.12, and the remaining three bits determine the phase shift to be applied as shown in Figure 5.13. The resultant "constellation pattern" resembles Figure 5.14.

At the fallback rate of 7200 bps, only three bits per baud are encoded and there is no amplitude change. At the 4800-bps fallback rate, two bits per baud are encoded and they specify only four phase shifts.

Except for the WE 209-type modem, most 9.6-kbps devices manufactured throughout the world adhere to the V.29 standard. This makes a V.29 modem popular for use on international leased lines because the selection of the modem to be placed on either end of the line may be restricted to one or a few models due to some countries' government restrictions. By using V.29, modems' compatibility among different vendor products is assured, which enables data transmission compatibility on international leased lines.

Although the V.29 modulation method provides compatibility with respect to modulation, many modems employing this standard are not compatible with one another. This lack of compatibility is attributable to the fact that several vendors designed proprietary modems using a V.29 "data pump" or chip set which performs the modulation process previously described. Most of these proprietary modems were designed to provide a pseudo full-duplex transmission capability over the two-wire public-switched telephone network. To accomplish this, modem designers added a microprocessor and memory to a V.29 data pump and developed several proprietary schemes to obtain a pseudo full-duplex transmission capability. One scheme involves adding a slow-speed reverse channel to a V.29 data pump to provide transmission at 300 bps in one direction and at 9600 bps in the other direction. Each modem monitors the flow of data in both directions and changes the assignment of the primary and reverse channels to correspond to the quantity of data flow in each direction.

Although data can flow in both directions simultaneously, each direction operates at a different speed. Thus, the modem is asymmetrical and provides users with the impression that it operates as a true full-duplex device. Asymmetrical transmission was incorporated by several modem manufacturers to support the communications requirements of personal computers. Included in an asymmetrical modem is an asynchronous-to-synchronous converter, which enables the asynchronous data flow of personal computers to be used with a modified V.29 pump that operates synchronously.

Figure 5.11.
QAM Modem
Constellation Patterns

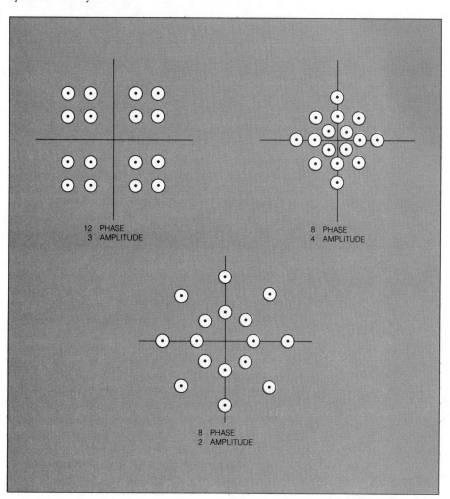

Figure 5.12.
Bit Q1 Determines
Amplitude
*(Source: CCITT
Recommendation V.29,
CCITT, Geneva, C.H.)*

Absolute Phase	Q1	Relative Signal Element Amplitude
0°, 90°, 180°, 270°	0	3
	1	5
45°, 135°, 225°, 315°	0	$\sqrt{2}$
	1	$3\sqrt{2}$

Figure 5.13.
Bits Q2, Q3, and Q4
Determine Phase Shift
*(Source: CCITT
Recommendation V.29,
CCITT, Geneva, C.H.)*

Q2	Q3	Q4	Phase Change*
0	0	1	0°
0	0	0	45°
0	1	0	90°
0	1	1	135°
1	1	1	180°
1	1	0	225°
1	0	0	270°
1	0	1	315°

*Note — The phase change is the actual on-line phase shift in the transition region from the center of one signaling element to the center of the following signaling element.

When asymmetrical modems reached the marketplace in the late 1980s, they were considered as potential successors to the V.22 bis modem discussed in Chapter 4 due to the high price of V.32 modems. Unfortunately for asymmetrical modem manufacturers, the lack of standards governing the asymmetrical transmission technique, as well as a significant reduction in the cost of V.32 modems (discussed in the next section in the chapter), inhibited their widespread acceptance. Today, most persons requiring high-speed data transmission on the PSTN use V.32 modems.

**Figure 5.14.
Signal Space Diagram
at 9600 bps**
*(Source: CCITT
Recommendation V.29,
CCITT, Geneva, C.H.)*

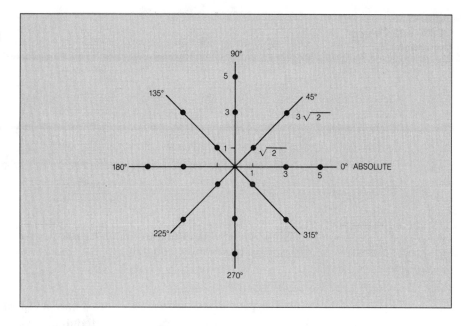

CCITT V.32

A recent CCITT recommendation that warrants attention is the V.32 standard. This standard is based on a modified quadrature amplitude modulation technique and is designed to permit full-duplex 9.6-kbps transmission over the switched telephone network. The key to the operation of a V.32 modem is a built-in echo canceling technique that enables transmitted and received signals to occupy the same bandwidth.

When the V.32 modem connects to another V.32 modem, two high speed channels in the opposite direction of one another are established as illustrated in Figure 5.15. Each of these channels occupies roughly the same bandwidth as the other channel. Intelligence built into the receiver in each modem permits the modem to cancel the effects of its transmitted signal, which enables each device to distinguish its sending signal from the signal being received.

Early V.32 modems required sophisticated circuitry to carry out echo canceling. The circuitry made the cost of V.32 modems two to three times the cost of V.29 modems, which provide the same data transmission rate on leased lines and was one of the contributing factors for the development of asymmetrical modems. Because firms manufacturing semiconductors developed chip sets to implement echo canceling the cost of V.32 modems significantly decreased during 1990. By 1991, the cost of

**Figure 5.15.
CCITT V.32 Channel
Derivation**

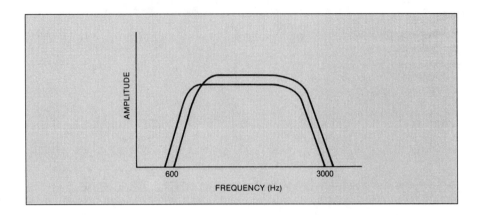

V.32 modems had declined to under $1000 per unit and they were in widespread use in most companies.

CCITT V.32 bis

Although CCITT V.32 bis was not a formal standard when this book revision was prepared, it can be expected to be promulgated within the near future. This proposed standard uses the same echo cancellation technique as V.32 but incorporates a different modulation scheme which enables a high-speed transmission of 14.4 kbps over the switched telephone network. This proposed standard is downward compatible with the V.32 recommendation, which will enable V.32 bis modems, when manufactured, to communicate with the large number of V.32 modems in use.

Higher Speed QAM Modems

To increase the data rate of modems beyond 9.6 kbps, several vendors developed modulation schemes whereby data was collected 2,400 times per second into a 6-bit symbol. This technique resulted in the use of a 64-point signal constellation to obtain a 14.4-kbps data transmission rate. The resulting constellation pattern was four times as dense as the V.29 constellation pattern (Figure 5.14), so the modem had high susceptibility to phase jitter and noise.

When phase jitter or noise occur, the signal points in the modem's constellation pattern are shifted or rotated during transmission from their proper location. The receiving modem, which is designed to select the nearest valid signal point, misinterprets a shifted or rotated signal point, which results in a transmission error. Because of the susceptibility of conventional 14.4-kbps QAM modems to transmission impairments, their throughput in many instances is lower than that obtainable with 9.6-kbps devices.

Figure 5.16 shows the proportion of noise to signal level increasing on a line when 9.6-kbps and 14.4-kbps QAM modems are used.

**Figure 5.16.
Modem Throughput
Variance**

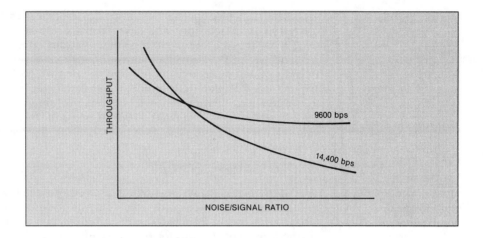

Because the constellation pattern of a 14.4-kbps modem is four times the density of a 9.6-kbps modem, 14.4-kbps modems are more susceptible to noise, which results in their throughput at a certain noise to signal ratio decreasing under that obtainable with a 9.6-kbps device. The reason the throughput declines is that the erroneous received signal points cause the transmission protocol of devices using the modems to attempt to correct the error by retransmission. The resulting retransmissions lower the modem's effective data throughput rate.

CCITT V.33

Conventional QAM modems' sensitivity to transmission impairments makes them unsuitable for use at data rates above 9.6 kbps on noisy circuits. Many long distance circuits have a fair degree of noise, so a mechanism was required to provide to the modulation method some immunity from the noise on the line. The application of Trellis Coding to QAM provided a significant degree of immunity, which resulted in the development of a series of modems that based operations on Trellis Coded Modulation (TCM).

In the TCM process, an encoder is employed to add a redundant bit to each group of bits used to generate a signal change. In a 14.4-kbps TCM modem, the resulting signal point is selected from a 128-point signal constellation pattern. The extra bit introduced by the encoder results in only certain sequences of signal points being valid. Thus, if a transmission impairment occurs that causes a signal point to be shifted, the receiving modem knows that certain points are invalid and compares only the observed point to valid points by selecting the valid signal point closest to the observed signal. By using TCM, the modem becomes only half as susceptible to noise as a conventional QAM modem. This permits higher data rates without decreasing the throughput of the modem that can occur because of the standard magnitude of noise commonly encountered on leased lines.

The V.33 modem is a 14.4-kbps device that uses TCM, is designed for operation on leased lines, and has a fallback rate of 9.6 kbps. Although the CCITT has yet to promulgate recommendations covering higher speed modems, several vendors have introduced 19.2-kbps TCM-based devices. In 1986, Codex Corporation became the first to introduce an "Eight-State Trellis Coded Modulation" modem, but Paradyne, NEC, and Fujitsu followed shortly with their own versions. Although the initial cost of 19.2-kbps modems exceeded $10,000 per unit, by mid-1990, several vendors were offering them for under $2,000, a price that encourages their widespread use.

DIGITAL TRANSMISSION

It is advantageous to transmit data in binary form, rather than converting it to analog form. However, digital transmission must be restricted to channels with greater bandwidth than the voice band.

In transmission systems which are not restricted by the bandwidth limitations of the voice-grade channel, it is advantageous to transmit the binary information from the source as binary data without conversion to analog form. The reasons for this were explained in Chapter 3. For end-user applications, the devices that connect between the business machine (DTE) and the channel usually are called limited distance adapters, wireline modems, or channel interface units.

The most obvious difference between voice-band modems and direct digital transmission units is the increased bandwidth required by the latter. Recall from Chapter 3 that this increase is about a factor of eight. Thus, digital transmission is restricted to channels with bandwidths greater than the 3 kHz voice band.

Line Coding

Unipolar Code

The NRZ code works well for the shielded and short travel paths within a machine, but is not suited for long distance use because residual DC shifts the "zero" level.

The waveform of binary signals normally used in computers and terminals is called unipolar; that is, the voltage representing the bits varies between 0 V and +5 V as Figure 5.17a shows. (The code shown is called NRZ, Non-Return to Zero, because the voltage does not return to zero between adjacent 1 bits.) This representation works well inside machines where the transmission paths are short and well shielded, but it is unsuitable for long paths because of the presence of residual DC levels and the potential absence of enough signal transitions to allow reliable recovery of a clocking signal. Signal conditioning devices (the aforementioned channel interface units) are used to convert the unipolar waveform to one of several different patterns that meet the goals of no long-term DC residual in the signal and strong timing content. Several of these signal patterns are shown in Figure 5.17b through 5.17e.

Figure 5.17.
Line Coding of Binary
Pulses

a. Unipolar NRZ

b. Polar NRZ

c. Bipolar (Alternate Mark Inversion)

Transition for each bit.

d. Diphase (Manchester)

e. Differentially Encoded Diphase

Polar NRZ Code

The simplest pattern that eliminates some of the residual DC problem is called a polar NRZ line code. It is shown in Figure 5.17b. This coding merely shifts the signal reference level to the midpoint of the signal amplitude. This has the effect of reducing the power required to transmit the signal by one-half compared with unipolar but has the disadvantage of having most of the energy in the signal concentrated around zero frequency, as illustrated in Figure 5.18.

**Figure 5.18.
Energy Distribution of
Encoded Pulses**

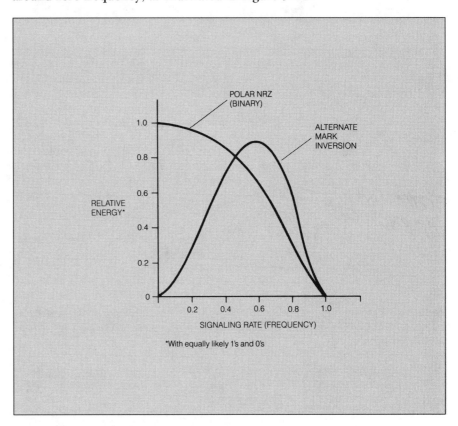

A more satisfactory coding scheme is that used in the so-called T1 digital transmission system. This scheme, called bipolar or alternate mark inversion, is illustrated in Figure 5.17c. This format has no residual DC component and has zero power in the spectrum at zero frequency, as Figure 5.18 shows. It achieves these goals by transmitting pulses with a

The bipolar (alternate mark inversion) coding scheme eliminates residual DC and has zero power in the spectrum at zero frequency. The polarity of every other 1 bit is inverted.

50% duty cycle (only half as wide as the pulse interval allows) and by inverting the polarity of alternate 1 bits that are transmitted. Note that the bipolar format is really a three-state signal (+V, 0 V, −V). This increase in the code space of the signal adds redundancy without increasing the bandwidth of the signal and makes performance monitoring easier. Assuring that long strings of zero bits do not occur (with an accompanying lack of timing information) is left to the transmitting terminal or channel interface.

Diphase Code

In diphase, coding, strong timing information is provided by having a transition for every bit, and residual DC is eliminated by having both polarities for every bit.

Another technique that has received considerable acceptance is called digital biphase, diphase, or Manchester coding. It is illustrated in Figure 5.17d. The diphase code provides strong timing information by supplying a transition for every bit, whether it be a one or a zero. If the diphase signal is differentially encoded as Figure 5.17e shows, it is even possible to determine the absolute phase of the signal because only a zero has a transition at the beginning of an interval. It also eliminates the residual DC problem by providing both a positive and negative polarity for every bit. However, all these desirable characteristics are gained at the expense of requiring twice the bandwidth of a bipolar signal. Also, for differentially encoded diphase, the error rate is doubled. The diphase scheme is used on the Ethernet local area network developed by the Xerox Corporation, Digital Equipment Corporation, and Intel Corporation.

The block diagram of a circuit to receive the bipolar signal and decode it into straight binary is shown in Figure 5.19. Note that the alternate mark inversion (AMI) pulse format is rectified into polar pulses inside the receiver where suppressing the DC component of the signal is no longer critical.

Repeaters

Because it is not possible to separate the noise from an analog signal once the two are mixed on a transmission path, both the noise and the desired signal are amplified in repeaters. The signal to noise ratio gets progressively worse as the path length increases.

The regenerative repeater used in digital transmission doesn't just amplify the input signal, it actually regenerates the binary signal so it is just like the original signal.

This is not true when digital signals are used because a different kind of repeater, called a regenerative repeater (Figure 5.20), can be used. This repeater doesn't just amplify but regenerates the pulses to restore the shape of the binary signal exactly as it was when it left the originating transmitter. This is a major advantage of the digital transmission technique as it is possible in principle, and to a large extent in practice, to reduce the error rate of the signal to as low a value as desired merely by putting the repeaters closer together.

**Figure 5.19.
Bipolar Decoder**
*(Source: Frank E.
Owen, PCM and Digital
Transmission Systems,
© 1982, McGraw-Hill,
Inc.)*

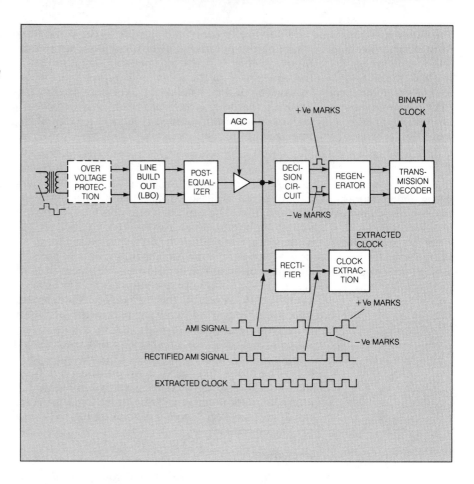

The regenerative re-
peater has phase and
frequency correction
circuits to compensate
for nonlinearities in the
transmission path.

The regenerative repeater, like the sending line terminal circuit, has some of the same functions as a modem. For example, it does certain electrical transformations on the input waveform to make it suitable for the transmission path. Both the sending and receiving ends of these operations can be studied by referring to Figure 5.20. On the input end, the line build-out (LBO) circuit matches the post-equalizer circuit with the length of the transmission cable on the input end. The post-equalizer circuit compensates for the frequency and phase nonlinearities of a standard length of input circuit, which is represented by the output of the LBO. The equalized input signal is amplified by an amplifier controlled by an automatic gain control (AGC) circuit, then the stabilized and normalized input goes to a clock extraction circuit and a decision circuit/regenerator. The clock extraction circuit, which is driven by the received data transitions, clocks the regenerator so that the original signal is regenerated exactly.

**Figure 5.20.
Regenerative
Repeater** *(Source:
Frank E. Owen, PCM
and Digital Transmission
Systems,* © *1982,
McGraw-Hill, Inc.)*

The signal is regenerated to its orginal shape.

WHAT HAVE WE LEARNED?

1. The bandwidth of a channel sets a limit on the modulation or baud rate of the channel.
2. The data rate through a channel can be increased by sending more than one bit per baud.
3. Synchronous modems modulate a carrier wave in phase or amplitude or both to send more than one bit per baud.
4. Synchronous modems send the clock signal along with the data, and are more expensive than asynchronous modems because of the additional circuitry necessary to recover the clock from the data.
5. Usually only phase modulation is used in 2400-bps modems, but both phase and amplitude modulation is used in 4800 and 9600-bps modems.

6. The most important transmission impairment that synchronous modems must deal with is differential delay distortion. Such modems have adaptive equalizers to correct for this distortion.
7. Accurate recovery of the signal in both synchronous modems and digital transmission of binary signals depends on having a sufficient number of one bits transmitted.
8. Asymmetrical transmission involves the assignment of different operating rates of transmission occurring in each direction.
9. Digital transmission uses regenerative repeaters instead of amplifiers to correct the line signal.

Quiz for Chapter 5

1. What is one principal difference between synchronous and asynchronous transmission?
   a. The bandwidth required is different.
   b. The pulse heights are different.
   c. The clocking is mixed with the data in asynchronous transmission.
   d. The clocking is derived from the data in synchronous transmission.

2. Synchronous modems cost more than asynchronous modems because:
   a. They are larger.
   b. They must contain clock recovery circuits.
   c. The production volume is larger.
   d. They must operate on a larger bandwidth.

3. The scrambler in a synchronous modem is in the:
   a. Control section.
   b. Receiver section.
   c. Transmitter section.
   d. Terminal section.

4. Binary codes are sometimes transformed in modems into:
   a. Hexadecimal.
   b. Huffman codes.
   c. Gray code.
   d. Complementary codes.

5. The digital-to-analog converter in a synchronous modem sends signals to the:
   a. Modulator.
   b. Transmission line.
   c. Terminal.
   d. Equalizer.

6. The receive equalizer in a synchronous modem is called:
   a. A compromise equalizer.
   b. A statistical equalizer.
   c. An adaptive equalizer.
   d. An impairment equalizer.

7. The receive equalizer reduces delay distortion using a:
   a. Tapped delay line.
   b. Difference engine.
   c. Descrambler.
   d. "Gearshift."

8. A Western Electric 201 modem operates with a carrier frequency of:
   a. 1000 Hz.
   b. 1200 Hz.
   c. 1800 Hz.
   d. 600 bauds.

9. The CCITT V.26 modem has a modulation rate of:
   a. 1200 Hz.
   b. 1200 bauds.
   c. 1560 cps.
   d. None of the above.

10. The transmission signal coding method for T1 carrier is called:
    a. Binary.
    b. NRZ.
    c. Bipolar.
    d. Manchester.

Multiplexing Techniques

ABOUT THIS CHAPTER

Until now we have primarily focused our attention upon communications between individual devices, such as a personal computer user transmitting information to a mainframe computer or an individual using a telephone to place a long distance call. Whenever there is a requirement for the use of two or more transmission paths that are partially or completely routed in parallel, there also exists an opportunity to economize upon transmission cost through multiplexing.

In this chapter we will focus our attention upon the multiplexing techniques used by communications carriers and business organizations to share transmission facilities. After examining communications carrier multiplexing techniques, including *f*requency *d*ivision *m*ultiplexing (FDM) and *t*ime *d*ivision *m*ultiplexing (TDM), we will conclude this chapter with a discussion of the applicability of those techniques to business organizations as well as the use of *s*tatistical *t*ime *d*ivision *m*ultiplexers (STDM) by those organizations.

MULTIPLEXING

Sharing a Channel

Just as modulation may be understood using the idea of sending code with a flashlight, so multiplexing has a simple example. Let's imagine that we have several letters to take to the post office. We could get into the car and take one letter, mail it, come back home and get the second letter, take it to the post office and mail it, come back to get the third . . . silly, right? Why not take all of the letters in the same trip, since they're all going to the post office?

This is what multiplexing amounts to: using a resource (in this case, the car going to the post office) to carry more than one message at a time. In the systems we are concerned with, a microwave system is a transmission facility (like the car), and a telephone call is the message (like the letter). The transmission facility is divided in either of two ways in order to share it; by frequency or by time.

Frequency Division Multiplexing

FDM translates the frequencies within each of several voice-band channels to different frequency channels that are combined and transmitted together.

Figure 6.1 shows the use of frequency division multiplexing (FDM) to carry more than one telephone conversation over a transmission channel. In effect, the frequencies in each call are changed so that they can be placed side-by-side in a wideband channel and transmitted as a group. At the other end, the frequencies in each call are changed back to the original frequencies. FDM was the mainstay of telephone transmission for many years; it is more efficient in terms of bandwidth than digital systems. The problem is that noise is amplified along with the voice. This fact, and the great decrease in cost of digital electronics, has led to the widespread replacement of FDM systems with time division multiplexing (TDM) systems.

Figure 6.1.
Frequency Division
Multiplexing *(Source:*
Andrew S. Tannebaum,
Computer Networks,
Prentice-Hall, Inc.)

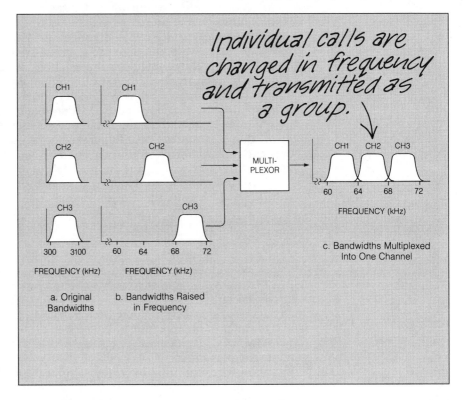

A second and perhaps more important reason for the tremendous reduction in the use of FDM during the past two decades was the conversion of most long distance communications carrier transmission facilities from analog to digital. This conversion resulted in voice conversations being digitized at a carrier central office and carried in digital format to another central office. At the distant central office, the digitized conversation was converted back into its analog form and routed to the destination telephone connected to that central office. By 1990, U.S. Sprint had converted all of its long distance circuits to digital and AT&T and MCI had converted in excess of 90 percent of their long distance transmission facilities. To obtain an appreciation for the method by which analog voice is converted into a digital format, let us examine digital modulation which forms the basis for the use of TDMs by communications carriers.

DIGITAL MODULATION

Sine waves are all we have to work with in transmitting over the analog telephone channel because it doesn't transmit pulses. Digital transmission systems will transmit pulses, and with them we can encode either analog or digital information by modulating pulses.

Digital modulation methods include: PAM, PWM, PPM, and PCM.

Figure 6.2 shows three ways to modulate a series of pulses to carry data. When the amplitude of the pulses is varied to represent analog information, the method is called *pulse amplitude modulation* (PAM). This method is very susceptible to electrical noise interference. In the second method, called *pulse width modulation* (PWM), the information is represented by varying the width of the pulses. Both of these techniques are used in telephone switching equipment, such as a *private branch exchange* (PBX). The third technique, which varies the position of pulses within a group of pulses (called the frame) to represent information, is called *pulse position modulation* (PPM).

Figure 6.3 shows the process of sampling an analog signal as in PAM, but the amplitudes of the samples are encoded into binary numbers represented by constant amplitude pulses that are transmitted. This process, called *pulse code modulation* (PCM) overcomes the noise interference problem of PAM. Most long distance telephone calls are transmitted by PCM.

PCM

PCM involves a three-step process: sampling, quantization, and coding.

The PCM system used by communications carriers employs a three-step process: sampling, quantization, and coding. During the sampling process, the analog signal is sampled 8000 times per second. This sampling rate is based upon the Nyquist theorem, which states that to faithfully reconstruct an analog signal the number of sample points must equal twice the maximum frequency of the signal. Since each voice channel has a bandwidth of 4 kilohertz (kHz), the sampling rate becomes 8000 samples per second.

Figure 6.2.
Pulse Modulation

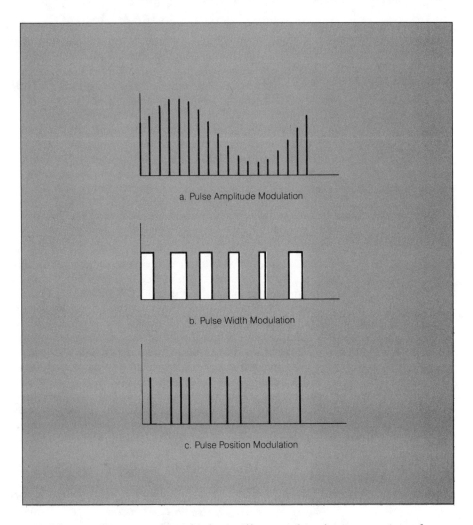

a. Pulse Amplitude Modulation

b. Pulse Width Modulation

c. Pulse Position Modulation

The resulting samples which are illustrated in the top portion of Figure 6.3 represent an infinite number of voltages. Thus, the second step in the PCM process, which is called quantization, reduces the PAM signal to a limited number of discrete amplitudes. The third step in the PCM process, which is known as coding, reduces the number of unique values of the PAM signal so they can be coded through the use of an 8-bit byte. For simplicity, the lower portion of Figure 6.3 used 4 bits to represent each PAM signal sample; however, in actuality, 8 bits are used.

**Figure 6.3.
Pulse Code
Modulation**

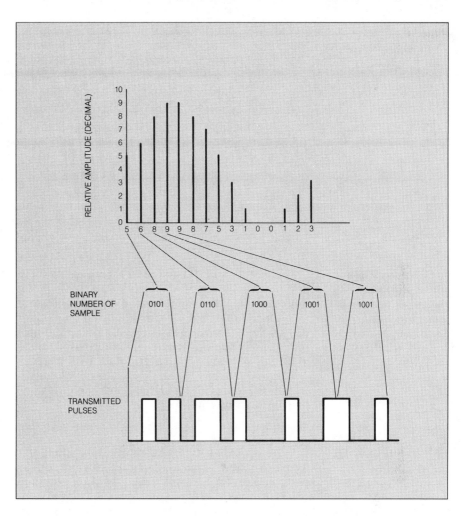

Early PCM systems were used to relieve cable congestion in urban areas.

One of the earliest uses of PCM systems was to relieve cable congestion in urban areas during the 1960s. At that time, communications carriers installed equipment called channel banks in their central offices. Each channel bank contained a codec, time division multiplexer, and line driver. The codec, which is an acronym for coder-decoder, accepts 24 analog voice signals and samples those signals, producing a series of PAM signals that are quantized and coded into 8-bit bytes. The TDM combines the digitized bit stream from each of the 24 inputs into one high-speed serial bit stream, while the line driver converts the electrical characteristics of the bit stream for transmission on the circuit linking channel banks. Figure 6.4 illustrates a channel bank system which was the forerunner of what is now commonly known as a *T-carrier transmission system*.

**Figure 6.4.
Channel Bank System**

CHANNEL BANK   CHANNEL BANK

ANALOG — CODEC : TDM — LD — R — LD — TDM : CODEC — ANALOG

SPAN LINE

Legend
CODEC - Coder - Decoder
R   - Repeater
LD   - Line Driver

Repeaters on a span line regenerate the digital pulses, removing any prior distortion to the pulses.

The repeater illustrated in Figure 6.4 actually represents a series of devices installed approximately 6000 feet from one another on the span line. Each repeater examines the digital pulses transmitted on the span line connecting a pair of channel banks and regenerates each pulse. Since the repeater "throws away" the old pulse and generates a new pulse, it removes any prior distortion. In comparison, amplifiers used with analog transmission boost the strength of an analog signal, including increasing any prior distortion to the signal. This explains why, in general, digital transmission provides a higher level of signal quality and lower error rate than analog transmission.

Framing

To provide a method for synchronization of transmission, a framing format was developed for use with channel banks. Currently, the most popular framing format is called D4, however, a new framing format called ESF is gaining in use.

Under D4 framing, the frame bit of 12 frames is used to provide a synchronization pattern.

Under the D4 framing format, which is illustrated in Figure 6.5a, a frame bit is used to prefix each group of 24 8-bit bytes, with each byte representing a digitized voice sample for each of 24 voice channels. Thus, a D4 frame contains $1 + 24 \times 8$, or 193 bits. The framing bits of 12 frames are used to develop a framing pattern which enables a receiving channel bank to synchronize itself to the transmission of data from a channel bank at the opposite end of a span line.

Figure 6.5.
D4 Framing Structure
and Framing Pattern

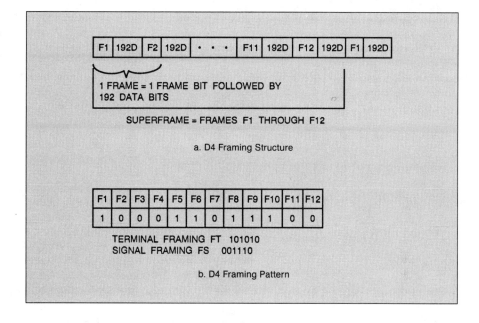

| F1 | 192D | F2 | 192D | • • • | F11 | 192D | F12 | 192D | F1 | 192D |

1 FRAME = 1 FRAME BIT FOLLOWED BY
192 DATA BITS

SUPERFRAME = FRAMES F1 THROUGH F12

a. D4 Framing Structure

F1	F2	F3	F4	F5	F6	F7	F8	F9	F10	F11	F12
1	0	0	0	1	1	0	1	1	1	0	0

TERMINAL FRAMING FT   101010
SIGNAL FRAMING FS   001110

b. D4 Framing Pattern

The framing bits in a D4 superframe are alternately designated as *terminal framing bits* (Ft) or *signal framing bits* (Fs). The terminal framing bits consist of the odd framing bits as illustrated in the lower portion of Figure 6.5. Under D4 framing, the Ft bits form an alternating pattern of 1s and 0s, enabling one frame to be distinguished from another. Thus, the sequence of terminal framing bits is also referred to as a *Frame Alignment Signal*.

The signal framing bits which represent the repeating pattern "001110" are the even frame bits. These bits are used to define multiframe boundaries and enable the extraction of signaling bits from frames. Signaling bits are used to carry such mechanical signaling information as on-hook, off-hook, dialed digits, and call progress information. The method used to provide signaling bits is called bit robbing and is beyond the scope of this book. Readers are referred to the book *Digital Networking and T-Carrier Multiplexing* authored by Gilbert Held and published by John Wiley & Sons, Inc., of New York for detailed information concerning digital transmission systems, including the bit robbing process.

ESF extends D4 framing to 24 consecutive frames, enabling synchronization patterns as well as performance measurement information to be transmitted.

A second framing format known as *extended superframe* or ESF extends D4 framing to 24 consecutive frames. Unlike D4 framing that contains a specific repeating pattern, ESF framing contains both fixed and variable patterns. Out of the 24 frame bits in an extended superframe, only six are used for a framing pattern for synchronization.

The remaining frame bits are used to transmit error performance and network monitoring information. Although only 30 percent of channel banks currently support ESF framing, this percentage is expected to increase due to the performance measurement data it provides.

The T-Carrier

The T-carrier provides a transmission path for multiplexing up to 24 voice conversations.

The span line illustrated in Figure 6.4 is now commonly referred to as a T-carrier. This circuit originally provided communications carriers with the ability to multiplex 24 voice conversations on one high-speed digital circuit.

Since each voice conversation is sampled 8000 times per second and each sample is encoded into 8 bits, the digitization rate per channel is 8000 samples/second × 8 bits/sample, or 64 kbps. The aggregate of 24 channels represents a data rate of 64 kbps × 24, or 1.536 Mbps. Since the framing rate is 8000 bits per second, the operating rate of the T-carrier is 1.536 Mbps + 8 kbps, or 1.544 Mbps.

Through the use of a T1 multiplexer, organizations can transmit voice, data, and video information on a common circuit operating at 1.544 Mbps.

Until the early 1980s, the use of T-carrier transmission facilities was limited to communications carriers. Since then, the use of the T-carrier has been made available to commercial organizations. In the digital transmission hierarchy of carrier facilities, the 1.544-Mbps transmission rate represents the first level in the hierarchy and is commonly referred to as a T1 transmission facility. As a result of the commercial availability of this transmission facility, a large number of independent companies began to manufacture T1 multiplexers. Through the use of this type of multiplexer, companies were able to integrate the transmission of voice, data, and video between locations, routing this mixture of data onto a common high-speed transmission line operating at 1.544 Mbps.

Figure 6.6 illustrates one example of the use of a T1 multiplexer by an organization which enables the integration of voice, data, and video transmission. In the example shown, the T1 multiplexer contains PCM cards which enable analog voice conversations routed from a Private Branch Exchange (PBX) to be digitized prior to being multiplexed. If a digital PBX was installed data could be directly multiplexed without the use of PCM cards.

Digital data is manipulated within a T1 multiplexer in a unipolar NRZ format as previously indicated in Figure 5-17a. Although this data representation format is commonly used by computer systems, electronic equipment, and the data terminal equipment (DTE) to data communications equipment (DCE) interface, it is unsuitable for transmission on a T1 transmission facility.

Bipolar coding enables a signal and power to be carried on a common line and separated by the use of a transformer.

When span lines were first routed between channel banks, communications carriers desired a method that would allow them to transmit both a digital signal and power on the same circuit, separating the signal from the power through the use of a transformer at each channel bank location. To obtain this capability, a signaling method that resulted in no residual DC voltage was required which would enable the use of transformers to separate the signal from the power carried on the line. The resulting line coding method that provided this capability is the bipolar *alternate mark inversion* (AMI) coding format previously illustrated in Figure 5-17c.

**Figure 6.6.
Typical T1 Multiplexer
Application**

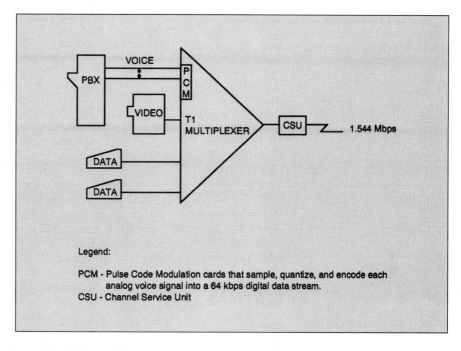

Legend:

PCM - Pulse Code Modulation cards that sample, quantize, and encode each
analog voice signal into a 64 kbps digital data stream.
CSU - Channel Service Unit

Most T1 multiplexers convert unipolar RTZ signals into bipolar AMI signals for transmission. However, prior to actual transmission on the T1 line the digital signal must be framed according to the line code supported by the communications carrier—D4 or ESF. The framing function is but one of several operations performed by the channel service unit (CSU). Other functions performed by CSUs include storing performance data when an ESF framing format is used, recognizing and responding to network codes transmitted by the communications carrier and equipment connected to the T1 line, and transmitting a minimum number of binary ones, the latter referred to as "ones density."

Ones Density

A minimum number of marks, referred to as "ones density," must flow on a digital transmission facility to enable repeaters to obtain timing from the data.

The requirement for a ones density level on T1 circuits resulted from the need of repeaters to maintain timing. If a long string of binary zeros was transmitted, the repeaters on a span line could conceivably lose timing. Thus, the CSU must be capable of ensuring that a binary one or mark pulse occurs every so often, which enables repeaters to obtain timing from the pulse.

Specifically, carrier requirements are such that the number of consecutive zeros must be less than 15 and each 8-bit byte must include at least one "1" bit. To support carrier ones density requirements several techniques are used, including binary 7 (B7) zero code suppression and binary 8 zero substitution, among others.

Under B7 zero code suppression, a 1 bit is substituted in bit position 7 of an all-zero byte. Although this technique ensures the carrier's ones density requirements are met, it also restricts data to seven usable bits instead of eight. This means that each 64-kbps voice channel multiplexed on a T1 line is restricted to 64 kbps $\times$ 7/8, or 56 kbps, when used for data transmission.

To understand why bit position 7 was selected for substitution, consider a worst-case scenario as illustrated in Figure 6.7. In this example, the 8-bit byte representing the 24th channel contains a mark in bit position 1 followed by the remainder of the byte's bit positions set to zero. If the framing bit following the 24th channel has a value of zero and is followed by an all-zero byte, 16 bit positions would be between marks if bit position 8 had its value altered to 1. Normally this would be more desirable as it represents the least significant position in a byte and would minimize its effect upon a digitized voice signal. However, selecting bit position 8 would then violate the carrier's ones density requirements, which resulted in the selection of bit position 7 for substitution.

B8ZS provides a clear channel capability, enabling data transmission to occur at 64 kbps on a voice channel.

Binary 8 Zero Substitution (B8ZS) was developed by Bell Laboratories and represents a considerable improvement over B7 Zero Suppression as it enables data to be transmitted at 64 kbps on a voice channel. This capability, in which a minimum ones density is obtained without corrupting data provides what is known as a clear channel. Under B8ZS coding, each byte of eight consecutive 0s is replaced by a code which includes an intentional bipolar violation. Figure 6.8 illustrates the B8ZS coding process.

B8ZS coding uses intentional bipolar violations to maintain a minimum ones density.

In examining Figure 6.8 the coding used becomes more meaningful if we review how bipolar coding normally functions. That is, under bipolar coding, marks or binary ones are encoded using alternating polarities, while spaces are encoded as a zero voltage level. Thus, the encoded byte, when the pulse preceding an all-zeros byte was positive, commences with bit position 4 high, which represents a bipolar violation. This is illustrated at A in Figure 6-8 Next, bit positions 5 and 7 are both encoded as negative marks which represents another bipolar violation. Since bits 4 and 8 are positive pulses while bits 5 and 7 are negative pulses, the encoded byte does not result in any DC voltage buildup although it violates bipolar coding rules. At the receiving CSU, the encoded byte is recognized as defining the occurrence of an all-zeros byte and the CSU then replaces the B8ZS code with eight binary zeros. Similarly, if the pulse preceding an all-zeros byte was negative, the all-zeros byte is encoded in the opposite manner as illustrated at B in Figure 6.8.

**Figure 6.7.
B7 Zero Code
Suppression Worst-
Case Scenario**

**Figure 6.8.
B8ZS Coding**

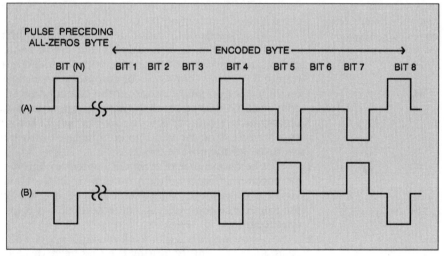

Note that the state of bit position 4 represents a bipolar violation with respect to the pulse preceding the all-zeros byte, while bit positions 5 and 7 represent a bipolar violation with respect to each bit position's polarity. Also note that there are an equal number of positive and negative pulses to prevent DC voltage buildup.

The bipolar violations contained in the B8ZS coding represent intentional bipolar violations. Other examples of intentional bipolar violations are loopback codes which when recognized by a CSU place it in a loopback mode of operation. Intentional bipolar violations do not represent coding errors. In comparison, unintentional bipolar violations represent coding errors resulting from line impairments whose measurement over a period of time provides an indication of the quality of a digital circuit.

Time Division Multiplexing

The T1 multiplexer which evolved from channel banks represents one of the earliest types of TDMs. Until T1 lines were made available for use by commercial organizations most TDMs were manufactured for use with analog leased lines or low-speed Dataphone Digital Service (DDS) digital transmission facilities. When used with analog leased lines, the aggregate data rate of the TDM is limited to 19.2 kbps, while its use with DDS limited its aggregate data rate to 56 kbps.

When used by commercial organizations the rationale for multiplexing is the same as for communications carriers—economics.

Most communications networks used by organizations include several TDM systems that are used primarily because of economics. When one circuit and a pair of multiplexers replace two or more data circuits, the savings that accrue from the elimination of data lines usually can pay for the required equipment in less than a year.

To understand the rationale for using multiplexers, consider an example where eight terminals located in San Francisco must communicate with a mainframe computer located in Chicago. If each terminal requires four hours of computer access per day and the cost of one hour of communications on the switched telephone network is $30, conventional dialing by each terminal operator to Chicago costs the organization $960 per day. If a month has 22 business days, the monthly cost for accessing the Chicago computer would slightly exceed $21,000, exclusive of the cost of modems.

When a number of terminal devices at one location require access to a computer at a second location, multiplexing should be considered. Figure 6.9 illustrates a network configuration that could be used to satisfy the San Francisco to Chicago communications requirements of the organization.

Assuming the cost of each multiplexer is $3,000 and the leased line costs $1,000 monthly, during the first year, the multiplexing method would cost $18,000, exclusive of modems. In the second year of operation, the cost of multiplexing would be reduced to $12,000 because we assume the equipment was purchased the first year. Thus, in this example, the two-year cost of multiplexing is $30,000, resulting in a substantial savings.

**Figure 6.9.
Using Multiplexers
to Reduce
Communications
Costs**

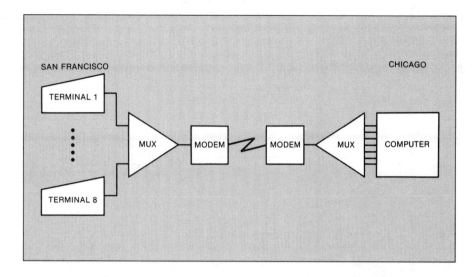

A second reason for the use of multiplexers is the relative fixed cost associated with their use. Multiplexer systems are connected to one another via leased lines that have rates which may increase slightly from year to year because of tariff changes. The cost of the multiplexer system is rather stable and predictable because the cost of the line is billed on a monthly basis based on the distance between locations and is not dependent on usage. In comparison, the cost of using the switched telephone network depends on many factors, including the duration of the call, the distance between calling and called parties, the day and time of day the call was originated and whether operator assistance was required. If only a few terminal users increase their connect time 15 minutes per day, the monthly cost of communications could substantially increase.

Operation

A TDM, as its name implies, uses time as a reference for multiplexing data. To understand the operation of a TDM as well as the limitations associated with this technology, let us examine how data from a few terminals or personal computers are multiplexed and demultiplexed. Figure 6.10 illustrates the multiplexing of data from three terminal devices at a remote location to a mainframe computer at a distant location. For simplicity of illustration, it was assumed that terminal 1 transmitted the character sequence "BA," while terminals 2 and 3 transmitted "DC" and "FE," respectively. The TDM at the remote location scans each port connected to a terminal for data, recognizing "A," "C," and "E" as input to ports 1, 2, and 3 of the multiplexer during the first scan. The TDM accepts data from each port and builds a multiplexing frame which represents the data from each port during the scan. Thus, frame 1 contains the character sequence "ECA," while frame 2 contains "FDB." In

**Figure 6.10.
The Multiplexing
Process**

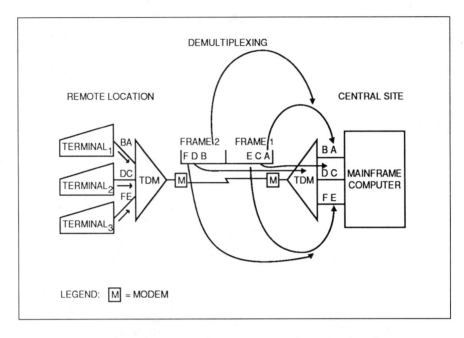

actuality, each TDM frame will also contain synchronization characters prefixing data as well as data from one or more scans.

The position of data within a TDM frame is used to ensure data is demultiplexed correctly.

At the receiving TDM the position of data in each frame is used to ensure the correct demultiplexing of data. As indicated in Figure 6.10, "A" is the first position of frame 1 which tells the TDM that byte of information should be output onto port 1 of the multiplexer. Similarly, the character "C" which is located in the second position and "E" which is located in the third position of frame 1 inform the multiplexer at the central site to output those characters onto ports 2 and 3, respectively. Next, the data in frame 2 is examined by the central site multiplexer. Since "B" is in position 1 it is output onto port 1. Next, "D" and "F" which are located in positions 2 and 3 of frame 2 are output onto ports 2 and 3. Thus, the TDM demultiplexing process depends upon the position of data within each frame.

Null characters are inserted into TDM frames to enable demultiplexing to occur based upon the position of data within a frame.

To understand the limitation of the TDM process, consider the actual operation of terminal devices. Terminal operators may be reading a manual, attempting to determine how to correct a programming error or how to respond to a message requesting a specific type of data entry. Other terminal operators may be diligently entering data or receiving information, while some operators are on a coffee break or simply thinking about the response they should enter to an application program they are accessing. Thus, at any instant in time it is highly probable that there is no data transmission activity from or destined to one or more terminal devices. Since a TDM demultiplexes by the position of data in each frame, the absence of activity could result in the misinterpretation of data. To prevent this from happening, a TDM will insert null characters in each frame whenever there is no activity when input from a port is sampled by the TDM scanning process.

At the receiving multiplexer, the null characters maintain the positioning within the frame required for demultiplexing to occur correctly; however, they are "stripped" by the receiving multiplexer and are not output to devices attached to the TDM.

Although the use of null characters ensures demultiplexing occurs correctly, it also indicates that the multiplexing process is not as efficient as it could be. For example, when several terminal users are on a break, thinking, or even entering data at a normal typing rate, most frames flowing between multiplexers contain a large percentage of null characters. Thus, for most periods of time, data transmission between TDMs is highly inefficient. Although a T1 multiplexer has the same inefficiency, its 1.544-Mbps operating rate enables the transmission of up to hundreds of devices to be carried on one very high speed line. In comparison, TDMs connected to analog or DDS circuits operating at much lower data rates are limited to supporting a much smaller population of devices. Thus, the inefficiency of TDMs is much more pronounced when used with analog or DDS transmission facilities and resulted in the development of a different type of multiplexer for use on those transmission facilities. This type of multiplexer, referred to as a *statistical time division multiplexer* (STDM), provides a much higher level of line utilization efficiency than TDMs and has essentially replaced the use of TDMs by many organizations.

STDMS

STDMs create variable length frames.

In comparison to TDMs that use fixed frames with data positioned in each frame, STDMs use variable length frames. To understand the operation of STDMs, let us examine how variable frames are created. In doing so we will discuss one of several methods that is used to create variable positional information within a multiplexing frame.

To understand the operation of STDMs, assume that eight terminal devices are connected to a multiplexer as illustrated in Figure 6.11a. Let us further assume that during one scan operation terminals 1, 2, 3, and 6 were active and transmitted the characters X, Y, Z, and Q, respectively. If the STDM employs a bit map character to denote the activity of each port during a scan, the multiplexer sets the bit position that corresponds to a port to a 1 if there is activity. Otherwise, a bit map position setting of 0 indicates no activity occurred on a port during the scan.

The frame construction example illustrated in Figure 6.11b indicates how the use of a bit map can reduce the size of a frame when some ports connected to the STDM are inactive. In this example, terminals 1, 2, 3, and 6 were active, hence, bit map positions 1, 2, 3, and 6 were set to 1s. Therefore, the character from each terminal can be added after the bit map to form a variable length frame without requiring the use of null characters since the bit map indicates the actual position of each character in the frame.

In general, an STDM can double to quadruple the number of asynchronous data sources serviced by a conventional TDM. This additional servicing capability is known as the multiplexer's service ratio. In addition to taking advantage of idle times, the STDM will strip start, stop, and parity bits from each asynchronous character prior to transmission and "rebuild" the character when it is demultiplexed. Some STDMs add data compression to a list of functions they perform, further increasing their service ratio.

Service Ratio

To understand the concept of an STDM's service ratio, first consider Figure 6.12a which illustrates the use of a conventional TDM connected to a modem operating at 9600 bps. When a conventional TDM is used to multiplex data, the aggregate input data rate cannot exceed the output data rate. Hence, up to eight terminals operating at 1200 bps could be serviced by the TDM resulting in a total input of 8 × 1200, or 9600 bps, being equal to the line operating rate.

A service ratio is a multiplier which indicates the average data input to an STDM based upon its line operating rate.

If the STDM's service ratio is 2, this means that on the average it can service an aggregate input twice the line operating rate, or 19200 bps. We say "on the average," because during a long period of time some terminals may be powered off and unused, some terminal operators are thinking about what to do next, and other terminal operators are entering data or receiving a response to their queries. Due to the previously explained STDM functions, over a prolonged period of time the multiplexer can accept an input data rate twice its output rate. However, consider a worst-case scenario in which each terminal is a personal computer and every terminal operator attempts to transmit a large file at the same time. In this situation the total input to the STDM becomes 19200 bps and the multiplexer cannot take advantage of idle times since each terminal is transmitting a continuous sequence of data. Even after stripping start, stop, and parity bits, the aggregate input data rate will exceed the line operating rate. Although the STDM contains a buffer area, as each terminal continues to transmit data the buffer area would eventually fill and overflow, resulting in a loss of data. To prevent the loss of data, STDMs will initiate flow control to turn off one or more devices whenever its buffer reaches a certain level of occupancy. Then, as data from its buffer is transmitted onto the line and the level of buffer occupancy decreases to a certain level the STDM will turn off flow control, allowing devices connected to the multiplexer to resume transmission.

**Figure 6.11.
STDM Operation**

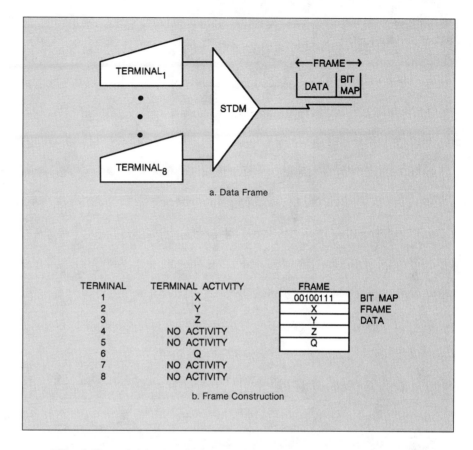

a. Data Frame

TERMINAL	TERMINAL ACTIVITY	FRAME	
1	X	00100111	BIT MAP
2	Y	X	FRAME
3	Z	Y	DATA
4	NO ACTIVITY	Z	
5	NO ACTIVITY	Q	
6	Q		
7	NO ACTIVITY		
8	NO ACTIVITY		

b. Frame Construction

The ability of STDMs to service on the average two to four times the aggregate data rate of the line connecting multiplexers resulted in their wide acceptance by most organizations. By 1990, almost 80 percent of all TDMs incorporated a statistical multiplexing process. Today conventional TDMs are primarily used where delays from the use of flow control cannot be tolerated—such as in T1 multiplexers where a delay in voice would be most annoying.

Figure 6.12.
STDM Service Ratio

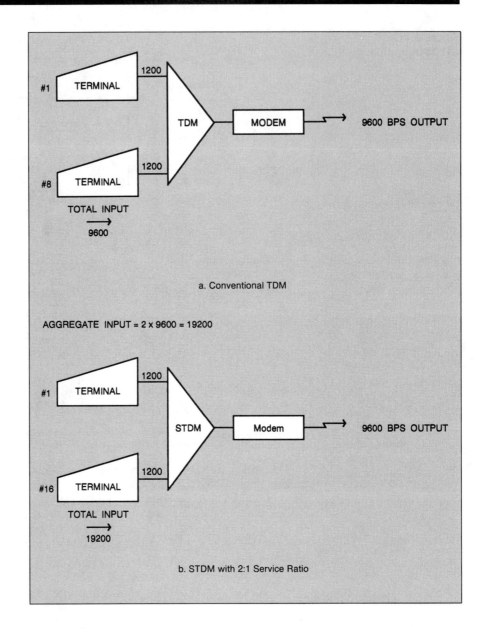

a. Conventional TDM

AGGREGATE INPUT = 2 x 9600 = 19200

b. STDM with 2:1 Service Ratio

WHAT HAVE WE LEARNED?

1. Multiplexing is the process of sharing the use of a transmission facility by time or by frequency.
2. The conversion of most long distance communications carrier transmission facilities from analog to digital resulted in a large replacement of FDM by TDM systems.

3. To faithfully reproduce an analog signal it must be sampled at a rate equal to twice the bandwidth it occupies.

4. Repeaters regenerate digital pulses, removing any prior distortion. In comparison, amplifiers boost the strength of analog signals, including increasing any prior distortion.

5. Framing is used to provide a method of synchronization between channel banks.

6. D4 framing is restricted to providing synchronization data while ESF framing enables the flow of performance measurement information as well as synchronization data.

7. Bipolar transmission allows a digital signal and power to carried on the same line and separated from one another by the use of transformers.

8. A minimum number of binary ones known as "ones density" must occur on a digital transmission line to enable repeaters to obtain timing from data.

9. Intentional bipolar violations which occur when two successive marks have the same polarity can be used to convey information or maintain a minimum ones density on a digital transmission facility.

10. When no activity occurs on a TDM input port the multiplexer will insert a null character into the frame it builds. This character maintains the correct positioning of data from all ports, enabling demultiplexing to occur by position of data within a frame.

Quiz for Chapter 6

1. Multiplexing is
   a. The process of increasing bandwidth on a channel.
   b. A technique that enables more than one data source to share the use of a common line.
   c. Mailing letters at the Post Office.
   d. The ability to share frequency by time.

2. One of the reasons frequency division multiplexing has essentially been replaced by time division multiplexing is because:
   a. There is more time than frequency.
   b. It is difficult to place channels side by side.
   c. Noise is amplified with voice when an FDM system is used.
   d. Most available frequencies have been used.

3. When the amplitude of pulses is varied to represent analog information the method is called:
   a. PCM
   b. PWM
   c. PAM
   d. PPM

4. The PCM sampling rate is 8000 samples per second because:
   a. That represents the maximum rate technology supports.
   b. This rate allows unique values.
   c. This rate allows the faithful reconstruction of an analog signal.
   d. This rate is easily produced by a sampling chip.

5. In general digital transmission provides a higher level of signal quality than analog transmission because
   a. Repeaters regenerate digital pulses and remove distortion while amplifiers increase an analog signal, including any prior distortion to the signal.
   b. Digital signals are smaller than analog signals and cannot be easily distorted.
   c. Analog signals are continuous and are not easily distorted.
   d. Digital signals are easier to sample than analog signals.

6. The D4 framing pattern contains a sequence of:
   a. 24 bits
   b. 4 terminal and 8 framing bits
   c. 8 terminal and 4 framing bits
   d. 12 bits

7. Bipolar signaling is used in place of unipolar signaling on T1 lines because:

a. Bipolar produces twice as many marks as a unipolar signal.

b. It allows transmission at polar locations.

c. Bipolar signaling reduces residual DC voltage buildup, allowing a digital signal to be separated from power through the use of a transformer.

d. It allows transformers to be spaced far from one another which reduces the cost of transmission.

8. B7 Zero Code Suppression is a technique which

a. Allows data to flow on a digital line.

b. Ensures each byte has at least one mark bit.

c. Is the latest clear channel encoding technique developed by Bell Laboratories.

d. Provides a clear channel transmission capability, allowing 64-kbps data transmission on a voice channel.

9. Intentional bipolar violations

a. Represent coding errors caused by line impairments.

b. Are used to convey information or maintain a minimum number of ones on a digital line.

c. Result in successive marks having opposite polarities.

d. Only occur in the laboratory.

10. Demultiplexing by a time division multiplexer occurs based upon:

a. The position of data within a frame.

b. The position of a frame within a group of frames.

c. The activity of a connected device.

d. The priority assigned to a connected device.

Fiber Optic and Satellite Communications

ABOUT THIS CHAPTER

This chapter is about transmission of data using light as a carrier. We will learn some of the history of the development of this form of communications, and why the technique has generated so much excitement in the communications world. We will learn why fiber optic systems work, and some of the terms used in describing their operation. Some current terrestrial and undersea fiber optic systems will be described. We will learn about the application of fiber optics to local area data networks. Finally, we will look at some of the techniques and considerations in transmitting data via geostationary satellites.

INTRODUCTION AND HISTORICAL PERSPECTIVE

Alexander Graham Bell was a very curious and inventive man. In 1880, four years after the invention of the telephone, he patented an "Apparatus for signaling and communicating, called Photophone." This device, illustrated in Figure 7.1, transmitted a voice signal over a distance of 200 meters using a beam of sunlight as the carrier. As the speech into the speaking trumpet vibrated the mirror, the light energy reflected onto the photovoltaic cell was varied. The electric current produced by the cell varied in accordance with the varying light energy.

The device demonstrated the basic principle of optical communications as it is practiced today. The two requirements for commercial success, however, were almost a hundred years away. These were a powerful and reliable light source, and a reliable and low-cost medium for transmission.

The use of light as a commercially feasible communications system had to wait until the development of the laser as a powerful, reliable light source, and the clad glass fiber as an inexpensive, reliable medium.

In 1960 the laser was recognized as the long-sought light source, and systems were tried using both the atmosphere and beam waveguides as the transmission medium. The application of a glass fiber with a cladding was proposed in 1966, and by 1970 fibers with losses of only 20 decibels per kilometer (dB/km) were demonstrated. Since then, progress in the invention and application of fiber optics has been startling. Fibers with losses of less than 0.2 dB/km have been demonstrated in the laboratory (in 1979), as have systems which can transmit at data rates in excess of 400 million bits per second (Mbps) for distances in excess of 100 km without repeaters or amplifiers. Advances in fiber optics threaten to obsolete satellite systems for some kinds of communications (point-to-point where large bandwidths are required, such as transoceanic telephone systems) only ten years after the satellite systems were commercially employed as the communications systems of the future.

Figure 7.1.
Alexander Bell's
Photophone

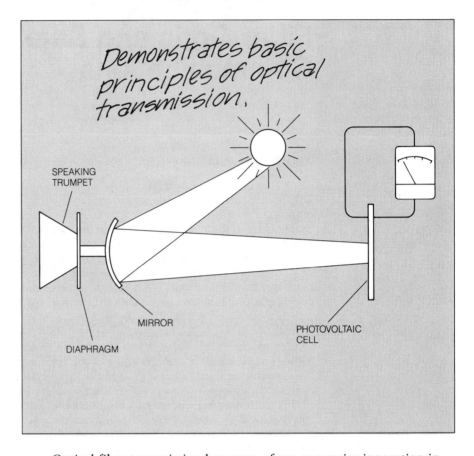

Optical fiber transmission has come of age as a major innovation in telecommunications. Such systems offer extremely high bandwidth, freedom from external interference, immunity from interception by external means, and cheap raw materials (silicon, the most abundant material on earth).

FUNDAMENTALS OF FIBER OPTIC SYSTEMS

Light rays are guided within the optical fiber by the phenomenon of light refraction. Refraction is the change in direction of light rays caused by the change in speed of propagation when they pass from one medium to another.

Optical fibers guide light rays within the fiber material. They can do this because light rays bend or change direction when they pass from one medium to another. They bend because the speed of propagation of light in each medium is different. This phenomenon is called refraction. One common example of refraction occurs when you stand at the edge of a pool and look at an object at the bottom of the pool. Unless you are directly over the object as shown in Figure 7.2a, it will appear to be farther away than it really is as indicated in Figure 7.2b. This is because the speed of the light rays from the object increases as they pass from the water to the air. This causes them to bend, changing the angle at which you perceive the object.

Snell's Law

How optical fibers work can be explained by Snell's Law, which states that the ratio of the sine of the angle of incidence to the sine of the angle of refraction is equal to the ratio of the propagation velocities of the wave in the two respective media. This is equal to a constant which is the ratio of the refractive index of the second medium to that of the first. Written as an equation, Snell's Law looks like this:

$$\frac{\sin A_1}{\sin A_2} = \frac{V_1}{V_2} = K = \frac{n_2}{n_1}$$

where,

A_1 and A_2 are the angles of incidence and refraction, respectively,

V_1 and V_2 are the velocities of propagation of the wave in the two media,

n_1 and n_2 are the indices of refraction of the two media.

Using Snell's Law, the light rays will be totally contained within the fiber optic material when the angle of incidence is greater than the critical angle.

The parameters are demonstrated graphically in Figure 7.3. In each case, A_1 is the angle of incidence and A_2 is the angle of refraction. The index of refraction of material 1, n_1, is greater than the index of refraction of material 2, n_2. This means that the velocity of propagation of light is greater in material 2 than material 1.

Figure 7.3a demonstrates how a light ray passing from material 1 to material 2 is refracted in material 2 when A1 is less than the critical angle. Figure 7.3b demonstrates the condition that exists when A1 is at the critical angle and the angle A2 is at 90 degrees. The light ray is directed along the boundary between the two materials.

As shown in Figure 7.3c, any light rays that are incident at angles greater than A_1 of Figure 7.3b will be reflected back into material 1 with angle A_2 equal to angle A_1. The condition in Figure 7.3c is the one of particular interest for optical fibers and it will be discussed further in following sections.

Fiber Composition

Optical fibers are constructed with three separate regions: the fiber core, the cladding around the core, and the protective outer sheath.

An optical fiber is a dielectric (nonconductor of electricity) waveguide made of glass or plastic. As shown in Figure 7.4, it consists of three distinct regions: a core, the cladding, and a sheath or jacket. The index of refraction of the assembly varies across the radius of the cable, with the core having a constant or smoothly varying index of refraction called n_c, and the cladding region having another constant index of refraction called n. For a fiber designed to carry light in several modes of

Figure 7.2.
Bending of Light Rays

AIR

90°

WATER

TRUE POSITION =
APPARENT POSITION

a. View from Directly Above

Speed of light rays slower in water than air.

A2

n_2

$n_1 > n_2$

A1

APPARENT
POSITION

TRUE
POSITION

b. View from an Angle

**Figure 7.3.
Index of Refraction**

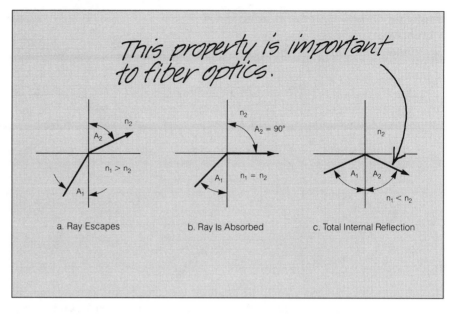

This property is important to fiber optics.

a. Ray Escapes   b. Ray Is Absorbed   c. Total Internal Reflection

propagation (called a multimode fiber), the diameter of the core is several times the wavelength of the light to be carried, and the cladding thickness will be greater than the radius of the core. Some typical values for a multimode fiber might be:

The angle at which light rays enter an optical fiber determines how the rays will propagate in the fiber—either parallel to the fiber axis, in a zigzag path, or not at all.

1. An operating light wavelength of 0.8 micrometers (μm).

2. A core index of refraction n_c of 1.5.

3. A cladding index of refraction n of 1.485 (= 0.99 $\times$ n_c).

4. A core diameter of 50 μm.

5. A cladding thickness of 37.5 μm.

The clad fiber would have a diameter of 125 μm and light would propagate as shown in Figure 7.5.

A light source emits light at many angles relative to the center of the fiber. In Figure 7.5, light ray A enters the fiber perpendicular to the face of the core and parallel to the axis. Its angle of incidence A_1 is zero, therefore, it is not refracted and travels parallel to the axis. Light ray B enters the fiber core from air ($n_1 = 1$) at an angle of incidence of A_{1B} and is refracted at an angle A_{2B} because n_2 is greater than n_1. When light ray B strikes the boundary between the core and the cladding, its angle of incidence, $A_{1'B}$, is greater than the critical angle. Therefore, the angle of refraction, $A_{2'B}$, is equal to $A_{1'B}$ and the light ray is refracted back into the core. The ray propagates in this zigzag fashion down the core until it reaches the other end.

**Figure 7.4.
Optical Fiber
Construction**

CORE

CLADDING   SHEATH

If the angle of incidence, A_{1C}, is too large, as it is for light ray C, the light ray will strike the boundary between the core and the cladding with an angle of incidence, $A_{1'C}$, less than the critical angle. The ray will enter into the cladding and propagate in, or be absorbed in, the cladding and jacket (which is opaque to light).

Multimode and Single-Mode Propagation

The angle at which light enters an optical fiber is called its mode of propagation. When a fiber carries more than one mode, it is a multimode fiber.

Much of the power in a single-mode fiber, which does not have a core diameter large enough to transmit more than one mode, is propagated in the cladding.

For optical fibers in which the diameter of the core is many times the wavelength of the light transmitted, the light beam travels along the fiber by bouncing back and forth at the interface between the core and the cladding. Rays entering the fiber at differing angles are refracted varying numbers of times as they move from one end to the other, and consequently do not arrive at the distant end with the same phase relationship as when they started. The differing angles of entry are called *modes of propagation* (or just modes), and a fiber carrying several modes is called a multimode fiber. Multimode propagation causes the rays leaving the fiber to interfere both constructively and destructively as they leave the end of the fiber. This effect is called *modal delay spreading*.

If, on the other hand, the diameter of the fiber core is only a few times the wavelength of the transmitted light (say a factor of 3), only one ray or mode will be propagated, and no destructive interference between rays will occur. These fibers are called *single-mode fibers*, and are the media that are used in most transmission systems. Figures 7.6a and b

**Figure 7.5.
Light Ray Paths in
Multimode Fiber**

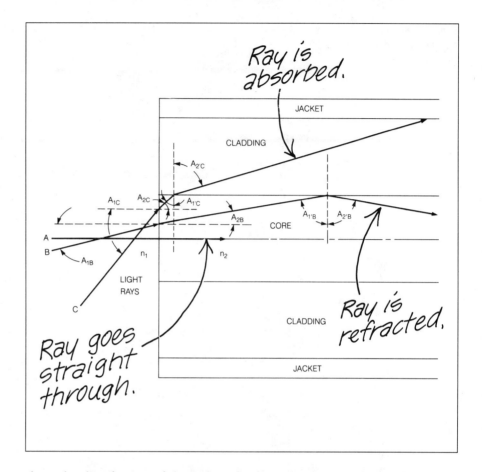

show the distribution of the index of refraction across, and typical diameters of, multimode, and single-mode fibers. One of the principal differences between single-mode and multimode fibers is that most of the power in the multimode fiber travels in the core, while in single-mode fibers a large fraction of the power is propagated in the cladding near the core. At the point where the light wavelength becomes long enough to cause single-mode propagation, about 20% of the power is carried in the cladding, but if the light wavelength is doubled, over 50% of the power travels in the cladding.

**Figure 7.6.
Refractive Index
Profiles**

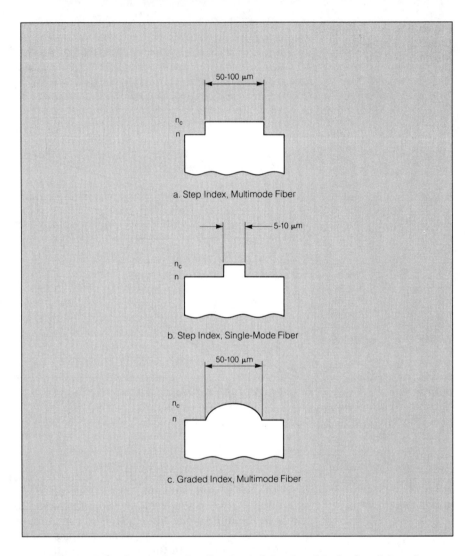

a. Step Index, Multimode Fiber

b. Step Index, Single-Mode Fiber

c. Graded Index, Multimode Fiber

Graded-index multimode fibers have fairly equal propagation delays due to a reduction in inter-modal dispersion.

Figure 7.6c shows the distribution of another kind of multimode fiber, called a graded-index fiber. The index of refraction varies smoothly across the diameter of the core, but remains constant in the cladding. This treatment reduces the inter-modal dispersion by the fiber, as rays traveling along a graded-index fiber have nearly equal delays. Other refractive-index profiles have been devised to solve various problems, such as reduction of chromatic dispersion. Some of these profiles are shown in Figure 7.7; the step and graded profiles are repeated for comparison.

Bandwidth

Material dispersion is the spreading of pulses that occurs when the light source sends light through the optical fiber at more than one wavelength.

The limitations on bandwidth in fiber optic systems arise from two main sources—modal delay spreading and material dispersion. Modal delay spreading was previously described, and is evident primarily in multimode fibers. Material dispersion arises from the variation in the velocity of light through the fiber with the wavelength of the light.

If the light source, such as a light-emitting diode (LED), emits pulses of light at more than one wavelength, the different wavelengths will travel at different velocities through the fiber. This causes spreading of the pulses. At a typical LED wavelength of 0.8 µm, the delay variation is about 100 picoseconds (ps) per nanometer (nm) per km. If the width of the spectrum emitted by the LED is 50 nm, pulses from the source will be spread by 5 nanoseconds (ns) per km. This will limit the modulation bandwidth product to about 50 to 100 MHz/km. Fortunately, at certain wavelengths (near 1.3 and 1.5 µm for some types of fibers), there is a null in the material dispersion curve, giving much better modulation bandwidth performance. Figure 7.8 shows the relationship of loss in doped silicon glass fibers versus light wavelength. Most current development work is aimed at making fibers, light sources, and detectors that work well at the loss nulls at 1.3 and 1.5 µm.

Attenuation

Signal power loss (attenuation) is a function of four factors: scattering, absorption, connections, and fiber bending.

The loss in signal power as the light travels down the fiber is called *attenuation*. Attenuation in the fibers is controlled mainly by four factors: radiation of the propagated light, called scattering; conversion of the light energy to heat, called absorption; connection losses at splices and joints in the fiber; and losses at bends in the fiber.

Scattering Losses

Scattering arises due to microscopic imperfections in the fiber, such as the inclusion of water in the glass. The effect of impurities in the transmission medium is evident when we look up at the sky and see a blue color. In fact, deep space has no color (appears as black), but due to the scattering of sunlight by the dust in the atmosphere, the sky appears as a bright blue.

Scattering occurs because of microscopic imperfections in the fiber.

There is a limit below which scattering cannot be reduced, no matter how perfectly the glass fiber is made, because of irregularities in the molecular structure of glass. This limit, called the Rayleigh scattering limit, is shown graphically in Figure 7.8. For light with a wavelength of 0.8 µm, it is about 2.9 dB/km. At a wavelength of 1.3 µm, the value is about 0.3 dB/km, and at 1.55 µm wavelength, the limit is about 0.15 dB/km. Commercially available glass fibers exhibit losses of about 3.5 dB/km at 0.8 µm, and 0.7 to 1.5 dB/km at 1.3 and 1.5 µm. There is less attenuation through 6 meters (about 20 feet) of good quality optical fiber glass than through an ordinary clean windowpane.

**Figure 7.7.
Different Refractive
Index Profiles for
Optical Fibers**

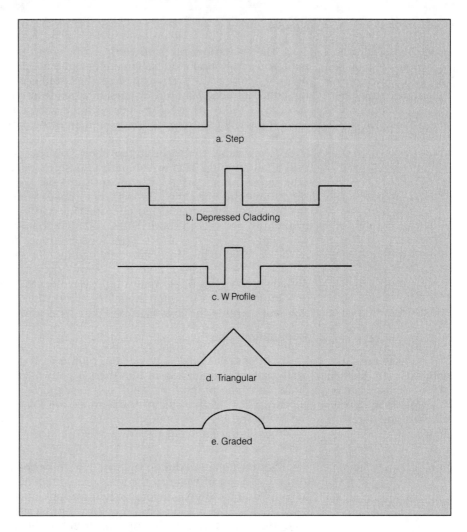

a. Step

b. Depressed Cladding

c. W Profile

d. Triangular

e. Graded

Scattering occurs be-
cause of microscopic
imperfections in the
fiber.

There is a limit below which scattering cannot be reduced, no matter
how perfectly the glass fiber is made, because of irregularities in the
molecular structure of glass. This limit, called the Rayleigh scattering
limit, is shown graphically in Figure 7.8. For light with a wavelength of
0.8 µm, it is about 2.9 dB/km. At a wavelength of 1.3 µm, the value is
about 0.3 dB/km, and at 1.55 µm wavelength, the limit is about
0.15 dB/km. Commercially available glass fibers exhibit losses of about
3.5 dB/km at 0.8 µm, and 0.7 to 1.5 dB/km at 1.3 and 1.5 µm. There is
less attenuation through 6 meters (about 20 feet) of good quality optical
fiber glass than through an ordinary clean windowpane.

Figure 7.8.
Net Spectral Loss
Curve for a Glass Core
(Source: James Martin,
Telecommunications
and the Computer,
Prentice-Hall, Inc. 1969)

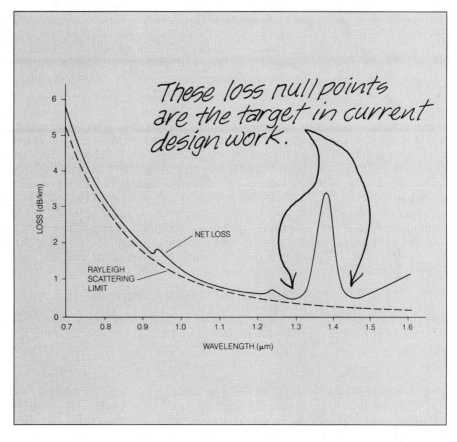

Absorption Losses

Opaque imperfections
also cause signal power
loss because, when a
light beam strikes
them, some of the
light's energy is con-
verted into heat.

Absorption refers to the conversion of the power in the light beam
to heat in some material or imperfection which is partially or completely
opaque. This property is useful, as in the jacket of the fiber, to keep the
light from escaping the cable, but is a problem when it occurs as
inclusions or imperfections in the fiber. Current fiber optic systems are
designed to minimize intrinsic absorption by transmitting at 0.8, 1.3, and
1.5 µm, where there are reductions in the absorption curve for light.

Connection Losses

A relatively large
amount of signal power
is lost at every connec-
tion point, particularly
at repair splices.

Connection losses are inevitable and represent a large source of loss in
commercial fiber optic systems. In addition to the installation connections,
repair connections will be required because experience has shown that a
typical line will be broken accidentally two or three times per kilometer
over a 30-year period. The alignment of optical fibers required at each
connection is a considerable mechanical feat. The full effect of the
connection is not obtained unless the parts are aligned correctly. The ends

of the fibers must be parallel to within one degree or less, and the core must be concentric with the cladding to within 0.5 µm. Production techniques have been developed to splice single-mode fibers whose total diameter is less than 10 µm by using a mounting fixture and small electric heater. Mechanical connectors have been developed which allow random mating of fibers with average connection losses of less than 0.3 dB.

Bending Losses

Bending the fibers also can cause signal loss because the light rays on the outside of a sharp bend cannot travel fast enough to keep up with the other rays and they are lost.

Bending an optical fiber is akin to playing crack-the-whip with the light rays. As light travels around the bend, the light on the outside of the bend must travel faster to maintain a constant phase across the wave. As the radius of the bend is decreased, a point is reached where part of the wave would have to travel faster than the local speed of light—an obvious impossibility. At that point the light is lost from the waveguide. For commercial single-mode fiber optic cables operating at 1.3 and 1.5 µm, the bending occurring in fabrication (the cables are made with the fibers wound spirally around a center) and installation does not cause a noticeable increase in attenuation.

Numerical Aperture and Acceptance Angle

The numerical aperture is the measure of a fiber's ability to gather light. The acceptance angle is the largest angle at which a light ray can enter and still propagate down the fiber.

The numerical aperture of the optical fiber is a measure of its light-gathering ability (much like the maximum f-stop of a camera lens). The optical power accepted by the fiber varies as the square of the numerical aperture, but unlike the camera lens f-stop, the numerical aperture does not depend on any physical dimension of the optical fiber.

The acceptance angle is the maximum angle that an entering light ray may have relative to the axis of the fiber and still propagate down the fiber. A large acceptance angle makes the end alignment less critical when splicing and connecting fibers.

FIBER OPTIC SUBSYSTEMS AND COMPONENTS

Fiber Production

Optical fibers are fabricated in several ways, depending on the vendor and purpose of the system. The core and cladding regions of the fiber are doped to alter their refractive indices. This doping is carried out by heating vapors of various substances such as germanium, phosphorus, and fluorine, and depositing the particles of resulting oxidized vapor or ''soot'' on high-quality fused-silica glass mandrels, called preforms. The preforms are a large-scale version of the core and cladding which is then heated to a taffy-like consistency and drawn down into the actual fiber. The core and cladding dimensions have essentially the same relationship in the final fiber as in the preform. Deposition of the dopants is done in one of three standard ways: outside, inside, and axial vapor deposition.

Light Sources

Light sources for fiber optic systems must convert electrical energy from the computer or terminal circuits feeding them to optical energy (photons) in a way that allows the light to be coupled effectively to the fiber. Two such sources currently in production are the surface *light-emitting diode* (LED) and the *injection laser diode* (ILD).

Light-Emitting Diodes

To convert the electrical energy of a computer or terminal to light energy for use by an optical fiber system, LEDs or ILDs are used.

A cross section of a surface LED is shown in Figure 7.9. It emits light over a relatively broad spectrum, and in addition disperses the emitted light over a rather large angle. This causes the LED to couple much less power into a fiber with a given acceptance angle than does the ILD. Currently, LEDs are able to couple about 100 microwatts (μW) of power into a fiber with a numerical aperture of 0.2 or more with a coupling efficiency of about 2%. The principal advantages of LEDs are low cost and high reliability.

**Figure 7.9.
Construction of Light-Emitting Diode for
1.3 μm Operation**

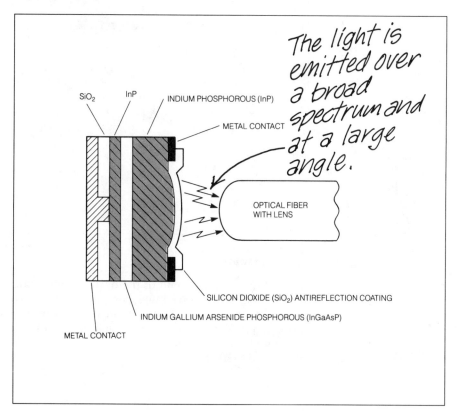

The light is emitted over a broad spectrum and at a large angle.

Injection Laser Diodes

A cross section of a typical ILD is shown in Figure 7.10. Because of its narrow spectrum of emission and its ability to couple output efficiently into the fiber lightguide, the ILD supplies power levels of 5 to 7 milliwatts (mW). At present, ILDs are considerably more expensive than LEDs and their service life is generally less by a factor of about 10. Other disadvantages of laser diodes are that they must be supplied with automatic level control circuits, the laser power output must be controlled, and the device must be protected from power supply transients.

**Figure 7.10.
Construction of
Injection Laser Diode**

CONTACT

OXIDE

LIGHT-EMITTING
LAYER

CONTACT

Narrow emission spectrum

Light Detectors

At the receiving end of the optical communications system, the receiver must have very high sensitivity and low noise. To meet these requirements, there is a choice of two types of devices to detect the light beam, amplify it, and convert it back into an electrical signal: the integrated p-i-n field-effect transistor (FET) assembly and the avalanche photodiode (APD).

Light detectors are used at the receiving end of the optical fiber to detect, amplify, and convert the light signal back into its original electrical form.

In the p-i-n FET device, a photodiode with unity gain (the p-i-n device) is coupled with a high-impedance front-end amplifier. This device combines operation at low voltage with low sensitivity to operating temperature, high reliability, and ease of manufacture.

The avalanche photodiode produces a gain of 100 or more; however, it also produces noise which may limit the receiver sensitivity. The APD devices require high voltage bias which varies with temperature. Receivers using APDs are so sensitive that they require as few as 200 photons to be detected at the receiver per bit transmitted at data rates of 200 to 400 Mbps.

WAVELENGTH MULTIPLEXING

Wavelength multiplexing, a technique similar to frequency division multiplexing, is used to send light signals from several sources down the same fiber.

A combination of single-mode fiber (low dispersion by the transmission medium), narrow output spectrum (power concentration at a single frequency), and narrow dispersion angle (good power coupling) from ILDs makes possible the extreme bandwidth-distance characteristics given for systems at the beginning of this chapter. The narrow ILD emission spectrum also makes it possible to send several signals from different sources down the same fiber by a technique called wavelength multiplexing. The ability to multiplex several analog signals in the frequency domain (FDM) has been described in detail in Chapter 6. As illustrated in Figure 7.11, wavelength multiplexing at optical frequencies is the equivalent of FDM at lower frequencies. Light at two or more discrete wavelengths is coupled into the fiber with each wavelength carrying a channel at whatever modulation rate is used by the transmission equipment driving the light source. Thus, the information capacity of each fiber is doubled or tripled.

TRANSMISSION SYSTEMS

Local and Intercity Systems—The FT3C System

Studies by AT&T of a digital lightwave transmission system indicated it would cost less than traditional systems because of differences in terminal multiplexing equipment requirements and cost.

An AT&T study in 1978 noted a striking advantage of installing a digital transmission system over comparable analog systems: $900.00 per circuit termination when interconnecting a number of digital switching machines. The savings come from the difference in requirement for terminal multiplexing equipment. The AT&T FT3C lightwave system was devised to provide the most economical digital transmission system possible with the current state of the fiber optic art. It uses wavelength multiplexing techniques to send three 90-Mbps signals over the same fiber, giving over 240,000 digital channels at 64,000 bps in a cable containing

**Figure 7.11.
Wavelength
Multiplexing**

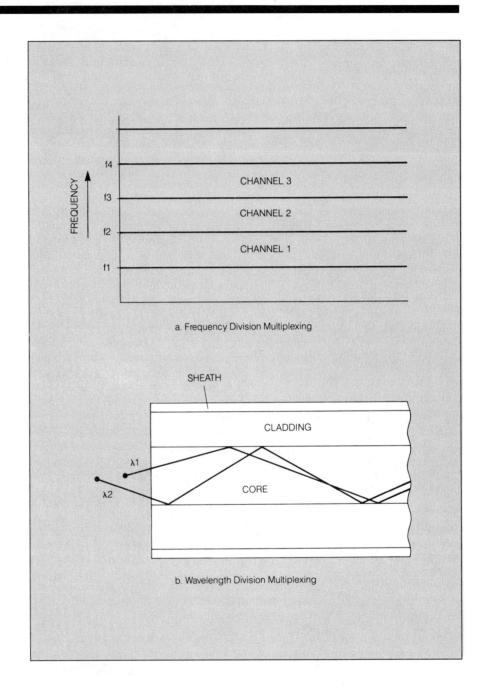

a. Frequency Division Multiplexing

b. Wavelength Division Multiplexing

144 optical fibers. The first application of the system was in the Northeast Corridor project by AT&T, between Boston and Washington, and in the North/South Lightwave Project on the West coast of the U.S. by Pacific Telesis, between San Francisco and San Diego. Figure 7.12a is a map of the Northeast Corridor system, which contains 78,000 fiber-kilometers of lightwave circuits. Figure 7.12b is a map of the North/South Lightwave Project. The two systems were placed in service in 1983 and have been considerably expanded since then.

The significant advantages associated with the use of fiber optic transmission systems resulted in tens of thousands of miles of fiber being installed during the 1980s. By early 1991 U.S. Sprint had converted 100 percent of their intercity transmission facilities from microwave to fiber, and AT&T and MCI Communications were working towards completing the conversion of their systems to fiber.

International Systems—The SL Underwater Cable

The advent of optical fiber technology for undersea cables provides point-to-point channel capacity equal to satellite systems at reduced cost and without long transmission delays, unstable environmental interference, induced noise, and broadcast of potentially sensitive information to half the world.

Undersea optical fiber cables can provide a data communications channel with a carrying capacity equal to satellite systems, but with greater security, less interference, less noise, and lower cost.

Undersea cable systems have some understandably difficult environmental requirements. The environment includes pressures of 10,000 pounds per square inch (psi) at depths of 7300 meters, salt water, and the possibility of mechanical damage from anchors and earth movement in shallow waters. An important requirement for these systems is that the regenerator spacing be as wide as possible to cut down on the system failure probability and the power requirements, since power must be fed from the ends of the cable.

A schematic of the SL Undersea Lightguide System is shown as Figure 7.13. It is comprised of a high-voltage power supply, a supervisory terminal, a multiplexor with inputs for several types of information, the cable light source, the cable itself, and the repeaters. The cable is made of a central core and a surrounding support as shown in Figure 7.14. The core has an outside diameter of 2.6 mm and consists of 12 optical fibers wound helically around a central copper-clad steel wire called a kingwire, all embedded in an elastomeric substance and covered with a nylon sheath. This assembly is in turn covered with a number of steel strands, a continuously welded copper tube, and an insulation of low-density polyethylene for electrical insulation and abrasion resistance. The outside diameter of the completed cable is 21 mm (about 0.8 in.).

Figure 7.12.
Fiber Optic Networks
(Source , J.R. Sauffer,
IEEE Journal on
Selected Areas in
Communications, Vol.
SAC-1, No. 3, April
1983. © 1983 IEEE)

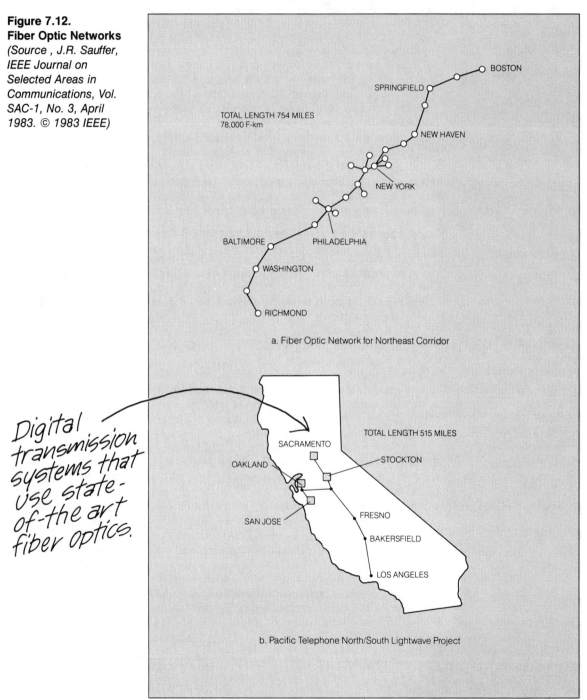

Digital transmission systems that use state-of-the art fiber optics.

Figure 7.13.
SL Undersea
Lightguide System
(Source, J.R. Sauffer,
IEEE Journal on
Selected Areas in
Communications, Vol.
SAC-1, No. 3, April
1983, © 1983 IEEE)

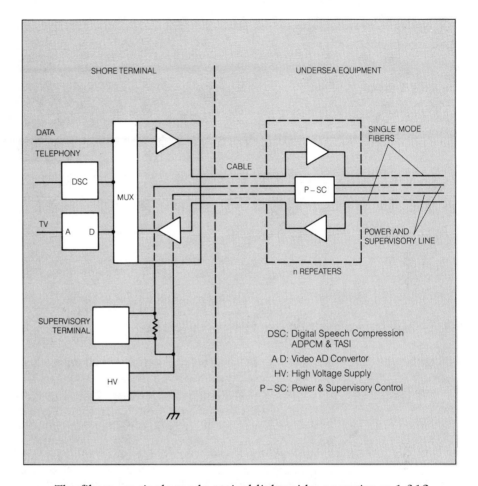

The fibers are single-mode optical lightguides operating at 1.312 µm. The data rate on each fiber pair is 280 Mbps, and repeaters are spaced every 35 km. The total capacity of the system is over 35,000 two-way voice channels. Inputs from binary data sources are multiplexed directly into the stream. Analog channels are first converted to binary by the adaptive delta modulation technique, then processed by a type of digital circuit (Digital TASI) that interleaves inputs from a number of input speech channels onto a smaller number of output channels. The light sources for the systems are ILDs operating near 1.3 µm with an average output power of 1 mW (0 dBm). Light detectors are indium-gallium-arsenide (InGaAs) p-i-n diode receivers followed by silicon bipolar transimpedance amplifiers. Three spare laser diodes, which can be switched in remotely if a failure occurs, are provided per circuit.

Figure 7.14.
Embedded Fiber Core
Cable *(Source, J.R. Sauffer, IEEE Journal on Selected Areas in Communications, Vol. SAC-1, No. 3, April 1983, © 1983 IEEE)*

By the late 1980s, several fiber optic undersea cables were laid across the Atlantic, linking New York to England, France, and Spain via light transmission. The successful operation of those systems resulted in communications carriers expanding their plans for fiber optic undersea cables. At the time this book revision was written several trans-Pacific and trans-Mediterranean fiber optic cables were in the process of being installed. By the mid-1990s, a large majority of voice, data, and video transmissions between the United States and Europe, Japan, and Australia will be routed via fiber optic cable between continents.

As the use of fiber optic cable has increased a corresponding decrease has resulted in the use of satellites for voice transmission. The primary reason for the wide acceptance of fiber optic cable over satellites is the immunity of the former to electromagnetic interference as well as the elimination of ½ second or longer delays associated with the use of satellites due to the signal having to traverse a distance of over 50,000 miles during transmission. Today most satellites are used for television and data transmission which are insensitive to transmission delays.

SATELLITE TRANSMISSION SYSTEMS

Basic Satellite Technology

Broad focus of the downlink signal and the propagation delay caused by the great distance between earth and satellite can present problems in two-way satellite communications.

Satellite communications systems are basically line-of-sight microwave systems with a single repeater. As stated in Chapter 3, the satellite is said to be in geostationary orbit, and is called a geostationary satellite, because the speed of the satellite is matched to the rotation of the earth at the equator. Because of the great distance of the satellite from the earth (about 22,300 miles) and antenna size limitations which limit focusing ability, the cone of coverage for a single satellite transmitter may be as large as the entire continental U.S.

For those transmission services which originate at a single point and flow to many points in one direction, such as television and radio signals, the large area of coverage is ideal. The relatively long delay between the instant a signal is sent and when it returns to earth (about 240 milliseconds (ms)) has no undesirable effect when the signal is going only one way. However, for signals such as data communications sessions and telephone conversations, which go in both directions and are only intended to be received at one other point, the large area of coverage and the delay can cause problems.

Data and telephone conversations usually proceed as a series of messages in one direction which are answered or acknowledged by messages in the other direction. When the delay between the message being sent and the reply or acknowledgement is long, the transmission rate of information slows down. In the case of voice messages, long delays between utterance and reply make the speaker think he or she has not been heard or understood. This leads to requests for repeating (the equivalent of negative acknowledgement in the data world) and increased frustration. There is also a serious privacy issue with communications intended for only one destination, but broadcast so that an entire continent can receive them. One of the factors causing the rush to all-digital transmission is the ease of encrypting information in digital form, so that when the inevitable interception of broadcast signals occurs, the information intercepted is at least somewhat difficult to decipher.

A satellite transmission system consists of one or more earth stations and a geostationary satellite which can be seen by the stations. Separate frequencies are assigned for sending to the satellite (the uplink) and receiving from the satellite (the downlink). The current frequency assignments for satellite systems are shown in Table 7.1.

The main components of a satellite system are the earth sending and receiving stations and a geosynchronous satellite equipped with transponders.

Satellites are equipped with multiple repeater units called transponders. Many systems have 10 or 12 transponders, but a new series of international satellites, called INTELSAT VI, have 46 transponders. Transponders are assigned different uses, but in the case of those used for voice or voice-equivalent data communications channels (nominal 4-kHz bandwidth), the transponder capacity may be as large as 3000 channels.

Table 7.1. Frequency Assignments for Satellite Systems

Uplink Frequencies	Downlink Frequencies
5.925–6.425 GHz	3.700–4.200 GHz
7.900–8.400 GHz	7.250–7.750 GHz
14.00–14.50 GHz	11.70–12.20 GHz
27.50–30.00 GHz	17.70–20.20 GHz

The INTELSAT VI satellite provides a total bandwidth, using frequency reuse techniques, of 3460 MHz.

Multiple Access Systems

Telephone switching systems and data multiplexers are designed based on the fact that not every telephone or terminal that can send information wishes to do so at the same time; or alternatively, the telephone or terminal user does not need or wish to pay for the entire capacity of a channel. These conditions are also true for the users of satellite systems. Several methods have been devised to allow sharing of the satellite and earth station resources among several users so that it appears that the transmission channel is dedicated to each user.

Frequency Division Multiple Access

Satellites using FDMA have the available bandwidth of a transponder divided into smaller segments.

Frequency Division Multiple Access (FDMA) is simply another example of the familiar data and voice transmission technique called frequency division multiplexing (FDM) used to allocate small portions of a large bandwidth (500 MHz for satellite transponders) to individual users. For instance, a telecommunications common carrier in a particular country, say Brazil, may want 132 voice-grade channels for sending voice and analog-coded data to various other countries. The bandwidth required on the current international satellite systems for this many channels is 10 MHz. Since one transponder has a bandwidth of 500 MHz, it could accommodate 50 users each requiring 132 channels. The Brazilian user might be allocated the frequency band between 5990 and 6000 MHz for the uplink to the satellite, and the corresponding downlink frequencies would be 3765 to 3775 MHz. Other users might be assigned similar portions of the bandwidth in the same transponder. For example, a Portuguese user might be allocated the 6220 to 6230 MHz uplink band and the 3995 to 4005 MHz downlink band. A Canadian user might operate on the 5930 to 5940 MHz uplink band and the 3705 to 3715 MHz downlink band. Figure 7.15 illustrates how the three users each have one uplink, all into a single transponder, but all users can receive all three downlinks. This arrangement makes possible simultaneous two-way transmissions between any of the three sites using only a part of one satellite transponder.

**Figure 7.15.
Multiuser Satellite
System**

Time Division Multiple Access

In TDMA, access to a satellite transponder is divided into discrete time frames.

Time Division Multiple Access (TDMA) is the equivalent of FDMA, but in the time domain rather than the frequency domain. TDMA works just like time division multiplexing (TDM) for land-based data and voice transmissions, with each satellite transponder having a data rate capacity of between 10 and 100 Mbps. During the time a station is sending on the uplink, it has available the entire data rate capacity of the transponder, but then it must stop sending for a short time to allow another station access to the transponder. The information flows to the satellite in frames, each frame containing one burst of information from each earth station allowed access to the single transponder. A typical format for a frame is shown in Figure 7.16. The sum of the durations of the individual bursts do not quite equal the frame time in order to give some guard time between bursts.

Timing for keeping the station bursts apart is a major problem, and is complicated by two facts. First, the satellites are not perfectly stationary in orbit (each one appears to travel in a small figure-8 pattern). Also, the time of travel of the signal between different earth stations and the same satellite is different because of different slant range distances. TDMA techniques allow the satellite transmitter to be operated at higher power levels than FDMA. This is permissible because only one carrier at a time

**Figure 7.16.
TDMA Transmission
Frames**

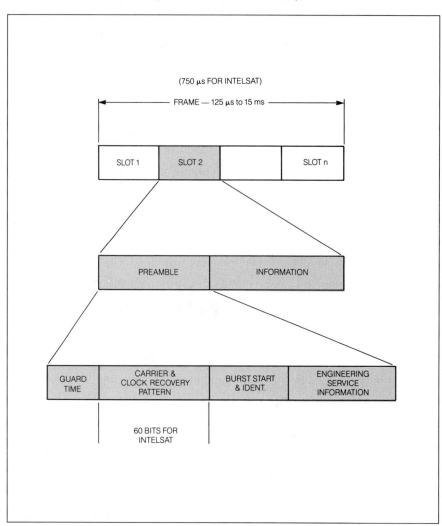

occupies the transponder, reducing the amount of intermodulation distortion generated.

Demand Assignment Multiple Access

DAMA is similar to FDMA except that channels are not assigned on a permanent basis.

Using the *Demand Assignment Multiple Access* (DAMA) technique, each satellite transponder is used much like a telephone switch; that is, a subchannel is assigned only when traffic is available to be carried on it. This is in contrast to the FDMA and TDMA techniques described previously, where channels are assigned to users on a permanent basis, even if there is no traffic demand. DAMA is a variant of FDMA in that a part or all of a transponder is divided into individual channels which can be accessed by all DAMA terminals on the ground which are serviced by the DAMA transponder. A central computer system, or a system of distributed and cooperating computers, on the ground keeps track of who gets which channel when. DAMA is particularly useful for loading transponders efficiently when each of several ground sites need only a few channels.

WHAT HAVE WE LEARNED?

1. Light travelling in an optical fiber obeys Snell's law.
2. Light can travel in a multimode optical fiber along several paths, or in a single-mode fiber along only one path.
3. The index of refraction of the glass making up an optical fiber varies across the diameter of the fiber, with the highest index in the middle of the fiber.
4. Fiber optic system bandwidth is limited by modal delay spreading, and material dispersion.
5. Fiber optic system transmission distance is limited by scattering, absorption, losses at connections, and losses at bends in the cable.
6. Fibers with varying index of refraction across the fiber are made by heating a preform which has been doped with metal salts such as germanium and phosphorus and drawing it down to a small diameter.
7. Transmitters for fiber optic systems are light-emitting diodes or semi-conductor injection lasers.
8. Receivers in fiber optic systems are avalanche photodiodes or integrated p-i-n field-effect transistors.
9. Satellite transmissions have four uplink bands and four downlink bands.
10. TDMA techniques allow the satellite transmitter to be operated at higher power levels than FDMA.

Quiz for Chapter 7

1. The requirements for a successful transmission system using light are:
   a. Powerful, reliable light source.
   b. Strong glass.
   c. Reliable, low-cost transmission medium.
   d. Powerful amplifiers.

2. The core of an optical fiber has:
   a. A lower index of refraction than air.
   b. A lower index of refraction than the cladding.
   c. A higher index of refraction than the cladding.
   d. None of the above.

3. For single-mode fibers, the core diameter is about:
   a. 10 times the fiber radius.
   b. 3 times the wavelength of the light carried in the fiber.
   c. 15 micrometers.
   d. 10 times the wavelength of the light carried in the fiber.

4. Over a period of 30 years, a kilometer of fiber optic cable is likely to be broken:
   a. Not at all.
   b. Once.
   c. 10 times.
   d. 2 or 3 times.

5. Deposition of dopants on fiber preforms is done by:
   a. Outside vapor deposition.
   b. Axial vapor deposition.
   c. Inside vapor deposition.
   d. All of the above.

6. A light-emitting diode is able to couple how much power into an optical fiber?
   a. 10 watts.
   b. 10 milliwatts.
   c. 100 microwatts.
   d. 1 picowatt.

7. Avalanche photodiode receivers can detect bits of transmitted data by receiving:
   a. 1 photon.
   b. 10 photons.
   c. 100 photons.
   d. 200 photons.

8. One unsolved problem with satellite systems is:
   a. Coverage.
   b. Privacy.
   c. Bandwidth.
   d. Access.

9. The AT&T FT3C fiber optic transmission system is designed to use how many light wavelengths?
   a. One.
   b. Two.
   c. Three.
   d. Ten.

10. The SL Undersea Lightguide system can carry how many two-way voice channels?
    a. 10,000
    b. 100,000
    c. 35,000
    d. 760

11. When the index of refraction is greater in Material 1 than it is in Material 2, the velocity of propagation in Material 1 compared to Material 2 is:
 a. Equal to or greater.
 b. Greater.
 c. Lesser.
 d. Equal.

12. The different angles of entry of light into an optical fiber where the diameter of the core is many times the wavelength of the light transmitted are called:
 a. Emitters.
 b. Modes.
 c. Sensors.
 d. Refractors.

13. In single-mode fibers, a large fraction of the power is propagated in the:
 a. Sheath.
 b. Core.
 c. Cladding.
 d. Air.

14. The loss in signal power as light travels down a fiber is called:
 a. Propagation.
 b. Scattering.
 c. Absorption.
 d. Attenuation.

15. The coupling efficiency of an LED light source to an optical fiber with a numerical aperture of 0.2 or more is:
 a. 60%.
 b. 10%.
 c. 2%.
 d. 0.1%.

16. The FT3C lightwave system contains the following number of fibers:
 a. 12.
 b. 144.
 c. 128.
 d. 64.

17. A geostationary satellite used for communications systems is:
 a. Stationary in the sky.
 b. Rotates with the earth.
 c. Positioned over the equator.
 d. Remains stationary relative to the earth's surface.
 e. a and c.
 f. b, c, and d.

18. Multiple repeaters in communications satellites are known as:
 a. Transponders.
 b. Detectors.
 c. Modulators.
 d. Stations.

19. In the current frequency assignments, how many frequency bands are there for the up-link frequencies?
 a. 16.
 b. 8.
 c. 4.
 d. 2.

20. The bandwidth required to send 132 voice-grade channels by FDM on an international satellite system is:
 a. 500 MHz
 b. 10 MHz
 c. 1320 MHz
 d. 50 MHz

Protocols and Error Control

ABOUT THIS CHAPTER

This chapter is about the rules that data communications systems use when communicating with each other, how they discover that an error has been made in transmission, and some methods that are used in correcting those errors. Since there are many data transmission schemes in use (for example, asynchronous and synchronous, half- and full-duplex), many sets of rules, called protocols, and many error detection and correction schemes have been devised. The most common of these techniques are explained in this chapter.

PROTOCOLS AND INTERFACES

A protocol is a set of rules defining the interactions between two machines or processes that are alike or that have similar functions. An interface is a set of rules controlling the interaction of two different machines or processes.

Protocols are agreements between people or processes (usually nowadays the processes are computer programs) about which may do what to whom, and when. A protocol is different from an interface. An interface is a set or rules, often embodied in pieces of hardware, controlling the interaction of two different machines or processes, such as a computer and a modem. A protocol, on the other hand, is a set of rules defining the interactions between two machines or processes that are alike or that have similar functions. The difference is illustrated in Figure 8.1. House A and House B look alike, but are occupied by a curious set of people. The British engineer on the top floor of house A needs to communicate with another engineer, also British, on the top floor of B. The only telephone, however, is guarded by a Swedish businessman on the bottom floor of each house. The engineer speaks no Swedish, and the Swede no English.

The two engineers, like most people who talk on the telephone, have a routine, worked out over long years, for communicating. The one answering says "Hullo." The one calling says "Hullo, this is Reggie." Then the first says "Oh, hullo, Reggie. How are you, old boy?" This is called a preamble. They then begin discussing Wimbledon, the weather, and even some business. At the end of most sentences, the one being questioned makes a reply, even if it is only a sound rather than a word or sentence. If one party does not hear some sort of reply from the other at fairly short intervals, he may say, "I say, are you still there?" If he still receives no reply, he may terminate the conversation and begin the whole process over. If one party does not understand the other, he will say, "What?", and the second party will repeat the last sentence. When the

**Figure 8.1.
Protocols and
Interfaces**

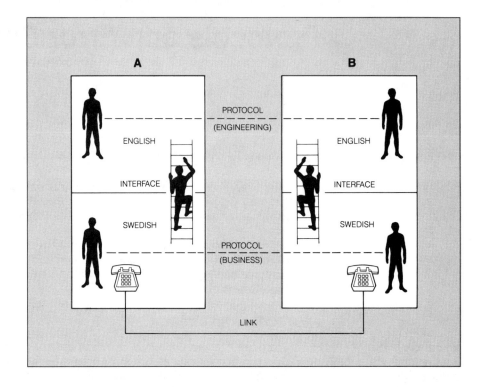

Protocols function for
machine communica-
tion much like the
formats and rules for
human conversations
and are used for the
same reasons.

conversation is over, the person terminating the call will say, "Well, goodbye for now." The called party will reply, "Goodbye.", and both will hang up. The Swedish businessman has a similar technique for conversing with his counterpart. All of these conventional conversational actions make up a protocol. As we shall see in the remainder of this chapter, protocols developed for communicating between processes in computers have all of the same mechanisms as those used between humans, for exactly the same reasons.

Even though our two engineers are able to communicate reliably with each other because they have a communications protocol, they still have the problem of no direct access to the communications channel, which is jealously guarded by the large Swedish businessmen. The solution is an interface. The engineers engage a person who stands midway up the stairs and who speaks both engineering English and business Swedish, and whose task it is to relay the conversation from the engineer (speaking in English) to the businessman (listening in Swedish), who relays it over the telephone to his Swedish counterpart in house B, who relays it in Swedish to another person halfway up the stairs, who finally conveys the messages in English to the called party. This seems like a clumsy and inefficient procedure and in many respects it is, but it is the same procedure used in millions of data communications systems to allow an applications program, communicating in one set of symbols (perhaps

ASCII) and at one rate of symbol production, to communicate through a teleprocessing monitor using another set of symbols (perhaps EBCDIC) at a vastly different rate, to a line interface program dealing with yet a third set of symbols (bits). The story of standard interfaces is told in Chapter 4. The story in this chapter is about protocols.

Elements of a Protocol

There are three main elements to any protocol: a character set, a set of rules for message timing and sequence, and error determination and correction procedures.

The basic elements of a communications protocol are a set of symbols, called a character set, a set of rules for the sequence and timing of messages constructed from the character set, and procedures for determining when an error has occurred in the transmission and how to correct the error. The character set will consist of a subset which is meaningful to people (usually called printing characters), and another subset which conveys control information (usually called control characters). There is a correspondence between each character and a group of symbols on the transmission channel. For instance the printing character A might correspond to the binary code 1000001. Several standard codes with equivalent sets of ones and zeros (bits), such as the ASCII discussed in a previous chapter, have been defined over the years. The set of rules to be followed by the sender and receiver gives the meaning, permissible sequences, and time relationships of the control characters and messages formed from the symbols. The error detection and correction procedure allows for the detection of and orderly recovery from errors caused by factors outside the control of the terminal at either end.

TELETYPEWRITER AND XMODEM PROTOCOLS

TTY protocols are the simplest ones in general use. The 58 characters in the character set of one TTY protocol were encoded by a 5-bit binary code.

The simplest protocols in general use are the ones associated with the transmission of start-stop or asynchronous data between teleprinter machines. For a long period after the development of the teleprinter, the machines were electromechanically controlled as we discussed in a previous chapter, and protocols had to be appropriate to a very simple mechanical controller in each machine. One of the first teletypewriter (TTY) protocols used a character set containing 58 symbols: 50 printing characters, a space, and seven control characters as shown in Figure 8.2. These symbols were encoded into a 5-bit binary code as shown (the octal representation is shown only for readers familiar with octal). The printing characters are the uppercase letters, the numbers, and 14 punctuation marks. Three control characters allow for carriage return (CR), line feed (LF), and ringing the terminal bell (BELL) to announce a message. Also provided are a NULL (or blank) character (which is not the same as a space) and a WRU character. WRU stands for "Who Are You", and causes a mechanical device in the teleprinter to send a character sequence identifying that particular terminal. The other two control characters are the FIGS character, which causes the machine to print numbers and punctuation, and the LTRS character, which causes the machine to print the uppercase alphabet. As mentioned in a previous chapter, this character set and associated binary code is commonly referred to as the Baudot code,

Figure 8.2.
CCITT Alphabet No. 2

BINARY	OCTAL	LTRS	FIGS
0 0 0 0 0	00	BLANK	BLANK
0 0 0 0 1	01	E	3
0 0 0 1 0	02	LF	LF
0 0 0 1 1	03	A	-
0 0 1 0 0	04	SPACE	SPACE
0 0 1 0 1	05	S	'
0 0 1 1 0	06	I	8
0 0 1 1 1	07	U	7
0 1 0 0 0	10	CR	CR
0 1 0 0 1	11	D	WRU
0 1 0 1 0	12	R	4
0 1 0 1 1	13	J	BELL
0 1 1 0 0	14	N	,
0 1 1 0 1	15	F	
0 1 1 1 0	16	C	:
0 1 1 1 1	17	K	(
1 0 0 0 0	20	T	5
1 0 0 0 1	21	Z	+
1 0 0 1 0	22	L	)
1 0 0 1 1	23	W	2
1 0 1 0 0	24	H	
1 0 1 0 1	25	Y	6
1 0 1 1 0	26	P	0
1 0 1 1 1	27	Q	1
1 1 0 0 0	30	O	9
1 1 0 0 1	31	B	?
1 1 0 1 0	32	G	
1 1 0 1 1	33	FIGS	FIGS
1 1 1 0 0	34	M	.
1 1 1 0 1	35	X	/
1 1 1 1 0	36	V	=
1 1 1 1 1	37	LTRS	LTRS

after Emile Baudot, who invented the first code with symbols of a fixed length.

The protocol for operation of a message system using the Baudot code goes something like this (the procedure varies somewhat according to the operator of the system):

1. A communications channel is connected between the two machines. This may be a temporary, dialed connection, or a permanent private line.

2. The sending machine sends a WRU, to verify that the receiving machine is the proper one for the message to be sent.

3. The sending machine sends a "Here is ...", which is normally the same sequence of characters which is sent when it receives a WRU, to identify the sender.

4. The sending machine sends a preamble or message header which identifies the name and address of the intended message recipient, the date and time of entry of the message into the system, the date and time of transmission, and the message sequence number assigned by the sender. In some systems, the sender will use two sequence numbers; one to count the number of messages sent by the sender that day, and the second to count the number of messages sent to the receiver's terminal that day.

5. At the end of the message, the sending machine sends another "Here is ..." and another WRU. The second WRU is to determine if the receiving machine is still connected to the line. The operator of the sending machine will, if the message is being sent manually, sometimes send several BELL characters, to alert a person at the receiving end that a message is ready for delivery.

Because the simple TTY protocol does not check for errors in the message, even low error rates will cause the received message to be gibberish and the sender will not know it.

This protocol has developed over many years of sending messages manually between individual terminals operated by people. You will note that it has all of the elements described in the opening paragraphs: a previously defined set of symbols and corresponding codes suitable for electronic transmission, a preamble, a message, and even a rudimentary error detection procedure (the invocation of the WRU at the beginning and end of the session). The same sort of protocol is used for teleprinter message systems even when one end of the system is a computer, as are all of the current public teleprinter networks.

The simple teletypewriter protocol described in the preceding does not work very well in the presence of even fairly low error rates on the path between the machines. Individual characters can be mutilated in such a way as to cause the receiving machine to begin printing gibberish, and the transmitter will never know. The WRU check at the end of a message assures only that the receiving machine received the WRU correctly and that the circuit is still good in the backwards direction, but says nothing about whether the message got through. To provide better assurance of correct transmission, two more techniques are sometimes used for simple protocols: character parity and echoplex.

Parity

Parity is the technique where a bit is added to every symbol for the purpose of error detection. It can either be even or odd parity.

The Communicator's Creed: "Now abideth faith, hope, and parity, but the greatest of these is parity."

The addition by the transmitter of another bit to the bits that encode a symbol for the purpose of error detection is called parity. The bit is always transmitted, and is usually set to the value that will cause the coded symbol to have an even number of one bits; thus, the scheme is called even parity. The parity bit is recomputed by the receiver. If the newly computed value gives the correct parity, all is well. If not, some indication is given to the receiving terminal, usually by substituting a special error character for the one received.

For an example of parity checking, consider the ASCII character M, which has a bit composition of 1 0 0 1 1 0 1 (see Figure 1.5). Because the character has four 1 bits, a 1 bit would be added if odd parity checking is used, whereas a 0 bit is used if even parity checking is employed. Figure 8.3 illustrates the formation of the parity bit for odd and even parity checking for the ASCII character M.

**Figure 8.3.
Parity Bit Formation
for ASCII Character M**

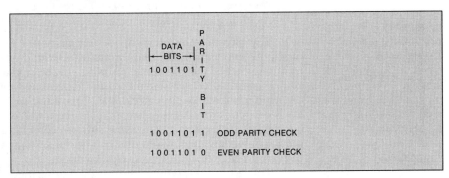

The parity scheme will detect single-bit errors in the transmitted symbols, but not multiple-bit errors. Error correction can occur by the receiver sending a message back which requests retransmission.

Echoplex

Echoplex is an error detection technique in which each character of a message is retransmitted by the receiver back to the originator as it is received.

Echoplex is perhaps not properly classed as an element of protocols, but we will discuss it here anyway. It is the technique of sending back (or echoing) each character by the receiver as the characters are received. The sender can then see by the copy printed locally whether the characters are making the round trip without being mutilated. When an echoed character is received in error by the original sender, it is not possible to tell whether the data were received correctly at the destination and scrambled on the return path, or were erroneous when received at the original destination. But at least some error indication is immediately available to the sender.

Checksums

In addition to character (or vertical) parity where a parity bit is added to each character, a block parity character may be added at the end of each message block.

In the preceding discussion on parity, the bit required to make the number of 1-bits in an individual character was added onto the end of the character and sent along with it. This scheme is sometimes called vertical redundancy checking (VRC), or vertical parity, because if one holds a punched paper tape with its length in the horizontal, each character will appear as a vertical column of holes across the tape. It is possible, and is common in some systems, to include a horizontal check character, which performs the parity function for each row of holes in the tape.

Figure 8.4 shows a set of characters represented as holes punched in a tape, with the vertical or character parity bit at the top of each character, and the horizontal or block parity character at the right. The block parity character is usually called a *checksum*, because it is formed by performing a binary addition without carry of each successive character. It also is sometimes referred to as a *longitudinal redundancy check* (LRC) character. It is sent as an extra character at the end of each message block. A system that uses both vertical parity and a checksum usually can detect all single-bit errors in a single character and some multiple-bit errors within a single character. In fact, this method of error detection is one of the three types supported by the BiSync protocol described later in this chapter.

**Figure 8.4.
Vertical and Horizontal Parity**

XMODEM Protocol

XMODEM protocol has an error checking technique that can be used between microcomputers. Messages are sent in blocks of 128 characters surrounded by control characters.

The XMODEM protocol was devised by Ward Christensen as a simple error checking scheme suitable for file transfer operations between microcomputers. It requires that one terminal or computer be set up by an operator or computer program as the sender and the other be set up as the receiver. Once the protocol is started, the transmitter waits for the receiver to send a Negative Acknowledge (NAK) character. The receiver meanwhile is set to send NAKs every 10 seconds. When the transmitter detects the first NAK, it begins sending messages as blocks of 128 data characters, surrounded by some protocol control characters. The beginning of each block is signaled by a Start Of Header (SOH) character. This is followed by a block number character in ASCII, followed by the same block number with each bit inverted. The bit inversion is known as the *1's complement* and results in the block number being followed by the 1's complement of the block number. A 128-character piece of the file is sent, followed by a checksum that is the remainder of the sum of all the 128 bytes in the message divided by 255. Mathematically, the XMODEM checksum can be represented as

$$\text{CHECKSUM} = R \left[\frac{\sum\limits_{1}^{128} \text{ASCII Value of Character}}{255} \right]$$

where,

R is the remainder of the division process.

Figure 8.5 shows the XMODEM protocol block format.

**Figure 8.5.
XMODEM Protocol
Block Format**

START OF HEADER	BLOCK NUMBER	1's COMPLEMENT OF BLOCK NUMBER	128 DATA CHARACTERS	CHECKSUM

The receiver checks each part of the received block as follows:

1. Was the first character an SOH?
2. Was the block number exactly one more than the last previous block received?
3. Were exactly 128 characters of data received?
4. Was the locally computed checksum identical with the last character received in the block?

If the receiver is satisfied, it sends an Acknowledge (ACK) back to the transmitter, and the transmitter sends the next block. If not, a NAK is sent, and the transmitter resends the block found in error. This process is continued, block by block, until the entire file is sent and verified. At the end of the data, the transmitter sends an End Of Text character. The receiver replies with an ACK and the session is terminated.

Even though the XMODEM protocol is very simple and easy to operate, it requires a computer at each end, and every file to be transferred must be set up manually.

There are several points to be made about the XMODEM protocol. First, it is very simple and easy to implement with a small computer, but it does require a computer at each end. Second, it requires manual setup for each file to be transferred. Third, the error detection technique (ordinary sum of the data characters) is unsophisticated and unable to detect reliably the most common type of transmission error, which is a noise burst which may last on the order of 10 milliseconds (the duration of about 12 bits at 1200 bps). Fourth, it is a half-duplex protocol; that is, information is sent, then the sender waits for a reply before sending the next message. Since operation of the XMODEM protocol generally assumes a full-duplex line, it is inefficient in use of the transmission facility.

In spite of the previously mentioned limitations, the XMODEM protocol and several derivatives, including XMODEM/CRC and ZMODEM, are supported by most asynchronous communications programs designed for operation on personal computers. The rationale for the widespread support of those protocols is related to the initial placement of the XMODEM protocol into the public domain. This action allowed software developers to use the protocol without cost. In addition, it provided communications compatibility between programs developed by different vendors which was extremely important in the 1970s when many software developers preferred to introduce proprietary protocols that only worked when two computer systems used the same software program.

Most of the asynchronous communications programs developed during the early 1980s eventually included XMODEM support. In the late 1980s, several derivatives of the XMODEM protocol gained acceptance due to the increased level of functionality they provided. Some new versions of the XMODEM protocol added CRC error checking, a process described later in this chapter. Other versions provided a full duplex transmission capability with CRC error detection, further increasing the efficiency of the protocol.

CONVOLUTIONAL CODING—CYCLIC REDUNDANCY CHECKS

Convolutional coding attaches a BCC to the end of each message block. The receiver recomputes BCC and compares it to the one transmitted to determine if the message was correctly received.

Several schemes have been devised to detect errors in binary communications systems using feedback or convolutional coding. These methods all append information computed at the transmitter to the end of each message transmitted to enable the receiver to determine if a transmission error has occurred. The added information is mathematically related to the messages and is therefore redundant. The receiver recomputes the value and compares the recomputed number with the number received. If the two are the same, all is well. If not, the receiver notifies the transmitter that an error has occurred, and the message is re-sent. These methods go by the name of *Cyclic Redundancy Checking* (CRC) and the values appended to the messages are called CRCs or *Block Check Characters* (BCCs). A CRC is calculated by dividing the entire numeric binary value of the block of data by a constant, called a generator polynomial. The quotient is discarded, and the remainder is appended to the block and transmitted along with the data.

The check character is determined by dividing the total binary value of the entire block by a constant called a gener-ator polynomial.

CRCs usually are computed using multiple section feedback shift registers with eXclusive-OR (XOR) logic elements between each section and at the end. A typical arrangement is shown in Figure 8.6. This register implements the CCITT/ISO High-level Data Link Control (HDLC) CRC, which is called CCITT-CRC. The circles with a + in the middle represent XOR logic elements. For B = 0 or B = 1, the two rules for XOR are

1. B XOR 1 = 0
2. B XOR 0 = B

The shift register is initialized to all 1s at the beginning of CRC calculation for a message. As each bit of the transmitted characters is applied to the transmission facility, it is also applied at point A of Figure 8.6, then the entire register is shifted right one bit. As the bits are transmitted and shifted, each 1 bit that appears at A also affects the state of the other XOR elements, and that effect is propagated throughout the register for several bit times after the bit initially appears. Thus, any bit continues to have an effect on the transmitted data for a considerable time after that bit is sent. When the last data bit has been sent, the bits in the CRC shift register are complemented and transmitted.

At the receiver, the identical process is performed, and when the end of the message including the CRC is detected, the CRC is tested for the unique value 0001110100001111. If this value is found, all is well and the CRC register is reset to all ones for the next message. If the special value is not found, the program is notified that a transmission error has occurred, and a negative acknowledgement is returned to the sender.

The CRC error detec-tion process has a very high rate of success in accurately detecting error bursts of up to 16 bits because of the history held in the shift registers.

The CRC process has the advantage that the current state of the shift register is the result of considerable past history. It is therefore unlikely that a burst of errors, such as normally occurs in serial data transmission, will produce a calculated CRC at the receiver that is the same as that which was originally sent. In fact, the 16-bit CRC calculation procedures, CRC-16 and CRC-CCITT, will detect all error bursts of 16 bits or less in

**Figure 8.6.
Shift Register
Implementation of
CCITT-CRC** *(Source:
John E. MacNamara,
Technical Aspects of
Data Communication,
© 1977, Digital Press,
Maynard, Mass.)*

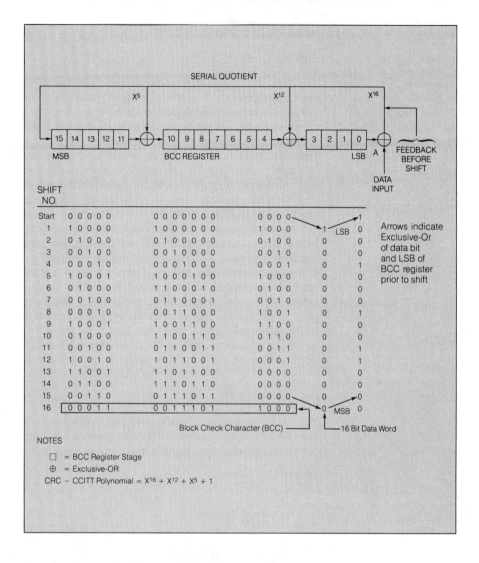

length. They will also detect over 99.9% of error bursts of greater than
16 bits. Another advantage of CRC is that it does not require the addition
of another bit per character sent as do the VRC and LRC schemes. It does,
however, require the sending of one or two (two for CRC-16 and
CRC-CCITT) extra characters at the end of each transmitted block.

CRC algorithms are usually implemented in hardware, and integrated
circuits have been developed to do the entire process for more than one
method (e.g., CRC-12, CRC-16, and CRC-CCITT). It is also possible to do
the calculations in software, with table lookup techniques providing
reasonable performance.

HALF-DUPLEX PROTOCOLS

Links

Data links, either point-to-point or multipoint, are the data communications equipment and circuits that allow two or more terminals to communicate.

The basic notion in link protocols is that of the data link. A data link is an arrangement of modems or other interface equipment and communications circuits connecting two or more terminals that wish to communicate. Probably the most widely used link protocol is comprised of the *Binary Synchronous Communications* procedures defined by IBM (usually abbreviated as BiSync or BSC). These procedures allow for operation on a data link in one direction at one time. BiSync can be operated on full-duplex circuits, but information still flows in only one direction at a time, so that in many cases the advantage of the full-duplex circuit is minimized.

For the purpose of discussion of protocols, the physical form of the link is important in that the procedures for connecting and disconnecting the link may be different depending on whether the link is permanently connected or dial-up, and also depending on the delay between when a data bit is sent and when it is received. This latter factor is of particular concern on satellite links due to the large difference in round-trip propagation delay between satellite links and terrestrial links. Regardless of the physical form of the link, however, the data are sent over it as a serial stream of symbols encoded as bits, and the control procedures between the ends of the link are effected using the transmission and recognition of line-control characters or control codes.

Point-to-Point Links

A point-to-point link is one that connects only two stations at one time as Figure 8.7a shows. Point-to-point links may be established on dedicated or dial-up circuits, and they may be half-duplex or full-duplex.

Multipoint Links

Multipoint links connect more than two stations at one time as Figure 8.7b shows. Obviously, some control procedure must be in place to designate which stations may use the link at any one time. For this purpose, one station on the multidrop lines is designated as the control or master station, and all other stations are designated as tributaries or slaves. The control station is the traffic director, designating which stations are to use the link by a polling and selection process. At any instant in time, transmission on a multipoint link will be between only two stations, with all other stations on the link in a passive receive mode.

**Figure 8.7.
Point-to-Point and
Multipoint Links**

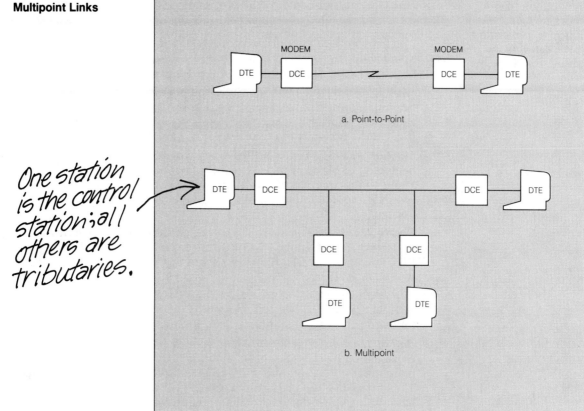

*One station
is the control
station; all
others are
tributaries.*

Transmission Codes—Character Sets

IBM's BiSync can be
used with three charac-
ter sets: set, EBCDIC,
and ASCII.

BiSync is defined by IBM to accommodate three character sets and
their associated binary codes. Each set consists of a set of graphics (letters,
numbers, and punctuation), a set of terminal control and format control
codes (BELL, Form Feed, WRU, etc), and a set of data link control codes
(Start of Text, End of Transmission, etc). The three sets are the: Six-Bit
Transcode (SBT), Extended Binary Coded Decimal Interchange Code
(EBCDIC), and United States of America Standard Code for Information
Interchange (USASCII, or more commonly, just ASCII).

The codes differ in number of bits per symbol encoded (6 for SBT, 7
for ASCII, and 8 for EBCDIC), and different numbers of characters in the
character set (64 for SBT, 128 for ASCII, and 144 for EBCDIC). There are
significant differences between the sets in such properties as the sorting
order between letters and numbers.

Link Control Codes

Various link control codes are used in BiSync to gain control of the data link and ensure that the proper actions occur.

Link control is effected by the proper recognition of control characters, and the taking of appropriate actions. The control codes used in BiSync are defined as follows:

Synchronous Idle (SYN)—Establishes and maintains synchronization between DCEs, and is used as a filler between data blocks.

Start of Header (SOH)—Identifies the beginning of a block of heading information. Headers are control information (such as addresses, priority, and message numbers) used by the system to process the text part of the message.

Start of Text (STX)—Identifies the end of a header and the beginning of block of text. Text is the part of the message from an applications program which is destined for another applications program and which must pass through the communications system unchanged.

End of Transmission Block (ETB)—Identifies the end of a block started with an SOH or STX. A BCC is sent immediately following an ETB. Receipt of an ETB requires a status reply (ACK0, ACK1, NAK, WACK, or RVI).

End of Text (ETX)—Terminates a block of data started by an STX or SOH which was transmitted as an entity. A BCC is sent immediately following an ETX. ETX also requires a status reply.

End of Transmission (EOT)—Indicates the end of message transmission by this station; the message may have contained one or more blocks. Receipt of an EOT causes all receiving stations to reset. The EOT is also used as a response to a poll when the polled station has nothing to send, and as an abort signal when the sender cannot continue transmission.

Enquiry (ENQ)—Requests a repeat transmission of a response to a message block if the original response is garbled or is not received. ENQ may also indicate the end of a polling or selection sequence, and is used to bid for the line when the line is a point-to-point connection.

Affirmative Acknowledgement (ACK0 or ACK1)—Indicates correct receipt of the last previous block, and that the receiver is ready to accept the next block. ACK0 and ACK1 are used alternately, and receipt of the wrong one is an indication of an error in the protocol. ACK0 is the correct response to a station selection (on a multipoint circuit) or a line bid (on a point-to-point circuit).

Wait-Before-Transmit Affirmative Acknowledgement (WACK)— Indicates a temporary not-ready-to-receive condition to the sending station and affirmative acknowledgement of the last previously received data block. The normal response to WACK by the sending station is ENQ, but EOT and DLE EOT are also valid. If ENQ is received after sending WACK, the sending station continues to send WACK until it is ready to continue sending data.

Negative Acknowledgement (NAK)—Indicates that the last previously received block was received in error, and that the receiver is ready to receive another block. NAK is also used as a station-not-ready reply to a station selection or line bid.

Data Link Escape (DLE)—Indicates to the receiver that the character following the DLE is to be interpreted as a control character.

Reverse Interrupt (RVI)—Indicates a request by a receiving station that the current transmission be terminated so that a high-priority message can be sent (such as a shutdown notice). RVI is also an affirmative acknowledgement to the last previous block received. In a multipoint circuit, RVI sent from the control station means the control station wishes to select a different station. When a sending station receives an RVI, it responds by sending all data that would prevent it from becoming a receiving station.

Temporary Text Delay (TTD)—Indicates that the sending station is not ready to send immediately, but wishes to keep the line. The receiving terminal reply to TTD is NAK. TTD normally is sent after two seconds if the sender cannot transmit the next block; this holds off the normal three-second abort timer at the receiving terminal. The response to TTD is NAK, and TTD may be repeated several times. TTD also is used as a forward abort, by sending EOT in response to the NAK reply.

Switched Line Disconnect (DLE EOT)—Indicates to a receiver that the transmitter is going to hang up on a switched line connection.

Code Sequences

Some control characters require a two-character sequence of standard characters.

Reference to the ASCII and EBCDIC code charts will reveal no code assigned to several of the control characters mentioned in the preceding listing. Such control codes are represented by two-character sequences of the characters that are defined in the charts. Table 8.1 gives the correspondence between these control characters and sequences of standard characters.

**Table 8.1.
Character Sequences for BiSync Control Characters**

BiSync Data Link Character	Character Sequences for Various Code Sets		
	ASCII	**EBCDIC**	**SBT**
ACK0	DLE 0	DLE 70	DLE -
ACK1	DLE 1	DLE /	DLE T
WACK	DLE ;	DLE ,	DLE W
RVI	DLE	DLE @	DLE 2
TTD	STX ENQ	STX ENQ	STX ENQ

Polling and Selection

In a BiSync link, the control station determines which tributary station is active on the link, as well as the direction of transmission.

The active participants on a BiSync link are managed by a control station which issues either a Poll or a Select message addressed to the desired tributary. The *Poll* is an invitation-to-send from the control to the tributary. This allows the tributary to send any messages desired to the control station. The *Select* is a request-to-receive notice from the control station, telling the tributary that the control station has something to send to it. The control station thus controls which station has the link, and the direction of transmission.

Stations on the data link are assigned unique addresses which may consist of from one to seven characters. The first character defines the station, and succeeding characters define some part of the station, such as a printer, as required. Some BiSync implementations repeat the station address for reliability purposes.

Message Blocks

Messages consist of one or more blocks of text, called the body of the message, surrounded by synchronization, header and error control characters. The beginning of each block is identified by the STX control character, and all blocks except the last in a message are ended either by an ETB or an ITB character. The last block of the message is ended by an ETX character.

Error Checking

Three types of error detection modes are used by BiSync: An odd parity check of each character including VRC/LRC, a BCC comparison using CRC-12, and a BCC comparison using CRC-16.

BiSync uses three types of error detection: VRC/LRC, CRC-12, and CRC-16. Table 8.2 shows under what conditions each is used. Transparency mode is described later in this section. The VRC is an odd-parity check performed on each character transmitted, including the LRC character at the end of the block. Each bit in the LRC character provides odd parity for the corresponding bit position of all characters sent in the block. Figure 8.8 illustrates the formation of the VRC and LRC for an eight character data block. Note that the LRC is formed in the same manner as the VRC; however, the LRC covers all characters in the data block, whereas the VRC covers individual characters.

In BiSync, the LRC character is called the Block Check Character (BCC) and is sent as the next character following an ETB, ITB, or ETX

Table 8.2.
Type of Redundancy Check

Code Set	No Transparency	Transparency Installed and Operating	Transparency Installed but Not Operating
EBCDIC	CRC-16	CRC-16	CRC-16
ASCII	VRC/LRC	CRC-16	VRC/CRC-16
SBT	CRC-12	CRC-12	CRC-12

Figure 8.8.
VRC/LRC Parity Check

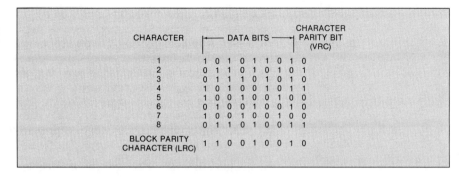

character. The BCC sent with the data is compared at the receiver with one accumulated by the receiver, and if the two are equal, all is well. The BCC calculation is restarted by the first STX or SOH character received after the direction of transmission is reversed (called a line turnaround). All characters except SYN characters received from that point until the next line turnaround are included in the calculation. If the message is sent in blocks with no line turnaround, each block will be followed by an ITB, then the BCC. The BCC calculation is then restarted with the next STX or SOH character received.

The Cyclic Redundancy Check codes are used for error checking in the same fashion as the LRC code. If the transmission code set is SBT, the CRC-12 method is used, since each transmitted character is only six bits. For EBCDIC, the CRC-16 scheme is always used. For the ASCII code set, IBM has specified that the VRC/LRC scheme be used in the nontransparency (standard) mode, and CRC-16 be used in transparency mode. Transparency mode is described in detail in the following.

Message Formats

Information is carried in BiSync as messages, and each message may have several parts: a synchronization sequence, a header, some text, and a block check sequence. Each part is identified by one or more control characters. In the case of messages used only for control, some parts such as the header, the text, or the BCC may be missing.

Synchronization

Establishing the synchronization required between sender and receiver requires a three step sequence: Bit synchronization, character synchronization, and message synchronization.

Unless the transmitter and receiver agree on the exact (to the bit) starting point of a message, they cannot communicate. Achieving this synchronization requires three steps:

1. The modems or other data communications devices at both ends of the circuit must acquire bit synchronization. The methods for doing this were discussed in Chapter 5.

2. The link interface equipment in the DTE must acquire character synchronization. This is done by searching the bit stream for a specific pattern of bits called a Synchronization Character (SYN). In

ASCII, the bit pattern for SYN is 0010110. To help insure against recognition of a false SYN, most systems including BiSync require transmission and detection of two successive SYNs before the next step in the synchronization process is taken. The two SYN characters taken as a control set are called a Sync Sequence, and are shown in most diagrams as a 0. In order to insure that the first and last characters of a transmission are correctly sent, some BiSync stations add a PAD character before the first SYN and after every BCC, EOT, and ACK. This stratagem was devised primarily to overcome hardware limitations in some early hard-wired BiSync terminals.

3. The program operating the protocol must acquire message synchronization. In other words, the program must be able to find the beginning of each message or control character sequence. This is achieved by a program search of the characters received after the sync sequence for a control character which is defined to begin a block of data or control sequence. Such characters are SOH, STX, ACK0/1, NAK, WACK, RVI, and EOT.

Heading

The character SOH begins the heading used in identifying the message type, numbering, priority and routing.

A heading is a sequence of characters beginning with the character SOH that is used for message type identification, message numbering, priority specification, and routing. Receipt of the SOH initiates accumulation of the BCC (but the SOH is not included in the BCC). The heading may be of fixed or variable length, and is ended by an STX.

Text

The text part of the message contains the information to be sent between application programs. The text begins with an STX and ends with an ETX. Text may be broken up into blocks for better error control. Each block begins with an STX and ends with an ETB, except for the last block which ends with an ETX. The normal end of a transmission is signaled by sending an EOT following the ETX. Control characters are not allowed within the body of a text block. If a control character is detected, the receiving station terminates reception and looks for a BCC as the next two characters.

Timeouts

Four BiSync time-outs functions prevent indefinite delays due to data errors or missing line turnaround signals.

Timeouts must be provided by the communications program or terminal to prevent indefinite delays caused by data errors or missing line turnaround signals. Four functions are specified in BiSync for timeouts: transmit, receive, disconnect, and continue.

Transmit timeout is normally set for one second, and defines the rate of insertion of synchronous idle (SYN SYN or DLE SYN) sequences in the data to help maintain bit and character synchronization.

Receive timeout is normally set for three seconds, and does several things:

1. It limits the time a transmitting station will wait for a reply.

2. It signals a receiving station to check the line for synchronous idle characters, which indicate that transmission is continuing. The receive timeout is reset each time a sync sequence is received.

3. It sets a limit on the time a tributary station in a multipoint circuit may remain in control mode. The timer is reset each time an end signal such as an ENQ or ACK is received as long as the station stays in control mode.

Disconnect timeout causes a station on a switched network to disconnect from the circuit after 20 seconds of inactivity.

Continue timeout causes a transmitting station sending a TTD to send another if it is still unable to send text. A receiving station must transmit a WACK if it becomes temporarily unable to receive within a two-second interval.

Transparent-Text Mode

Data communications often requires the sending of information that is in binary instead of in a character code. A transparent-text mode is used for this purpose.

It is often necessary in communicating between machines to send data that do not represent characters but instead represent some purely arbitrary quantity or object. An example is the binary representation of a computer program. In such a case, it is likely that some of the data will have the same bit pattern as a BiSync control character. Transparent-text mode, sometimes called transparency, allows such data to be sent without being misinterpreted by the communications program. The basic technique in transparency is to precede each true control character with the DLE character as Figure 8.9a shows. If a DLE bit pattern appears in the text of the message, it also is preceded by a DLE. Thus, a bit pattern is interpreted as a control character only if preceded by a DLE. The resulting message after processing by the link interface program to remove the DLE is shown in Figure 8.9b. Note that any DLE DLE sequence in the text has the first DLE suppressed and the second sent along as part of the data.

FULL-DUPLEX PROTOCOLS

On-line applications using CRT terminals required a protocol for full-duplex operations that contained a powerful error detection and correction system that prevented aliasing.

The Binary Synchronous Communications procedures were devised at a time when most data communications circuits were operated at 2400 bits per second, and were two-wire half-duplex circuits connecting remote job entry card reader/printer terminals to mainframes. As on-line applications using remote CRT terminals became more cost-effective, and four-wire private line circuits became available, the demand for a communications protocol that could handle full-duplex operations arose. The requirements for such a protocol were:

**Figure 8.9.
BiSync Transparency
Mode**

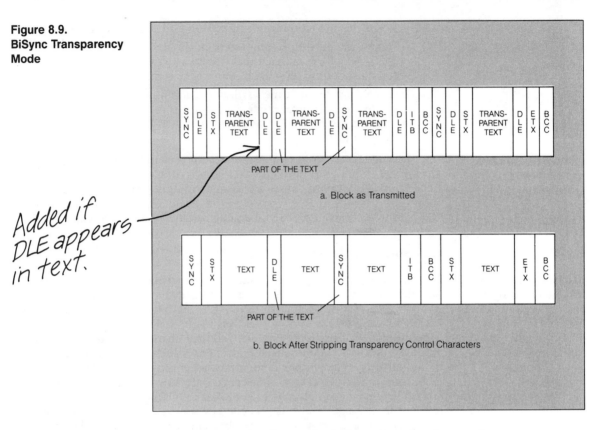

*Added if
DLE appears
in text.*

a. Block as Transmitted

b. Block After Stripping Transparency Control Characters

1. Messages must flow in both directions simultaneously.

2. It must be possible to have more than one message in the channel at one time (BiSync allows only one).

3. Transparency must be designed in, not tacked on as an afterthought.

4. The protocol must allow switched network, half-duplex, and multi-point operation, as well as full-duplex point-to-point.

5. The error detection and correction scheme must be powerful, and must prohibit the problem of aliasing.

The last condition is a particularly difficult one. *Aliasing* occurs when a message fragment caused by a transmission error is interpreted as a good message at the receiver; that is, when a bad or broken message "looks like" a good message. This can be a serious problem, especially in critical applications such as funds transfer and military command and control. Much design effort in the international standards organizations and in private companies was devoted to development of protocols that prevented the aliasing problem. This led to the development of three widely used schemes: two of them were alike in principle and operation and in requiring special hardware, but promulgated by different organizations. The third, developed at Digital Equipment Corporation, uses a different technique, but can operate with standard character-oriented line interface equipment.

High-Level Data Link Control Procedures

Protocols to prevent aliasing must determine where a true message block begins and ends and what part of the message is to be included in the CRC. HDLC is one of these.

The critical issue in preventing aliasing is the determination of where a legal message block begins and ends, and exactly what part of the information taken in by the receiver is to be included in the CRC. As a result of work done at IBM by J. Ray Kersey and others in the early 1970s, a protocol was proposed and later adopted as an international standard by the International Standards Organization in 1979. It is called the *High-level Data Link Control* (HDLC) procedures. In HDLC, the message synchronization indicator (called a Flag) is generated by a hardware circuit, and other hardware circuits prevent any data being transmitted from having the same pattern as the Flag. The Flag then becomes a kind of out-of-band framing signal, much like the break signal in the teletypewriter protocol.

Data is examined on a bit-by-bit basis in HDLC, thus, it is called a bit-oriented protocol.

Since the data being transmitted are examined on a bit-by-bit basis to screen out possible aliases of the Flag; HDLC and other similar protocols, such as IBM's *Synchronous Data Link Control* (SDLC), are referred to as *bit-oriented protocols*, or BOPs. Unlike BiSync and DDCMP (which will be described later) the text part of messages sent using the HDLC protocol may, in principle, be any arbitrary number of bits long, and HDLC is defined to allow this. In practice, like BiSync and DDCMP, most implementations of BOPs restrict the text (and in fact all of the message including the Flag) to be an integral multiple of the number of bits in a character (almost always eight).

In HDLC, all information is carried by frames that may be of three types: information frames (I-frames), supervisory control sequences (S-frames), or unnumbered command/responses (U-frames). Figure 8.10 shows one information frame as a rectangular block divided into its six fields: a beginning Flag (F1) field, an Address field (A), a Control field (C), an Information field (I), a Frame Check Sequence (FCS) field, and a final Flag (F2) field. S-frames and U-frames have the same fields except that the I field is left out.

I-frames perform information transfer, and independently carry message acknowledgements, and Poll or Final bits. S-frames perform link supervisory control such as message acknowledgements, retransmit requests, and requests for temporary holds on I-frame transmissions (like a WACK in BiSync). U-frames provide a flexible format for additional link control data by omitting the frame sequence numbers and thus providing a place for an additional 32 command and 32 response functions. The fields in the HDLC frame are used as follows:

Flag field: Every frame begins and ends with a Flag, which is the bit pattern 01111110. The same Flag may end one frame and begin the next. Every station connected to a link must continuously search the received data for the Flag.

Address field: In command frames, the address identifies the destination station for the command. In response frames, the address identifies the station sending the response.

Control field: The control field carries commands and responses, according to Table 8.3.

Figure 8.10.
HDLC Format *(Source: Stephen Bigelow Understanding Telephone Electronics, 1991, Sams, Division of Macmillan Computer Publishing)*

Each information frame is divided into six fields.

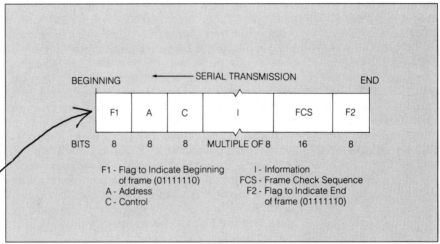

Table 8.3.
Control Field Contents

HDLC Frame Format	Bits in Control Field							
	1	2	3	4	5	6	7	8
I-frame (Information transfer commands/ responses)	0	N(S)[1]			P/F[2]	N(R)[3]		
S-frame (Supervisory commands/responses)	1	0	S[4]		P/F	N(R)		
U-frame (Unnumbered commands/responses)	1	1	M[5]		P/F	M		

Notes:

[1]N(S) is the transmitting station send sequence number, bit 2 is the low order bit.
[2]P/F is the Poll bit for primary station transmissions, and the final bit for secondary station transmissions.
[3]N(R) is the transmitting station receive sequence number, Bit 6 is the low-order bit.
[4]S are supervisory function bits.
[5]M are modifier function bits.

In HDLC, there are six fields in an information frame, but only five fields in other frames, which are supervisory control sequences or unnumbered command/responses.

Information field: The information field may contain any sequence of bits, which in principle need not be related to a particular character set or data structure. In practice, the information field is almost always an integral multiple of one character in length, which is usually eight bits.

Frame Check Sequence (FSC) field: The FSC (or CRC) for HDLC is the CCITT-CRC as previously discussed.

In order to ensure that the Flag is unique, the transmitting hardware must monitor the bit stream continually between the beginning and ending Flags for the presence of strings of five one-bits in a row. If such a string occurs, a zero-bit is inserted (called bit stuffing) by the hardware after the fifth one-bit so the string will not "look like" a Flag. The added zero-bit is removed at the receiver. This procedure makes any appearance of strings of one-bits greater than five in number either a Flag, an error on the transmission line, or a deliberately sent fill pattern between frames of all one-bits. One method of aborting transmission of a frame is to begin transmitting continuous ones.

Specification in the protocol of a unique, hardware-generated Flag pattern and the length of the Address, Control, and FCS fields provides complete transparency for the Information field. The hardware prevents any bit pattern sent by the applications program from having more than five continuous ones, and the hardware-added zeros are stripped from the data stream as it passes through the receiver. Also, the position of the FCS is defined by receipt of the ending Flag, so that the residual pattern in the CRC register can be immediately compared with the fixed value (0001110100001111).

A normal message sequence involves sending frames from a transmitting station (data source) to a receiving station (data sink), and having the receiving station acknowledge receipt of the transmission by sending a frame back to the sender.

The order of bit transmission is defined for addresses, commands, responses, and sequence numbers to be low-order bit first, but the order of bit transmission for the information field is not specified. The FCS is transmitted beginning with the coefficient of the highest order term (x^{15}). An invalid frame is defined as one that is not properly bounded by Flags, or is shorter than 32 bits between Flags. Invalid frames are ignored (in contrast with frames that have a bad FCS, which require a NAK).

HDLC Semantics

The preceding discussion dealt with what is called the syntax of HDLC. The syntax is the definition of the bit patterns and order of sending bits that will make correctly formed messages; that is, those that are legal in the protocol. In order to understand what happens when HDLC is used, however, it is necessary to define the semantic content of messages; that is, the meanings that should be assigned to correctly formed messages.

The normal sequence of messages in HDLC consists of the transfer of one or more frames containing I-fields from a data source (the transmitting station) to a data sink (the receiving station). The receipt is acknowledged by the sink by sending a frame in the backwards direction. The source must retain all transmitted messages until they are explicitly acknowledged by the sink. The value of N(R) indicates that the station transmitting the N(R) has correctly received all I-frames numbered up to N(R)-1. I-frames and S-frames (see Table 8.3) are numbered, the number going from 0 to 7 (for unextended control fields). An independent numbering sequence is carried for each data source/data sink combination. The response from a sink may acknowledge several (but not more than 7) received messages at one time, and may be contained in an I-frame being sent from the sink to the source.

A data link consists of two or more communicating stations, so for control purposes it is necessary to designate one station as the primary station, with responsibility for managing data flow and link error recovery procedures. Primary stations send command frames. Other stations on the link are called secondary stations, and they communicate using response frames. Primary stations can send to secondaries using the Select bit in the control field of an I-frame, or a primary may allow a secondary to send by sending a Poll bit.

Secondary stations may operate in one of two modes; a *Normal Response Mode* (NRM) or an *Asynchronous Response Mode* (ARM). In NRM, the secondary may send only in response to a specific request or permission by the primary station. The secondary station explicitly indicates the last frame to be sent by setting the final bit in the control field. In ARM, the secondary may independently initiate transmission without receiving an explicit permission or Poll from the primary.

Space does not permit covering HDLC in greater detail. The interested reader is referred to International Standards ISO 3309-1979 (E), ISO 4335-1979 (E), and ISO 6256-1981 for the complete definition of the HDLC protocol. There is a data link control procedure standard promulgated by the American National Standards Institute (ANSI) in the United States called *Advanced Data Communications Control Procedures* (ADCCP), which is functionally equivalent to HDLC.

Synchronous Data Link Control

SDLC developed by IBM has the same frame format and is similar in function to HDLC.

The standard full-duplex synchronous data link control protocol used by the IBM Corporation in products conforming to their System Network Architecture is called *Synchronous Data Link Control* (SDLC). It is functionally equivalent to HDLC, but with these exceptions:

1. SDLC information fields must be an integral multiple of 8 bits long.

2. Current IBM products support only the Unbalanced Normal operation with Normal Disconnected mode class or procedures as defined in ISO DIS 6159 and DIS 4335/DAD1.

3. SDLC contains additional commands and responses not defined in the ISO Elements of Procedure, for example, a TEST command and response. Figure 8.11 shows the frame structure of SDLC (which is the same as HDLC) along with the common modes, commands, and responses. A close examination of this illustration will help you understand the SDLC format and the differences between HDLC and SDLC.

Digital Data Communications Message Protocol

DDCMP is character oriented rather than bit oriented.

At about the same time SDLC was being developed at IBM, George Friend, Steven Russell, and Stuart Wecker were given the task of developing a synchronous protocol at Digital Equipment Corporation. The requirements were similar to those given before for full-duplex protocols, but with one important additional item: the protocol must run on existing data communications hardware, and preferably on asynchronous as well as synchronous links. The result was the Digital Data Communications Message Protocol, or DDCMP.

DDCMP is a character oriented protocol rather than a bit oriented protocol as is SDLC. Therefore, DDCMP requires no special bit stuffing and destuffing hardware and can be used with various types of line interfaces, including asynchronous units. The method of specifying the length of a message in order to look for the BCC at the right time is inclusion of a 14-bit count field in the header. This is a count of the number of characters in the information field of the message. Because error-free transmission depends on the count field being detected correctly, the header of DDCMP messages is a constant length and has its own BCC, which is checked before setting up to receive the information part of the message. The format of DDCMP messages is shown in Figure 8.12. A detailed study of this figure reveals the bit pattern of the various fields in the frame for different types of messages.

The DDCMP does not require any special hardware to perform successfully on synchronous, asynchronous, or parallel data channels.

DDCMP has two principal advantages and some disadvantages. One advantage is that it is usable without special hardware on asynchronous, synchronous, or even parallel data channels. Another advantage is that the sequence number field allows for up to 255 messages to be outstanding on the channel at one time, a requirement when operating full-duplex channels over satellite links. On the other hand, it does not support a go-back-N or selective reject mode of operation, and it is, in principle, more vulnerable to the aliasing problem than bit-oriented protocols. It also has been mistakenly criticized for inefficiency because of the inclusion of a BCC after the header on the equivalent of I-frames. In fact, for messages of average length, DDCMP is somewhat more efficient than bit-stuffing protocols because of the extra bits added by the hardware in the bit-oriented schemes. In practice, aliasing has not caused noticeable problems with DDCMP.

Figure 8.11.
SDLC Format *(Source: Kenneth Sherman, Data Communications: A User's Guide, © Reston Publishing Co., Reston, VA.)*

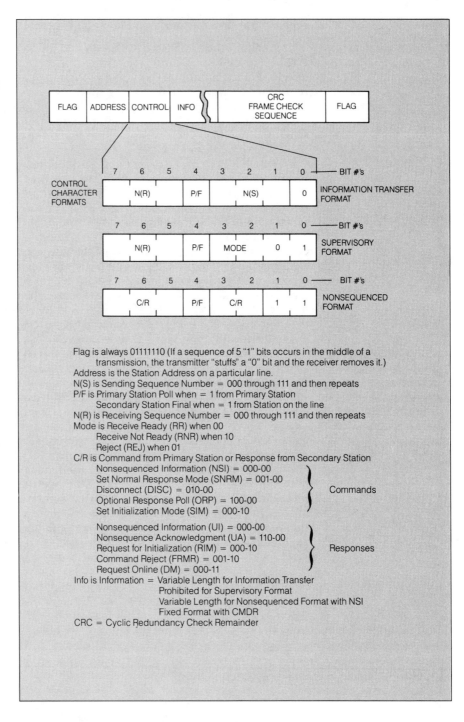

Flag is always 01111110 (If a sequence of 5 "1" bits occurs in the middle of a
transmission, the transmitter "stuffs" a "0" bit and the receiver removes it.)
Address is the Station Address on a particular line.
N(S) is Sending Sequence Number = 000 through 111 and then repeats
P/F is Primary Station Poll when = 1 from Primary Station
Secondary Station Final when = 1 from Station on the line
N(R) is Receiving Sequence Number = 000 through 111 and then repeats
Mode is Receive Ready (RR) when 00
Receive Not Ready (RNR) when 10
Reject (REJ) when 01
C/R is Command from Primary Station or Response from Secondary Station
Nonsequenced Information (NSI) = 000-00 ⎞
Set Normal Response Mode (SNRM) = 001-00 ⎟
Disconnect (DISC) = 010-00 ⎬ Commands
Optional Response Poll (ORP) = 100-00 ⎟
Set Initialization Mode (SIM) = 000-10 ⎠

Nonsequenced Information (UI) = 000-00 ⎞
Nonsequence Acknowledgment (UA) = 110-00 ⎟
Request for Initialization (RIM) = 000-10 ⎬ Responses
Command Reject (FRMR) = 001-10 ⎟
Request Online (DM) = 000-11 ⎠
Info is Information = Variable Length for Information Transfer
Prohibited for Supervisory Format
Variable Length for Nonsequenced Format with NSI
Fixed Format with CMDR
CRC = Cyclic Redundancy Check Remainder

Figure 8.12.
DDCMP Message
Format in Detail
(Source: John E.
MacNamara, Technical
Aspects of Data
Communication,
© 1977, Digital Press,
Maynard, MA.)

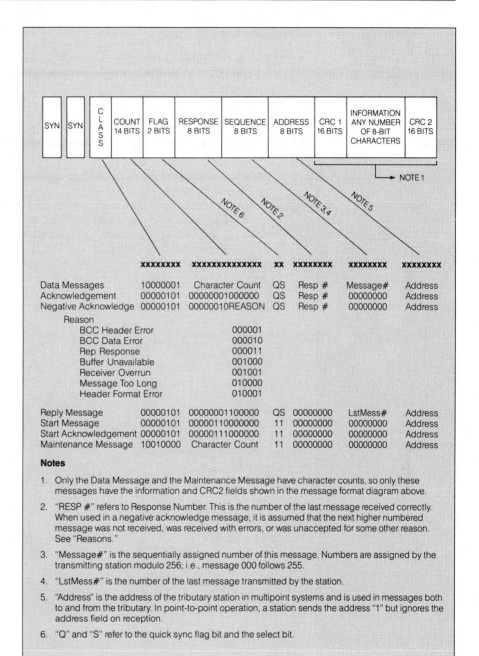

		XXXXXXXX	XXXXXXXXXXXXXX	XX	XXXXXXXX	XXXXXXXX	XXXXXXXX
Data Messages		10000001	Character Count	QS	Resp #	Message#	Address
Acknowledgement		00000101	00000001000000	QS	Resp #	00000000	Address
Negative Acknowledge		00000101	00000010REASON	QS	Resp #	00000000	Address

Reason

BCC Header Error	000001
BCC Data Error	000010
Rep Response	000011
Buffer Unavailable	001000
Receiver Overrun	001001
Message Too Long	010000
Header Format Error	010001

	XXXXXXXX	XXXXXXXXXXXXXX	XX	XXXXXXXX	XXXXXXXX	XXXXXXXX
Reply Message	00000101	00000001100000	QS	00000000	LstMess#	Address
Start Message	00000101	00000110000000	11	00000000	00000000	Address
Start Acknowledgement	00000101	00000111000000	11	00000000	00000000	Address
Maintenance Message	10010000	Character Count	11	00000000	00000000	Address

Notes

1. Only the Data Message and the Maintenance Message have character counts, so only these messages have the information and CRC2 fields shown in the message format diagram above.

2. "RESP #" refers to Response Number. This is the number of the last message received correctly. When used in a negative acknowledge message, it is assumed that the next higher numbered message was not received, was received with errors, or was unaccepted for some other reason. See "Reasons."

3. "Message#" is the sequentially assigned number of this message. Numbers are assigned by the transmitting station modulo 256; i.e., message 000 follows 255.

4. "LstMess#" is the number of the last message transmitted by the station.

5. "Address" is the address of the tributary station in multipoint systems and is used in messages both to and from the tributary. In point-to-point operation, a station sends the address "1" but ignores the address field on reception.

6. "Q" and "S" refer to the quick sync flag bit and the select bit.

WHAT HAVE WE LEARNED?

1. Protocols are rules for communications between processes that are alike. Interfaces are rules for communicating between processes that are different.
2. Data communications protocols are made up of symbols to be communicated, a code set translating those symbols to a binary code, and rules for the correct sequencing of the symbols.
3. Parity is a method of adding redundancy to coded symbols to help detect errors in transmission.
4. XMODEM is a simple protocol used in asynchronous transmission between microcomputers.
5. A Cyclic Redundancy Check is a number calculated from the data transmitted by the sender and recalculated by the receiver that allows the data to be checked for errors in transmission.
6. The most widely used code sets in the U.S.A. are ASCII and EBCDIC.
7. Protocols must be suitable for use on dial and private line connections, and for point-to-point and multipoint network arrangements.
8. The most widely used protocols in the U.S.A. are TTY, XMODEM, BiSync, SDLC, and DDCMP.

Quiz for Chapter 8

1. Communications protocols always have a:
  a. Set of symbols.
  b. Start of header.
  c. Special Flag symbol.
  d. BCC.

2. The Baudot code uses how many bits per symbol?
  a. 9
  b. 7
  c. 5
  d. 8

3. When transmitting odd-parity coded symbols, the number of bits that are zeros in each symbol is:
  a. Odd.
  b. Even.
  c. Unknown.
  d. None of the above.

4. In the XMODEM protocol, the sender waits for what character from the receiver before beginning transmission?
  a. WACK
  b. ACK
  c. RVI
  d. NAK

5. If each character in an XMODEM block has an ASCII value of 50 what would be the value of the checksum added to the block?
  a. 50
  b. 23
  c. 41
  d. 25

6. Which of the following is not a valid rule for XOR:
  a. 0 XOR 0 = 0
  b. 1 XOR 1 = 1
  c. 1 XOR 0 = 1
  d. B XOR B = 0

7. Which of the following BiSync control codes are not defined in the EBCDIC character set?
  a. STX
  b. ACK0
  c. ENQ
  d. TTD

8. How many messages may be outstanding (unacknowledged) on a BiSync link?
  a. 1
  b. 2
  c. 4
  d. 8

9. Which code set is used in BiSync when using VRC/LRC but not operating in transparency mode?
  a. EBCDIC
  b. ASCII
  c. SBT
  d. Fieldata

10. The escape character that identifies control characters in BiSync Transparency mode is:
  a. ESC
  b. SYN
  c. DLE
  d. RVI

11. One primary difference between DDCMP and SDLC is:

   a. DDCMP does not have a transparent mode.

   b. SDLC does not use a CRC.

   c. DDCMP has a message header.

   d. DDCMP does not require special hardware to find the beginning of a message.

Alternatives in Local Area Networks

ABOUT THIS CHAPTER

This chapter begins by describing the characteristics of an ideal local area network (LAN) and the major obstacles to achieving the ideal. The most common types of existing LAN architectures; contention-access based coaxial cable systems, token-passing systems, polled-access based coaxial cable systems, and frequency-division broadband systems, are discussed through examples of existing LANs. The chapter continues with a discussion of the application of digital telephone switching systems as LANs. These digital systems have been developed during the same time as the LANs and have the capability to provide many of the same services.

WHAT IS LAN?

A LAN is a data communications facility located within a single building or campus that provides all high-speed switched connections to its terminal processors and peripheral devices.

In its most basic form, a LAN is a data communication facility providing high-speed switched connections between processors, peripherals, and terminals within a single building or campus. Historically, LANs have evolved from the data processing or office processing industry where economics suggest relatively expensive storage devices and printers should be shared by multiple computers. Thus, LANs have evolved partly in response to the emergence of low-cost computing and its need for high-cost peripherals. Indeed, the first generation LANs were actually one form of distributed computer systems using proprietary high-speed data links between processing nodes and peripheral equipment.

LAN Versus Other Techniques

A perspective of a local area network as a digital communications facility is shown in Figure 9.1, which depicts the bandwidth versus distance capabilities of three data communications technologies: computer buses, voiceband data links, and LANs. The computer buses are internal to a computer mainframe and achieve very high data transfers by using high clock rates (for example, a few MHz) and parallel transmission (for example, 32 bits per clock cycle). Such systems are economical and practical only at distances up to a few meters. Voiceband data transmission uses readily available telephone wire pairs with modems. These systems are virtually unlimited in distance, but the standard analog telephone channel usually restricts voiceband data rates to 19,200 bps for leased lines or 9600 bps for switched (dial-up) connections. From a cost effectiveness point of view, 1200 and 2400 bps are very popular for dial-up data communications.

**Figure 9.1.
Distance Versus Data
Rate Comparison**

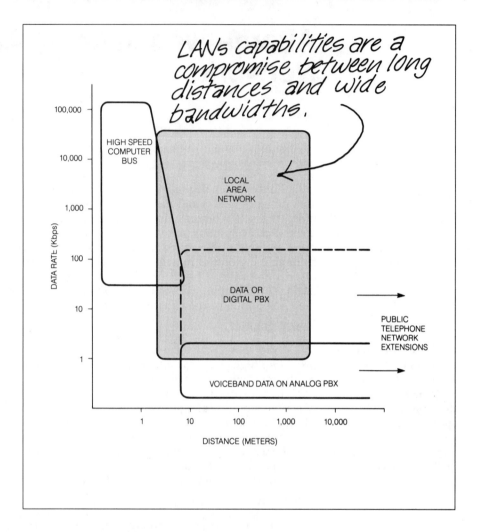

Each of the three data communications technologies have their own particular strengths and weaknesses when considering bandwidth vs. distance trade-offs.

As can be seen in Figure 9.1, the capabilities of a typical LAN represent a compromise between long distances and wide bandwidths. Some computer architectures have moved in on the region occupied by LANs by moving away from high-speed parallel buses to more loosely coupled distributed systems. Thus, the LAN region is overlapped on the left edge by distributed computer systems. Similarly, newly developing digital telephone systems are overlapping the LAN region on the bottom by providing moderate data rates (up to a few hundred kilobits per second) as a low-cost addition to basic telephone service.

The distance versus data rate aspect of a local area network depicted in Figure 9.1 actually represents only one level of definition of a LAN. As the market and technology have grown, so has the recognition that a LAN should solve or alleviate more problems pertaining to data communications than merely the data transmission problem. The data communications manager or service organization responsible for a particular building or campus is typically concerned with a variety of applications and associated types of equipment. If these different applications can be supported by one transmission facility, one type of hardware and software interface, and one set of maintenance procedures, total systems costs are reduced and overall administration is greatly simplified. For example, Figure 9.2, illustrates a local area network serving several independent applications.

The next section presents the attributes of an ideal local area network—one that is *all* supportive of *all* applications. In the succeeding sections, present day LANs are described and compared to the ideal as a means of contrasting one type of LAN to another.

THE IDEAL LAN

The ideal LAN should provide the same ease of access and equipment utilization that is found in a building's ac circuit.

The ideal LAN would be an information distribution system that is as easy to use as the conventional ac power distribution system in a building. Thus, adding a data terminal, processor, or peripheral to a local area network should require nothing more than plugging it into a conveniently located access port. Once plugged in, it should communicate intelligently with any other device on the network. This ideal system is summarized by the features that make the ac power system so easy to use:

1. One-time installation.
2. Widespread access.
3. Application independence.
4. Excess capacity.
5. Easy maintenance and administration.

The features identified in this list have been developed over the years to minimize life cycle costs for supplying ac power within a building. Although the costs of a typical installation can be reduced by wiring only to locations with immediate electrical needs, the costs of only small amounts of rewiring to supply additional locations at a later date would more than offset the initial savings. In order to achieve a one-time installation, it is necessary to provide widespread access; that is, an electrical outlet at virtually every location where one may be needed. Furthermore, the capacity at every outlet is generally greater than the needs of the electrical appliances that connect to it. Adding wiring or rewiring becomes necessary only for particularly high-power consuming devices (for example, those needing 240 volts or dedicated, high-current circuits).

If an information distribution system were available with all the desirable properties listed in the preceding, it would mean that

**Figure 9.2.
Local Area Network
Supporting Multiple
Independent
Applications**

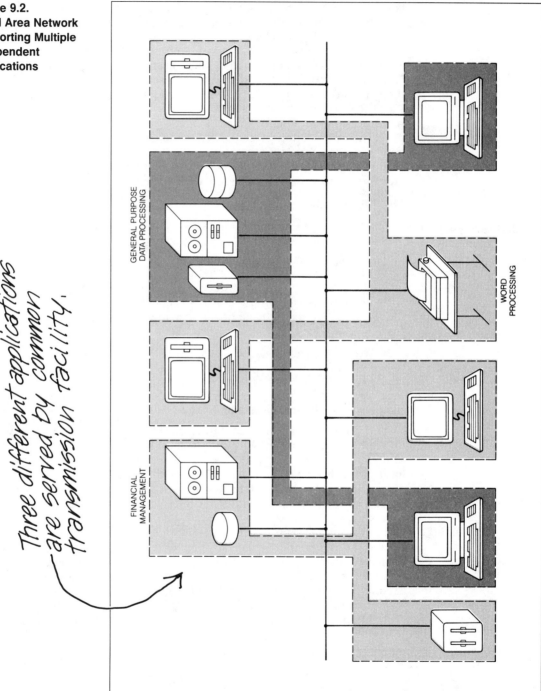

*Three different applications
are served by common
transmission facility.*

telephones, data terminals, printers, and storage devices could be moved as easily as unplugging and plugging in a lamp. Moreover, the equipment could be supplied by a variety of vendors. Although such an ideal system does not now exist, local area networks of several forms represent some of the first steps in the development of such a system.

Major Obstacles to the Ideal LAN

There are four major obstacles that must be overcome in the development of the ideal LAN.

The major obstacles to overcome in the development of the ideal system are summarized in the following:

No Single Standard

Due to the continually changing status of LANs and competitive nature of the vendors, a variety of local area network standards exist—both official and de facto. The situation is improving, however, because even the dominant suppliers who have been protecting their proprietary interfaces are being pressured by a maturing market to release interface specifications.

Diverse Requirements

The communications needs of a modern office building include voice, video, high-speed data, low-speed data, energy management, fire alarm, security, electronic mail, etc. These systems present transmission requirements that vary greatly in terms of data rates, acceptable delivery delays, reliability requirements, and error rate tolerance.

Costly Transmission Media

Being able to deliver tens of megabits per second to one device and only a few thousand bits per second to another implies that the lower rate devices are burdened with a costly transmission media. The best economic solution must involve a hierarchical network design (one with stepped levels of capacity) that allows twisted pair connections for low and medium data rate devices (a low step) feeding into a backbone high bandwidth transmission system (a higher step) such as coaxial cable or optical fibers.

Sophisticated Functional Requirements

Providing a network with the desired data rates and distances is only one item that must be considered in the data communications problem. Before one data device can communicate intelligently with another, numerous higher level communications functions must be compatible. These include codes, formats, error control, addressing, routing, flow control, access control, configuration management, and cost allocations.

The ISO Model

A formal hierarchical identification of all data communications network functions has been established by the International Standards

Organization (ISO) and referred to as the *ISO Model for Open Systems Interconnection* (OSI). This model, shown in Figure 9.3, identifies seven distinct levels of functional requirements pertaining to data communications networks. The lower three levels of this model were originally proposed by CCITT to encourage vendor commonality in interfacing to public packet switching networks. This standard, designated as the CCITT recommendation X.25, is described in detail in Chapter 10, along with the ISO model.

**Figure 9.3.
ISO Model for Open Systems
Interconnection**

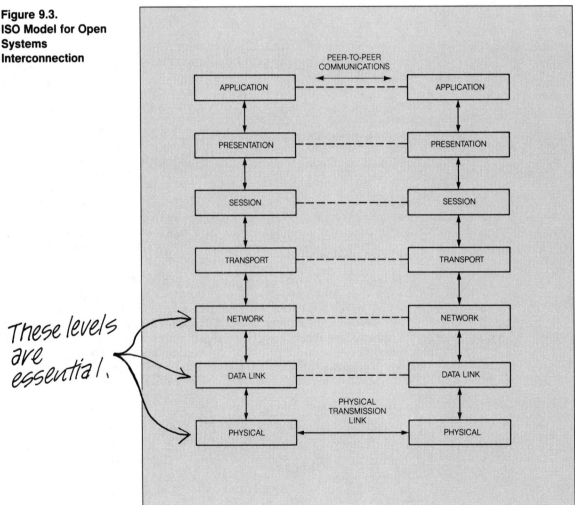

These levels are essential.

A formal data communications hierarchy model containing seven levels of functional requirements has been established by the Internal Standards Organization.

Realization of the ideal LAN would require all levels of functions included in the OSI standard; however, not all levels of the OSI standard need to be implemented to provide effective communications in a LAN. If only the lower levels of the standard exist, a LAN can usefully support the multiple applications shown in Figure 9.2. In essence, the transmission media and lower level interfaces are common so that data can be exchanged within virtual subnetworks; for example, the financial management group indicated in Figure 9.2. However, a device in one subnetwork cannot communicate intelligently with a device in another subnetwork because each application is using unique higher level implementations. This LAN would allow messages to be exchanged between these dissimilar terminals, but the message would not be understood. Nevertheless, the backbone LAN permits flexible location and relocation of the various attached equipment.

ETHERNET (CSMA/CD)

Ethernet, which uses baseband coaxial cable as its carrier medium, was a joint effort by Xerox, Digital Equipment, and Intel and was the first commercially available LAN.

Although the Ethernet was not the first data communications network to technically qualify as a local area network, it is the most important because it represents the first major product offering with nonproprietary communications interfaces and protocols. Using an experimental design developed in a Xerox Corporation research laboratory; Xerox, Digital Equipment, and Intel teamed to define some commercial products based upon jointly published communications standards. This action has invited other manufacturers to develop compatible products. The marketing strategy has been successful enough to establish the Ethernet interface as a standard even on systems utilizing transmission media different from the baseband coaxial cable used in the Ethernet.

The Ethernet architecture is based in concept on the Aloha satellite communications network developed at the University of Hawaii. The Aloha system allows multiple distributed devices to communicate with each other over a single radio channel using a satellite as a transponder. One station communicates with another by waiting until the radio channel is idle (determined by carrier sensing) and then sending a packet of data with a destination address, source address, and redundant check bits to detect transmission errors. All idle stations continuously monitor incoming data and accept those packets with their address and valid check sums. Whenever a station receives a new packet, the receiving station returns an acknowledgement to the source. If an originating station receives no acknowledgement within a specified time interval, it retransmits the packet under the assumption that the previous packet was interfered with by noise or by a transmission from another station at the same time. (The latter situation is referred to as a collision.) The Ethernet employs the same basic system concept using coaxial cable distribution throughout a building or campus.

Physical Layer

The transmission media of the Ethernet was originally restricted to the use of conventional "thick" coaxial cable using baseband transmission at 10 Mbps. Other media now used for Ethernet transmission includes "thin" coaxial cable and twisted-pair wire. Both types of coaxial cable media support the use of a bus technology, while the use of twisted-pair wire requires the use of a star topology for an Ethernet LAN. Baseband transmission implies data is transmitted without the use of a carrier and with only one channel defined in the system. When a station is transmitting, it uses the entire 10-Mbps capacity of the system. Data are encoded using a Manchester code as shown in Figure 9.4. This line code provides a strong timing component for clock recovery because a timing transition always occurs in the middle of every bit. In this type of coding, each bit period is divided into two complementary halves—a negative-to-positive voltage transition in the middle of the bit period designates a binary "1," while a positive-to-negative transition represents a binary "0." The Manchester line code has the additional property of always maintaining equal amounts of positive and negative voltages. This prevents the build-up of a dc component which simplifies the implementation of decision thresholds in the data detectors.

**Figure 9.4.
Manchester Line Code**

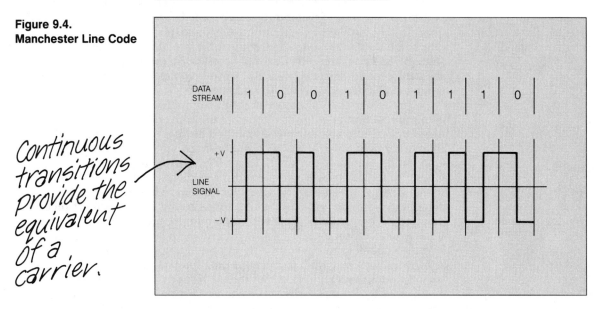

Continuous transitions provide the equivalent of a carrier.

The Manchester Code provides a form of carrier in its continuous transition. Multiple stations can enter or leave the line without causing traffic interruptions by using passive taps.

Although the data are not transmitted with a carrier per se, the continuous transitions of the Manchester code provide the equivalent of a carrier so the channel is easily monitored for activity (for example, by a carrier sense technique). Multiple access to the coaxial cable is provided by passive taps, thereby allowing station connections (called drops) to be added or removed without disrupting traffic in the system.

Another requirement of the transmission link and its associated access electronics is that, while transmitting, a transceiver must be capable of detecting the existence of another active transmitter. This is referred to as collision detection. Thus, the three basic steps for accessing an Ethernet are denoted CSMA/CD for: Carrier Sense, Multiple Access with Collision Detection.

The ability to detect collisions allows colliding stations to release the channel after using it for only a short period of time. A conventional Aloha system (one without collision detection), on the other hand, transmits entire messages without knowing if a collision has occurred. Because an Ethernet station checks for carrier presence before transmitting, collisions occur only if two stations begin transmitting within a time interval equal to the propagation delay between the stations. By restricting the maximum distance between transceivers to 2500 meters, the collision window is limited to 23 microseconds (μs) including amplifier delays.

Once a station begins transmitting, it can be sure that no collision will occur if none is detected within a round-trip propagation time of 46.4 μs. Since one bit time is 0.1 μs at 10 Mbps, the collision detection decision is made within 464 bit times. The maximum length of a frame is 12,144 bits, thus the collision detection feature will detect a collision very early in the frame to save significant transmission time that would be wasted if the entire frame were transmitted before detection.

A transceiver must be able to detect any other active transmitters on the line while it is transmitting. This is collision detection.

Whenever a collision occurs, all colliding stations detect the condition and wait individually random amounts of time before retrying the transmission. Thus, the stations do not wait for acknowledgement time outs to trigger a retransmission. (Acknowledgements are unnecessary at this level of the protocol, but may be used at a higher level to ensure that the message was received at the final destination.) By waiting random amounts of time before transmitting, the probability of repeated collisions is reduced. In heavy traffic conditions, the average delay before retransmission begins to increase after 10 unsuccessful attempts. After 16 collisions, no further attempts are made to transmit that message and the station is notified of the error by the transceiver.

In preparation for transmitting a data frame, the physical layer must insert a 64-bit preamble so that all receivers on the network can synchronize to the data stream before the desired data frame begins. The preamble consists of alternating 1s and 0s, ending in two 1s to signify the start of a frame.

Physical Layer Interface

Standard Ethernet transceiver cable connectors are 15-pin D-shell connectors (MIL-C-24308 or equivalent). The transceiver has a male connector while the station apparatus has a female connector, thus, the interconnecting cable must have one of each type. The pin assignments are:

1.	Shield	9.	Collision Presence −
2.	Collision Presence +	10.	Transmit −
3.	Transmit +	11.	Reserved
4.	Reserved	12.	Receive −
5.	Receive +	13.	Power
6.	Power return	14.	Reserved
7.	Reserved	15.	Reserved
8.	Reserved		

Data Link Layer

The data link is concerned with message frame format, message addressing, and error checking; and as such is largely independent of the medium-dependent physical channel.

The data link layer is primarily concerned with message packaging and link management. It is largely independent of the medium-dependent physical channel. The message packaging function includes:

1. *Framing:* Identifying the beginning and end of a message.
2. *Addressing:* Specified fields for source and destination addresses.
3. *Error checking:* Redundant codes for detecting channel errors.

The format of a frame is shown in Figure 9.5. The preamble is not shown because its generation and removal are functions of the physical layer. Similarly, the end of a frame is provided by the removal of the carrier sense signal detected by the absence of a bit transition following the last bit of the cyclic redundancy code (CRC). Notice that frame sizes must be an integral number of bytes, ranging from 64 to 1518 bytes. (At 8 bits per byte, that's 512 to 12,144 bits). The TYPE field is reserved to indicate which of several possible higher level protocols might be in use.

System Configurations

By using point-to-point cables and repeaters, several multidrop segments can be connected to add flexibility to Ethernet systems.

Besides the single cable system indicated in Figure 9.3, other Ethernet configurations are possible where several multidrop segments (possibly one in each of several buildings) are interconnected with point-to-point cables and repeaters. Figure 9.6 shows a typical configuration of a multisegment system. The following specifications apply:

1. Maximum Lengths:
   1500 meters of multidrop cable.
   1000 additional meters of point-to point cable between cable segments.

300 additional meters in six transceiver cables.
50 meters in a single transceiver cable.

2. Maximum Number of Stations:
    1024

Another series of configurations is obtainable through the use of 10Base-T, which is a more modern standard which allows the construction of 10-Mbps Ethernet LANs over unshielded twisted-pair wire. Under the 10Base-T standard, which is also referred to as IEEE 802.3i standard, workstations are cabled using twisted-pair wire to *medium access units* (MAUs). Each MAU normally has a built-in *attachment interface unit* (AIU) which can be cabled to a coaxial transceiver attached to a coaxial cable. Thus, workstations can be configured in a star topology and cabled to a bus structured backbone cable that serves to interconnect MAUs. Figure 9.7 illustrates a hybrid Ethernet media configuration in which personal computer workstations are cabled to MAUs via the use of twisted-pair wire. The MAUs, in turn, are connected to a coaxial cable which not only links MAUs, but, in addition, provides access to a mainframe computer.

Other CSMA/CD Systems

Besides the Ethernet, numerous other LANs have been developed by personal computer manufacturers using CSMA/CD for network access. Most of these systems have focused on supporting communications between personal computers and utilize both coaxial cables and twisted pair for transmission media. Various broadband LANs (discussed in a later section) also support CSMA/CD access on one or more rf channels.

**Figure 9.5.
Ethernet Data Link
Frame Format**

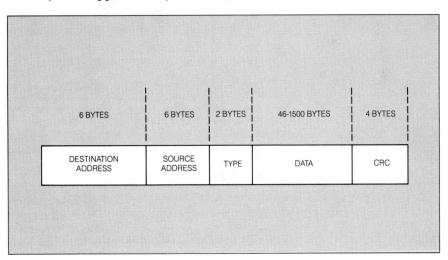

6 BYTES	6 BYTES	2 BYTES	46-1500 BYTES	4 BYTES
DESTINATION ADDRESS	SOURCE ADDRESS	TYPE	DATA	CRC

Figure 9.6.
A Typical Large-Scale
Ethernet Configuration
(Source: Ethernet
Specification
Version 2.0)

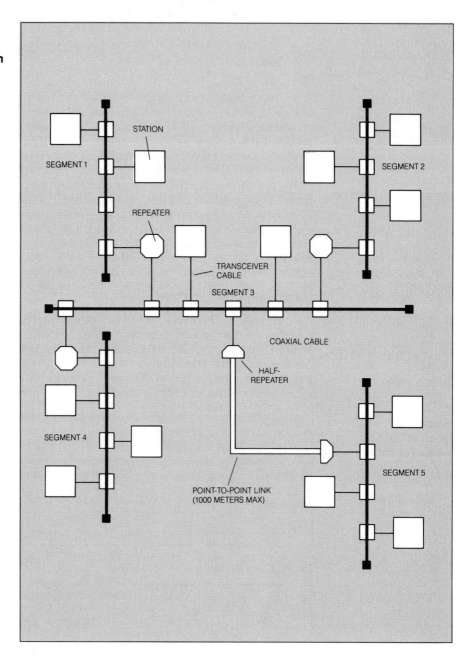

**Figure 9.7.
Hybrid Ethernet Media
Configuration.**

Legend:

PCW = personal computer workstation

AIU = attachment interface unit

CT = coaxial transceiver

TOKEN PASSING NETWORKS

Token passing networks provide access to the network by only one station at a time; the one with the token that is ready to send a message.

Because access to a CSMA network involves a certain amount of contention (competition) between stations trying to send a message at the same time, the behavior of the network must be analyzed and controlled in a statistical manner. Token passing networks, on the other hand, provide a different access procedure. Access is determined by which station has the token; that is, only one station at a time, the one with the token, is given the opportunity to seize the channel. The token is passed from one idle station to another until a station with a pending message receives it. After the message is sent, the token is passed to the next station. In essence, a token passing network is a distributed polling network.

Token topologies can be either a token passing ring or a token passing bus; each has its own peculiar strengths and weaknesses.

Two basic topologies (configurations or arrangements) exist for token passing networks: Token Passing Rings and Token Passing Buses. In a token passing ring, shown in Figure 9.8, the closed loop topology defines the logical topology (that is, the order in which the token is circulated). A token passing bus, shown in Figure 9.9, has more operational flexibility because the token passing order is defined by tables in each station. If a station (for example, a printer) never originates communications, it will be a terminate-only station and need not be in the polling sequence. If a station needs a high priority, it can appear more than once in the polling sequence.

Figure 9.8.
Token Passing Ring

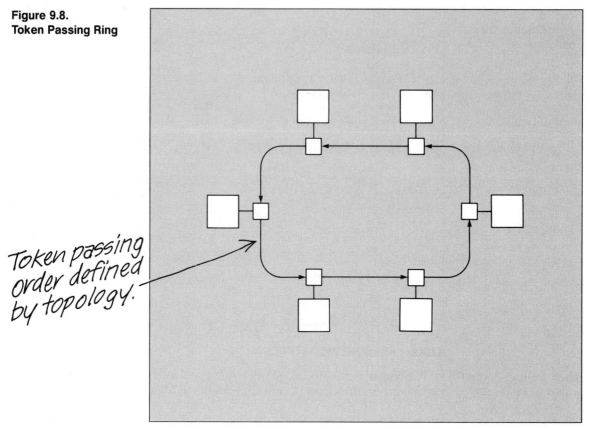

Token passing order defined by topology.

Besides the operational differences between bus and ring topologies, other major contrasts are:

1. A ring requires an active interface module in series with the transmission link. A bus uses a passive tap like a CSMA system.

2. The point-to-point nature of a ring's transmission links implies the signal quality is easily controlled. Multiple taps in a linear bus system, on the other hand, each contribute to signal distortions.

3. A ring has no inherent (built-in) distance limitation (as does the bus) because there is no delay dependence in its operation, and the access taps at each station serve as regenerative repeaters to the digital signals.

4. A bus allocates the entire channel to an active device. The channel of a ring can be subdivided into time division multiplexed subchannels for time continuous lower data rate applications. Figure 9.10 shows a ring with time division multiplexed subchannels. Such a system is also referred to as a loop, and typically requires a unique control node to define framing for the subchannels. Access to the TDM channels is distributed by passing tokens.

5. The ring topology is ideally suited to the particular capabilities of fiber optic transmission. As discussed in a previous chapter, optical fibers provide very wide bandwidth and complete elimination of electrical interference, but they are presently practical only as point-to-point transmission links.

ARCNET

ARCNet is a type of token passing bus. Its topology is a hybrid bus/star.

The forerunner of token passing networks in the U.S. is the Attached Resource Computer Network, ARCNet, developed by Datapoint Corporation. Initially, the network and protocol were kept proprietary, but the data link protocol, interface specs, and even integrated circuits were made publicly available in 1982. Functionally, the ARCNet is a token passing bus, but the physical topology, shown in Figure 9.11, is a hybrid bus/star. Rather than distribute taps along a linear bus as suggested in Figure 9.9, the ARCNet uses hubs with individual ports to connect *Resource Interface Modules* (RIMs) to the transmission media.

Figure 9.9. Representative Access Sequence in Token Passing Bus

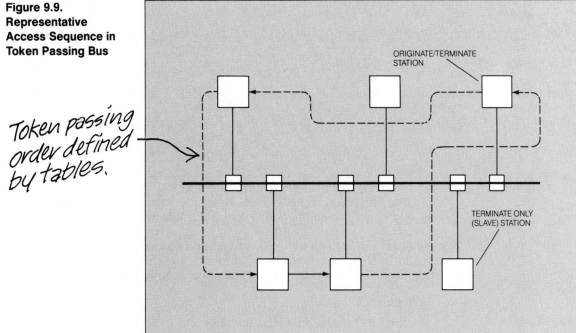

Token passing order defined by tables.

ORIGINATE/TERMINATE STATION

TERMINATE ONLY (SLAVE) STATION

**Figure 9.10.
Time Division
Multiplex Loop**

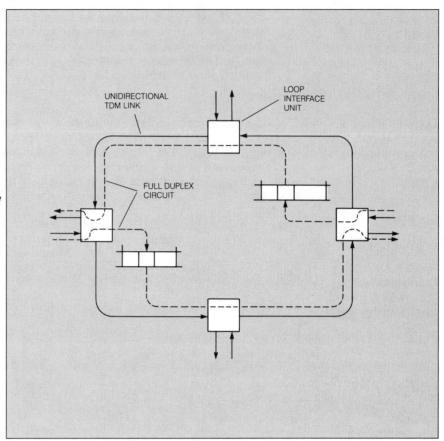

*Access to
TDM channels
is distributed
by passing
tokens.*

The hub based architecture is an effective means of controlling the signal quality because the hub isolates each RIM port from the main coaxial cable. Unidirectional (one-way) amplifiers in the hubs provide zero insertion loss and suppress reflections because only one direction of transmission is enabled at a time. Amplifier switching is possible because a token passing network only transmits in one direction at a time.

Physical Layer

The ARCNet interconnects the hubs and RIMs with RG62 coaxial cable using baseband transmission at 2.5 Mbps. Although 2.5 Mbps is a relatively low data rate. ARCNet uses inexpensive coax and can be configured (laid out) with as much as four miles between stations. The

RG62 coaxial cables with a baseband transmission rate of 2.5 Mbps are used to connect the hubs and RIMs in a ARCNet.

**Figure 9.11.
Representative
ARCNet Configuration**

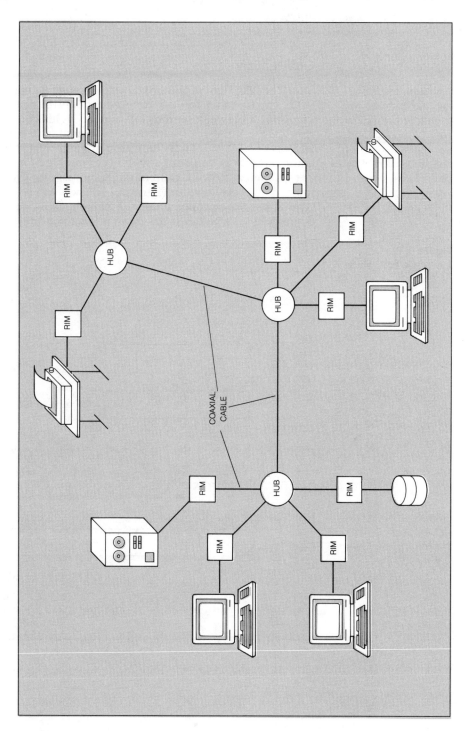

cable length between a hub and a RIM is limited to 2000 feet, but a four-mile span can have up to a maximum of ten hubs in a series path.

Link Protocol

There are five basic message formats used in link protocol: four control message and one data carrier. Eight bits are used in all address fields.

The ARCNet employs five basic message formats as shown in Figure 9.12. The first four formats are used for control messages while the fifth carries data between stations. All address fields consist of 8 bits which restricts the number of stations to 255 (address 0 is reserved as a broadcast address to all stations). As indicated in Figure 9.12, the destination address (DID) is duplicated with every message for error protection.

A logical flow diagram of the token passing procedure implemented in every RIM is shown in Figure 9.13. Upon receiving a token (message type 1) with the proper address, a RIM chooses one of two paths, depending on whether it has transmit data pending. If data are pending,

**Figure 9.12.
Message Formats in
ARCNet**

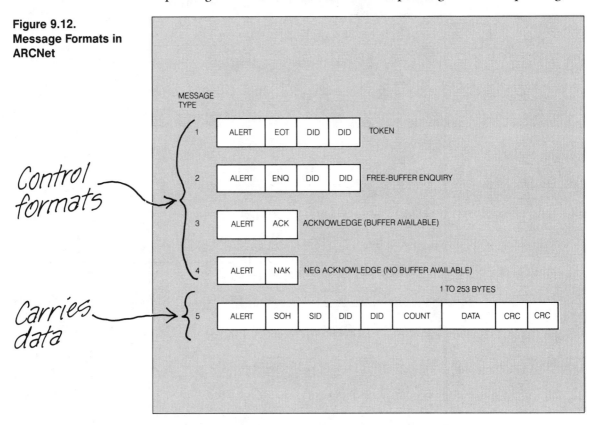

the RIM sends a free-buffer request (message type 2) to the desired destination RIM inquiring whether it is ready to receive. The destination RIM responds with an ACK (message type 3) if it has buffer space available, or a NAK (message type 4) if it does not.

Figure 9.13.
Flow Diagram of
Token Passing
Procedure in ARCNet

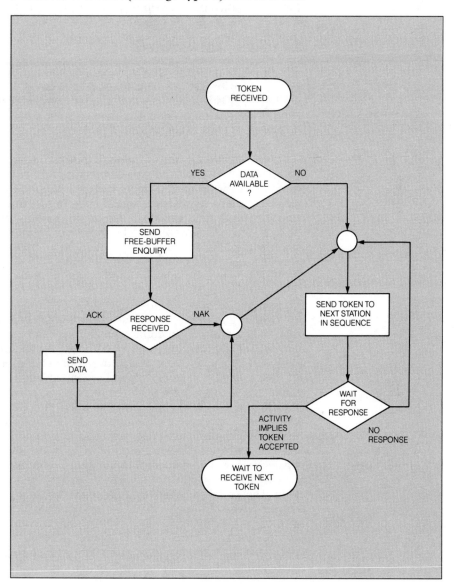

After a RIM has transmitted its data or determined that it cannot, it passes the token to the station with the next higher address. After sending the token, the RIM monitors the channel to see if it is accepted. The occurrence of a message type 1, 2, or 5 indicates the token is accepted. No response on the channel within 74 μs implies the intended station is off-line and the token should be passed to the station with the next higher address.

IBM TOKEN-RING NETWORK

In the mid-1980s, IBM introduced its token-ring network based upon the use of token passing. This token-ring network uses a logical ring topology that is physically wired as a star, with workstations connected to a wiring concentrator known as a *multistation access unit* (MAU). MAUs are cabled to each other to form a ring, in effect resulting in a star-ring topology for the token-ring network.

Figure 9-14 illustrates the wiring of workstations to each MAU. Each workstation uses a twisted-pair connection for ''ring-in'' and a second twisted pair for ''ring-out,'' with the data flowing from station to station in one direction to represent a logical ring. In addition to functioning as a central wiring point, the MAU also controls access of each workstation to the LAN. This is accomplished by the use of relays in each MAU port, enabling the MAU to simply short the relay to bypass a workstation. To obtain access to the LAN a workstation raises a 5-volt signal which causes the MAU to open the relay on the port and add the workstation to the ring. This technique enables all inactive stations on a ring to be automatically bypassed which serves to maximize LAN performance.

Although three networks are shown connected to one MAU in Figure 9.14, in actuality, up to eight workstations can be connected. A token-ring network is expanded to support additional workstations through the use of additional MAUs, with the MAUs interconnected to form a ring.

IBM, as well as several third-party manufacturers, produce token-ring adapter cards that can be installed in personal computers to allow PCs to be cabled to MAUs. The original IBM token-ring network operated at 4 Mbps and supported a maximum of 72 device connections which is the equivalent of interconnecting nine MAUs. This network for which 4-Mbps token-ring adapter cards are used in PCs can use shielded or unshielded twisted-pair wiring. A second IBM token-ring network operates at 16 Mbps and extends the support of devices to 250 but requires the use of shielded cable. The 16-Mbps network requires the use of 16-Mbps token-ring adapter cards. Although IBM and third-party manufacturers market 4/16-Mbps token-ring adapters that can operate at either data rate, all devices on a LAN must be set to operate at either 4 or 16 Mbps. This means that users migrating from a 4-Mbps token-ring network to 16 Mbps must change all adapters for the LAN to operate at the higher rate.

Bridges

Bridges are devices that connect LANs at the ISO data-link level. In a token-ring network, a local bridge can be used to connect two adjacent

**Figure 9.14.
Wiring Workstations to
a MAU**

token-ring LANs into one LAN. One example of a local bridge is an IBM PS/2 Model 55 personal computer containing two token-ring adapter cards, with each card cabled to the MAU of a local token-ring network. Figure 9.15 illustrates the use of a local bridge to connect two token-ring networks.

Local and remote bridges can be used to interconnect LANs

A second type of bridge is a remote bridge. This type of bridge is used to connect token-ring networks located at a distance from one another that requires interconnection via the use of a communications carrier transmission facility. When two LANs are connected by remote bridging, a remote bridge must be installed on each LAN. In place of a second token-ring adapter, each remote bridge would contain a serial communications port, allowing the device to be connected to a modem or a DSU/CSU, which, in turn, would be connected to an analog or digital transmission facility. The remote bridge examines addressing information in each token-ring frame and upon recognition of an address on the distant LAN routes the frame via the serial port of the device onto the communications carrier transmission facility linking the remote LANs together. Figure 9.16 illustrates the use of remote bridges to interconnect two LANs located remotely from one another.

Figure 9.15.
Using a Local Bridge

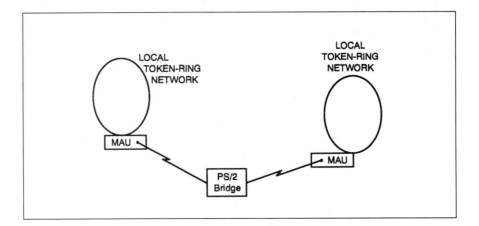

Figure 9.16.
Using Remote Bridges

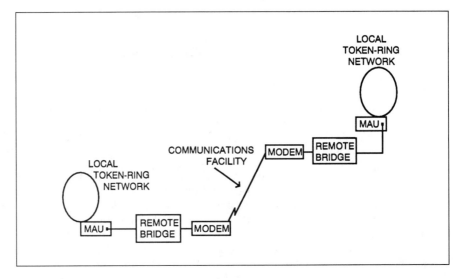

Gateways

To provide an interconnection capability for accessing mainframe computers, IBM markets several products that can be equipped with token-ring adapters and function as gateway devices. Two examples of such products are the IBM 3174 control unit with *token-ring adapter* (TRA) and the IBM 3725 *token-ring interface coupler* (TIC). The 3174 control unit can be located locally or remotely from a mainframe computer and allows up to 32 terminal devices to share access to the mainframe over a common cable or transmission facility. When equipped with a TRA the 3174 can serve as a local or remote LAN gateway for accessing an IBM mainframe.

Since the maximum data rate of a 3174 is 56 kbps, the use of a TRA on that device can result in degraded performance if too many LAN users attempt to access the mainframe simultaneously. To provide an increased level of gateway access the IBM 3725 *front-end processor* (FEP) can be equipped with a TIC which allows the FEP to be directly connected to a 4-or 16-Mbps token-ring network. Figure 9.17 illustrates several methods by which the IBM 3174 control unit and the IBM 3725 front-end processor can provide token-ring network users with access to an IBM mainframe computer.

**Figure 9.17.
Gateway Access to an
IBM Mainframe**

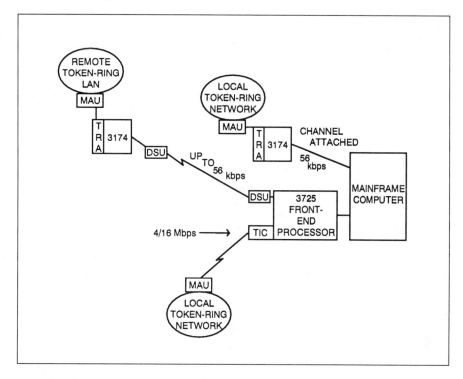

BROADBAND NETWORKS

Frequency division multiplexing over wide bandwidth coaxial cables is used by broadband local area networks to transmit on multiple channels. This technique was developed by the cable TV industry.

Broadband local area networks use wide bandwidth coaxial cables with frequency division multiplexing (FDM) to establish multiple channels within a system. The FDM channels are typically 6 MHz wide following the standards and technology developed by the CATV (cable TV) industry. Since the usable bandwidth of a CATV cable is 300 to 400 MHz, there can be as many as 50 to 60 separate channels. Often separate FDM channels are used for separate applications.

The power and attraction of a broadband network is evident in Figure 9.18. Notice that the transmission system supports not only a data network, but also closed-circuit TV distribution, point-to-point voice telephone circuits, and point-to-point data circuits.

Use of a broadband system for data transmission requires modems in the physical interface equipment. If the modems are assigned to a fixed frequency (channel), the associated station can communicate only with other stations assigned to the same frequency. If frequency agile modems (modems that have a tuner to allow changing channels) are used, the stations can switch between the FDM channels to gain access to much larger networks.

Physical Layer

Single-cable systems use a dual-frequency architecture; one frequency for sending, one for receiving on the same cable.

Broadband LAN systems utilize either one or two cables routed to every station. Single-cable systems are patterned after customary CATV systems where the FDM channels are separated into two groups as shown in Figure 9.19. One group of frequencies carries signals from the transmitter of all station interfaces to a frequency translation module referred to as the head end. The head end amplifies the received signals and shifts them to the second group of frequencies, whereupon they travel back along the cable to the receivers of every station interface. Thus, a single channel in a functional sense requires a pair of FDM channels in a physical sense. The dual-frequency architecture permits the use of unidirectional amplifiers as shown in Figure 9.19.

An alternative to the dual-frequency approach is the dual-cable architecture shown in Figure 9.20. Each station interface transmits on a particular channel in one cable and receives on the same channel in the second cable. The head end no longer provides FDM group translation; in fact, it may be nothing more than a passive cable-to-cable connection.

Whichever physical architecture is used, the advantage of unidirectional amplification appears in the maximum distance specifications of broadband networks. Distance limits of 5 to 30 miles are typical except in cases where access protocols like CSMA/CD restrict the allowable propagation times.

Data Link Layer

There is no single standard for broadband networks. Only the FDM channels have been given specific frequency assignments to allow interface with CATV systems.

Due to the flexibility and multiple services supported by broadband networks, no one standard configuration or agreement on operation has come about or is likely to come about. The only thing that appears to be a standard is the assignment of FDM channels which must be standardized to interface with CATV systems. Suppliers of data communications services on broadband cables generally have decided to use the data link protocols of the baseband systems. In particular; both Ethernet and ARCNet access protocols are available for rf channels on a broadband network. Thus, the OSI goal of separating the physical layer from the higher layers has proven to be useful by allowing data communications suppliers these options.

**Figure 9.18.
Broadband LAN
Supporting Multiple
Services**

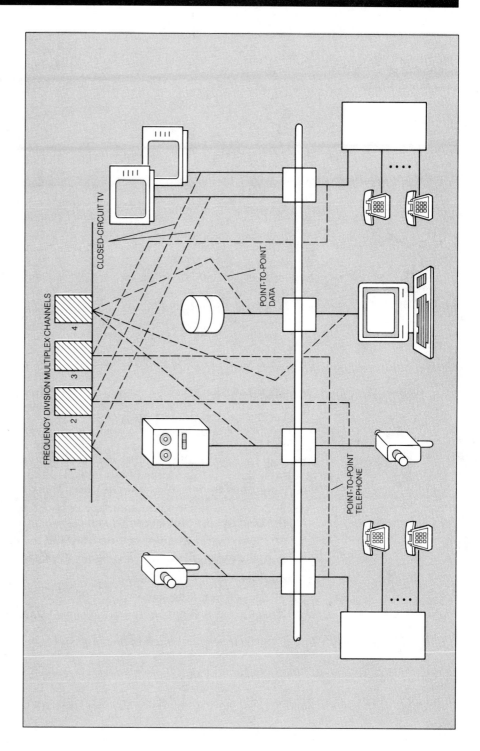

**Figure 9.19.
Dual-Frequency/
Single-Cable
Broadband Network**

*One cable,
two
frequencies*

LAN STANDARDS

Local area network standards (as with other communication standards) get established in two ways: by dominant manufacturers who attract plug compatible competitors, and by official standards organizations. The leading official standards organization for LANs in the U.S. is the IEEE 802 Standards Committee. This committee has several working groups responsible for establishing these LAN standards:

1. 802.1—Coordinating the interface between OSI Levels 1 & 2 with the five higher level layers.

2. 802.2—Logical data link standard similar to HDLC and ADCCP.

3. 802.3—CSMA/CD standard similar to Ethernet.

4. 802.4—Token Bus standard.

5. 802.5—Token Ring standard.

**Figure 9.20.
Dual-Cable/Single-
Frequency Broadband
Network**

*Two cables,
one
frequency*

Logical Link Control—IEEE 802.2

The IEEE 802 standards committee separated the OSI Data Link Layer into LLC and MAC layers.

In order to accommodate multiple LAN access methods, the IEEE 802 standards committee separated the OSI Data Link Layer into two sublayers: a *logical link control* (LLC) sublayer and a *media access control* (MAC) sublayer as shown in Figure 9.21. Under working group 802.2, the LLC control procedures have been defined to be basically the same as the CCITT X.25 Link Access Procedure HDLC in a balanced mode (LAPB). The balanced mode is used for peer structured networks wherein any station can originate communication directly with any other station.

LLC control procedures are similar to CCITT's X.25 Link Access Procedure HDLC in a balanced mode.

Two basic types of services are provided within 802.2 LLC. The Type 1 service involves unacknowledged "connectionless" operation wherein the source station sends a message to another station (or stations) without having established a logical connection for sequencing and acknowledging messages. This mode of operation is intended for transmission of messages that are not essential and for systems wherein higher levels provide error recovery and sequencing functions (as in Ethernet).

**Figure 9.21.
Relationship of IEEE
802 Partition to ISO
Reference Model**

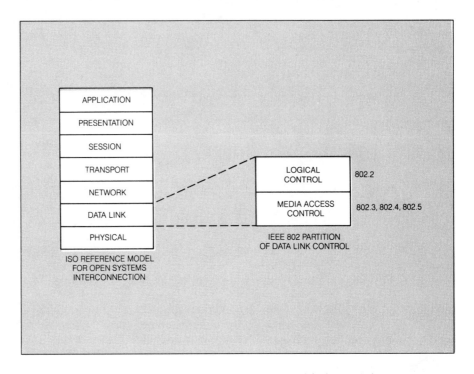

The Type 2 service is the more conventional balanced data communications service which establishes logical connections between two LLCs. Each LLC can send and receive both messages and responses. Each LLC also has the responsibility of ensuring complete and accurate deliveries of its outgoing messages.

CSMA/CD—IEEE 802.3

The IEEE 802.3 standard defines the MAC sublayer for CSMA/CD and a corresponding physical layer for connection to a baseband coaxial cable. The standard is basically patterned after the Ethernet specification with certain options in the frame format as shown in Figure 9.22. The address fields can be 16 bits long instead of Ethernet's 48 bits, but all addresses in a particular network must be of the same length. The 2-byte type field of Ethernet has been replaced by a 2-byte length field which designates the number of data bytes in the following message data field.

Variations in the physical layer allow signaling rates of 1, 5, 10, and 20 Mbps. A multidrop coaxial cable segment is limited to 500 meters (with 100 stations) instead of 1500 meters in Ethernet, but there can be as many as five coaxial cable segments in a IEEE 802.3 system.

The IEEE 802.3 standard is similar to the Ethernet specification but has 16-bit address fields, instead of 48.

Figure 9.22.
IEEE 802.3 Format for
CSMA/CD

PREAMBLE	DESTINATION ADDRESS	SOURCE ADDRESS	LENGTH	DATA	CRC
	2 OR 6 BYTES	2 OR 6 BYTES	2 BYTES		4 BYTES

Token-Passing Ring Access—IEEE 802.5

The IEEE 802.5 standard defines a token-passing ring method in which access to a shared medium is obtained by the passing of a token. The token, which is a predefined sequence of bits, provides a receiving workstation on a token-ring LAN with the right to transmit a frame or a sequence of frames onto the ring.

Once a workstation receives a free token, it builds a frame that includes the destination address of its transmission, its source address, and an information field as well as a frame check sequence; the latter is used for frame verification similar to the manner in which a CRC or BCC is used. As the frame circulates around the ring, each workstation examines the destination address. If the destination address matches the address of the workstation, the workstation receives data from the information field and sets a field in the frame to indicate the successful receipt of the frame. As the frame continues around the ring it returns to the originator which notes the successful transfer of information in the frame. The originator now generates a new token, which provides other workstations with the ability to gain access to the transmission medium.

VOICE AND/OR DATA PBX

As LAN technology has been developing, PBXs have been evolving and using more digital electronics in voice switched services.

The local area networks described in the preceding sections have evolved primarily from the data processing or office equipment industry; therefore, they are strongly influenced by data communications applications. At the same time that LAN technology has been developing, voice telephone systems called private branch exchanges (PBXs) have been incorporating more and more digital electronics as a means of providing switched voice service. As shown in Figure 9.23, the conventional PBX architecture utilizes dedicated twisted pair wires from every station to the central node (switch). Connection requests are signaled by an off-hook signal and dialed digits or "hot line" addresses stored in the memory of the switch controller. Once a connection is established, the associated transmission channels are dedicated to that connection for its duration.

The data PBX depicted in Figure 9.23 provides an economical solution to several data communications problems.

PBXs are not capable of effectively handling high speed processor-to-processor communications because of 50-kbps to 1-Mbps transmission rate range.

1. A terminal can be switched to different computers (CPUs) for different applications, to modems for external dial-up connections, or to data multiplexers for efficient use of external leased lines.

2. The distance between the computer ports and the data terminals is extended to as much as several thousand feet. The standard EIA specification for the RS-232 interface is limited to 50 feet (although RS-232 interfaces are often used over longer distances).

3. The switch acts as a port concentrator; that is, many external device ports can be handled by a few computer ports. The switch accomplishes this by connecting only active terminals to the computer ports. This greatly reduces the number of ports required in each computer.

Although twisted pair wires are relatively inexpensive and easy to install, they restrict the capacity of the data channels to a range of 50 kbps to 1 Mbps, depending on distance. Thus, the data PBX is a viable solution for data entry and medium rate interactive terminal communications, but not for high-speed processor-to-processor communications.

Integrated Voice/Data PBXs

Digitization of PBX Systems will enable control information to be multiplexed onto the voice signal wires allowing only one or two wires to handle multiple lines instead of the normal 25 pairs.

Beginning in the mid-1970s, PBXs began utilizing digital technology in their switching matrices because, despite the cost of voice digitization at line interfaces, the total switch cost is lower due to economics in the matrix. More recently, the point of digitization has begun to move from within the central equipment to the voice stations themselves. The main motivations for digitizing in the instruments are:

1. To easily multiplex control information (which is inherently digital) onto the same pair or pairs of wires that carry the voice signals (typically 64 kbps). This allows sophisticated multiline telephones to operate over one or two pairs of wires. Conventional analog telephone systems use expensive 25-pair cables for multiline key sets.

**Figure 9.23.
Representative
Application of a
Data PBX**

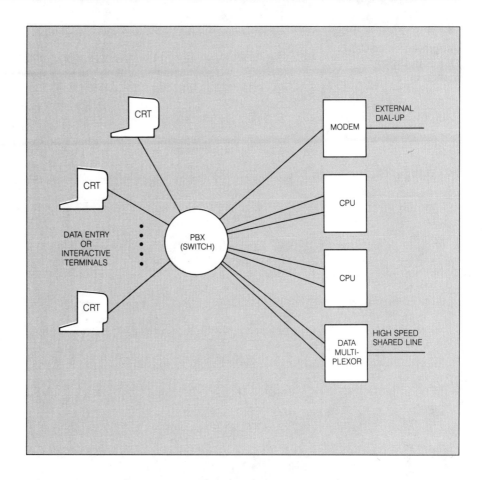

2. To multiplex data channels on the same pairs of wires used for voice so one installation can simultaneously provide voice and data communications.

Initially, the digital instruments could be cost justified only in sophisticated applications. As the cost of digital instruments decreased, however, it became possible to cost justify an all-digital system, thus providing 64-kbps digital channels at every location of a telephone. The widespread presence of 64-kbps digital channels makes it easier to add other digital transmission services as shown in Figure 9.24.

LAN COMPARISONS AND TRENDS

Each of the LAN system architectures presented in the previous sections have unique technical and operational advantages and disadvantages. The following paragraphs contrast the systems in terms of the properties of an ideal LAN.

**Figure 9.24.
Integrated Voice/Data
PBX with Digital
Instruments**

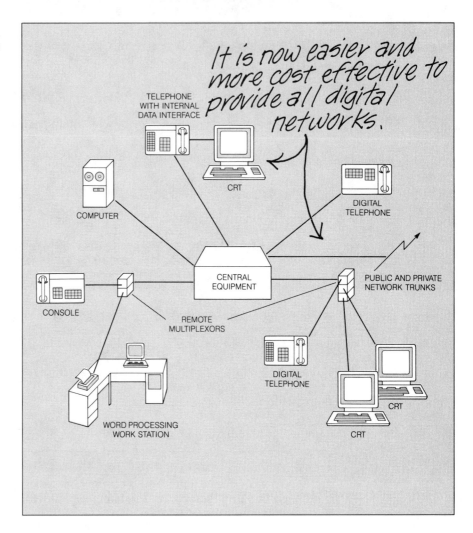

One-Time Installations

The overall goal of a one-time installation is not satisfied in practice by any of the LAN architectures. Even a telephone system, which is a necessity in every building, typically requires significant rewiring as people move, if only from one side of an office to another.

Widespread Access

Before widespread access becomes a reality for an information distribution network, the cost of significant numbers of unused ports must be reduced. Even though telephone twisted pairs are relatively inexpensive, unused telephone ports typically represent a significant hidden cost in terms of the electronics interfaces that the wires are connected to in the central equipment. Distributed access architectures like CSMA or token passing do not produce hidden costs for unused ports as long as the maximum number of ports is not exceeded.

Application Independence

A major prerequisite for an information network to support multiple applications is the support of higher level data communications functions. The suppliers of coaxial cable based LANs are generally most advanced in this regard although it is more a matter of market orientation than a technology difference. The CSMA and token passing systems also provide a high data rate for those applications that need it.

Excess Capacity

In one sense, the CSMA or token passing architectures are ideal because the entire capacity of the system is available at every port. A port can use as much bandwidth as it needs. On the other hand, this feature limits the system capacity. If the total bandwidth requirements of the stations exceed the system bandwidth, the needed expansion is either very costly or impossible.

In contrast, circuit switched (PBX) architectures can be expanded almost without limit. The bandwidth delivered to every port remains unchanged as more stations are added.

Easy Maintenance and Administration

The most difficult systems to maintain are the broadband systems because of the tight gain requirements of the amplifiers and equalizers. From a data communications point of view, the integrated voice/data PBX is the easiest to maintain since well established procedures already exist for the voice services. Furthermore, PBX suppliers are accustomed to providing turnkey system support for the life of the installation. However, due to product background, they typically do not support higher level communication requirements.

No single LAN system architecture has suffi-cient capabilities to provide all possible data communication transmission needs. Each one has its own special qualities and technical advantages and disadvantages.

No presently available single LAN system architecture can economically satisfy the needs of all communications within a building or campus. Nor is it likely that one system will ever evolve to economically fulfill these needs. Thus, there will always be a need for either separate systems tailored to specific applications or possibly hybrid systems employing the best features of selected individual architectures. One such hybrid architecture that is beginning to evolve is shown in Figure 9.25. This illustration depicts an integrated voice/data PBX that collects terminal traffic and switches it onto high-speed multiplexed computer to PBX interfaces (CPIs). Communications between processors (CPU) and their shared high-speed peripherals is best accomplished with a high-speed coaxial cable or fiber optic LAN. The advantage of the configuration in Figure 9.25 is that low-speed, short messages to and from the terminals are not contending for the high-speed facility optimized for file transfers.

WHAT HAVE WE LEARNED?

1. LANs provide high-speed switched connections between such data equipment as computers, storage devices, printers, word processors, and display terminals at distances up to a few thousand meters.
2. The usefulness of a LAN is maximized if it provides higher level data communications support in addition to basic transmission and switching functions.
3. Communications functions within a network should be partitioned in a hierarchial manner to isolate the implementation of major functional components from each other.
4. A myriad of LAN architectures are possible, but the most prevalent are:
    a. Contention access based coaxial cable systems (for example, Ethernet).
    b. Token-passing systems (for example, IBM token-ring network).
    c. Polled access based coaxial cable systems (for example, ARCNet).
    d. Frequency division broadband systems based on cable television technology and practice.
5. Some of the incompatibilities that traditionally arise in LAN equipment supplied by different vendors is being resolved by IEEE standards committee 802.
6. Digital PBXs for telephone switching are being designed to carry data in addition to basic telephone service. Although these systems do not provide the very high data rates of a conventional LAN, they represent a very economical alternative to a LAN for moderate data rate switched connections.

**Figure 9.25.
Hybrid PBX/LAN
Network**

A hybrid system allows tailoring to specific needs.

CRT

TAPE

CPU

DISK

PBX

COMPUTER-PBX
INTERFACE (CPI)

CRT

PRINTER

CPU

DISK

CRT

VOICE/COMPUTER ACCESS
NETWORK

COMPUTER
NETWORK

Quiz for Chapter 9

1. Which of the following transmission systems provides the highest data rate to an individual device?
   a. Voiceband modem.
   b. Local area network.
   c. Computer bus.
   d. Digital PBX.

2. Which of the following systems provides the longest digital transmission distances?
   a. Voiceband modem.
   b. Local area network.
   c. Computer bus.
   d. Digital PBX.

3. Which of the following is a characteristic of a LAN?
   a. Parallel transmission.
   b. Unlimited expansion.
   c. Low cost access for low bandwidth channels.
   d. Application independent interfaces.

4. Which of the following transmission media is not readily suitable to CSMA operation?
   a. Radio.
   b. Optical fibers.
   c. Coaxial cable.
   d. Twisted pair.

5. Which of the following functions is not provided as part of the basic Ethernet design?
   a. Access control.
   b. Addressing.
   c. Automatic retransmission of a message.
   d. Multiple virtual networks.

6. Which of the following is not a useful property of a Manchester line code for an Ethernet?
   a. Continuous energy.
   b. Continuous clock transitions.
   c. No dc component.
   d. No signal change at a 1 to 0 transition.

7. Which of the following data communications functions is generally provided for in a LAN?
   a. Data link control.
   b. Applications processing.
   c. Flow control.
   d. Routing.

8. The purpose of the preamble in an Ethernet is:
   a. Clock synchronization.
   b. Error checking.
   c. Collision avoidance.
   d. Broadcast.

9. Which of the following is possible in a token-passing bus network?
   a. Unlimited number of stations.
   b. Unlimited distances.
   c. Multiple time division channels.
   d. In-service expansion.

10. Which of the following is not possible in a token-passing loop network?
    a. Unlimited number of stations.
    b. Unlimited distances.
    c. Multiple time division channels.
    d. In-service expansion.

11. Which of the following LAN architectures can be expanded to the greatest total system bandwidth?
    a. Digital PBX.
    b. CSMA/CD baseband system.
    c. Token-passing network.
    d. Broadband cable system.

12. Which of the following systems is the most capable of servicing a wide range of applications?
    a. Digital PBX.
    b. CSMA/CD baseband system.
    c. Token passing network.
    d. Broadband cable system.

13. Which of the following is a characteristic of a token passing ring as opposed to a token passing bus?
    a. Signal quality control.
    b. Passive interface (tap).
    c. Flexible polling sequence.
    d. Priority access capabilities.

14. Which of the following is not a characteristic of the hub architecture of ARCNet?
    a. Directionalized transmission.
    b. RIM port isolation.
    c. Zero insertion loss amplifiers.
    d. Alternate routing.

15. Which of the following can not be provided in a broadband LAN?
    a. Frequency agile modems.
    b. Closed-circuit TV.
    c. Voice circuits.
    d. Fiber optic transmission.

16. Which of the following is not possible in a digital (data) PBX using twisted pair transmission?
    a. Computer port concentration.
    b. 64-kbps data circuits.
    c. High speed file transfers.
    d. Transmission up to several thousand feet.

17. Which of the following is not a motivation for digitizing a voice signal in the telephones of a digital PBX?
    a. Simplified control signaling.
    b. Lower cost telephones.
    c. Fewer wire pairs.
    d. Multiplexed voice and data channels.

Architectures and Packet Networks

ABOUT THIS CHAPTER

This chapter deals with several data networking architecture concepts; that is, the way data networks are arranged or structured. These include the concept of architectural levels or layers. Without emphasizing architectural structure or terminology, previous chapters have actually described data networking and switching on two different levels: the physical level and the link level. Packet networks, which involve a third architectural level, are discussed in this chapter. The CCITT X.25 standard packet switching architecture is described; then the Open Systems Interconnection (OSI) Reference Model is explained along with its relationship to X.25 and other systems.

PROTOCOL LAYERING

A protocol is a set of rules governing a time sequence of events that take place between peer entities; that is, between equipment or layers on the same level.

Physical Layer

In a previous chapter, we discussed the mechanical, physical, electrical, logical, and functional relationships between the various wires and signals in a serial interface and how the bits of data are passed through them between a Data Terminal Equipment (DTE) and Data Circuit-terminating Equipment (DCE). We showed, for example, that bits passing through the transmit data wire from a source DTE should eventually pass through a receive data wire to a sink DTE. These are called physical layer or level one protocols.

Level one protocols deal with the physical layer of data communication; that is, the passing of the bits through the wires to and from DTEs. Link protocols cover a higher level of architecture; they are concerned with all aspects of maintaining order within the link.

Link Layer

In a previous chapter, we discussed means by which various fields, such as address, text, and error checking, may be present within the same bit stream. A number of specific link protocols were discussed, showing techniques which are used to define (without any possibility of confusion) the boundaries of the fields within a bit stream, send information to a specific terminal on a multipoint link, check for and correct transmission errors, and generally maintain order within the link.

Architecturally speaking, link protocols are at a higher level (a more "intelligent" level) than physical protocols; yet all of the information used in the link protocol is actually contained in the bit stream transmitted through the serial interface. Conceptually, we speak of the link protocol fields as embedded (contained within) or layered within the physical protocol bits.

Network Layer

The highest level of protocol architecture is the network layer. This layer is used to route data link-to-link through a network.

At the third architectural level is the network layer. Protocols at this layer may be used to route data from link to link through a network containing intelligent nodes called packet switches. The method by which this routing and associated administration takes place is called the network layer protocol. The network layer protocol information, called the packet header, is embedded in the information field of a link-level frame. The packet switch uses part of this information to route the data to the next link, and so on. The packet header, together with the user data, is called a packet.

PACKET NETWORKS

Packet networks function with the help of special intelligent switching nodes. A network node joining three or more links is called a DSE.

A packet network is a special kind of data network containing intelligent switching nodes. Packet networks have the following general characteristics:

1. Prior to transmission, each data message is segmented into short blocks of specified maximum length, and each block is provided with a header containing addressing and sequencing information. Each packet becomes the information field of a transmission at the link protocol level which usually contains error control capabilities.

2. The packets are passed very quickly from node to node, arriving in a fraction of a second at their final destination.

3. The node computers do not archive (store) the data. Messages are "forgotten" by the sending node as soon as the next node checks for error (if required), and acknowledges receipt.

The terms DTE and DCE have been discussed previously. In packet networks, an additional term is introduced—the *Data Switching Exchange* (DSE). A DSE is a network node joining three or more links. Figure 10.1 shows the relationship between DTEs, DCEs, and DSEs in a packet network. The point where the serial interface cable connects to the DCE is sometimes referred to as the network gateway.

Unlike level one switching, in which a specific link is dedicated to a particular message or group of messages, data packets are forwarded from DSE to DSE in such a way that packets from many sources and to many sinks may pass through the same internode link at different moments during the same short period of time.

**Figure 10.1.
Two-Node Packet
Network**

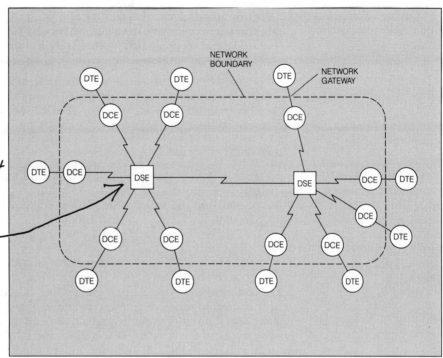

The DSE is an intelligent switching node joining three or more links.

Advantages of Packet Switching

Packet switching can offer significant advantages over other data communication techniques.

Depending on the situation, packet switching can offer several possible advantages over other data communications techniques:

1. For data applications in which the amount of traffic between terminals cannot justify a dedicated circuit, packet switching may be more economical than transmission over private lines.

2. For applications in which data communication sessions are shorter than a minimum chargeable time unit for a telephone call, packet switching may be more economical than dialed data.

3. Because destination address information is inherently a part of the packet, a large number of messages may be sent to many different destinations as fast as the source DTE can turn them out. Depending on the type of packet service being used, there might not be any connection time delay before transmitting packets containing actual data.

4. Because of the intelligence built into the network (that is, computers at each node), dynamic routing of data is possible. Each packet travels over the route established by the network as the best available path for that packet at that time. This characteristic can be used to maximize efficiency and minimize congestion.

5. Built-in intelligence also facilitates a "graceful degradation" property of the packet network because, whenever there is a failure of a link or node, packets may be automatically rerouted around the defective portion of the network.

6. Because of the intelligence within the network, a rich array of basic communication services is possible. Examples are: error detection and correction, message delivery verification, group addressing, reverse billing, message sequence checking, and diagnostics.

X.25 PACKET SYSTEMS

The primary emphasis of the X.25 standard is to describe what a terminal and its associated network must be able to do; not describe the terminal and network themselves.

The CCITT X.25 standard for packet switching systems is one of the most significant networking architectures affecting data communications for the present and the foreseeable future. The X.25 standard is actually only a part of a much larger collection of CCITT recommendations on public data networks. To fully understand the subject, one must study the entire "X" series.

The X.25 standard itself describes the physical, link, and network protocols *in the interface between the DTE and DCE at the gateway* to a packet switching network. At first glance, the concept of describing a packet network in terms of gateway parameters may seem peculiar, but from the users' point of view, it's all that's needed. In voice telephone network terms, if we were to collect all of the standards relating to the physical, electrical, logical, and functional properties of local loops and their signals into one document, we would have the telephone network 0equivalent of X.25. As shown in Figure 10.2, X.25 relates a data terminal to the gateway of a packet network in precisely the same way that local loop signaling standards relate a telephone to the central office of a telephone network.

If we had never seen a telephone or placed a telephone call, our knowing all there is to know about a local loop and its signaling wouldn't teach us much about the design of the telephone or of the network; but we would know how to use them. Similarly, the X.25 standard describes neither the data terminal nor the packet data network, but X.25 reveals a great deal about what the terminal and the network must be able to do. It is for this reason that the X.25 has taken on so much importance.

As already mentioned, the X.25 standard specifies three separate protocol layers at the serial interface gateway. The physical-level characteristics of X.21 (or X.21 bis) are specified as the physical layer protocol ("bis" is the Swiss/French equivalent of "alternate form"). X.21 uses a 15-pin synchronous interface which has not enjoyed enthusiastic acceptance in the U.S. because of the popularity of RS-232 and V.35 which existed before X.21. In recognition of this fact, the CCITT has endorsed X.21 bis as a suitable alternate. X.21 bis specifies V.24/V.28 (essentially the equivalent of RS-232), X.26/IS-4902 (essentially the equivalent of RS-449), and V.35 at their appropriate respective bit rates. Since U.S. vendors generally provide RS-232 or V.35, no change is required.

**Figure 10.2.
Analogy Between X.25
and the Total
Specifications for a
Local Loop**

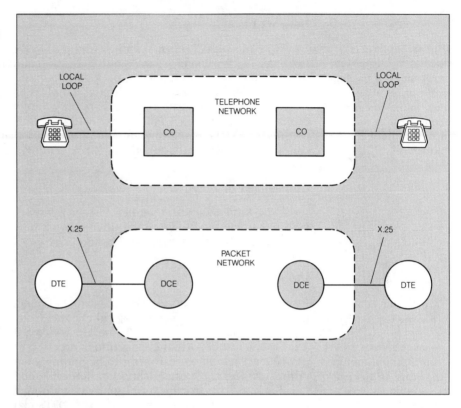

Link Level

The protocol at the link level, LAPB, provides for two-way simultaneous communications between the DTE and DCE at the network gateway.

At the link level, the protocol specified is a subset of HDLC, referred to in X.25 terminology as LAPB (Link Access Procedure Balanced). (An older version of X.25 used a link protocol called LAP which is being phased out.) LAPB provides for two-way simultaneous communication between the DTE and DCE at the network gateway. LAPB frame structure is identical with that of SDLC which was explained in a previous chapter. The delimiter (flag), abort, idle channel, transparency (zero insertion), frame sequencing, flow control, and error control mechanisms are identical with those of SDLC. The differences in the LAPB procedures and the SDLC procedures are mainly in the areas of line control and addressing; these will be explained later.

Network Level

The packet level of X.25 is the network level, and it is transmitted as an information field in the command frame. At least three octets are used in the header.

The network level of X.25 is referred to in the standard as the packet level. All X.25 packets are transmitted as information fields in LAPB information command frames. A packet contains at least a header of three or more octets. (An octet is a group of eight bits.) Most packets also contain user data, but some packets are only for control, status indication, or diagnostics. (The preceding terms will be explained in later text and illustrations.) The maximum amount of user data that can be included in a data packet is determined by the network vendor, but is usually 128 octets.

Capabilities of X.25

The X.25 standard, together with its references, specifies two essential services which must be offered by carriers in order to be in full compliance with the standard. These are *Virtual Call Sevice* and *Permanent Virtual Circuit Service*.

Virtual Call Service

Virtual connections are made and disconnected by using special, nondata carrying packets that have a unique bit stream. In a virtual connection no fixed physical path actually exists in the network.

In Virtual Call Service (VC), a virtual "connection" normally must be established first between a logical channel from the calling DTE and a logical channel to the called DTE before any data packets can be sent. Establishment of a virtual connection is precisely the functional equivalent of placing a telephone call prior to beginning a telephone conversion. The virtual connection is established and disestablished using special packets having unique bit streams, but usually containing no data. Once the connection has been established, the two DTEs may carry on a two-way dialog until a "clear request packet" (disconnect) is sent.

The VC connection is referred to as "virtual" because a fixed physical path does not really exist through the network. The intelligence in the network simply relates a specified logical channel number at one DTE to that at the other DTE.

A given DTE may have many logical channel numbers active in the same X.25 interface at the same time. (That statement was important. Read it again.) Once a virtual connection has been established, say, between logical channel #319 on one DTE and, say, #14 on another DTE, then the actual data packet headers need refer only to logical channel numbers. The intelligent network keeps up with their conversational relationship; that is, a data packet from logical channel #319 at the one DTE will appear on logical channel #14 at the other, with the network performing the conversion. Further details on this subject will be given later.

Permanent Virtual Circuit Service

After a PVC has been established only data packets are sent between the terminals on the carrier-assigned logical channels.

Permanent Virtual Circuit (PVC) service is the functional equivalent of a private line service. As in VC, no end-to-end physical pathway really exists; the intelligent network relates the respective logical channels of the two DTEs involved. No special packets are sent by the DTE to establish or disestablish connections. A PVC is established by requesting it in writing from the carrier providing the packet network service, and it remains in effect until disestablished by written request. Terminals between which a PVC has been established need only send data packets on the carrier-assigned logical channels as required. Since a DTE may have many logical channels active at the same time within the X.25 interface, some may be assigned as PVCs while others are used for setting up VCs as required—all in the same X.25 interface!

For both VC and PVC, the network is obligated to deliver packets in the order submitted, even if the physical path changes due to circuit loading, failure, or whatever. Costwise, the relationship between VC and PVC is similar to that between long distance telephone and private line services. Other standard packet network features, such as error control, diagnostics, etc., are equivalent for VC and PVC.

Facilities

Facilities are optional features available to customers to customize VC service.

In CCITT terminology, a facility is an optional feature offered with a service, sometimes at extra cost. X.25 specifies a rich array of facilities for VC and PVC services. In any case, the final choice of services and facilities is up to the customer.

Examples of facilities for VC service are fast select, incoming calls barred, outgoing calls barred, closed user group, and reverse billing. Fast select gives the user the capability to send and receive data to and from a number of different remote stations very quickly and efficiently without actually establishing regular virtual connections. Such a capability has many potential uses for distribution of electronic mail, polling of inventories, etc.

LAPB Procedures

Space does not allow a complete discussion of the link layer protocol of X.25; however, the following information provides general knowledge of the LAPB procedures. A thorough treatment is included in the X.25 standard, and examples of operation are included in ISO 4335 Addendum 2.

LAPB provides for two-way simultaneous transmission on a point-to-point link between a DTE and a DCE at the packet network gateway (Figure 10.1). Since the link is point-to-point, only the address of the DTE or the address of the DCE may appear in the A (address) field of an LAPB frame. These addresses are shown in Figure 10.3. The A field refers to a link address, not to a network address. The network address of the destination terminal is embedded in the packet header (PH), which is part of the I field.

Figure 10.3.
Commands Versus
Responses in LAPB

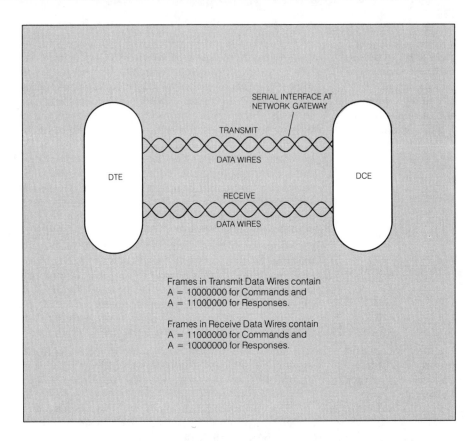

SERIAL INTERFACE AT
NETWORK GATEWAY

TRANSMIT
DATA WIRES

RECEIVE
DATA WIRES

DTE

DCE

Frames in Transmit Data Wires contain
A = 10000000 for Commands and
A = 11000000 for Responses.

Frames in Receive Data Wires contain
A = 11000000 for Commands and
A = 10000000 for Responses.

Commands and re-
sponses may be made
by both the DTE and
the DCE. The function
of a frame depends on
the direction it is mov-
ing and the value of A.

Both stations (the DTE and the DCE) may issue commands and responses to each other as shown in Figure 10.3. Whether a frame is a command or a response depends on a combination of two factors:

1. Which direction is it moving; that is, is it on the transmit data wires from the DTE or the receive data wires toward the DTE.

2. What is the value of A?

Because of the addressing scheme, there can be no uncertainty even if frames are moving in opposite directions at the same time between DTE and DCE.

Tables 10.1 and 10.2 show the legitimate commands and responses, respectively, in the LAPB frame, along with their respective control octet values. Explanations of the abbreviations and terms are given in the following paragraphs.

**Table 10.1.
LAPB Commands**

Command Name	Content of Control Octet Bit Number			
	8 7 6	**5**	**4 3 2**	**1**
I (Information)	N(R)	P	N(S)	0
RR (Receiver Ready)	N(R)	P	0 0 0	1
RNR (Receiver Not Ready)	N(R)	P	0 1 0	1
REJ (Reject)	N(R)	P	1 0 0	1
SABM (Set Asynchronous Balanced Mode)	0 0 1	P	1 1 1	1
DISC (Disconnect)	0 1 0	P	0 0 1	1

**Table 10.2.
LAPB Responses**

Response Name	Content of Control Octet Bit Number			
	8 7 6	**5**	**4 3 2**	**1**
RR (Receiver Ready)	N(R)	F	0 0 0	1
RNR (Receiver Not Ready)	N(R)	F	0 1 0	1
REJ (Reject)	N(R)	F	1 0 0	1
UA (Unnumbered Acknowledgement)	0 1 1	F	0 0 1	1
DM (Disconnect Mode)	0 0 0	F	1 1 1	1
FRMR (Frame Rejected)	1 0 0	F	0 1 1	1

Explanation of LAPB Commands and Responses

Most frames in LAPB operations are commands. Response frames are issued only when a command frame with P = 1 is received.

During LAPB operation, most frames are commands. A response frame is compelled when a command frame is received containing P = 1; such a response contains F = 1. All other frames contain P = 0 or F = 0.

SABM/UA is a command/response pair used to initialize all counters and timers at the beginning of a session. Similarly, DISC/DM is a command/response pair used at the end of a session. FRMR is a response to any illegal command for which there is no indication of transmission errors according to the frame check sequence (FCS) field.

I commands are used to transmit packets; that is, in the I field. Packets are never sent as responses. N(S) is a 3-bit packet counter capable of counting from 0 through 7 (000 through 111 in binary). After seven packets have been sent, the counter simply rolls over to 000 again for the next value of N(S).

While N(S) counts packets sent from one end of the link, the value of N(R) indicates the next value of N(S) expected to be returned from the other end of the link. By updating the value of N(R), a station acknowledges correctly received packets in the same way as SDLC frames are acknowledged. For example, if a DTE sends an I command (a packet) for which N(S) = 5 and P = 1, and the DCE returns an RR response with N(R) = 6 and F = 1, the DTE knows that the packet was received correctly. If N(R) = 5 and F = 1, the packet was received incorrectly. No more than seven unacknowledged packets can be outstanding, as an ambiguity would result.

In checkpointing, a type of LAPB error detection, RR is the response by a station that has no packets to send but must answer a compelled response.

RR is what a station sends when it needs to send something, but has no packets to send. For example, a compelled response to an I command might be an RR with F = 1. This procedure is called checkpointing. Checkpointing is one of the techniques which LAPB makes available for error detection.

REJ is another way of requesting retransmission of frames. RNR is used for flow control to indicate a busy condition. It prevents further transmissions until cleared by an RR.

Packet-Level Procedures

The most interesting feature of X.25 is the network (packet) layer protocol. Remember that the packets are contained in the I command frames at the link (frame) level, and that each packet has a header of at least three octets. Most, but not all, packets contain user data; other packets are used for control, status indication, or diagnostics. Figure 10.4 illustrates the general layout of X.25 packet headers.

Data Packets

Data Packets are packets where Bit #1 in Octet #3 of the header has a value of 0. A data packet can have up to 128 octets of user data.

A packet which has 0 as the value of Bit #1 in Octet #3 of the header is a Data Packet. Data packet headers normally contain three octets. A standard X.25 data packet contains up to 128 octets of user data following the header. Figure 10.5 illustrates the layout of a typical data packet. (This chapter is not intended to cover all possible ramifications and extensions of X.25. There is, for example, the provision for modulo 128 P(S) and P(R) counters, each of which requires 7 bits. A data packet header in such a system would require a minimum of four octets.)

It was pointed out earlier that X.25 specifies two essential services; namely, Virtual Call (VC) and Permanent Virtual Circuit (PVC) services. Once a VC has been set up, the operation of data packets under VC service is identical with that under PVC. In the paragraphs that follow, operation under PVC will be described first, then the additional concerns of VC, such as call setup, will be described.

There are three parts to Octet #3 of the data packet header: two 3-bit fields, P(S) and P(R) and a 1-bit field M. When M has a value of 1, it indicates that more data packets are to follow as a single unit.

Theoretically, every X.25 gateway interface may support up to 16 logical channel groups, each containing up to 256 logical channels, for a grand total of 4096 simultaneous logical channels per gateway. It is up to the company that establishes the network to say how many it will actually support in each type of service—that is, PVC and VC.

Notice in Figure 10.5 that Octet #3 of the data packet header contains two 3-bit fields, P(S) and P(R), and a 1-bit field M. M is the "more data" mark; when it is 1, additional data packets will follow which are to be considered as a unit; when it is 0, no more packet will follow in this unit. P(S) and P(R) are data packet counters, each of which may vary from 000 through 111 (0–7). They roll over to 000 again after passing 111. (These are not the same as N(S) and N(R) discussed earlier.) Only

Figure 10.4.
General Layout of
X.25 Packet Headers
(Source: CCITT,
Recommendation X.25,
CCITT, Geneva, C.H.)

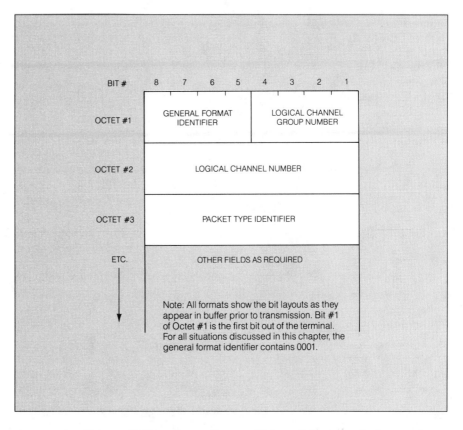

data packets have a P(S) counter; there will be a P(S) in each data packet sent across the DTE to DCE interface at the network gateway (Figure 10.1) and a P(S) in each data packet sent from DCE to DTE at the network gateway.

By definition, P(R) is the amount of the next expected value of P(S) from the other direction on that logical channel (this will be explained below). The values of P(S) and P(R) relate to each other within a logical channel at the network level in exactly the same way that N(S) and N(R) relate to each other on a point-to-point link. The Ns are not related to the Ps, however, because the Ns refer to all packets sent in a link, and the Ps refer only to data packets sent in a particular logical channel within that link.

The use of P(S) and P(R) is illustrated in Figure 10.6. A sequence of two-way simultaneous (full-duplex) transmissions of data packets within a logical channel across a DTE/DCE interface at a packet network gateway is

The values of P(S) and P(R) are related within a logical channel at the network level. P(R) is the amount that P(S) is expected to be in the next packet that is coming from the other direction on that particular logical channel.

Figure 10.5.
Typical CCITT X.25
Data Packet
(Source: CCITT.
Recommendation X.25,
CCITT, Geneva, C.H.)

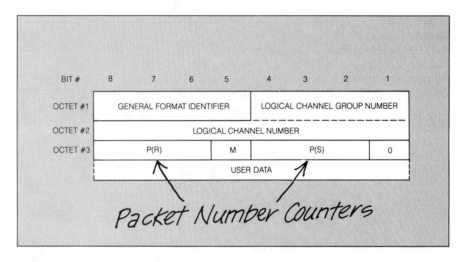

illustrated. In this illustration, each rectangle represents a packet; the first number in the rectangle is the value of P(S) and the second is the value of P(R) in that packet's header. Inspection of the sequence in Figure 10.6 will confirm two facts already implied:

1. The values of P(S) in a particular direction in a logical channel proceed in numerical order: 0, 1, 2, 3, etc.

2. The value of P(R) sent in a packet is not updated to i until the entire packet whose value of P(S) is i − 1 has been completely received error free. Such update is an acknowledgement of all packets in that logical channel through P(S) = i − 1.

The dynamic establishment and disestablishment of a VC using special packets is very similar to that of placing and terminating a telephone call on the public telephone network, as indicated in Tables 10.3 and 10.4. Inspection of these tables reveals that seven new packet names have been introduced. An event occurring on one side of the network is usually paired with a complementary event on the other side. For example, a Call Request Packet from calling DTE to DCE at one interface results in an Incoming Call Packet from DCE to called DTE at another interface. Table 10.5 shows the packet type identifiers (Octet 3 of header) for these pairs of packet types.

**Figure 10.6.
Values of P(S) and
P(R) for a Sequence of
Data Packets**

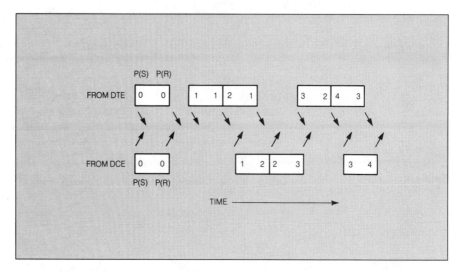

**Table 10.3.
Network Analogies for
Call Establishment**

Telephone Network	X.25 Packet Network
Place call	Send "Call Request" Packet
Hear telephone ring	Receive "Incoming Call" Packet
Pick up handset of ringing phone	Send "Call Accepted" Packet
Hear "Hello"	Receive "Call Connected" Packet
Fail to answer ring	Send "Clear Request" Packet*
No answer, busy, or fast busy	Receive "Clear Indication" Packet
Hang up	Send "Clear Confirmation" Packet*

With cause shown in packet

**Table 10.4.
Network Analogies
After Establishment
of Call**

Telephone Network	X.25 Packet Network
Hang up to disconnect	Send "Clear Request" Packet
Hear other person hang up	Receive "Clear Indication" Packet*
Hang up after other person hangs up	Send "Clear Confirmation" Packet
Call disconnected by network	Receive "Clear Indication" Packet*

With cause shown in packet

Figure 10.7 shows a "normal" sequence of a VC setup, two-way simultaneous data transfer, and terminal-initiated disconnect. Note that the four packet type identifiers of Table 10.5 are simply passed through the network without the network modifying them.

**Table 10.5.
Packet Type
Identifiers for Call
Setup and Clearing**

DTE to DCE	DCE to DTE	Octet #3
Call Request	Incoming Call	0 0 0 0 1 0 1 1
Call Accepted	Call Connected	0 0 0 0 1 1 1 1
Clear Request	Clear Indication	0 0 0 1 0 0 1 1
DTE-initiated—	Network-initiated—	
Clear Confirmation	Clear Confirmation	0 0 0 1 0 1 1 1

**Figure 10.7.
A "Normal" VC
Sequence**

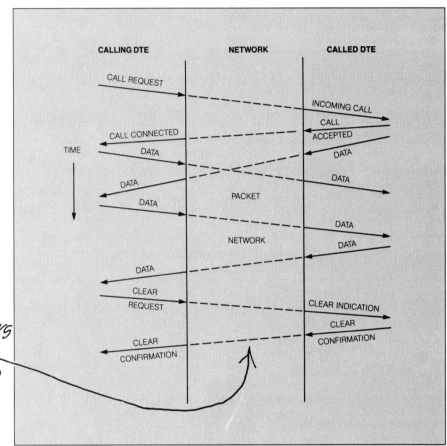

The packet type identifiers are passed without being changed.

Figure 10.8 shows what happens when a VC does not complete. If the VC is refused by the called DTE, the called DTE sends **Clear Request**. If the VC is refused by the network, the calling DTE receives **Clear Indication**.

Figure 10.8.
VC Not Completed

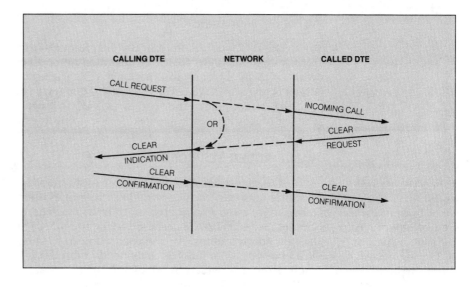

Call Request/Incoming Call Packets

The numbers assigned
to the ends of a logical
channel do not have to
be the same. The intel-
ligent switcher will
make the appropriate
connection as required
regardless of the end
numbers.

The logical channel
numbers used in VC
service will come from
a pool of numbers
available when the call
is made. The numbers
at the opposite inter-
faces are different.

The headers of the Call Request/Incoming Call pair of packets are
the most complex of the various header formats. Not only do they contain
the basic three octets shown in Figure 10.4, but they also contain
destination addressing and facility selection information. In certain cases,
they also contain user data.

The *logical channel numbers* (LCNs) and *logical channel group
numbers* (LCGNs) for PVC service are assigned by the carrier from the
ranges of numbers that the carrier decides to designate for PVC service.
The numbers assigned to opposite ends of a given logical channel do not
have to be the same. Different numbers could be assigned to the opposite
ends of the channel, and the intelligent switches within the network
would make the appropriate conversions as the packets pass to and fro.

In the case of VC service, the numerical values of logical channels at
the opposite interfaces are never the same; the network always converts
these numbers to and fro. The channel numbers used are assigned from a
pool of numbers available at the time of call set up.

In placing a Call Request, a calling DTE will select the highest logical
channel number which does not exceed a limit specified by the carrier and
which is not already being used on another VC. The network will then pair
the selected logical channel number with that VC from that calling DTE. At
the destination end, the network will select the lowest logical channel
number which is not less than a limit specified by the carrier and which is
not already in use with that called DTE. The network will then pair that
logical channel number with that VC to that called DTE. The two DTEs
engaged in PVC or VC transactions each never know (or care) what LCGN or
LCN is being used by the other DTE/DCE interface.

VC Destination Addressing

The DTE Address field in the Call Request/Incoming Call Packet format contains digits which are handled much like telephone numbers, with up to 14 digits on international VCs. The arrangement of these 14 digits is given in X.121. For domestic calls, fewer digits are required.

There are many other details in X.25 that cannot be covered here and the list of facilities and diagnostic codes continues to grow. The reader is referred to the standard for details.

VALUE-ADDED SERVICES

Enhanced, or value-added, services are provided by some carriers to overcome some of the shortcomings of X.25 that can arise when a terminal does not meet some of the prerequisites for full X.25 use.

X.25 describes a highly flexible basic point-to-point service through a public network. To the user whose terminals operate in the X.25 packet mode, have a significant amount of traffic to send to many locations, and connect via a DTE/DCE serial interface to an X.25 network gateway, X.25 has few shortcomings. For the user who cannot meet all of these criteria, X.25 does have limitations. Enhanced (value-added) service offerings, such as those provided by AT&T Information Systems, U.S. Sprint (formerly GTE Telenet), BT Tymnet (formerly Tymnet), and others, seek to address these and other matters:

1. Broadcast services (sending the same data at the same time to many receivers).
2. Dial access. (Since the DTE/DCE interface is intended as a two-way simultaneous synchronous gateway, packet-mode access normally cannot be provided via the public telephone network.)
3. Conversion to lower speed start-stop transmission for low-volume terminals.
4. Code and protocol conversion services.

The CCITT has provided guidance with regard to item 3, as will be shown later.

THE X SERIES OF RECOMMENDED STANDARDS

Services, facilities, terminals, and interfaces are covered by CCITT sections X.1 through X.39. Network architecture, transmission, switching, and all remaining areas are covered by sections X.40 through X.200.

As stated earlier, X.25 is part of the "X" series of recommended standards for public data networks begin promulgated (made public) by the CCITT. The X series is classified into two categories: X.1 through X.39, which deal with services, facilities, terminals, and interfaces; and X.40 through X.199, which deal with network architecture, transmission, signaling, switching, maintenance, and administrative arrangements. From a packet network user viewpoint, the most important X standards are listed in the following with their titles and brief descriptions.

X.1—International User Classes of Service in Public Data Networks

Assigns numerical class designation to different terminal speeds and types.

X.2—International User Services and Facilities in Public Data Networks

Specifies essential and additional services and facilities.

X.3—Packet Assembly/Disassembly Facility (PAD) in a Public Data Network

Describes the packet assembler/disassembler which normally is used at a network gateway to allow connection of a start-stop terminal to a packet network.

X.20 bis—Use on Public Data Networks of DTE Designed for Interfacing to Asynchronous Duplex V-Series Modems

Allows use of V.24/V.28 (essentially the same as EIA RS-232).

X.21 bis—Use on Public Data Networks of DTE Designated for Interfacing to Synchronous V-Series Modems

Allows use of V.24/V.28 (essentially the same as EIA RS-232) or V.35.

X.25—Interface Between DTE and DCE for Terminals Operating in the Packet Mode on Public Data Networks

Defines the architecture of three levels of protocols existing in the serial interface cable between a packet-mode terminal and a gateway to a packet network.

X.28—DTE/DCE Interface for a Start-Stop Mode DTE Accessing the PAD in a Public Data Network Situated in the Same Country

Defines the architecture of protocols existing in a serial interface cable between a start-stop terminal and an X.3 PAD.

X.29—Procedures for the Exchange of Control Information and User Data Between a PAD and a Packet Mode DTE or Another PAD

Defines the architecture of protocols behind the X.3 PAD, either between two PADs or between a PAD and a packet-mode terminal on the other side of the network.

X.75—Terminal and Transit Call Control Procedures and Data Transfer System on International Circuits Between Packet-Switched Data Networks

Defines the architecture of protocols between two public packet networks.

X.121—International Numbering Plan for Public Data Networks

Defines a numbering plan including code assignments for each nation.

Interrelationships Between X Standards

Many X standard sections touch on other sections with great detail or add depth to specific areas of concern. In some cases a section will describe conditions that must be met before other sections become applicable.

Figure 10.9 shows the interrelationships between many of these X standards. In summary: X.25 specifies the relationship between a packet-mode DTE and a packet network. X.28 specifies the relationship between a start-stop (asynchronous) DTE and an X.3 PAD which must reside between a nonpacket DTE and a packet network. X.29 specifies additional relationships over and above those in X.25 which a packet-mode DTE must satisfy when communicating with a nonpacket mode DTE through a packet network and PAD. X.29 also covers the relationships between two PADs when two nonpacket mode DTEs are communicating through a packet network.

The CCITT envisioned the X.3 PAD as being within the packet network; that is, behind the DCE. The 1980 version X.3 covers the PAD only for start-stop (asynchronous) terminals, but it leaves open the future possibility of covering other nonpacket terminals; for example, IBM BSC. A number of stand-alone X.3 PADs are now marketed for connection of various start-stop and non-start-stop DTEs to packet networks.

Frame Relay

Although X.25 based packet networks have gained widespread acceptance, their data handling ability in an era of increasing use of fiber optic cable represents a severe limitation. The growth in the installation of fiber optic cable for the transmission of voice, data, and video between communications carrier central offices has reduced the potential of transmission errors to under 1 in 10^9 bits from 1 in 10^5 typically encountered on analog transmission facilities. However, the use of X.25 packet networks results in the flow of packets through numerous data switching exchanges, with each DSE performing error checking and sometimes performing flow control procedures, both of which introduce delays that adversely affect the throughput of data.

Although X.25 error-checking procedures were necessary when packet networks were established using analog leased lines to interconnect DSEs, for many communications applications where data flows over fiber optic cable, the use of a series of error checking procedures is both unnecessary and detrimental to developing high-speed transmission that effectively uses available bandwidth. Recognizing this limitation to X.25, a form of fast packet switching referred to as *frame relay* was developed.

**Figure 10.9.
Relationships Between
Some "X" Interface
Standards**

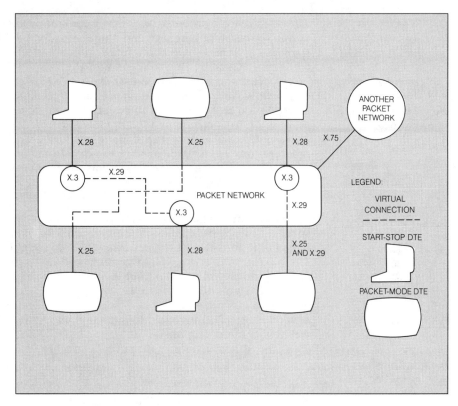

Frame relay can be considered as a logical progression of X.25 packet switching. Under frame relay, a majority of error checking and flow control functions performed in an X.25 network are eliminated. As a result, frame relay transmission occurs at the 1.544 Mbps DS-1 rate which is significantly higher than obtainable using X.25 packet networks.

OPEN SYSTEMS IN INTERCONNECTION REFERENCE MODEL

OSI/RM is a reference model for data communication architectures. It has been redrafted by the CCITT and designated CCITT X.200.

In 1983, the International Organization for Standardization (ISO) culminated six years of intensive effort to develop and publish a guideline—a reference model—for describing data communications architectures. The resulting document, International Standard #7498, has been redrafted by the CCITT using its own terminology, and the redraft has been designated CCITT X.200. The generic name for both documents is Open Systems Interconnection Reference Model (OSI/RM)—usually called simply OSI.

OSI defines a consistent language and boundaries for protocols so that systems that follow OSI can communicate with one another. However, OSI itself is not a protocol.

OSI is not a protocol nor does it contain protocols. What OSI does is define a consistent language and boundaries for establishing protocols such that systems which abide by its rules should be "open" to one another—that is, be able to communicate.

Decades of frustration caused by incompatibility between competitive and/or geographically distinct communications systems have created such an appetite for the establishment of cooperative systems that there is a virtual stampede toward global standardization of data communications architectures. Many standard committees in several organizations are now engaged in the development of protocols for the various layers in the numerous systems to which OSI will apply.

OSI Layers

OSI defines a complete architecture having seven layers. There is no specific reason why it is seven instead of six or eight; the functions that must be performed just happened to fall into roughly seven groupings. The lowest three layers (physical, link, and network) correspond closely to the physical, link, and packet levels of X.25. Protocols have been and are being developed for other kinds of systems, such as facsimile, integrated voice/data networks, videotex, etc. Even if the protocols were never written, OSI has had a tremendous impact in standardizing the way we view communications.

There are seven layers to any architecture as defined by OSI. The three lowest levels correspond roughly to the physical, link and packet levels of X.25.

The official names of the seven layers are, from top to bottom:

7. Application   3. Network
6. Presentation   2. Link
5. Session   1. Physical
4. Transport

Each successive step up the list takes one to a higher level of system supervision. In terms of the protocols, lower levels involve successively more embedded headers. Figure 10.10 shows how the seven levels relate for a system whose lower three layers correspond to X.25. (In this case, NH is the packet header.) The concept of layers was previouisly discussed in Chapter 9.

An Analogy

The basic requirements to establish, maintain and terminate communications without error are similar whether verbal or computer communications are being used.

Whenever people communicate, whether by computer or verbally, they invoke protocols at all seven levels of OSI. Without going into the laborious details and vocabulary of the OSI standard, we shall illustrate the OSI categorizations of the seven levels from top to bottom for a typical telephone call.

1. Physical Layer Concerns—These are the actual sounds being uttered into the mouthpiece and heard from the receiver.
2. Link Layer Concerns—Talk when you're supposed to and listen when you're supposed to. Ask for a repeat if there is something you don't understand. Tell the other party to slow down if he's talking too fast.

**Figure 10.10.
Seven Embedded
Layers of OSI**

USER — USER DATA — USER

APPLICATION — AH USER DATA — APPLICATION

PRESENTATION — PH DATA UNIT — PRESENTATION

SESSION — SH DATA UNIT — SESSION

TRANSPORT — TH DATA UNIT — TRANSPORT

NETWORK — NH DATA UNIT — NETWORK

X.25 PACKET

LINK — F A C DATA UNIT (I FIELD) FCS F — LINK

X.25 FRAME

PHYSICAL — BITS — PHYSICAL

COMMUNICATION PATH

PHYSICAL TRANSMISSION MEDIA

These correspond roughly to the equivalent layers of X.25.

3. Network Layer Concerns—Dial the number and listen for call-progress signals. Redial if you get a busy signal or if cut off. Disconnect when the conversation is completed.

4. Transport Layer Concerns—What is the most cost-effective way to handle this call (or these calls) consistent with priorities? What long distance carrier(s) should be used?

5. Session Layer Concerns—Can this situation be handled in one call or several? Will other people need to be brought in at different times? Who will control the discussion in a multiparty conversation? Who will reestablish the call if we're cut off?

6. Presentation Layer Concerns—Are we talking the same language and dialect?

7. Application Layer Concerns—Am I talking to the right person? Who is paying for this call? Is this the best time to talk, or should I call back later? Does the other party have a pencil and paper to take notes?

Anyone who has used a telephone in everyday business situations can relate to all seven levels of the reference model just described. By reflecting on X.25, the reader should be able to identify the analogies to the packet, link, and physical layer protocols.

WHAT HAVE WE LEARNED?

1. When protocols are layered, the higher level layers are embedded inside fields of less intelligent layers.
2. Packet switching involves fast store-and-forward computers at each network node.
3. X.25 is an international standard packet switching architecture specifying three layers of protocols at the network gateway.
4. When properly used, X.25 networks provide a fast, reliable, accurate, flexible, and cost effective data communications alternative.
5. X.25 specifies two services: Virtual Call service is analogous to a telephone call; Permanent Virtual Circuit service is analogous to a private line.
6. X.25 doesn't provide for dial access or for start-stop transmission, but enhanced services do.
7. A single X.25 interface can handle many logical channels at the same time.
8. X.25 is but a part of a larger group of CCITT standards on public data networks.
9. X.25/X.121 provides for an extremely large worldwide population of terminals.
10. Frame relay is a form of fast packet switching in which error checking and flow control is minimized.
11. Open Systems Interconnection is a reference architectural model which is revolutionizing the way we view telecommunications.

Quiz for Chapter 10

1. The electrical state of the control leads in a serial interface is a concern of:
   a. The physical-layer protocol.
   b. The link-layer protocol.
   c. The network-layer protocol.
   d. None of the above.

2. The X.25 standard specifies a:
   a. Technique for dial access.
   b. Technique for start-stop data.
   c. Data bit rate.
   d. DTE/DCE interface.

3. The X.25 standard is:
   a. Required for all packet switching networks.
   b. A recommendation of the CCITT.
   c. A complete description of a public data network.
   d. Used by all packet terminals.

4. The X.25 standard for packet networks is analogous to:
   a. PBX standards for a telephone network.
   b. Handset standards for a telephone.
   c. Local loop standards for a telephone network.
   d. Switching standards for a telephone network.

5. The value of the "A" field in an LAPB frame specifies:
   a. The calling DTE for a virtual call.
   b. The called DTE for a virtual call.
   c. The data sink for a VC or PVC.
   d. One of the two ends of a serial interface.

6. A group of packets from a source through an X.25 packet system to a sink:
   a. Arrive in the same order sent for VC, but not for PVC.
   b. Arrive in the same order sent for PVC, but not VC.
   c. Arrive in the same order sent for both VC and PVC.
   d. None of the above.

7. The value of N(S) is related to the value of P(S) as follows:
   a. N(S) − P(S) = number of outstanding packets.
   b. N(S) − P(S) = number of outstanding frames.
   c. N(S) − P(S) = number of active logical channels in a link.
   d. They are not related.

8. A protocol is a set of rules governing a time sequence of events that must take place.
   a. Between peers.
   b. Between nonpeers.
   c. Across an interface.
   d. None of the above.

9. The OSI Reference Model defines the functions for seven layers of protocols:
   a. Including the user and communications medium.
   b. Not including the user or communications medium.
   c. Including the communications medium but not the user.
   d. Including the user but not the communications medium.

10. The X.25 standard covers how many OSI layers:
    a. Three
    b. Four
    c. Seven
    d. None

11. Architecturally, link protocols are at a level:
    a. Lower than physical protocols.
    b. Higher than physical protocols.
    c. The same as physical protocols.
    d. None of the above.

12. A data packet is a packet header together with:
    a. A network layer.
    b. An administrative layer.
    c. User data.
    d. A packet switch.

13. A network node joining three or more links is a:
    a. DSE.
    b. DTE.
    c. DCE.
    d. DTE and DCE.

14. The X.25 standard specifies how many separate protocol layers at the serial interface gateway:
    a. 8
    b. 2
    c. 4
    d. 3

15. The LAPB frame structure and the frame structure of SDLC are:
    a. Opposite.
    b. Identical.
    c. Reversed.
    d. None of the above.

16. Establishing a virtual "connection" is functionally equivalent to:
    a. Placing a telephone call prior to a conversation.
    b. Connecting a virtual memory.
    c. Physically connecting a DTE and DCE.
    d. None of the above.

17. In X.25 network layer protocol, the data packets normally contain:
    a. One octet of header plus data.
    b. Two octets of header plus data.
    c. Three octets of header plus data.
    d. Four octets of header plus data.

18. The OSI reference model is:
    a. Worthless.
    b. A protocol.
    c. Not a protocol.
    d. None of the above.

19. Layer 1 of the OSI model is the:
   a. Link layer.
   b. Physical layer.
   c. Network layer.
   d. Transport layer.

20. The applications layer of the OSI model is the:
   a. Seventh layer.
   b. Sixth layer.
   c. Fifth layer.
   d. Fourth layer.

Network Design and Management

ABOUT THIS CHAPTER

The user's terminal is the source and sink of all user data, but good network design and management is usually necessary in order to make data communications networks usable and affordable. By network design, we mean the selection of various circuit parameters and/or the selection and interconnection of various devices to accomplish design goals.

This chapter covers the goals, principles, and tools of efficient network design and management. Many of the administrative principles of network management, such as planning and budgeting, are similar to other kinds of management. The technical aspects to be discussed here include network design goals and throughput timing, networking devices, interconnection, fault isolation, fault correction, and quality assurance.

Any network, no matter how simple or complex, may be incorporated into a larger network. The approach of this chapter is to start with the principles of good network design for basic point-to-point networks, establishing a solid basis for these, and then to discuss some of the technologies for building more complex networks.

NETWORK DESIGN GOALS

To achieve an optimum cost of a data network vs. application balance, factors other than equipment cost must enter into the final cost determination.

The greatest motivation for network design is cost. Cost includes a multitude of factors other than the prices of the terminals and networks. For example, the costs of local area networks are usually justified on the basis of higher speed, because the time of the people and computers who use these networks is expensive. In other situations, communications reliability is the basic cost justification. In many cases, the failure of a data communications system to function properly when needed can cost a business far more than the price of the system.

If price were no object, most data networks would be a simple point-to-point data channel. Indeed, if a point-to-point channel can be kept busy at a reasonably high bit rate for transmitting data that's worth sending, then it may be the most cost-effective way to handle a particular data communication task.

On the other hand, many data applications cannot cost-justify dedicated channels because of insufficient quantity and/or priority of the data. In such cases, it is sometimes possible to combine data from more than one source into a single long-haul transmission path by use of multiplexers and other networking devices. While the use of such techniques may allow cost justification of the application, the addition of equipment is likely to reduce reliability and to increase the time and effort required to find and correct a problem.

The underlying objective of data networking is to strike a satisfactory balance between the accurate, timely, and secure delivery of user data and total cost. The term "satisfactory" implies that the user who is paying for the delivery system is satisfied with it.

Accuracy

Previous chapters have discussed the subject of accuracy in terms of error control. Not all data transmissions are required to be error-free; for example, overseas telex messages and cablegrams which contain human-language messages do not suffer loss of meaning if a word is occasionally misspelled. On the other hand, the transfer of accounting information between financial institutions requires a high level of accuracy.

Timeliness

The timely delivery of data involves: The amount of data to be transmitted, the importance and priority of the information, the average rate of transfer of error-free data, and the availability of the network to the user.

Timeliness involves four general aspects which are discussed in the following:

Amount of Data

Obviously, the amount and priority of data will have an impact on the throughput rate required, but cost must be considered in establishing these parameters. In some extreme situations, the amount of data may be so great that the best way to transfer it will be by physically transporting truckloads of magnetic tape! At the other extreme, a satisfactory "networking" solution might be a simple low-speed transmission over a dialed point-to-point telephone channel.

Priority of Data

As a general rule, the importance and frequency of testing is directly proportional to the importance and priority of the data. An Italian proverb asserts, "Good things cost less than bad ones." While this proverb doesn't apply universally to data communications, it does remind us that the best solution isn't always the cheapest. There are numerous situations, for example in industrial process control and manufacturing, in which a total failure of a data link could cost a company more than $10,000 an hour. In such cases, reliability, testing, and planning for alternative methods obviously are of extreme importance.

Information Throughput Rate

The information throughput rate, properly known as the *Transfer Rate of Information Bits* (TRIB), will be covered in detail in the next section. Basically, TRIB is the average rate of transfer of the actual error-free bits of user data, not counting overhead bits.

Availability of the Network

Availability of the network is determined by three factors: access time, mean time between failures (MTBF), and mean time to restore service (MTRS). For private lines and permanent virtual circuits, access time is of no concern; for dialed connections and virtual calls, the time delay to establish the call might be significant in comparison with the transmission time if the amount of data is small. MTBF usually refers to the time between "hard" (permanent) failures; but if the error rate becomes high enough, the TRIB can nosedive even though the connection still exists. MTRS may involve either a temporary restoration, as in the case of dialed backup for a private line, or it may simply refer to repair time if no alternative service is available.

Security

As more and more confidential and proprietary information is being transmitted through data communication systems, the security of this information becomes more important.

Security is receiving increasing attention as data communication is used more and more for significant and important matters of everyday life. Many sources of information are now available which cover this area in detail. Besides the physical aspects of security, data communication security involves both privacy and authentication. Privacy refers to secrecy (use of codes) and protection from unauthorized access (use of passwords). Authentication has to do with ensuring that a data message hasn't been tampered with between source and sink, and with verifying that the sender of the message is as claimed.

In certain kinds of transmissions, authentication is more important than any other aspect of networking mentioned so far. For example, a Swiss bank receiving an international telex from another bank containing instructions to transfer funds between accounts will be interested in knowing whether extra zeros have been added to the amount, whether account numbers have been modified, and whether the claimed source of the message is authentic.

In summary, data network design involves a complex series of interrelated judgments involving these and other factors:

1. Cost of the delivery system
2. Priority of the data
3. Response time required
4. Throughput rate
5. Accessibility
6. Reliability
7. Testing
8. Contingency Planning
9. Privacy
10. Authentication

TRANSFER RATE OF INFORMATION BITS

The TRIB is a result of several factors other than the data link bit rate. In almost all cases, the TRIB is less than the bit rate at the serial interface.

As mentioned earlier, TRIB is sometimes called information throughput rate. By definition,

$$\text{TRIB} = \frac{\text{Number of information bits accepted by the sink}}{\text{Total time required to get those bits accepted}}$$

Due to the burst nature of most data transmission, TRIB has meaning only as an average over a period of time. Although the data link bit rate has a

The major parameters that adversely affect the TRIB are transmission overhead and delays.

lot to do with TRIB, other factors may at times have as much or more influence. For example, if the channel is noisy, a higher bit rate may increase the error rate to such an extent that the TRIB actually goes down.

TRIB is almost always less than the bit rate at the serial interface. (In a few sophisticated data compression systems, the TRIB may appear to exceed the actual interface bit rate because the receiver puts out more bits than were actually transmitted.) Two other parameters that usually affect TRIB are transmission overhead and delays. Both of these parameters are closely tied to the coding and blocking of the data and to the protocols used. For example, if the protocol requires that acknowledgement of a block must be received by the sender before the next block is transmitted, there will be round trip delays added to the denominator of the TRIB definition given previously. In such instances, block length and delays can have a substantial effect on TRIB. Besides bit rate, the factors that should be considered in estimating TRIB are:

1. Noninformation bits sent with the data. These include:
    a. Start and stop bits if asynchronous transmission is used.
    b. Parity bits if ASCII code is used.
    c. Redundant (or "stuffed") zeroes if a bit-oriented link protocol (SDLC/HDLC) is used.
    d. Filler bits used by teleprocessing system utilities to fill out partial data blocks, if any.

2. Noninformation characters in the message stream. Depending on the link protocol used, these may include:
    a. Sync characters or flags.
    b. Address characters.
    c. Control characters (STX, ACK, etc.) or control byte.
    d. Error-checking characters (BCC or FCS).
    e. Transparency characters (DLE) and pads.

3. Noninformation messages required in the administration of the link protocol. These are the initialization, connect, disconnect, polling and status messages, etc. They usually are not counted in TRIB calculations if the sessions are sufficiently long for them to have a negligible effect.

4. Carrier turn-on delay. This is the period of time between request-to-send from the terminal and clear-to-send from the modem. It is also known as "modem turnaround time." It is required only when a modem is operating with switched carrier on an analog circuit. Normally this situation would apply on a circuit which cannot support the bit rate of the modem two ways simultaneously, such as a dialed connection at 4800 bps. It also applies to at least the remote (secondary) stations, and sometimes to all stations, on a multipoint circuit. The amount of the delay, if any, is programmed into the modem at the time of installation, based on the modem manufacturer's recommendations for the particular circuit type and bit rate. It can be from a few milliseconds to a few hundred milliseconds.

TRIB also is affected by transmission delays, buffer delays, response time computations, number of filler bits, and the transmission error rate.

5. Modem propagation delay. All synchronous modems operating on voice-grade circuits buffer the data both on transmit and receive. Depending on bit rate, the delay can be in the range of 2 to 10 milliseconds (ms) per modem.

6. Circuit propagation delay. Microwave radio signals, including communication satellite signals, and signals in optical fibers travel at near the speed of light. Electrical signals in local wires and cables travel somewhat slower. Also, many local telephone systems contain buffers of various types. As a rule of thumb, estimate 6 ms for local equipment on each end, and 1 millisecond for each 150 miles of cross-country terrestrial circuit. This gives [12 + (miles/150)] milliseconds for terrestrial one-way delay. Depending on latitude and longitude, satellite signals travel 45,000 to 50,000 miles in propagating from one satellite earth station to another; they also are buffered in the satellite and in the earth stations. As a rule of thumb, estimate 350 ms from user-to-user (one way), including terrestrial links between respective earth stations and users.

7. Other propagation delays due to buffering. Most devices used in creating complex networks for data communications store groups of received bits in buffers before retransmitting those bits on the next link. Multiplexers, concentrators, and other types of communications processors are examples of such devices. Depending on the number of bits so buffered and the circuit length, the buffer delays in some systems can exceed all other propagation delays in the transfer of data. Buffer delays are normally included in the equipment specifications provided by the manufacturer.

8. Computation time for response and other interlock time delays. While the time for data calculations normally wouldn't be considered in TRIB, processing time required to check for transmission errors and fabricate an appropriate response should be included since it is a communications function. Also, systems which allow multiple blocks to be sent between acknowledgements often require time gaps or filler bits between successive blocks.

9. Error rate. For blocked data, if the error rate is not large, it is usually sufficient to estimate TRIB by first assuming no errors, then making an adjustment based on the block error rate (BLER). For example, if 1% of the blocks contain an error, the block error rate is said to be 1%. This means that 1% of the blocks will need to be retransmitted; thus the TRIB will be lowered by approximately 1% due to errors.

Example of TRIB Calculation

Problem: How long will it take to transmit 10,000 records a distance of 500 miles every day on a dialed connection at 4800 bps using BSC protocol? There are 80 EBCDIC characters per record, and 2 records per block, thus, there are 5000 blocks containing 160 characters. What is the TRIB?

The first step in calculating TRIB is to determine the propagation delays.

Solution: Since the connection is dialed at 4800 bps, the carrier must be switched, which means there will be a carrier turn-on delay in each direction for each block (one for data, one for acknowledgement). From the modem manufacturer's recommendations, this is established as 100 ms. Other delays include:

1. Circuit propagation delay which, for a terrestrial 500 mile circuit, would be about 15 ms.
2. Modem propagation delay which, according to the modem operation manual, is 4 ms.
3. Computation delay which, according to measurements on the actual terminals, is 10 ms for the receiving terminal and negligible for the transmitting terminal.

Assume that each data transmission block includes:

1	leading pad character
4	sync characters
1	STX character
160	data characters (2 records at 80 characters each)
1	EOB or ETX character
2	character lengths of BCC
1	trailing pad
170	characters

The next step is to determine the character count in the data block and acknowledgement block, and the transmission time required at the data rate.

Thus, each block has 170 characters including overhead, but not counting DLE characters that would be sent if transparency is required. If each character requires 8 bits, the transmission time actually needed to send a data block at 4800 bps will be:

$$\frac{170 \times 8}{4800} = 283 \text{ ms}$$

Assume that each acknowledgement block includes:

1	leading pad character
4	sync characters
2	character lengths of ACK0/ACK1
1	trailing pad character
8	characters (all overhead)

The transmit time actually needed to send an acknowledgement block will be:

$$\frac{8 \times 8}{4800} = 13 \text{ ms}$$

The calculation is completed by combining all delay times to obtain round-trip time per block, which results in the total time for all blocks. The total time divided into the actual data bits transferred gives the TRIB value.

Including delays, the *round-trip* time to send 1 block will be:

```
100  ms near-end carrier turn-on
283  ms data block transmission
  4  ms transmit modem propagation
 15  ms circuit propagation
  4  ms receive modem propagation
 10  ms sink terminal calculation
100  ms far-end carrier turn-on
 13  ms acknowledgement block transmission
  4  ms transmit modem propagation
 15  ms circuit propagation
  4  ms receive modem propagation
552  ms or 0.552 second round-trip time per block
```

The total time needed to send 5000 blocks, neglecting retransmissions due to errors, is $0.552 \times 5000 = 2760$ seconds, or 46 minutes. If we assume that 1% of the blocks will contain at least 1 bit in error, then the time will be lengthened by about 1%. The actual number of information bits transmitted is 160 characters per block $\times$ 8 bits per character $\times$ 5000 blocks = 6,400,000 bits. If errors are not counted, then:

$$\text{TRIB} = \frac{6,400,000 \text{ bits}}{2760} = 2319 \text{ bits/sec}$$

Maximizing TRIB

It will be noted that the TRIB in the example just given is less than half of the modem bit rate of 4800 bps! Major factors contributing to this poor result were the modem carrier turn-on delay (modem turnaround) and the fact that acknowledgement of each block had to be received before the next block could be transmitted. (Note that the total of these times accounted for almost 40% of the round trip time.)

Several actions can be taken that would improve the TRIB. Installing a two-way simultaneous channel might provide the desired improvement, if the added expense of a private line is justified.

Persons who are unfamiliar with the type of calculation just illustrated often assume that the best way to improve throughput is to increase modem speed. To attempt such a remedy in this example would probably result in lower (not higher) TRIB, since it is likely that the modem turnaround, modem propagation delay, and error rate all would be higher. Not only would the modems cost more, but also the dialing and redialing required to obtain a connection that would operate satisfactorily at a higher bit rate would be both time-consuming and frustrating to the operator—if it would work at all.

One possible approach to improvement of TRIB in the example shown might be to eliminate modem turnaround entirely by installing a two-way simultaneous channel. At 4800 bps, this would require a private line. Comparison of private-line tariffs with those for dialed connections for the distance and amount of data involved will reveal that dialing is considerably less expensive.

Other possible approaches to improving TRIB performance include changing to a different protocol or increasing block length.

Still another approach to TRIB improvement might be to change to a different protocol. SDLC is capable of allowing acknowledgement of up to

7 frames with only one response. However, to change from BSC to SDLC link protocol would require expensive software and probably hardware modifications in both terminals.

The best way to improve the TRIB in this case would be to increase block length. Assuming sufficient buffer capacity in both terminals, an increase of block length from 2 records to 10 records would result in a total round-trip time of 1.619 seconds per block, with only 1000 blocks required to be sent. The total time needed would be 27 minutes, a daily saving of 19 minutes of long distance calling. The new TRIB would be 3953 bps, an increase of 70%.

Caution: Increasing block length always increases the block error rate because there is a greater exposure to the probability of error in a long block. For a block length increase of 500%, the BLER will increase by roughly the same factor. In the example, if the block error rate had really been 1% before (very high for such a short block), it would be about 5% now. This would erode some of the time saving.

Optimum Block Length

Exact matching to the optimum block length often is not practical because of what the blocking program can accomplish or because long-term changes in error rates and delays cause the optimum block length to change.

Figure 11.1 illustrates how block length affects TRIB, all other factors being equal. For every short blocks, the TRIB is low (as illustrated in the previous calculations) because overhead is a significant proportion of the total transmission. For very long blocks also, the TRIB is low because there is a significant probability of error within the block, and most blocks have to be retransmitted. Somewhere between the extremes, there is a block length, L_M, which yields maximum TRIB. Whether L_M is optimum depends on several factors besides TRIB:

1. If the error rate is low, the value of L_M may be so large as to be impractical, particularly for an interactive data system in which fast response is more important than throughput.

2. Quite often, the memory capacity of the terminals is not sufficient to handle a block length of L_M.

3. The utility programs that actually perform the blocking of data usually won't allow a precise match with L_M.

4. Long-term changes in error rates and delays make precise matching impractical anyway.

Regardless of these considerations, the network designer should make reasonable estimates of TRIB, be aware of the major impairments to faster TRIB, and ensure that the combination of factors is ''best'' for each situation.

NETWORKING DEVICES

Several types of special-purpose devices exist for improving cost-effectiveness of data networks. The basic purposes and advantages of the main types are given in the paragraphs that follow. The reader is referred to Chapter 6 for detailed information concerning the operation and utilization of multiplexers.

Figure 11.1.
Block Length (L_M) for maximum TRIB

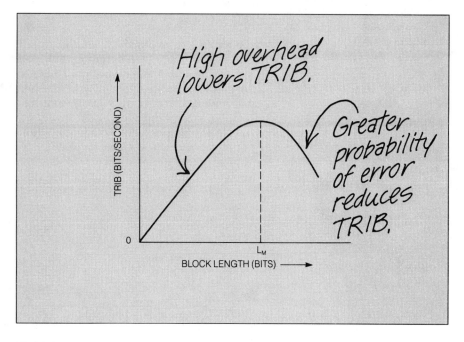

Multiplexers

Both the FDM and the TDM have advantages and disadvantages that must be considered to determine which to use in a particular application.

Multiplexers are devices that allow the combination of several data channels independently into one physical circuit. Data streams so combined can be separated and recovered at the opposite end of the system. There are two main types: frequency-division multiplexers (FDMs) and time-division multiplexers (TDMs). FDM has the advantage that it can be used on multipoint circuits, but the individual channels usually must each be for start-stop data. TDM can be used if all channels are point-to-point and generally allows faster bit rates and potentially more channels than FDM at less cost.

TDMs are of two types: classical (or dumb) TDMs and statistical (or smart) TDMs. Dumb TDMs should be used if the duty cycles of the data channels to be multiplexed are relatively high. A high duty cycle means that the channel is actually carrying bits most of the time. Since dumb TDMs send even idle (marking) bits when a channel becomes inactive, they waste a lot of potential capacity when the duty cycles are low.

Whenever usage statistics indicate a low duty cycles as the normal mode of utilization of most of the channels to be multiplexed, a statistical multiplexer system is usually a good choice. These devices send only data bits (no idle bits), so they can appear to have a higher total bit rate than the actual rate if there is a high percentage of idle bits coming from the terminals.

Modem Sharing Devices

Modem sharing devices allow several terminals to share the serial interface of one modem.

Modem sharing devices (MSDs) do just that: They allow several remote terminals at one site on a common multipoint circuit to share a single modem at that site. MSDs do not multiplex; they simply provide a means of sharing the serial interface of one modem among several terminals.

When a modem sharing unit is used, transmission occurs via polling and broadcast. To understand the operation and utilization of a *modem sharing unit* (MSU) consider Figure 11.2 in which three terminals share access to a common modem via a MSU.

Figure 11.2.
Modem Sharing Unit Enables Transmission via Polling and Broadcasting

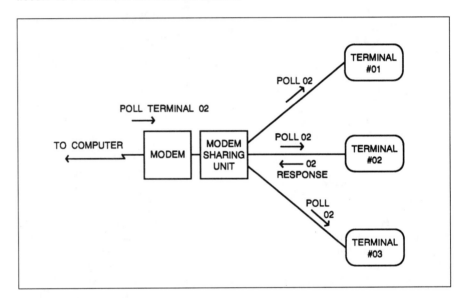

Line Bridging Devices

A useful networking device is the protocol converter; a microprocessor which converts data from one protocol to another.

Line bridging devices allow two or more analog circuits to be shared as one. Bridges are not multiplexers: They allow one modem to be used with circuits to more than one destination. Telephone companies and users can use bridges to create multipoint analog circuits from point-to-point segments.

Modem Eliminators

Modem eliminators are used to connect two DTEs together directly. They also are called null modems.

Protocol Converters

Protocol converters are microprocessors which convert data operating in one protocol, say start-stop ASCII, to another, say IBM BSC. A dial-up X.3 PAD for converting start-stop to X.25 is an example of a protocol converter.

INTERCONNECTION OF NETWORKING DEVICES

When actually making the physical connections between the various types of networking devices, be sure that all equipment manuals and interface standards are thoroughly understood.

The last section contained only a partial listing of devices intended to interconnect digital serial interfaces. Space does not allow a discussion of the numerous possible alternative requirements in the actual interconnection of leads between devices, terminals, modems, etc.

Probably the best advice that can be given is to study the equipment manuals and the interface standards themselves. As an alternative, the reader is referred to the book *Data Communications Networking Devices, Second Edition* by Gilbert Held and published by John Wiley & Sons for specific information concerning the operation and utilization of over 25 networking devices. Fortunately, all standard digital serial interfaces have been designed so that no actual damage can be caused by interconnecting two devices incorrectly. In the case of uncertainty, a programmable break-out box, (discussed in the next section) can be a handy tool for trying different combinations until the connection works.

In addition to the physical mating of pins and receptacles when connecting two serial interfaces together, particular attention should be given to:

1. Which is the driver (Source) of signal and which is the receiver (sink) of signal. Each pin-receptacle pair must contain one of each. For example, pin 2 of an RS-232 connector involves a driver in a DTE and a receiver in a DCE.

2. Stand-alone TDMs are generally schizophrenic; that is, the terminal ports each behave as DCEs communicating with DTEs, and the trunk port behaves as a DTE communicating with a DCE. TDMs generally are manufactured with female receptacles on all ports, both terminal and trunk, requiring male-to-male cables between the trunk port and trunk DCE. When extending such a TDM port by use of a remote channel, special care must be given to control, data, and timing leads. The TDM manual should be read to obtain specific information.

3. Whenever synchronous devices are interconnected, special attention should be given to clocking. Remember that the DCE is normally the source (driver) for both the transmit clock and receiver clock. However, when two DCEs are interconnected, one DCE must accept external clocking, and it must be programmed (optioned) for external clocking, usually by an internal switch setting. The presence of clock pulses on the external clock pin is not sufficient to make a modem accept external clocking.

4. Digital transmission systems normally will not accept external clocking, since their timing comes from a central network clock.

FAULT ISOLATION

Fault detection usually is pretty easy; fault isolation is more complicated. The first question is, "Is the problem in a terminal or in the communications system?" Troubleshooting data terminals is beyond the scope of this book. If the terminals pass self-test procedures, but still will not communicate, chances are good that the problem is in the communications system.

Loopback Tests

In the loopback test, which is a basic data communication fault isolation technique, faults are successively isolated by the process of elimination.

One of the basic techniques for isolation of faults in data communications is the loopback test. In a loopback, the output at the far end of a system or subsystem is connected to the input of the return path. Then the output of the return path is examined in relation to the input to the outgoing path.

Figure 11.3 illustrates how successive loopbacks can be used to isolate a fault on a simple point-to-point data link which uses an analog circuit. The local modem is first self-tested using an analog loopback at its far terminals (point A). If it passes the test, the loop is removed from the local modem. Then the local modem and the analog circuit are tested together using a remote analog loopback at the near terminals (point B) of the remote modem. If that test also appears satisfactory, then the remote analog loop is removed and the entire data link is tested end-to-end round-trip using a digital loopback at the far terminals (point C) of the remote modem. (Loopbacks at points B and C are useful only if the channel is full-duplex.) Using a process of elimination, the location of the fault can be narrowed to either the local modem, the analog circuit, or the remote modem.

Figure 11.3.
Loopback Test Points

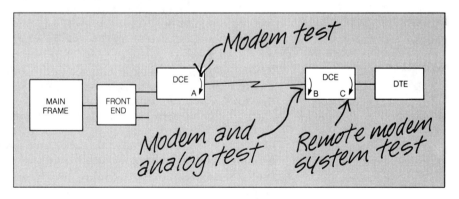

Loopbacks cannot determine which side of a path, outgoing or return, is faulty, but only the person who has to repair it really needs that information. End-to-end tests can distinguish the direction of the fault, but that often requires at least modest training of a person at the remote site.

Not only should one know what parameters of the faulty device can be tested, but the capabilities, limitations, and special requirements of the test system/equipment also should be known.

Caution Number One

Know what is being tested when performing a self-test on a device. As with terminals, no self-test ever tests all of the circuitry. For example, Figure 11.4 shows that a self-test of a modem doesn't check data continuity through the line transformers and through the RS-232 interface circuitry. The latter problem can be very treacherous. Whenever practical, use external tests to be sure.

**Figure 11.4.
Some Modem Circuitry
Is Not Tested in
Self-Test**

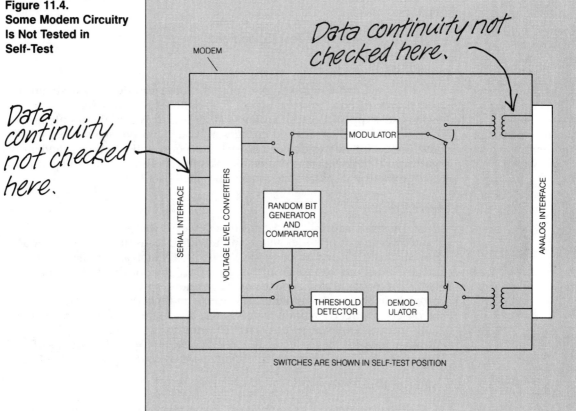

Caution Number Two

Most analog data circuits are designed to operate with a substantial drop in signal level from input to output; for example, there is 16-dB loss each way in a private-line voice-grade circuit to be used for data. When an analog loopback is performed at the remote end without inserting gain at that point, the input signal for the return path is 16 dB lower than it should be. Such a low-level signal can cause both the analog return path and the local modem receiver to operate improperly, perhaps giving a false indication. Many systems that provide for remote analog loopbacks automatically insert gain in the loopback path to avoid this problem. If the modems used in the test depicted in Figure 11.3 are not so equipped, then a different procedure should be used. For example, perform a self-test on each modem, then with an assistant at the far end, perform an end-to-end test.

Data Communications Test Equipment

Amplifier-Monitor

A wide variety of test equipment is available to assist in the detection and isolation of faults in data communication systems.

The self-contained battery-operated audio amplifier-speaker-monitor, sometimes called a "watergate box," is readily available at retail electronic supply stores for around $20 or less. It is useful not only for detecting modem carrier and changes in modem output signals, but it's also the easiest way to detect a noisy circuit or to tell whether a modem is putting out tone-dial or pulse-dial signals. It can also be used to monitor call progress and answer-back tones on dialed data links.

Breakout Box

The basic specialized data testing device is the breakout box, so-named because it provides access to individual leads in the serial interface between a DTE (such as a terminal) and a DCE (such as a modem). Prices range from about $60 to about $250 for breaking out the 25 leads of an RS-232 interface. Price depends on ruggedness, on whether the unit is programmable (leads can be crisscrossed), and whether data activity can be observed directly without a voltmeter. The higher priced units feature built-in battery power, full tri-state LED monitoring of leads, programmability, ruggedness, and DIP switches to open the circuits of individual leads. They may also provide positive and negative test voltages.

Bit Error Rate Tester

The next step up in acquisition of specialized data test equipment would be a *bit error rate tester* (BERT). RS-232 BERTs range in price from under $500 to around $3000, depending on whether block error (BLERT) and error-second measurements are to be included, whether start and stop bit insertion/deletion is required (if asynchronous multiplexers are in the circuit), and various automatic indicator features. Some models also feature programmable message generators for checking out teleprinters.

High-speed BERT/BLERTs in the multimegabit per second range can cost much more.

Decibel Meter

If analog voice-grade circuits are used extensively, a decibel (dB) meter is a wise investment for checking transmit and receive levels. A basic dB meter costs around $200. Persons considering purchase of a dB meter should consider a combination unit. Excellent portable meters with digital display are available. Such a meter which can read dBm, relative dB, frequency, relative frequency, voltage, current, and resistance costs about $400 to $500. Such an expenditure is not recommended unless testing on analog circuits is expected to be a common occurrence.

Oscilloscope

An oscilloscope, used with a breakout box for access, is an important error isolation and testing tool.

A multichannel oscilloscope (or scope for short) with x-y inputs can be used in conjunction with a breakout box for observing serial interface signals and/or in conjunction with a modem for detecting certain impairments on analog circuits. Examples of the use of a dual-trace scope in the RS-232 interface would be to measure modem turnaround time, to check for crosstalk interference between timing leads, and to observe degradation of signals in long serial interface cables.

With synchronous modems having signal-space (constellation) pattern generators, an x-y oscilloscope becomes a powerful instrument for detecting phase hits, phase jitter, amplitude hits, harmonic distortion, dropouts, and impulse noise in analog circuits. With other modems, a scope can be used to observe eye patterns for harmonic distortion, phase jitter, and certain types of hits.

Scopes which are suitable for these purposes generally cost in the range of $800 to $3000, depending on compactness, maximum data rate, and number of channels.

Voice Frequency Test Set

A voice-frequency test set permits measurement of frequency response, noise, and distortion of voice-grade analog circuits.

For the really serious user of data over voice-grade analog circuits, a voice frequency test set is a device which can quantify the major parameters of a voice-grade analog circuit. Standard capabilities include frequency response (amplitude received versus frequency for constant amplitude transmitted), C-message noise in dBrnc, C-message notched noise (S/N) in dB, and audio monitoring. Costs can range from $1500 upward, depending on the degree of automation in the tests and additional test functions provided. While the less expensive units do not provide for measurement of envelope delay distortion (one of the two parameters affected by C-conditioning), large amounts of delay distortion often are accompanied by large amounts of attenuation distortion which is much easier to measure. Voice frequency test sets normally should be used in pairs to provide end-to-end testing.

Data Link Content Monitor

A data link content monitor monitors and displays signals crossing the serial interface. Some allow specified sequences to be stored for later analysis.

Many large users of data communications have painfully discovered that the general purpose computer is not an efficient device for debugging data link and network protocols. Nor is it the best device for bit error rate testing of wideband data channels, T1 multiplexers and the like. The computer time, programmer time, and other expensive resources saved in a single project often can pay for the purchase of test equipment to cover these areas.

One equipment category is the basic RS-232 data link content monitor at approximately $2000 to $6000. This device simply monitors and displays signals passing across the serial interface. The display is normally in terms of characters, if appropriate, or it can be in binary or hexadecimal in the case of uncoded data. Pricing varies with the number of codes, the type of display, the ability to trap (or freeze) and display specific sequences, the amount of memory, scrolling of trapped memory contents, speed of the device with and without recording in memory, and whether the conditions of various nondata leads in the serial interface are recorded with the data for later analysis.

Simulator

Since a simulator is actually a special-purpose computer, it can be programmed to simulate a computer port, remote terminal, or network gateway for system development.

Monitor devices are excellent for diagnosing protocol problems in data links, but they are not efficient for system development. This function is best handled by a simulator. Such a device can be user-programmed to simulate a computer port, remote terminal, or network gateway in order to "exercise" the hardware/software system being developed. Simulators are actually special-purpose computers utilizing easy-to-learn high-level programming languages. They also can be programmed to operate effectively as content monitors, BERTs, and BLERTs. Prices range from $1000 to $25,000, depending on protocols supported, speed, serial interfaces supported, amount of memory, type of display, ease of programming, and portability. The newer units provide simulation up through the packet level (OSI Level 3) of X.25/X.75 protocols.

Protocol Analyzer

The protocol analyzer is the most sophisticated type of data communications test equipment currently marketed. The protocol analyzer obtains its name from the major functions it performs—protocol analysis. In doing so, the protocol analyzer monitors the bit stream flowing on a communications circuit or a LAN cable and decodes the bits into characters that represent the format and information content of the protocol. When designed explicitly for use on LANs, the protocol analyzer is usually referred to as a LAN analyzer. When designed for use on LANs and WANs the protocol analyzer is referred to as an enterprise analyzer. For example, a protocol analyzer monitoring an HDLC transmission would convert the bit sequence 01111110 to a flag character and then indicate the start or end of a frame of information. Other features incorporated into most protocol analyzers include the ability to analyze several communications protocols, perform data simulation, and BERT and BLERT testing.

The entry of digital electronics into data communications is having a tremendous influence on network control systems.

systems constitutes a powerful fault isolation and correction technique.

The cost effectiveness of a network control system based on testing and dedicated side channels to carry test information in the analog link must be weighed in view of the inroads being made by digital transmission systems. Digital segments don't support analog side channels. As digital transmission systems replace analog systems over the next few years, this type of control scheme will become less practical. A new generation of

Most protocol analyzers include a built-in breakout box, keyboard, on-line storage, and a display in a common housing. Due to the almost ubiquitous status of personal computers, some protocol analyzer manufacturers designed their products as adapter boards which are inserted into the system unit of a PC. When obtained as an adapter board, the protocol analyzer uses the keyboard, on-line storage, and display of the computer, significantly reducing the cost of the analyzer. Prices of protocol analyzers range from $1500 for devices manufactured on adapter boards for use in personal computers to over $25,000 for stand-alone protocol analyzers designed to decode the most recent protocols, such as signaling on the ISDN D channel.

Figure 11.5 illustrates a Digilog 800 protocol/performance analyzer. This device contains a color monitor, hard disk, and floppy disk, as well as a full function keyboard. In addition to decoding a number of protocols, the Digilog 800 provides numerous performance statistics based upon line monitoring of different protocols. The screen shown in Figure 11.5 is a "fill in the blank" menu system which enables operators to easily develop programs and obtain performance measurements or decode different protocols.

Figure 11.5.
Digilog 800 Protocol/
Performance Analyzer
(Courtesy Digilog Corp.)

Network Control System

Many companies which operate large complex data networks have found the timely isolation of faults to be so important as to cost-justify the installation of a centralized network control system as depicted in Figure 11.6. Such systems commonly use the low end of the frequency spectrum of the voice-grade circuit to carry a special interrogation and reporting "side channel." Such systems add significantly to the cost of each modem in the system.

**Figure 11.6.
Network Control
System**

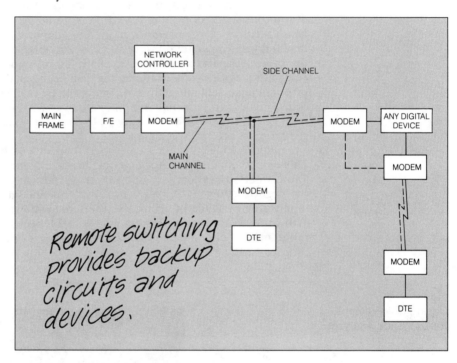

In a large complex data network, it may be cost effective to add a centralized network control system to assist in fault detection and isolation.

A modem which is addressed by the central unit can be commanded to perform certain tests and report the results back for display or recording. Such tests as continuity, level of received signal, and condition of an RS-232 lead can be accurately conducted without interrupting or modifying data flow. Other tests, such as self-tests and loopbacks, do cause interruption of data flow. Many of the more sophisticated systems can be user programmed to perform interruptive tests automatically during off-hours when actual interruption of data is unlikely. Test results can be automatically logged and compared with former test results to detect changes in circuit parameters.

Network control systems usually have a scheme for remote switching of circuits and devices to provide backup in the event of failures. The combination of remote testing and remote backup of data communications network control systems based on digital interrogation and reporting is now beginning to replace the analog systems.

RESTORATION OF SERVICE

Providing reliable service restoration promptly and economically is a challenging task.

Given enough planning and money, prompt and reliable restoration of data communications service is easy, but to make it economical is a little harder.

The planner for data communications backup should consider the following questions:

1. What is the frequency and length of downtime to be expected?

2. Can steps be taken to decrease the frequency and length of downtime without incurring additional costs; that is, are you getting what you already are paying for?

3. What will be the extra costs incurred due to complete outage of the service for the frequency and duration indicated?

4. Can these extra costs be reduced by a reduced-capability backup; for example, backing up a 4800 bps private line using a 1200 bps dialed connection?

5. What are the actual costs of all relevant backup schemes? Include the cost of personnel time as well as the cost of backup. The cost of backup must include the operating costs, such as dialed connection charges, as well as initial investment and installation costs.

Getting the Most for the Money

Existing systems performance often can be improved by closely examining the existing system and established procedures.

Before designing and implementing a backup technique, a review of current procedures might improve the frequency and duration of downtime.

1. Is there ongoing positive communication not only with the people in the user's own organization, but also with suppliers of equipment and services?

2. Do users have a thorough knowledge of the capabilities and limitations of all data communications system facilities, software, and hardware at their disposal, particularly the capabilities and limitations of self-contained test features?

3. Are there well-designed restoration procedures, agreed to in advance by all concerned and strictly followed?

4. Are new systems benchmark tested as they are placed in service, and then tested on a regular schedule to detect changes in circuit parameters?

5. Are exceptions (failures) documented, and are repeat offenders discovered?

6. Is there an ongoing in-house training program to ensure that each individual in the organization can properly handle all appropriate

parts of the above five points for those portions of the system within his or her purview?

Rapport With Suppliers

Close personal rapport between supplier and customers at all levels is of utmost importance to the smooth, efficient restoration of service of a communications system.

Central to any cost-effective service-restoration program is a firmly established positive rapport with all major suppliers of equipment and services—especially with key individuals such as telephone company (telco) personnel. Many data-link failures can be traced directly or indirectly to a breakdown in people-to-people communications between vendors and users. For example, in the case of an organization like a telephone company with many levels of personnel that deal with the customer, the rapport between supplier and customer must exist at all levels: Data technicians should be on a first-name basis with telco testboard personnel, technician supervisors with testboard supervisors, data communications operations manager with the telco network operations manager, and so on. When such rapport exists, several symptoms will be apparent:

1. Employees on both sides will be more helpful and understanding, especially in high-pressure situations.

2. Information on new testing and quality assurance techniques will flow easier. The user will gain a better understanding of the built-in test capabilities in the vendor's services and equipment; in fact, technicians on both sides will be eager to share their excitement over some new piece of test gear or a new discovery.

3. Better confidence in each other's abilities will emerge and will give rise to more of a supplier-user team approach.

4. The vendor employee will often render assistance above and beyond what is required and expected.

Data communications managers who succeed in cultivating this kind of rapport with their major vendors consider it among their greatest assets. In particular, they are careful to establish and follow good procedures for the testing of systems and proper reporting of problems to the vendor. Inherent in this process is the careful development of an escalation and reporting system.

Escalation and Reporting

Clearly established procedures must be developed to ensure that the proper level of management is involved in the correction of problems in a timely manner.

Through meetings with all concerned, the data communications manager should develop a very specific escalation schedule. This schedule should show exactly who becomes involved at increasing levels of authority, what calls are placed, and at what levels when a particular type of problem fails to show progress toward resolution after a specific time lapse. All persons involved in this schedule should be involved in its development, should ''sign-off'' on it, should have a personal copy of the finished product, and should have no cause for negative feelings whenever it is invoked.

Before asking for help from higher levels or from the vendor, it is absolutely vital that the user exhaust all means at his disposal to make use of test facilities available to him—especially self-tests. Remember the story about the little boy who cried "wolf"? Nothing can damage credibility and rapport faster than to blame the vendor when the problem is another vendor or in-house.

The personnel involved in system and data subsystem testing should be thoroughly familiar with the capabilities and limitations of the tests and the test equipment.

Personnel responsible for data subsystem and system testing must be thoroughly familiar with self-tests and their limitations, and with the meaning of any other tests for which they have equipment. Troubles should be reported only after such testing has been adequately documented, and escalation should be invoked only after the lack of progress in problem resolution has been documented.

Such documentation of problems and their resolution should be permanently recorded and reviewed with the vendor at regular intervals. This review aids in spotting areas of recurring difficulties and possibly degrading facilities and components, so these can be serviced before a "hard" failure occurs. This is why the benchmarking of newly acquired facilities is important.

Finally, appreciation should be expressed when appropriate. Nothing will make an employee of a vendor work harder for a user than an appreciation letter to his boss for good work done in the user's behalf.

Backup Techniques

Thought must be given to backup systems to keep priority lines in at least partial operation while repairs are being made. In high-priority situations, a duplicate hot-standby private line is often used.

Even the best procedures will not totally eliminate failures of circuits and equipment. When priority of data requires backup during the repair process, decisions must be made in the areas of providing spare parts for on-premise equipment (such as multiplexer boards and power supplies), providing complete standby devices (such as modems), providing an alternate physical communication medium (such as dialed backup), and determining who will do what when a failure occurs.

In high-priority situations, it isn't uncommon to find duplicate hot-standby private lines to backup the regularly used private lines. In such cases, it's important that the backup be provided via diversely routed circuits, even to the extent of using different entry points into the user's buildings.

The majority of backup plans provide for dialed backup, often with reduced capability. The following factors should be considered:

1. Backup on the public telephone network is generally limited to 9600 bps.

2. Depending on several factors, including distance from the modem to the central office, satisfactory dialed connections at 9600 bps may not be attainable, requiring fall-back to 7200 or 4800 bps.

3. If full-duplex backup is required at bit rates greater than 1200 bps, two calls may be required. This doubles the cost of providing backup. Some users provide only half-duplex backup for a full-duplex circuit; however, this type of fall-back may require changing the link protocol option selections whenever backup is invoked.

4. If the circuit to be replaced is multipoint, full backup will require simultaneous calls to each remote site that is affected; that is, six calls to fully backup a three-drop full-duplex circuit. Some users provide backup of a multipoint line to only one remote site at a time, which reduces the number of dialable lines required in the data center.

Suppliers of network control systems generally have system-integrated provision for remotely controlled backup and switching of circuits, modems, multiplexers, or anything else money can buy. For the less sophisticated user, stand-alone devices are available from a number of suppliers.

Figure 11.7 illustrates a typical stand-alone arrangement to provide remotely controlled full-duplex dialed backup of a multipoint circuit. The central site bridge provides for simultaneous transmission and reception on the private line and each pair of central office business lines. Because of the high cost for usage of a multiplicity of dialed connections, most users prefer manually dialed backup to ensure control over long-distance charges.

**Figure 11.7.
Dialed Backup of a
Multipoint Analog
Circuit**

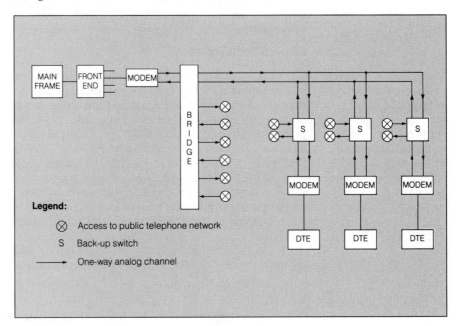

There are several methods that may be used to provide dialed backup service. In high-priority situations, alternate paths should be provided for both the private line and the remote DCE.

There are several schemes for the operation of the "S" switches in Figure 11.7. One typical scheme for operation of one "S" switch is as follows:

1. The central site technician places a call on one business line to the appropriate line connected to an "S" switch. The switch "answers" the call and places the call on "hold," starting an abort timer.

2. Then the operator places a second call to the other line. If the call comes in before the abort timer runs out, the switch will answer and connect the modem to both dialed lines; if not, it will abort the first call.

3. The "S" switch will revert back to the private line if either no modem carrier is detected within a specified interval or the carrier is interrupted. More sophisticated types of "S" switches require reception of special coded commands both for switching away from the private line and for returning to it.

Some high-priority systems require the ability to substitute another path for both the private line and the remote DCE. Figure 11.8 shows such a configuration. The operation is similar to that in Figure 11.7, except for the position and arrangement of the switch within the circuit. As indicated in the drawing, this arrangement is also useful for backing up a digital link.

**Figure 11.8.
Dialed Backup of a
Digital Link**

WHAT HAVE WE LEARNED?

1. The underlying objective of data networking is to strike a balance between the accurate timely delivery of user data and total cost.
2. Any network, no matter how simple or complex, may be incorporated into a larger network. A larger network cannot be optimized until its component parts are individually optimized.
3. Information throughput rate involves many factors besides the modem bit rate.
4. Classical time division multiplexers provide a powerful tool for combining data transmission link requirements into a smaller number of higher speed links. Statistical TDMs may be even more powerful if the duty cycles of individual links to be combined are low.
5. Frequency division multiplexers can be useful if the links involve low-speed multipoint data transmission.
6. Other useful networking devices include sharing devices, modem eliminators, and protocol converters.
7. Loopbacks are a common and simple technique for testing data communications components and networks.
8. Test equipment for data communications falls into two generic categories: digital testing and analog testing.
9. Good network design includes appropriate planning for contingencies and procedures for restoring service.
10. Dialed backup is a common technique for restoring service on analog and digital transmission systems.

Quiz for Chapter 11

1. Which of the following is not considered a primary objective of data networking?
   a. Security.
   b. Packet switching.
   c. Timeliness.
   d. Accuracy.

2. On a point-to-point data channel using an analog circuit, TRIB is:
   a. Higher than the modem bit rate.
   b. Equal to the modem bit rate.
   c. Lower than the modem bit rate.
   d. Not related to the modem bit rate.

3. The block length that gives maximum TRIB:
   a. Increases as the error rate increases.
   b. Decreases as the error rate increases.
   c. Isn't related to error rate.
   d. Is called the optimum block length.

4. Smart TDMs:
   a. Are always better than dumb TDMs.
   b. Are always better than FDM.
   c. Are the same as modem sharing devices.
   d. May be better than dumb TDMs if the data terminals have a low duty cycle.

5. FDM devices can operate:
   a. On multipoint analog data channels.
   b. More efficiently than dumb TDMs.
   c. More efficiently than smart TDMs.
   d. Like modem sharing devices.

6. Protocol converters are:
   a. The same as multiplexers.
   b. The same as TDMs.
   c. Usually operated in pairs.
   d. Usually not operated in pairs.

7. Null modems are a type of:
   a. Modem eliminator.
   b. Modem.
   c. Multiplexer.
   d. Protocol converter.

8. A basic technique for isolating data communication faults is:
   a. Calling the telephone company.
   b. Performing a loopback test.
   c. Calling the DTE service department.
   d. Simulating the system on a special-purpose computer.

9. The main purpose of a data link content monitor is to:
   a. Determine the type of switching used in a data line.
   b. Determine the type of transmission used in a data link.
   c. Detect problems in protocols.
   d. Measure bit error rates.

10. The most sophisticated type
of data communications test
equipment is the:
  a. simulator.
  b. protocol analyzer.
  c. DTE.
  d. breakout box.

11. Full-capability dialed backup
of a multipoint full-duplex
4800-bps private line having
4 remote drops requires:
  a. 4 calls.
  b. Either 4 or 8 calls.
  c. 8 calls.
  d. Can't tell.

ISDN

ABOUT THIS CHAPTER

ISDN, which is the acronym for *Integrated Services Digital Network*, augurs the potential for the development of a universal digital network that provides integrated voice and data on common telephone company facilities. In this chapter, we'll examine the idea behind ISDN, its architecture, and some of the benefits that can be expected from it in the not-too-distant future.

CONCEPT

The need to transmit human speech resulted in the development of a telephone system that was originally designed for the transmission of analog data. Although the telephone system satisfied the basic need to transmit human speech, its design required the conversion of digital signals produced by computers and terminals into an analog format for the transmission of digital data. This conversion was awkward and expensive because modems were required at both ends of a telephone channel to do the digital-to-analog and analog-to-digital conversions.

A rapid decrease in the cost of semiconductors and the evolution in digital signal processing resulted in the application of digital technology to the telephone network. In the 1960s, telephone companies began to replace the electromechanical switches located in their central offices with digital switches. By the early 1970s, several communications carriers were offering end-to-end transmission services in which unipolar digital data from terminals and computers were converted first into a modified bipolar digital format, then through a series of digital repeaters in the network, the data was transmitted to its destination. At its destination, data was converted back to its original unipolar digital format. The unipolar to bipolar signal conversion enabled the telephone company to space repeaters farther apart, reducing the construction cost of the digital network. Figure 12.1 illustrates the use of amplifiers and repeaters on analog and digital circuits.

The amplifier used on analog circuits amplifies the entire signal to include any signal impairments. The digital repeater, which is also known as a data regenerator, regenerates a new digital pulse, eliminating any distortion to the pulse that occurs as it travels on a digital circuit.

Because analog amplifiers increase the size of an analog signal to include any previous distortion, whereas digital repeaters regenerate a digital pulse and eliminate any previous distortion to the digital signal, the

**Figure 12.1.
Amplifiers Versus
Repeaters**

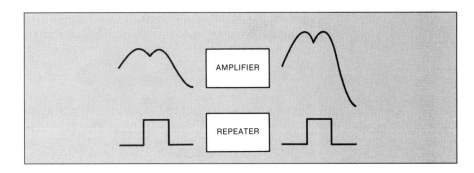

error rate on a digital network is significantly lower than that on an analog facility. In addition, the devices required to perform the unipolar to bipolar and bipolar to unipolar signal conversion are much less expensive than the modems required for signal conversion on analog facilities.

By the mid-1980s, most telephone companies had incorporated a large amount of digital technology into their plant facilities so that a significant portion of the lines connecting telephone company central offices transported speech in digital form, although speech continued to be carried in analog form from the subscriber to the central office. At the central office, speech is digitized for transmission over the backbone network of the telephone system. Similarly, at the central office closest to the destination of the telephone conversation, the digitized speech is reconverted into its analog format, then transmitted to the subscriber's telephone.

The progression of telephone systems technology in the use of digital technology forms the basis for ISDN. Thus, ISDN can be viewed as an evolutionary progression in the conversion of the analog telephone system into an eventual all-digital network, enabling both voice and data to be transported end to end in a digital format.

Besides integrating voice and data, ISDN provides a level of communications capability above that obtainable with conventional analog technology. When voice and data are integrated, subscribers will be able to talk on the telephone and use a computer or terminal at the same time over a common subscriber line. For business, this capability should improve the productivity of office workers and reduce the cost of wiring buildings and offices because there should be no need to install separate wires to each desk for voice and data. Thus, ISDN offers subscribers a level of efficiency beyond that obtainable through the utilization of conventional facilities.

For individual subscribers, ISDN may result in the offering of a series of new functions accessible to their homes over existing telephone wire. Electronic meter reading, slow scan video, electronic mail, and other applications can be expected to be offered to individual subscribers and businesses.

ISDN ARCHITECTURE

Two methods of access to ISDN have been defined—Basic access and Primary access. ISDN *Basic access* deals with the connection and operation of individual telephone instruments and terminals to the digital network. *Primary access* governs the method by which many Basic access subscribers can be connected to the network over a common line facility.

Basic Access

Basic access defines a multiple channel connection that is derived by the time division multiplexing of data on twisted pair wiring. This multiple channel connection links an end-user terminal device directly to a telephone company office or to a local Private Automated Branch Exchange (PABX). Figure 12.2 illustrates the channel format of the ISDN Basic access method.

**Figure 12.2.
ISDN Basic Access
Channel Format**

As shown in Figure 12.2, Basic access consists of two bearer (B) channels and a data channel. The three channels are multiplexed by time onto a common twisted pair wiring media. Each bearer channel can carry one digitized voice conversation or data stream at a transmission rate of 64 kbps. Digitized voice in ISDN is encoded by sampling voice 8,000 times per second and encoding each sample in 8 bits, which results in a 64-kbps data rate. The inclusion of two bearer channels enables Basic access to provide the subscriber with the ability to simultaneously transmit data and conduct a voice conversation on one telephone line or to be in conversation with one person and receive a second telephone call. In the latter case, assuming subscribers have an appropriate telephone instrument, they could put one person on hold and answer the second call, all on one line! With analog technology, two physical lines are required. In fact, a Basic access ISDN line can be used to connect up to eight different devices that can be independently accessed via one standard telephone circuit. This expanded access is permissible because the D channel is designed to control the B channels through the sharing of network signaling functions and for the transmission of packet switched data.

Under the Basic access format, up to three channels can be used to provide simultaneous data streams.

To illustrate the expanded capability of ISDN Basic access over conventional telephone service, consider Figure 12.3. Figure 12.3a indicates how you might connect a telephone, fax machine, and computer modem to the public switched telephone network via the installation of three separate telephone lines between your home or office and the telephone central office. Figure 12.3b shows the same equipment connected to a Basic access ISDN line, which, in effect, is one telephone line onto which digitized data is multiplexed. Note that although up to eight devices can share access to the same ISDN Basic access line only two devices can simultaneously operate at 64 kbps since only two B channels are contained on a Basic access line. It is anticipated that the capability to transmit packet switched data will enable the D channel to be used to provide many new applications, including monitoring home alarm systems and reading of utility meters on demand.

**Figure 12.3.
ISDN Basic Access
Versus Conventional
Telephone Access**

a. Conventional Telephone Access   b. Using ISDN Basic Access

Primary Access

Primary access is a multiplexing arrangement whereby a grouping of Basic access users shares a common line facility. Primary access is designed to directly connect a PABX to the ISDN network. This access method eliminates the need to provide individual Basic access lines when a group of terminal devices shares a common PABX that could be connected directly to an ISDN network via a single high speed line. Because of the different methods used to multiplex digitized voice conversations between telephone company offices in North America and Europe, two Primary access standards have been developed.

In North America, Primary access consists of a grouping of 23 B channels and one D channel to provide a 1.544-Mbps composite data rate. This data rate is more commonly known as the standard T1 carrier data rate which was described in Chapter 6. The D channel in Primary access, and each B channel, operates at 64 kbps. Multiplying 24 channels by 64 kbps results in a data rate of 1.536 Mbps, which is precisely 8 kbps fewer than the T1 carrier's 1.544-Mbps data rate.

The T1 carrier used in North America is not the same as that used in Europe due to different methods of signaling.

A North American T1 carrier consists of 24 digitized voice channels. Each voice channel is sampled 8,000 times per second, and 8 bits are used to encode the digitized value of each sample, Thus, a 64-kbps data rate is required to transmit a digitized voice conversation. To permit synchronization of the T1 signal, a single bit, known as a framing bit, is added to the data stream. The framing bit represents 24 channels, as illustrated in Figure 12.4. One sample of 24 channels of digitized voice is represented therefore by 193 bits. Because the sampling occurs 8,000 times per second, the data rate of a T1 carrier is $193 \times 8,000$ or 1.544 Mbps.

Figure 12.4.
The T1 Frame

In Europe, the T1 carrier consists of 30 digitized voice channels and 2 separate signaling channels. Because each channel operates at 64 kbps, the resulting T1 carrier data rate is 2.048 Mbps.

Network Characteristics

The major characteristics of an ISDN network follow and form the basis of business' and telephone companies' desire for the development of this new network.

ISDN integrates voice, data, and video services.

ISDN has a digital end-to-end connection that provides high transmission quality.

ISDN has improved and expanded services because of B and D channel data rates.

ISDN is more efficient and productive.

ISDN offers advances in device connectivity.

The digital nature of ISDN integrates voice, data, and video services, which alleviates the need for subscribers to obtain separate facilities for each service. Because an ISDN network is designed to provide end-to-end digital transmission, pulses can be regenerated easily throughout the network, resulting in the generation of new pulses to replace distorted ones.

In comparison, analog transmission facilities use amplifiers to boost the strength of transmission signals, but they also increase any impairments in the analog signal. Because regeneration is superior to amplification, digital transmission has a lower error rate and provides a higher transmission signal quality than an equivalent analog transmission facility.

Basic access provides three signal paths on a common line, and ISDN, too, offers to subscribers the potential of improvements and expansion to existing services. For existing services, current analog telephone line bandwidth limitations preclude data transmission rates more than 19.2 kbps occurring on the switched telephone network. In comparison, under ISDN, each B channel can support a 64-kbps transmission rate, whereas the D channel can operate at 16 kbps. In fact, if both B channels and the D channel were in simultaneous operation, a data rate of 144 kbps would be obtainable on a Basic access ISDN circuit, exceeding by a factor of seven the current analog circuit data rates.

Because each Basic access channel consists of three multiplexed channels, different operations can occur simultaneously without requiring the subscriber to acquire separate multiplexing equipment. Thus, a subscriber could receive a call from one person, transmit data to a computer, and have a utility company read his or her electric meter, all at one time. With the ability to conduct as many as three simultaneous operations on one line, the subscriber gains efficiency and productivity. Efficiency should increase because one line now can support several simultaneous operations, whereas the productivity of the subscriber can increase because of the ability to receive telephone calls and conduct a conversation while transmitting data.

Advances in device connectivity to the ISDN network can be expected to occur in two areas. At the physical interface, an eight-pin modular plug and jack will provide a command interface that will enable devices to be portable between jacks. This will eliminate special cabling, and usually, additional telephone company installation charges for the movement of devices between offices. Digital telephones and other instruments can be expected to have an intelligent reporting capability. When a telephone is moved from one office to another, simply plugging it into a jack will result in it reporting its extension and location to a PBX. This capability will permit employees who are moving within an organization to immediately receive telephone calls at their new location without waiting for the company to reprogram the PBX.

Telephone Equipment and Network Interface

A key element of ISDN is a small set of compatible multipurpose user-network interfaces developed to support a wide range of applications. These network interfaces are based on a series of reference points for different user terminal arrangements that define these interfaces. Figure 12.5 illustrates the relationship between ISDN reference points and network interfaces.

**Figure 12.5.
ISDN Reference Points
and Network
Interfaces**

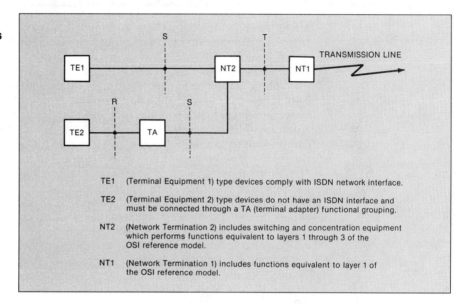

TE1   (Terminal Equipment 1) type devices comply with ISDN network interface.

TE2   (Terminal Equipment 2) type devices do not have an ISDN interface and must be connected through a TA (terminal adapter) functional grouping.

NT2   (Network Termination 2) includes switching and concentration equipment which performs functions equivalent to layers 1 through 3 of the OSI reference model.

NT1   (Network Termination 1) includes functions equivalent to layer 1 of the OSI reference model.

The ISDN reference configuration consists of functional groupings and reference points at which physical interfaces may exist. The functional groupings are sets of functions that may be required at an interface, whereas reference points are employed to divide the functional groups into distinct entities.

The TE (Terminal Equipment) functional grouping is comprised of TE1 and TE2 type equipment. Digital telephones, conventional data terminals, and integrated voice-data workstations are examples of TE equipment. TE1 type equipment complies with the ISDN user-network interface and permits such equipment to be connected directly to an ISDN "S" type interface that supports multiple B and D channels.

TE2 type equipment are devices with non-ISDN interfaces, such as RS-232 or the CCITT X- or V-Series interfaces. This type of equipment must be connected through a TA (Terminal Adapter) functional grouping, which is used to convert a non-ISDN interface (R) into an ISDN interface (S). The TA does both a physical interface conversion and protocol conversion, permitting a TE2 terminal to operate on ISDN.

The NT2 (Network Termination 2) functional group includes devices that do switching and data concentration functions equivalent to the first

The Terminal Adapter (TA) can be expected to play a key role in the use of ISDN as it permits equipment with a non-ISDN inter-face to be connected into an ISDN network.

three layers of the OSI reference model. Typical NT2 equipment can include PABXs, LANs, terminal controllers, concentrators, and multiplexers.

The NT1 (Network Termination 1) functional group is the ISDN digital interface point and is equivalent to layer 1 of the OSI Reference Model. Functions of NT1 include the physical and electrical termination of the loop, line monitoring, timing, and bit multiplexing. In Europe, where most communications carriers are government-owned monopolies, NT1 and NT2 functions may be combined into a common device, such as a PABX. In such situations, the equipment serves as an NT12 functional group. In comparison, in the United States, the communications carrier may provide only the NT1, whereas third-party equipment would connect to the communications carrier equipment at the T interface.

The last interface which occurs at reference point U is a two-wire connection (Basic access) or four-wire (Primary access) connection between the customer premises (NT1) and the carrier's central office. From this reference point to the central office data flows in a special compressed transmission format (2B1Q) in which 2 binary bits (2B) are encoded in one quaternary symbol (1Q). When transmission occurs in the 2B1Q format up to four signal levels can occur, with each level defining the encoding of two bits of data. Table 12.1 indicates the relationship between the four allowed signaling states and the composition of the encoded pairs of bits. Figure 12.6 illustrates an example of 2B1Q coding (top) and the resulting relationship between the quaternary symbol and the encoded binary pairs.

**Table 12.1.
2B1Q Relationship**

Quaternary Signal Level	Encoded Bit Values
−3	00
−1	01
+3	10
+1	11

Through the use of 2B1Q encoding, the Basic access 160-kbps data rate is achieved via a 4-kilobaud rate. This allows the large base of conventional copper pair wiring previously installed between customer premises and communications carrier central offices to be used to support ISDN transmission.

**Figure 12.6.
2B1Q Encoding
Example**

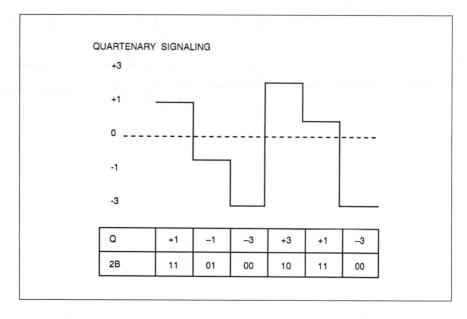

QUARTERNARY SIGNALING

Q	+1	−1	−3	+3	+1	−3
2B	11	01	00	10	11	00

Refer to the CCITT I recommendation series for detailed information about ISDN reference points and network interfaces.

By providing a set of standardized network interfaces, both pre- and post-ISDN terminals will be able to share the benefits of using ISDN. Pre-ISDN terminal devices will be connected to ISDN facilities by Terminal Adapters, which will convert a non-ISDN interface (R) into an ISDN interface (S). With several well publicized field trials of ISDN being conducted in the United States and abroad, it is only a matter of time until commercial ISDN offerings become available for selection by many analog telephone subscribers. Similar to the manner in which "plastics" was used as the all-encompassing word of the future in a popular 1960s movie, "ISDN" can be expected to be its replacement for the late 1990s.

WHAT HAVE WE LEARNED?

1. ISDN can be viewed as an evolutionary process because communications carriers have been converting their facilities to digital technology since the 1960s.
2. Access arrangements to the ISDN network include Basic and Primary access.
3. The multiple channels on one ISDN physical line are obtained through time division multiplexing.
4. Multiple channels on one ISDN physical line permit multiple voice or voice and data transmission to occur at the same time on a common circuit.

5. The Basic access D channel on which data is transmitted in packet form can be expected to be used for such new applications as monitoring home alarm systems and reading of utility meters as well as for the transmission of signaling information to control the operation of the B channels.

6. Non-ISDN equipment can be connected to ISDN lines through the use of terminal adapters.

Quiz for Chapter 12

1. The data rate of the ISDN Basic access B channel is
   a. 32 kbps
   b. 64 kbps
   c. 144 kbps
   d. 192 kbps

2. The data rate of the ISDN Basic access D Channel is
   a. 64 kbps
   b. 16 kbps
   c. 8 kbps
   d. 144 kbps

3. The equation that defines the composition of an ISDN Basic access line is
   a. 2B + D
   b. B + D
   c. B + 2D
   d. 2B + 2D

4. In North America, the equation that defines the composition of an ISDN Primary access line is
   a. 30B + D
   b. 2B + D
   c. B + D
   d. 23B + D

5. The network interface that will permit equipment without an ISDN interface to be connected into an ISDN interface is known as
   a. TE1
   b. TE2
   c. TA
   c. TE

6. The number of channels on which different operations can occur simultaneously on one ISDN Basic access line is
   a. 1
   b. 2
   c. 5
   d. 3

7. Digital telephones and integrated voice-data workstations are examples of what type of ISDN equipment?
   a. TE
   b. TA
   c. NT2
   d. TP

8. The transmission of data on an ISDN line between a customer's premises and a carrier's central office is encoded using:
   a. quadrature amplitude modulation
   b. 2B1Q encoding
   c. hexadecimal encoding
   d. octal encoding

Glossary

Amplifier: A device used to increase the strength of an analog signal.

Analog Signal: A signal, such as voice or music, that varies in a continuous manner. Contrast with digital signal.

ASCII (American Standard Code for Information Interchange): A 7-bit code established by the American National Standards Institute to achieve compatibility between data services. Equivalent to the international ISO 7-bit code.

Attenuation: The difference between transmitted and received power due to transmission loss through equipment, lines, or other communication devices.

Bandwidth: The frequency range between the lowest and highest frequencies that are passed through a component, circuit, or system with acceptable attenuation.

Baseband: The frequency band occupied by a single or composite signal in its original or unmodulated form.

Basic Access: The method whereby individual telephone instruments and terminals will be connected to a digital network.

Baud: A unit of signaling speed equal to the number of signal events per second. Not necessarily the same as bits per second.

Binary Coded Decimal (BCD): A system of binary numbering where each decimal digit 0 through 9 is represented by four bits.

Binary Synchronous Communications (BSC or BiSync): A communication protocol developed by IBM which has become an industry standard. It uses a defined set of control characters and control character sequences for synchronized transmission of binary coded data between stations in a data communications system.

bis: Meaning second in Latin, this term is used as a suffix to denote a secondary version of a CCITT modem standard.

Bit: Contraction of binary digit. The smallest unit of information. A bit represents the choice between a one or zero value (mark or space in communications terminology).

Bit Rate: The speed at which bits are transmitted, usually expressed in bits per second. Not necessarily the same as baud rate.

Block: A sequence of continuous data characters or bytes transmitted as a unit. A coding procedure is usually applied for synchronization or error control purposes.

bps (bits per second): A measure of the information transfer rate of a data channel.

Bridge: A device that connects LANs at the ISO data link level.

Buffer: A storage device used to compensate for a difference in rate of data flow, or time of occurrence of events, when transmitting data from one device to another.

Byte: A binary element string operated upon as a unit and usually shorter than a computer word. Eight-bit bytes are common.

Carrier: A signal suitable for modulation by another signal containing information to be transmitted. The carrier is usually a sine wave for analog systems.

CCITT: (Consultative Committee for International Telephone & Telegraph) A standards-making body whose recommendations are more closely followed in Europe than North America.

Channel, Voice Grade: A channel, generally with a frequency range of about 300 to 3400 Hz, suitable for transmission of speech or data in analog form. Data transmission rates of 9600 bps may be achieved by modulation techniques that produce a baud rate of 2400.

Character: A letter, figure, number, punctuation, or other symbol contained in a message or used in a control function.

Character Set: The characters that can be coded and/or printed by a particular machine.

Code: A set of unambiguous rules specifying the way in which characters may be represented.

Common Carrier: A company that furnishes communication services to the general public and which is regulated by appropriate state or federal agencies.

Conditioning, Line: The addition of equipment to a leased voice-grade channel to improve analog characteristics to allow higher rates of data transmission.

Constellation Pattern: The pattern obtained from plotting the location of each bit combination modulated by a modem through phase and amplitude changes.

Contention: The facility provided by the dial network or a port selector which allows multiple terminals to compete on a first-come-first-served basis for a smaller number of computer ports.

Data Communications Equipment (also Data Circuit-Terminating Equipment) (DCE): The equipment that provides the functions required to establish, maintain, and terminate a connection, and provides the signal conversion required for communication between data terminal equipment and the telephone line or data circuit.

Data Terminal Equipment (DTE): A computer or business machine that provides data in the form of digital signals at its output.

dBm: Decibel referenced to one milliwatt. Used in communications circuits as a measure of signal power. Zero dBm equals one milliwatt into a specified impedance, often 600 ohms.

Decibel (dB): A logarithmic measure of the ratio between two powers, P_1 and P_2. The equation is: $dB = 10 \log_{10} P_2/P_1$

Delay Equalizer: A corrective network which is designed to make the phase delay or envelope delay of a circuit or system substantially constant over a desired frequency range.

Delay, Propagation: The time required for a signal to travel from one point to another in a component, circuit, or system.

Demodulation: The process of recovering data from a modulated carrier wave. The reverse of modulation.

Dial-Up Line: A communications circuit that is established by a switched circuit connection using the telephone dial network.

Dibit: A group of two bits. In four-phase modulation, such as differential phase shift keying (DPSK), each possible dibit is encoded as one of four unique carrier phase shifts. The four possible states for a dibit are 00, 01, 10, and 11.

Digital Repeater: A data regenerator that, on the detection of the rise of a digital pulse's leading edge, regenerates the pulse.

Digital Signal: A discrete or discontinuous signal; one whose various states are identified with discrete levels or values.

Distortion, Delay: Distortion resulting from nonuniform speed of transmission of the various frequency components of a signal through a transmission medium. Also called group delay.

Distortion, Harmonic: The result of nonlinearities in the communication channel that cause harmonics of the input frequencies to appear in the output.

Distortion, Linear (or Amplitude): An unwanted change in signal amplitude so that the output signal envelope is not proportional to the input signal envelope, but no frequency related distortion is involved.

Echo Suppressor: A device that allows transmission in only one direction at a time. They are inserted in telephone circuits to attenuate echoes on long distance circuits. They are not desirable in data communications circuits because they increase the turnaround time.

Equalization: The process of reducing the effects of amplitude, frequency, and/or phase distortion of a circuit by inserting networks to compensate for the difference in attenuation and/or time delay at various frequencies in the transmission band.

Filter: A network designed to transmit electrical signals having frequencies within one or more frequency bands and to attenuate signals of other frequencies.

Frame Relay: A form of fast packet switching in which error checking and flow control is minimized.

Frequency Division Multiplexer: A device which divides the available transmission frequency range into narrower bands, each of which is used for a separate channel.

Frequency Response: The change in attenuation with frequency relative to the attenuation at a reference frequency. Also called attenuation distortion.

Frequency Shift Keying (FSK): A form of frequency modulation commonly used in low-speed modems in which the two states of the signal are transmitted as two separate frequencies.

Full-Duplex: Refers to a communications system or equipment capable of simultaneous two-way communications.

Gateway: Hardware and software that permits devices located on a local area network to access the facilities of another network.

Half-Duplex: Refers to a communications system or equipment capable of communications in both directions, but in only one direction at a time.

Handshaking: Exchange of predetermined codes and signals between two data terminals to establish a connection.

Interface: A shared boundary defined by common physical interconnection characteristics, signal characteristics, and meanings of interchanged signals.

Intermodulation Noise: Spurious frequencies, such as sum and difference frequencies, which are the products of frequencies transmitted through a nonlinear circuit.

ISDN (Integrated Services Digital Network): A future offering designed to provide a universal digital network that will permit the integration of voice and data on a common telephone company facility.

Jitter: A tendency toward lack of synchronization caused by mechanical or electrical changes.

Kilostream: A digital network that operates in the United Kingdom.

Line: (1) A circuit between a customer terminal and the central office. (2) The portion of a transmission system, including the transmission media and associated repeaters, between two terminal locations.

Link: A circuit or transmission path, including all equipment, between a sender and a receiver.

Local Area Network: A communications network that is restricted to a small geographical area, usually within a building or on a campus, and that has cabling normally installed and/or controlled by the organization that operates the network.

Loop, Local: The pair of wires between a customer terminal and the central office.

Loopback Test: A test of communications link performed by connecting the equipment output of one direction to the equipment input of the other direction and testing the quality of the received signal.

Mark: One of the two possible states of a binary information element. The closed circuit and idle state in a teleprinter circuit. See Space.

Modem (MOdulator/DEModulator): A type of DCE that at the transmitting end converts digital data to an analog signal for transmission on telephone circuits. A modem at the receiving end converts the analog signal to digital form.

Modulation: The process of varying some characteristic of the carrier wave in accordance with the instantaneous value or samples of the intelligence to be transmitted. Amplitude, frequency, and phase are the characteristics commonly varied.

Multiplex: To interleave or simultaneously transmit two or more messages on a single channel.

Multistation Access Unit: A device that enables workstations on a LAN to be cabled in a star configuration.

Noise: Random electrical signals, introduced by circuit components or natural disturbances, which tend to generate errors in transmission.

PABX (Private Automatic Branch Exchange): A device that is installed on a customer's premises and that permits a large number of telephones to automatically access the switched telephone network by using a smaller number of lines connecting the PABX to the telephone company network.

PBX (Private Branch Exchange): Telephone switching equipment dedicated to one customer and connected to the public switched network.

Personal Computer: A computer with processing power based on a microprocessor and designed primarily for use by one person.

Polling: The individual selection of multiple terminals by a controller to allow transmission of traffic to/from all terminals on a multidrop line in an orderly manner.

Port: An interface on a computer configured as data terminal equipment and capable of having a modem attached for communication with a remote data terminal.

Primary Access: A multiplexing arrangement whereby many ISDN Basic access subscribers can be connected to a digital network over a common line facility.

Protocol: The rules for communication between like processes, giving a means to control the orderly communication of information between stations on a data link.

Protocol Analyzer: A device that decodes a bit stream being monitored into characters that represent the format and information content of a transmission protocol.

Redundancy: The portion of the total information contained in a message which can be eliminated without loss of essential information.

Repeater: A communications system component which amplifies or regenerates signals to compensate for losses in the system.

Serial Transmission: A method of information transfer in which the bits comprising a character are sent in sequence one at a time.

Slow Scan Video: The process whereby still video images are transmitted frequently to provide the appearance of video motion.

Space: One of the two possible states of a binary information element. The open circuit or no current state of a teleprinter line. See Mark.

Start Bit or Element: The first bit or element transmitted in the asynchronous transmission of a character to synchronize the receiver.

Stop Bit or Element: The last bit or element transmitted in the asynchronous transmission of a character to return the circuit to the at-rest or idle condition.

Statistical Multiplexer: A multiplexer which uses the idle time of connected devices to carry data traffic from active devices.

Symbol: The graphical representation of some idea which is used by people. Letters and numbers are symbols.

TA (Terminal Adapter): A device that is used to permit equipment with a non-ISDN interface to be connected to that digital network.

ter: Meaning third in Latin, this term is used as a suffix to denote a third version of a CCITT modem standard.

TE1 (Terminal Equipment 1): Devices that comply with the ISDN network interface and can be connected directly to the digital network.

TE2 (Terminal Equipment 2): Devices that do not have an ISDN interface and must be connected by using a TA (terminal adapter) to the digital network.

Terminal Emulation: Software or firmware that enables a personal computer or terminal to duplicate the screen attributes of a terminal.

Time Division Multiplexer (TDM): A device that permits the transmission of two or more independent data channels on a single high speed circuit by interleaving the data from each channel on the circuit by time.

Transmission, Asynchronous: Transmission in which each information character is individually synchronized, usually by the use of start and stop elements.

Transmission, Synchronous: Transmission in which the sending and receiving instruments are operating continuously at substantially the same frequency and in which the desired phase relationship may be maintained by means of correction.

Trellis Coded Modulation: A modem modulation process in which one or more redundant bits is added to each group of bits used to generate a signal change. The extra bit or bits permits only certain sequences of signal points to be valid, resulting in a lowering of the error rate.

Turnaround Time: The actual time required to reverse the direction of transmission from sender to receiver or vice versa when using a half-duplex circuit. Time is required for line propagation effects, modem timing, and computer reaction.

UART (Universal Asynchronous Receiver/Transmitter): A device which performs asynchronous communication functions by converting parallel digital output from a DTE into serial bit transmission and vice versa.

2B1Q: An encoding technique used on ISDN lines in which two binary bits (2B) are encoded in one quaternary (1Q) symbol.

Bibliography

A History of Engineering & Science in the Bell System: The Early Years (*1875-1925*), Whippany, NJ: Bell Telephone Laboratories, Inc., 1975.

Bell Laboratories Record, Whippany, NJ: Bell Telephone Laboratories, Inc., November 1980.

Bellamy, John. *Digital Telephony*, New York: John Wiley & Sons, Inc., 1982.

Bigelow, Stephen. *Understanding Telephone Electronics*, 3rd Ed, Carmel, IN: Sams, a Division of Macmillan Computer Publishing, 1983.

CCITT Recommendations V.29, X.21, and X.25, CCITT, Geneva, C. H.

Doll, Dixon. *Data Communications; Facilities, Networks and Systems Design*, New York: John Wiley & Sons, 1978.

EIA Standard RS-232-C (and others), Electronic Industries Association.

Freeman, R.L. *Telecommunication System Engineering*, New York: John Wiley & Sons, Inc., 1980.

Freeman, R.L. *Telecommunication Transmission Handbook*, 2nd Ed., New York: John Wiley & Sons, Inc., 1981.

General Information—Binary Synchronous Communications, IBM Publication Nr. GA27-3004, IBM Systems Development Division, Publications Center.

General Information—IBM Synchronous Data Link Control, IBM Publication Nr. GA27-3093-2, IBM Systems Development Division, Publications Center.

IEEE Transactions on Communications, IEEE Communications Society, August 1980, Vol. COM-28.

Kreager, Paul. *Practical Aspects of Data Communications*, New York: McGraw-Hill Book Co., 1983.

Martin, James. *Telecommunications and the Computer*, Englewood Cliffs, NJ: Prentice-Hall, Inc., 1969.

McNamara, John E. *Technical Aspects of Data Communications*, 2nd Ed., Digital Press, 1982.

Members of the Technical Staff. *Transmission Systems for Communications*, Revised 4th Ed., Whippany, NJ: Bell Telephone Laboratories, Inc., 1971.

Members of the Technical Staff and the Technical Publications Department. *Engineering and Operations in the Bell System*, Whippany, NJ: Bell Telephone Laboratories, Inc., 1977.

Notes on the Network, American Telephone & Telegraph Co., 1980.

Owen, Frank E. *PCM and Digital Transmission Systems*, New York: McGraw-Hill, Inc., 1982.

Parameters of Telephone Network Design, IBM Publication Nr ZZ-11-3201-0, IBM World Trade Corp., Jan. 1977.

Sherman, Kenneth. *Data Communications: A User's Guide*, Reston Publishing Co., 1981.

Stauffer, J.R. *IEEE Journal on Selected Areas in Communications*, Vol. SAC-1, No. 3, April 1983.

Tanenbaum, Andrew S. *Computer Networks*, Englewood Cliffs, NJ: Prentice-Hall, Inc.

Index

1's complement, 218
2B1Q, 348

A

absorption losses, 193
Acknowledge (ACK) character, 219
aliasing, 230
alternate mark inversion (AMI),
   154-155, 168
amplifier, 343
amplitude
   binary signals, 127
   sine waves, 92
analog signals, 343
   bandwidth, 84
   carrier systems frequency divi-
      sion multiplexing (FDM), 85
   data transmission, 89-90
   delay distortion, 134
   modulation, 91-92
ANSI (American National Standards Institute), 9
ANSI.SYS device driver, 14
ARCNet (Attached Resource
   Computer Network), 255-260
   link protocol, 258-260
   physical layer, 256-258
   Resource Information Modules
      (RIMs), 255
ASCII (American Standard Code
   for Information Interchange), 9,
   11-14, 343
   character set, 67-68
   escape (ESC) character, 13-14
   teleprinters, 14
   terminals, 38-41

asynchronous data transmission,
   54-60, 348
   electromechanical method,
      55-57
   electronic receiving circuit,
      57-58
   stop bits and timing errors, 59
   teleprinter terminals, 31
asynchronous modems, 89-123
   auto-answer, 119-120
   answer mode, 95
   interfaces, 89
   low-speed operation, 93, 95-96
   originate mode, 95
Asynchronous Response Mode
   (ARM), 234
attenuation, 343
   fiber optics, 191-194
avalanche photodiode (APD),
   196-197

B

B7 zero code suppression, 169-170
B8 Zero Substitution (B8ZS),
   170-172
bandwidth, 343
   analog and digital signals, 84
   effects on transmission channel,
      82-83
   fiber optics, 191
   synchronous signaling, 128
baseband, 343
basic access, 343
batch processing, 15-16
batch terminals, 41
baud, 96, 343
Baudot code, 8-9, 213-215
Baudot, Emile, 8-9
Bell, Alexander Graham, 183

Bell modems
    113-type, 96
    212A-type, 96-97
binary coded decimal (BCD), 11, 343
binary signals, 127
binary synchronous communications (BSC), 222-223, 343
    Block Check Character (BCC), 226-227
    character sets, 223
    error checking, 226-227
    link control codes, 224-225
    message
        blocks, 226
        formats, 227-229
    polling and selection, 226
binary system, 6-7
bipolar
    inversion, 154-155
    signaling, 32
bis, 343
bit-mapping, 48
bit-oriented protocols (BOP), 231
bits, 6, 67, 343
Block Check Character (BCC), 220, 226-227
blocks, 343
bounded message carriers, 69
bps (bits per second), 343
bridges, 21-22, 344
    local, 261
    remote, 261
    token-ring network, 260-261
broadband Local Area Network (LAN), 263-266
    data link layer, 264
    frequency division multiplexing (FDM), 263-264
    physical layout, 264
buffers, 344
bytes, 7, 344

C

Carrier Sense, Multiple Access with Collision Detection (CSMA/CD), 249, 251, 268
carrier systems, 85-86, 90, 344
    analog and digital, 85-86
CCITT, 344
    International Alphabet No. 2, 9
    V.26 synchronous modems, 141-142
    V.27 synchronous modems, 142-143
    V.29 9600-bps modems, 146-151
    V.32 bis synchronous modem, 150
    V.32 synchronous modem, 149-150
    V.33 synchronous modem, 151-152
    X.21 recommendations, 117-119
cellular radio systems, 81-82
channel service unit (CSU), 169
channels, sharing, 161
characters, 8, 344
    binary-coded-decimal (BCD), 11
    echoing, 216
    escape (ESC), 13-14
    mapping, 48
    sets, 223, 344
coaxial cable, 73-74
code sequences and half-duplex protocols, 225
codec, 165
common carrier, 344
communication codes, 7-14, 344
    American Standard Code for Information Interchange (ASCII), 9, 11-14

Baudot code, 8-9
CCITT International Alphabet
    No. 2, 9
characters, 8
Extended Binary-Coded-
    Decimal Interchange Code
    (EBCDIC), 9-11
modern codes, 9
signaling elements, 8
standard codes, 8
computers
    batch processing, 15-16
    buses vs. Local Area Network
        (LAN), 241-242
    data communications, 15-23
    history, 15-21
    LANs (local area networks),
        20-21
    on-line processing, 16
    interfaces, 106-107
    see also personal computers
connection losses, 193-194
constellation pattern, 344
contention, 344
control characters, 213
    half-duplex protocols, 225
convolutional coding and error
    checking, 220-222
crosstalk, 73
CRT (cathode ray tube) terminals,
    37-51
    alternate input devices, 47
    ASCII terminals, 38-41
    display, 47-49
    dumb, 38-39
    ergonomics, 44
    features, 49-50
    keyboards, 44-47
    non-ASCII, 41-43
    parts, 44-49
    PROM (programmable ROM),
        39

ROM (read-only memory), 39
    smart, 38-39
    terminal emulator program,
        40-41
    user-programmable, 38-39
    vs. teleprinter terminals, 34-37
    Wyse WY-50, 49
current loop, 112-113
    equipment, 32
Cyclic Redundancy Checking (CRC)
    as error checking, 220-221

D

D4 framing format, 166-167
data circuit-terminating equipment
    (DCE), 344
data communications, 1-27
    basic description, 23-27
    binary system, 6-7
    communication codes, 7-14
    computers, 15-23
    DTE-DCE interface, 26-27
    early systems, 2
    form and content of information,
        24-26
    importance, 1-2
    industry changes, 23
    PBX (Private Branch Exchange),
        270
    protocols, 25-26
    receivers, 23
    redundancy, 69
    signaling standards, 100
    telegraph, 2-6
    transmission path, 23
    transmitter, 23
    two-state communication
        systems, 6
data communications equipment
    (DCE), 24, 100, 344

data communications test equipment
  amplifier-monitor, 318
  bit error rate tester (BERT), 318-319
  breakout box, 318
  data link content monitor, 320
  decibel meter, 319
  network control system, 322-323
  oscilloscope, 319
  protocol analyzer, 320-321
  simulator, 320
  voice frequency test set, 319
data compression and decompression, 98
data link, 222
  Ethernet, 250
Data Service Unit (DSU), 24
Data Switching Exchange (DSE), 280
data terminal equipment (DTE), 24, 100, 344
data terminals, 31-60
  ASCII, 38-41
  batch, 41
  clustered, 42
  CRT (cathode ray tube), 37-51
  data transmission, 51-60
  IBM 3270 series, 42-43
  non-ASCII, 41-43
  personal computers as, 50-51
  teleprinters, 31-37
data transmission
  analog, 89-90
  asynchronous, 54-60
  data terminals, 51-60
  error checking, 60
  framing, 52
  isochronous, 60
  non-indirect, 89
  parallel, 51-53

serial, 51-53
  start-stop codes, 60
  timing, 52
dBm, 344
decibel (dB), 344
DeForest triode, 73
delay equalizer, 345
Demand Assignment Multiple Access (DAMA), 207
demodulation, 345
descramblers, 136
devices, networking, 312-323
dial-up line, 345
dibits, 139
  phase shift keyed (DPSK) modulation, 96-97
dielectric waveguide, 185
differential phase shift keying (DPSK), 139-144
digital carrier systems, 85-86
  time division multiplexing (TDM), 85
Digital Data Communications Message Protocol (DDCMP), 235-237
digital modulation
  B7 zero code suppression, 169-170
  B8 Zero Substitution (B8ZS), 170-172
  framing, 166-167
  multiplexing, 163-177
  ones density, 169-172
  private branch exchange (PBX), 163
  pulse amplitude modulation (PAM), 163
  pulse code modulation (PCM), 163-166
  pulse position modulation (PPM), 163
  pulse width modulation (PWM), 163

statistical time division multiplexing (STDM), 175-177
T-carrier transmission system,
168-169
time division multiplexing
(TDM), 172-175
digital repeater, 345
digital signals, 345
bandwidth, 84
digital transmission
line coding, 152-155
repeaters, 155-157
synchronous modems, 152-157
synchronous signaling, 127-128
digital-to-analog converter, 132
diphase code, 155
display for CRT terminals, 47-49
distortion, 345
dot matrix printers, 35-36
double-current signaling, 32
DTE-DCE interface, 26-27
dumb CRT terminals, 38-39
vs. smart CRT terminals, 39-40

E

EBCDIC (Extended Binary-Coded-
Decimal Interchange Code), 9,
11
echo suppressor, 345
electric amplifiers, 73
electricity, 2
electrothermal printing, 36
equalization, 345
equalizers
receivers, 134-136
transmitter, 132
error checking
Binary Synchronous Communications (BSC) procedures,
226-227

Block Check Characters (BCC),
220
checksums, 217
convolutional coding, 220-222
Cyclic Redundancy Checking
(CRC), 220-221
echoplex, 216
parity, 216
ESC (escape) character, 13-14
ESF (extended superframe) framing
format, 166-167
Ethernet, 247-252, 268
Carrier Sense, Multiple Access
with Collision Detection
(CSMA/CD), 249, 251
data link layer, 250
physical layer, 248-250
system configurations, 250-251

F

fault isolation
data communications test
equipment, 318-323
loopback tests, 316-318
feedback shift registers, 130
fiber optics, 75-76, 183-202
attenuation, 191-194
bandwidth, 191
FT3C system, 197, 199
historical perspective, 183-184
injection laser diodes (ILD), 196
international systems, 199-202
laser, 183
light detectors, 196-197
light sources, 195-196
light-emitting diodes (LED), 195
local and intercity systems, 197,
199
optical fiber, 184-185, 187
refraction, 184, 186

SL underwater cable, 199, 201-202
Snell's Law, 185
subsystems and components, 194-197
system fundamentals, 184-190, 193-194
transmission systems, 197, 199-202
wavelength multiplexing, 197
filters, 345
flow control, 108-110
Fourier analysis, 92
Frame Alignment Signal, 167
frame relay, 296-297, 345
framing
channel service unit (CSU), 169
D4 format, 166-167
digital modulation, 166-167
ESF (extended superframe) format, 167
frequency and sine waves, 92
Frequency Division Multiple Access (FDMA), 204
frequency division multiplexing (FDM), 85, 162-163, 204, 313, 345
broadband Local Area Network (LAN), 263-264
frequency modulation (FM) and radiolink systems, 79
frequency response, 345
frequency-shift keying (FSK), 95, 97, 345
FT3C fiber optic system, 197, 199
full-duplex, 91, 346
2400-bps 4-wire synchronous modems, 139-142
4800-bps 4-wire synchronous modems, 142-144
asynchronous private line modems, 120

full-duplex protocols, 229-237
Digital Data Communications Message Protocol (DDCMP), 235-237
High-level Data Link Control (HDLC) procedures, 231-234
Synchronous Data Link Control (SDLC), 234

G

gateways, 21-22, 346
token-ring network, 262-263
Gauss, Carl Friedrich, 2
glossary, 343-348
graded-index optical fiber, 190
Gray code, 130
groundwave, 76

H

half-duplex, 91, 346
2400-bps 2-wire synchronous modems, 139-142
4800-bps 2-wire synchronous modems, 142-144
9600-bps 2-wire synchronous modems, 144-146
9600-bps /full-duplex 4-wire synchronous modems, 144-146
asynchronous private line modems, 120
half-duplex protocols, 222-229
code sequences, 225
control characters, 225
headings for messages, 228
link control codes, 224-225
link protocols, 222
message formats, 227-229

polling and selection, 226
timeouts, 228-229
transmission codes, 223
transparent-text mode, 229
handshaking, 346
Hayes Smartmodem 1200 modem,
121-123
high-frequency (HF) radio, 76
high-frequency radiotelephone,
76-77
High-level Data Link Control
(HDLC) procedures, 231-234
Asynchronous Response Mode
(ARM), 234
data links, 234
fields, 232-233
Normal Response Mode (NRM),
234
semantics, 233-234

I

IBM
3270 series terminals, 42-43
PS/2 Model 30, 50
IEEE 802.2, 267-268
IEEE 802.3, 268
IEEE 802.5, 269
impact printers, 35-36
information symbols, 67-69
injection laser diodes (ILD), 196
ink-jet printing, 36
integrated voice/data PBX (Private
Branch Exchange), 270-271
INTELSAT VI satellites, 203-204
interfaces, 211-213, 137, 346
intermodulation noise, 346
ISDN (Integrated Services Digital
Network), 331-339, 346
architecture, 332-335
basic access, 333-334
characteristics, 336
concept, 331-332
primary access, 334-335
telephone equipment and
network interface, 337-339
ISO (International Standards
Organization), 9
Model for Open Systems Interconnection (OSI), 245-247
isochronous data transmission, 60

J–K

jitter, 346

keyboard send-receive (KSR)
teleprinter terminals, 32-34
keyboards for CRT terminals, 44-47
layout, 44-45
numeric keypads, 46
programmable, 45-46
QWERTY, 44-45
special keys, 46-47
kilostream, 346

L

LANs (Local Area Networks), 20-21,
241-273, 346
see also networks
ARCNet (Attached Resource
Computer Network),
255-260
bridges, 21-22
broadband, 263-266
Carrier Sense, Multiple Access
with Collision Detection
(CSMA/CD), 268
comparisons and trends,
271-273
Ethernet, 247-252, 268
gateways, 20-22

IBM token-ring network,
    260-263
ideal system, 243-247
IEEE 802.2, 267-268
IEEE 802.3, 268
IEEE 802.5, 269
ISO Model for Open Systems
    Interconnection (OSI),
    245-247
logical link control (LLC),
    267-268
major obstacles, 245
media access control (MAC),
    267-268
PBX (Private Branch Exchange)
    as, 269-271
requirements, 245
routers, 21-22
standards, 266-269
token passing networks,
    253-255, 269
transmission media costs, 245
vs. computer buses, 241-242
vs. voiceband data transmis-
    sion, 241
LAPB (Link Access Procedure
    Balanced), 283
    commands and responses,
    287-288
    procedures, 285-286
laptop computers, 34
lasers, 183
Lempel-Ziv compression
    algorithm, 98
light detectors, 196-197
light-emitting diodes (LED), 195
line, 346
    bridging devices, 314
    conditioning, 344
line coding for digital transmis-
    sion, 152-155
line-of-sight (LOS) microwave
    radio systems, 78-80

link, 346
link control codes, 224-225
    Binary Synchronous Communi-
        cations Procedures (BSC),
        224-225
link protocols, 222-223
local bridge, 261
local loop, 346
logical channel group numbers
    (LCGNs), 293
logical channel numbers (LCNs),
    293
logical link control (LLC), 267-268
longitudinal redundancy check
    (LRC), 217
loopback tests, 316-318, 346

M

mark, 346
mean time between failures
    (MTBF), 307
mean time to restore service
    (MTRS), 307
media access control (MAC),
    267-268
memory-mapped display, 48
message blocks, 226
message carriers, 69-82
    bounded, 69
    cellular radio systems, 81-82
    coaxial cable, 73-74
    fiber optic systems, 75-76
    high-frequency radiotelephone,
        76-77
    line-of-sight (LOS) microwave
        radio systems, 78-80
    microwave radio, 78-80
    radiolink systems, 78-80
    satellite radiolink systems,
        80-81
    unbounded, 69

waveguides, 74-75
wire pairs, 70-73
microwave radio, 78-80
modal delay spreading, 188
modem eliminators, 314
modem sharing devices (MSDs),
    314
modem sharing unit (MSU), 314
modems, 89-91, 346
    300-baud, 93, 95-96
    analog transmission, 89-90
    asynchronous, 89-123
    auto-answer, 119-120
    baud rate, 96
    Bell
        113-type device, 96
        212A, 96-97
    carriers, 90
    CCITT X.21 recommendations,
        117-119
    current loop interface, 112-113
    data compression, 98
    data decompression, 98
    full-duplex
        asynchronous private line,
            120
        transmission, 91
    half-duplex
        asynchronous private line,
            120
        transmission, 91
    handshaking, 91
    Hayes Smartmodem 1200,
        121-123
    interfaces, 91, 100-120
    nonstandard, 97-98
    Packetized Ensemble Protocol,
        98-99
    protocol, 91
    RS-232 interface, 100-103
    RS-232C interface, 102-106
    RS-366 interface, 116

    RS-422A interface, 113-114
    RS-423A interface, 114
    RS-449 interface, 114-116
    RS-530 interface, 116
    sine wave as carrier, 92
    smart, 121-123
    synchronous, 127-157
    telephone channel restrictions,
        90-91
    to computer interface, 106
    Trailblazer, 99
    types, 119-120
    V.22 bis, 97
    V.22 standard, 97
    V.24 interface, 100-101
    V.24 bis, 98
modulation, 132, 346
    analog, 91-92
    dibit phase shift keyed (DPSK),
        96-97
    frequency-shift keying (FSK), 95,
        97
    quadrature amplitude (QAM),
        145-146
    synchronous modem types,
        144-146
    vestigial sideband, 145
Morse, Samuel B., 2-3, 5
multimode propagation, 188-190
multiple access systems
    Demand Assignment Multiple
        Access (DAMA), 207
    Frequency Division Multiple
        Access (FDMA), 204
    satellites, 204-207
    Time Division Multiple Access
        (TDMA), 205-207
multiplexing, 161-177, 313, 346
    digital modulation, 163-177
    frequency division (FDM),
        162-163, 313
    sharing channels, 161

time-division (TDM), 313
wavelength, 197-198
multipoint link protocols, 222
multistation access unit (MAU),
260, 346

N

Negative Acknowledge (NAK)
character, 218
networking devices, 312-323
fault isolation, 316-323
interconnection, 315
line bridging devices, 314
modem eliminators, 314
modem sharing devices
(MSDs), 314
modem sharing unit (MSU),
314
multiplexers, 313
protocol converters, 314
networks
see also LANs (Local Area
Networks)
accuracy, 306
architecture, 279-300
backup techniques, 325-327
design, 305-327
mean time between failures
(MTBF), 307
mean time to restore service
(MTRS), 307
packet, 280-297
protocol layering, 279
restoring service, 323-327
security, 307
TELEX, 14
timeliness, 306-307
token passing, 253-255
bus, 253-255
ring, 253-255, 269

token-ring, 260-263
Transfer Rate of Information
Bits (TRIB), 306-312
TWX, 14
value added services, 294
X series recommended standards, 294-296
neutral signaling, 32
noise, 347
non-ASCII terminals, 41-43
nonimpact printers, 36-37
nonstandard modems, 97-98
Normal Response Mode (NRM),
234
null modems, 314
numeric keypads, 46
Nyquist, Harry, 83-84
Nyquist theorem, 163

O

on-line processing, 16
ones density, 169-172
Open System Interconnection
Reference Model (OSI/RM),
297-300
optical fiber, 184
acceptance angle, 194
composition, 185, 187-188
graded-index, 190
modal delay spreading, 188
multimode fiber, 187
numerical aperture, 194
production, 194
propagation, 187-190
single-mode fibers, 188-189
OSI, 297-300
layers, 298-300

P

p-i-n FET (field-effect transistor),
    196-197
PABX (Private Automatic Branch
    Exchange), 347
packet networks, 280-297
    Data Switching Exchange
        (DSE), 280
    packet switching advantages,
        281-282
    X.25 standard, 282-295
packet-level procedures, 288-295
    Call Request/Incoming Call
        packets, 293
    data packets, 288-292
    VC destination addressing, 294
Packetized Ensemble Protocol
    Modems, 98-99
palmtop personal computers, 34
parallel data transmission, 51-53
parity, 216
Parkinsons's Law, 84
PBX (Private Branch Exchange),
    347
    as Local Area Network (LAN),
        269-271
    data communications, 270
    digital modulation, 163
    integrated voice/data, 270-271
Permanent Virtual Call Service
    (PVC), 285
personal computers, 20, 33-34
    see also computers
    as terminals, 50-51
    connectivity to control units, 43
    IBM PS/2 Model 30, 50
    laptops, 34
    palmtops, 34
    vs. user-programmable
        terminals, 40

point-to-point link protocols, 222
Polar NRZ code, 154-155
polar signaling, 32
polling, 347
    half-duplex protocols, 226
ports, 347
primary access, 347
printers, 35-37
programmable keyboards, 46
PROM (programmable ROM), 39
protocols, 25-26, 211-219, 347
    aliasing, 230
    analyzer, 347
    bit-oriented (BOP), 231
    boundaries, 298-300
    checksums, 217
    control characters, 213
    converters, 314
    echoplex, 216
    elements, 213
    full-duplex, 229-237
    half-duplex, 222-229
    layering, 279-280
    link, 222
    link layer, 279-280
    longitudinal redundancy check
        (LRC), 217
    network layer, 280
    parity, 216
    physical layer, 279
    printing characters, 213
    symbols, 213
    Synchronous Data Link Control
        (SDLC), 231
    teletypewriter (TTY), 213-216
    vertical redundancy checking
        (VRC), 217
    XMODEM, 218-219
pulse amplitude modulation (PAM),
    163
pulse code modulation (PCM),
    163-166

pulse position modulation (PPM), 163
pulse width modulation (PWM), 163

Q–R

quadrature amplitude modulation (QAM), 145-146
QWERTY keyboard, 44-45

radio, high-frequency (HF), 76
radiolink systems, 78-79
    satellite, 80-81
receive-only (RO) teleprinter terminals, 32-34
receivers, 23
    descramblers, 136
    equalizer, 134-136
    synchronous modems, 132-136
    timing recovery, 136
    training, 134
redundancy, 69, 347
refraction, 184, 186
regenerative repeaters, 155-157
remote batch data communications, 41
remote bridge, 261
remote job entry (RJE), 41
repeaters, 155-157, 347
Resource Information Modules (RIMs), 255
ROM (read-only memory), 39
routers, 21-22
RS-232 interface, 26, 100-103
    computer to modem, 106
    computer to serial printer, 106-107
    computer to video display terminal (VDT), 106
    connections, 106-107

DB-25 connector, 101
distance limitations, 110-111
electrical and functional interfaces, 101
flow control, 108-110
ground limitations, 111-112
limitations, 110-112
mechanical interface, 101
nonstandard usage, 107-108
speed limitations, 111
RS-232C interface, 102-106
    Carrier Detect (CD), 104-105
    Clear to Send (CTS), 104
    Data Carrier Detect (DCD), 104-105
    Data Set Ready (DSR), 104
    Data Signal Rate Selector, 105
    Data Terminal Ready (DTR), 104
    Protective Ground (GND), 102-103
    Received Data (RD), 104
    Received Line Signal Detector, 104-105
    Request to Send (RTS), 104
    Ring Indicator (RI), 105
    secondary channels, 106
    Signal Ground (SG), 102-103
    synchronous modems, 105
    Transmitted Data (TD), 104
RS-366 interface, 116
RS-422A interface, 113-114
RS-423A interface, 114
RS-449 interface, 114-116
RS-530 interface, 116

S

satellite radiolink systems, 80-81
satellites
    basic technology, 202-204
    communications, 18
    INTELSAT VI, 203-204

multiple access systems,
204-207
transmission systems, 202-207
scattering, 191-192
scramblers, 130-131
serial data transmission, 51-53
serial printers, 35-36
to computer interface, 106-107
serial transmission, 347
Shannon, Claude, 82-83
Shannon's Law, 83
signal framing bits (Fs), 167
signaling elements, 8
sine waves, 92
single-current signaling, 32
single-mode fibers, 188-189
single-mode propagation, 188-190
Six-Bit Transcode (SBT), 223
skywave, 76
slow scan video, 347
smart CRT terminals, 38-39
vs. dumb CRT terminals, 39-40
smart modems, 121-123
Snell's law, 185
space, 347
start bit, 347
Start Of Header (SOH) character,
218
statistical time division multiplexing (STDM), 175-177, 347
service ratio, 176-177
stop bit, 347
symbols, 347
Synchronous Data Link Control
(SDLC), 231, 234
synchronous modems, 127-157
2400-bps
full-duplex 4-wire, 139-142
half-duplex 2-wire, 139-142
4800-bps
full-duplex 4-wire, 142-144
half-duplex 2-wire, 142-144

9600-bps
half-duplex 2-wire, 144-146
half/full-duplex 4-wire,
144-146
CCITT
V.26, 141-142
V.27, 142-143
V.29 9600-bps, 146-151
V.32, 149-150
V.32 bis, 150
V.33, 151-152
components, 128-137
differential phase shift keying
(DPSK), 139-144
digital transmission, 152-157
dual speed technique, 135-136
gearshift, 135-136
higher speed QAM, 150-151
modulation types, 144-146
receivers, 132-136
RS-232C interface, 105
standards, 138-152
terminal control section, 137
transmitters, 129-132
Trellis Coded Modulation
(TCM), 151-152
Western Electric
model 201, 139-141
model 208, 143-144
synchronous signaling, 127-128
synchronous transmission, 348

T

T-carrier transmission system, 165,
168-169
alternate mark inversion (AMI),
168
T1 carrier, 335
TE1 (Terminal Equipment 1), 348
TE2 (Terminal Equipment 2), 348
telegraph, 2-6

telephone, channel restrictions on modems, 90-91
teleprinter terminals, 14, 31-37
  asynchronous transmission, 31
  bipolar signaling, 32
  communications, 31-32
  double-current signaling, 32
  interaction with computers, 33
  keyboard send-receive (KSR), 32-34
  neutral signaling, 32
  polar signaling, 32
  receive-only (RO), 32-34
  serial printers, 35-36
  single-current signaling, 32
  unipolar signaling, 32
  vs. CRT terminals, 34-37
teletypes, 31
teletypewriter (TTY), 14
  protocol, 213-216
TELEX network, 14
terminal adapter (TA), 347
terminal control section, 137
terminal emulation, 348
  program, 40-41
terminal framing bits (Ft), 167
terminals
  see data terminals, CRT terminals, *and* teleprinter terminals
thermionic vacuum tubes, 73
Time Division Multiple Access (TDMA), 205-207
time division multiplexing (TDM), 85, 172-175, 205-207, 313, 348
  operation, 173-175
timing circuits, 129
token passing networks, 253-255
  ring network, 253-255, 269
token-ring network, 260-263
  bridges, 260-261
  gateways, 262-263

multistation access unit (MAU), 260
Trailblazer modem, 99
Transfer Rate of Information Bits (TRIB), 306-312
  calculation example, 309-311
  maximizing, 311-312
  optimum block length, 312
transmission channels, 67-69
  bandwidth effects, 82-83
  bandwidth requirements, 84
  handling capacity, 82-83
  intersymbol interference, 83-84
transmission codes, 223
transmission path, 23
transmitters, 23
  digital-to-analog converter, 132
  equalizer, 132
  Gray code, 130
  modulator, 132
  scrambler, 130-131
  synchronous modems, 129-132
  timing circuit, 129
transparent-text mode, 229
Trellis Coded Modulation (TCM), 151-152, 348
two-state communication systems, 6
TWX network, 14

U

UART (Universal Asynchronous Receiver/Transmitter), 348
unbounded message carriers, 69
unipolar code, 152-153
unipolar signaling, 32
user-programmable terminals, 38-39
  vs. personal computers, 40

V

V.22 bis modem, 97
V.22 modem standard, 97
V.24 interface, 100-101
V.25 standard
    facilities, 285
    LAPB (Link Access Procedures
      Balanced), 285-288
V.42 bis modems, 98
VC destination addressing, 294
vertical redundancy checking
    (VRC), 217
vestigial sideband modulation, 145
video display terminals (VDT), 37
    to computer interface, 106
Virtual Call Service (VC), 284
voice grade channels, 344
voiceband data transmission vs.
    Local Area Network (LAN), 241

W

waveguides, 74-75
wavelength multiplexing, 197-198
Western Electric
    201 synchronous modem,
      139-141
    208 synchronous modem,
      143-144
wire pairs, 70-73
Wyse WY50 terminal, 49

X

X series recommended network
    standards, 294-296
    frame relay, 296-297
    interrelations between X
      standards, 296
X.25 standard, 282-295
    Call Request/Incoming Call
      packets, 293
    data packets, 288-292
    LAPB (Link Access Procedure
      Balanced), 283
    link level, 283
    logical channel group numbers
      (LCGNs), 293
    logical channel numbers (LCNs),
      293
    network level, 284
    packet-level procedures, 288-295
    Permanent Virtual Call Service
      (PVC), 285
    Virtual Call Service (VC), 284
XMODEM protocol, 218-219
    1's complement, 218
    Acknowledge (ACK) character,
      219
    checksum, 218
    Negative Acknowledge (NAK)
      character, 218
    Start Of Header (SOH) character,
      218

Answers to Quizzes

Chapter 1

1. **d**
2. **b**
3. **a**
4. **c**
5. **c**
6. **b**
7. **b**
8. **a**
9. **c**
10. **c**
11. **b**

Chapter 2

1. **c**
2. **a**
3. **b**
4. **b**
5. **c**
6. **c**
7. **a**
8. **a**
9. **b**
10. **c**
11. **c**
12. **a**
13. **b**
14. **c**
15. **a**
16. **c**
17. **b**
18. **a**
19. **c**
20. **a**

Chapter 3

1. **c**
2. **b**
3. **d**
4. **d**
5. **b**
6. **d**
7. **a**
8. **c**
9. **b**
10. **c**

Chapter 4

1. **c**
2. **a**
3. **b**
4. **a**
5. **b**
6. **c**
7. **b**
8. **a**
9. **c**
10. **b**

Chapter 5

1. **d**
2. **b**
3. **c**
4. **c**
5. **d**
6. **c**
7. **a**
8. **c**
9. **b**
10. **c**

Chapter 6

1. **b**
2. **c**
3. **c**
4. **c**
5. **a**
6. **d**
7. **c**
8. **d**
9. **b**
10. **a**

Chapter 7

1. **a and c**
2. **c**
3. **b**
4. **d**
5. **d**
6. **c**
7. **d**
8. **b**
9. **c**
10. **c**
11. **c**
12. **b**
13. **c**
14. **d**
15. **c**
16. **b**
17. **f**
18. **a**
19. **c**
20. **b**

Chapter 8

1. **a**
2. **c**
3. **c**
4. **d**
5. **d**
6. **b**
7. **b and d**
8. **a**
9. **b**
10. **c**
11. **d**

Chapter 9

1. **c**
2. **a**
3. **d**
4. **b**
5. **c**
6. **d**
7. **a**
8. **a**
9. **d**
10. **d**
11. **a**
12. **d**
13. **a**
14. **d**
15. **d**
16. **c**
17. **b**

Chapter 10	Chapter 11	Chapter 12
1. a	1. b	1. b
2. d	2. c	2. b
3. b	3. b	3. a
4. c	4. d	4. d
5. d	5. a	5. c
6. c	6. d	6. d
7. d	7. a	7. a
8. a	8. b	8. b
9. b	9. c	
10. a	10. b	
11. b	11. c	
12. c		
13. a		
14. d		
15. b		
16. a		
17. c		
18. c		
19. b		
20. a		

You're On The Cutting Edge
with Sams' Audio & Video Books

Handbook for Sound Engineers, Second Edition
Glen M. Ballou, Editor-in-Chief
1,500 pages, 73/8 x 91/4, $99.95 USA
0-672-22752-5

Radio Operator's License Q&A Manual, Eleventh Edition
Milton Kaufman
550 pages, 73/8 x 91/4, $24.95 USA
0-672-48444-7

Camcorder Survival Guide
Robert I. Wolenik
200 pages, 51/2 x 81/2, $14.95 USA
0-672-22759-2

Check Out These Titles from Sams!

Advanced Digital Audio
Ken C. Pohlmann
500 pages, 73/8 X 91/4, $39.95 USA
0-672-22768-1

Audio Systems Design and Installation
Philip Giddings
350 pages, 73/8 X 91/4, $59.95 USA
0-672-22672-3

Compact Disc Troubleshooting & Repair
Neil Heller & Thomas Bentz
208 pages, 73/8 X 91/4, $24.95 USA
0-672-22521-2

Introduction to Professional Recording Techniques
Bruce Bartlett
416 pages, 73/8 X 91/4, $29.95 USA
0-672-22574-3

The MIDI Manual
David Miles Huber
250 pages, 73/8 X 91/4, $24.95 USA
0-672-22757-6

Moderm Recording Techniques
David Miles Huber & Robert A. Runstein
400 pages, 73/8 X 91/4, $29.95 USA
0-672-22682-0

Principles of Digital Audio, Second Edition
Kenneth C. Pohlmann
474 pages, 73/8 X 91/4, $29.95 USA
0-672-22634-0

Radio Handbook, Twenty-Third Edition
William I. Orr, Editor
672 pages, 73/8 X 91/4, $39.95 USA
0-672-22424-0

Sound Recording Handbook
John M. Woram
600 pages, 73/8 X 91/4, $49.95 USA
0-672-22583-2

Sound System Engineering, Second Edition
Don Davis & Carolyn Davis
688 pages, 73/8 X 91/4, $49.95 USA
0-672-21857-7

Understanding Data Communications, Second Edition
Revised by Gilbert Held
304 pages, 73/8 X 91/4, $19.95 USA
0-672-27270-9

Understanding Fiber Optics
Jeff Hect
456 pages, 73/8 X 91/4, $24.95 USA
0-672-27066-8

Understanding Telephone Electronics, Third Edition
John L. Fike & George E. Friend, Revised by Stephen J. Bigelow
320 pages, 73/8 X 91/4, $24.95 USA
0-672-27350-0

VCR Troubleshooting & Repair, Second Ecition
Gregory R. Capelo & Robert C. Brenner
400 pages, 73/8 X 91/4, $19.95 USA
0-672-22749-5

Video Scrambling and Descrambling for Satellite and Cable TV
Rudolf Graf & William Sheets
256 pages, 73/8 X 91/4, $24.95 USA
0-672-22499-2

SAMS

See your local retailer or call 1-800-428-5331.

Stay Current with Sams' Electrical Books!

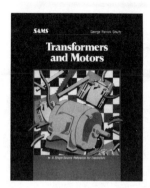

Sams' First Books Get You Started Fast!

Sams Guarantees Your Success In 10 Minutes!

The *10 Minute Guides* provide a new approach to learning computer programs. Each book teaches you the most often used features of a particular program in 15 to 20 short lessons—all of which can be completed in 10 minutes or less. What's more, the *10 Minute Guides* are simple to use. You won't find any "computer-ese" or technical jargon— just plain English explanations. With straightforward instructions, easy-to-follow steps, and special margin icons to call attention to important tips and definitions, the *10 Minute Guides* make learning a new software program easy and fun!

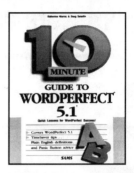

10 Minute Guide to WordPerfect 5.1
Katherine Murray & Doug Sabotin
160 pages, 51/2 x 81/2, $9.95 USA
0-672-22808-4

10 Minute Guide to MS-DOS 5
Jack Nimersheim
160 pages, 5 1/2 x 81/2, $9.95 USA
0-672-22807-6

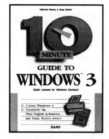

10 Minute Guide to Windows 3
Katherine Murray & Doug Sabotin
160 pages, 5 1/2 x 81/2, $9.95 USA
0-672-22812-2

10 Minute Guide to PC Tools 7
Joe Kraynak
160 pages, 5 1/2 x 81/2, $9.95 USA
0-672-30021-4

10 Minute Guide to Lotus 1-2-3
Katherine Murray & Doug Sabotin
160 pages, 51/2 x 8 1/2, $9.95 USA
0-672-22809-2

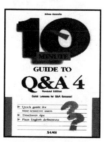

10 Minute Guide to Q&A 4, Revised Edition
Arlene Azzarello
160 pages, 51/2 x 81/2, $9.95 USA
0-672-30035-4

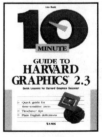

10 Minute Guide to Harvard Graphics 2.3
Lisa Bucki
160 pages, 51/2 x 81/2, $9.95 USA
0-672-22837-8

SAMS

See your local retailer or call 1-800-428-5331.

Turn to Sams For Complete
Hardware and Networking Information

The Business Guide to Local Area Networks
William Stallings
400 pages, 73/8 X 91/4, $24.95 USA
0-672-22728-2

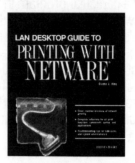

LAN Desktop Guide to Printing with NetWare
Donna J. King
350 pages, 73/8 X 91/4, $39.95 USA
0-672-30084-2

More Hardware & Networking Titles

**The First Book of Personal Computing
Second Edition**
W.E. Wang & Joe Kraynak
275 pages, 73/8 X 91/4, $16.95 USA
0-672-27385-3

The First Book of PS/1
Kate Barnes
300 pages, 73/8 X 91/4, $16.95 USA
0-672-27346-2

**IBM PC Advanced Troublshooting &
Repair**
Robert C. Brenner
304 pages, 73/8 X 91/4, $24.95 USA
0-672-22590-5

**IBM Personal Computer
Troubleshooting & Repair**
Robert C. Brenner
400 pages, 73/8 X 91/4, $24.95 USA
0-672-22662-6

**Interfacing to the IBM Personal
Computer, Second Edition**
Lewis C. Eggebrecht
432 pages, 73/8 X 91/4, $24.95 USA
0-672-22722-3

**LAN Desktop Guide to E-mail
with cc:Mail**
Bruce Fryer
350 pages, 73/8 X 91/4, $24.95 USA
0-672-30243-8

**Microcomputer Troubleshooting &
Repair**
John G. Stephenson & Bob Cahill
368 pages, 73/8 X 91/4, $24.95 USA
0-672-22629-4

**Understanding Local Area Networks,
Second Edition**
Stan Schatt
300 pages, 73/8 X 91/4, $24.95 USA
0-672-27303-9

SAMS

See your local retailer or call 1-800-428-5331.